The Left Bank Revisited

THE LEFT BANK REVISITED:

Selections from the Paris *Tribune* 1917-1934

Edited with an Introduction
by Hugh Ford

Foreword by Matthew Josephson

The Pennsylvania State University Press
University Park and London

Library of Congress Cataloging in Publication Data

Ford, Hugh D   1925−   comp.
  The Left Bank revisited.

    1. Americans in Paris. 2. Paris−Intellectual
life. I. The Chicago tribune. European ed.
II. Title.
DC715.F67   301.45'11'13044361   76-136964
ISBN 0-271-01144-0

Library of Congress Catalog Card Number 76-136964
International Standard Book Number   0-271-011440
Copyright © 1972 by The Pennsylvania State University
All Rights Reserved
Designed by Glenn Ruby

For Ralph Jules Frantz,
the Paris *Tribune*'s last Managing Editor

Contents

II The People

Music

Theater

Little Magazines and Little Presses

Book News and Reviews

Illustrations

The drawing of Ford Madox Ford is courtesy of Georg T.
Hartmann. All other drawings are from the *Chicago Tribune*,
European Edition (1917-1934) and are reprinted with the
permission of the *Chicago Tribune*.

Foreword

In the early nineteen-twenties when we Americans of the younger generation went to spend our wander-years in France as apprentice artists and writers in self-imposed "exile," we thought and wrote a good deal about the United States. We felt that we loved it—at a distance—and that Paris was "our second country." Maxim Gorky, a tramp laborer in early days, in his memoirs described the Black Sea waterfront and the grimy shops of his youth as his "universities." For us the terraces of the Montparnasse cafés giving on the lively Paris street scene were our "university" during an important stage of our lives.

This selection of articles and sketches from the Paris *Tribune* furnishes us with a rich and useful documentation for one of the most interesting periods in the history of U.S. cultural and social life: it was the era of the so-called Lost Generation that was never really lost but enjoyed a prodigious success. In the nineteenth century most Americans were quite insular, tending to pay little heed to what went on in the world outside their great island-continent, which they were occupied in building up. But the generation that lived through World War One thought a great deal about Europe; former soldiers or ambulance drivers at the battlefronts, as well as others who had not seen action in war, were prompted to return or to visit France, and conceived a great love affair with that beautiful old capital of the avant-garde that was Paris. For a long time the United States had imported the latest clothing fashions from Paris; now American youth exported themselves to Paris to seek out new fashions in literature and the arts, in manners and morals. Some stayed for a long season or a year; a minority remained to form a colony of expatriates who had found that the quality of life pleased them.

Why did so many Americans migrate to Paris at the time? Henry James in the 1870s had acclaimed it as the "great literary workshop of Europe." A generation later Ezra Pound became a professed exile first in London, then in Paris; he exhorted his fellow poets in America to quit their "half-savage" country and join him abroad. Initially only a few followed him—not until the great war had ended did the transatlantic migration of young Americans, poets and otherwise, begin in earnest.

Some literary historians have attributed the movement of Americans to Paris to the inspiration of Harold Stearns. A New Englander and Harvard graduate, Stearns at the age of thirty had won some prominence as an author and as the editor of *Civilization in the United States,* a symposium in which he and thirty other writers and scholars contributed essays surveying different aspects of modern American society. The consensus of opinion held that the nation's materialism and puritanism left it with only a poor sort of civilization. Stearns, who regarded himself as a spokesman for American intellectuals, called bravely for wine, then banned by Prohibition, and for sexual freedom. But *Civilization in the United States* was little read by the young persons who came to Paris then. By the time it appeared in 1922, hundreds upon hundreds of Americans had already settled on the banks of the Seine, including Harold Stearns himself who had left Greenwich Village in the summer of 1921. In Paris he sat in cafés, drank his drinks, and read Anatole France without fear of the law; he supported these habits by covering the race tracks as a reporter for the Paris *Tribune*.

When I arrived there in 1921, I found quite a group of my friends or acquaintances on hand; there was the budding novelist John Dos Passos; there was E. E. Cummings writing poems in abundance and with him my Columbia College classmate Slater Brown, who figured in Cummings' story of their wartime prison experience, *The Enormous Room*. Malcolm Cowley had also turned up with a fellowship to a French university; Ramon Guthrie, a wartime aviator, was there studying Provençal poetry; while Robert M. Coates of Yale had quit his advertising job in New York to settle down in the Café Dôme with other young American poets and prosateurs. Not long afterward the young newspaper reporter Ernest Hemingway arrived. A group of young American musicians studying composition with Nadia Boulanger was on hand, including Aaron Copland and Virgil Thomson, who lived on tiny grants or remittances from America. Also a more numerous group of young painters, including Niles Spencer, Stuart Davis, and Julian Levi, worked all day at the Academie Julian. Like the composers, these impecunious young artists were destined to fame; in later years their canvases were to be collected by America's leading museums.

Nearly five years later, when Hemingway's *The Sun Also Rises* became a best-seller, the floodgates were opened for tourists to Paris. Thousands of Americans came from the East, the West, and the Main Streets of the midlands—all evidently filled with the resolve to become full-fledged members of the Lost Generation that the novel so provocatively invoked. It would be incorrect to assume, however, that either Hemingway, or Harold Stearns before him, "invented" the Paris of the American expatriates. Change had been under way for years before they spoke up: the great Armory Show of 1913 that opened in New York and traveled to Chicago had revealed the cubist Picasso and the futurist Duchamps, who inspired young American artists with admiration for the School of Paris. By 1919 America was becoming less and less provincial: the realistic novels of Dreiser and Anderson were winning the public.

But the change was gradual. Men like Van Wyck Brooks—impatient with the generally amiable, old-fashioned authors of the "Howells-and-James Age" who still filled up the publishing offices of New York with their dated and genteel prose—called for a new day. The older generation cried out in anger at the "outlandish" new authors who were appearing in their midst and who, like Edgar Lee Masters and Amy Lowell, dared to write in free verse! The cultural lag weighed upon the advocates of the new literature; their work was often subjected to severe censorship by the U.S. Post Office. Nevertheless, the younger generation, whose outlook had been shaken up by the war, looked toward the wider cultural horizons represented by Paris and the civilization of old Europe in whose tragic history America had become so deeply involved.

Gertrude Stein had come to Paris almost as far back as one could remember, but she thought and wrote constantly about America, though it gave her no audience. She held that the United States was for her "the most important country in the world—but a parent's place is never the place to work in," and shrewdly added that it was a good thing for a writer looking at his own civilization "to have the contrast of another culture before him." This for me is one of the most illuminating statements of what advantages the Paris of the twenties offered.

The social center of the American community consisted of three neighboring cafés at the corner of the Boulevard Montparnasse and the Raspail. The sharply etched vignettes of the Montparnasse scene in *The Sun Also Rises* serve as an excellent tourist's guide:

> ... I walked past the sad tables of the Rotonde, to the Select. There were a few people inside at the bar, and outside, alone sat Harvey Stone. He had a pile of saucers in front of him and he needed a shave.

This was Harold Stearns as we saw him, little disguised as a gruff minor character in Hemingway's novel. He was one of those who had come to Paris with the purpose of writing a great book, but remained immobilized at the café.

The Paris *Tribune* articles render the background of the surge of artistic creativity inspired by life on the Left Bank, which had its pedantic moments. Many American habitués talked night and day about life, art and beauty, or about Picasso and Joyce; but Elliot H. Paul observes that they seem to have read "only parts of Ulysses," that they sound like "self-made Freudians . . . and open to ridicule." Alex Small finds their talk full of gossip about personalities, and he mistrusts their boasts of sexual prowess. Though they prated of *escape* or *freedom*, still "the shadow of the M. E. Church hung over the tawdry (American) bums of Montparnasse"—"Living in France, they stick to each other, and seldom read French or speak it badly."

"I came to Europe to get culture. Is this culture? . . . I might as well go back to Greenwich Village and rot there." This is Miss Djuna Barnes, a very attractive and talented lady, as quoted by Robert McAlmon in his memoirs, *Being Geniuses Together*. Like an errant Calvinist he replied: "It's nicer to go to hell in Paris."

Elliot H. Paul is compassionate toward the bohemians and gypsies in the cafés. What if they sleep late and idle on the terraces? Is it not just as well that "they are not merely successful magazine writers and wallpaper designers?" Many were called, but few were chosen. The bohemians and phoneys provided some comic relief; and at all events they composed a provisory audience for the tiny number of geniuses sprinkled amongst them.

In Paris, as in most Latin cities, the café was not only the home away from home, it was the open forum where one encountered fellow beings without formality, or prior letter or telephone call, upon a neutral terrain. The café audience surveyed the street scene with its ever changing actors: Arab rug peddlars, newsboys, flower sellers and professional women trotting back and forth on the pavement, or resting nearby. From a café terrace I saw Raymond Duncan, the brother of Isadora, in flowing Grecian robe and open sandals worn in winter; I saw the high T-model Ford coupe that carried those two solid women in veils and dust hats: Gertrude Stein and Alice B. Toklas—an impressive, an unforgettable pair. Picasso, in his prime, with Matisse and Derain, used to appear at the Rotonde of a Sunday. Kings among artists, they were approachable, merry and forthright. But when they found there were too many Americans, they ceased to come. At the café tables the tall talk grew even taller.

Overblown accounts of the "roaring twenties" in Paris have been given us by literary historians who were too young to have been at the scene. Even the estimable Richard Blackmur has gibed at the "expatriates of the arts and the bars" who lived as "parasites" and were "continually intoxicated by their postwar freedom from all moral and practical obligations." Others have represented us as abandoning ourselves to orgies of wine and lechery with the native coquettes—all at low cost, thanks to the favorable currency exchange. These canards have been finally disproved by the sober testimony of the Paris *Tribune* journalists who show that most of the literary expatriates were too poor to buy much in the way of drinks. Of the group of young Americans I knew, nearly all were living frugally on from $60 to $80 a month, and that in several cases (such as my own) included the support of a wife. Our standard of living was about that of the Paris workingmen or clerks, and yet we were never happier. In the 1860s the young Emile Zola had written, "*Ce n'est pas une honte d'être pauvre à Paris*," and this held true for the 1920s as well. My wife and I, after our arrival from the States, had taken an unheated furnished room in the Latin Quarter and ate suppers in a *pension* for university students of all nations at 25 cents per meal. We could then enjoy a delightful lunch at a *crêmerie* in Montparnasse where omelette, wine, and strawberries cost about 20 cents. At the café in the evening we used to cling to our coffee or beer for hours on end and no one minded. We were almost never heedful of our poverty, though it was endured in Europe's glittering capital of luxury, for we were working and learning our craft, publishing our first essays and stories in our own small transatlantic reviews. A mere handful of the more exuberant and proverbially noisy

Americans created the legends of alcoholism by getting themselves arrested regularly during the festivities of Bastille Day.

Paris was of course enjoyable for the rich also. Robert McAlmon lived on alimony and stood treat to everybody in Montparnasse. Peggy Guggenheim, then married to a Paris-born American, Lawrence Vail, was a generous hostess, who also bestowed small annuities upon poets like Djuna Barnes and Mina Loy, and helped the famous anarchist leader Emma Goldman. A job on the Paris *Tribune* or the *Herald* was a rare privilege won by only a few of those who applied; it meant a regular income of 250 francs a week—riches enough, I discovered when I found work on a small English newspaper during the winter months. In the winter, tourist business slackened; the staffs of the English-language newspapers were usually thinned down; my friends on the Paris *Tribune* would hole up in a cheap hotel for the cold weather, and live on credit by pledging their trunk of clothes with the proprietor until spring came.

At first there was little real contact between Americans and Frenchmen of letters. Gertrude Stein in all her years in Paris lived within her own walls, so to speak, and showed little interest in the modern French writers—not even in the marvellous Apollinaire whom she often saw with Picasso. Ezra Pound's knowledge of the French seemed to stop with the symbolists of the 1890s. It was my good fortune to meet and establish friendships with some young French writers who were my contemporaries, and who in 1922 formed the surrealist movement that succeeded dadaism in France. A valuable literary commerce grew up between us: they were as eager to learn all they could about American films, music, and literature as I was to learn about the European avant-garde. For the little reviews, *Secession* and *Broom,* I translated some of the poets such as Louis Aragon and Paul Eluard; I also introduced E. E. Cummings and Malcolm Cowley to my surrealist friends.

It was Eugene Jolas and his quarterly review, *transition,* that provided a most valuable artistic commerce between Americans and the French and German moderns. Born in New Jersey, the son of immigrants from Lorraine, he was brought back to Metz when he was two years old and grew up speaking French and German as well as English. At sixteen he himself emigrated to the United States and in time became a skilled newspaper reporter in New Orleans and New York. After the war he came to Paris and worked for the *Tribune* to which he contributed his series, "Rambles through Literary Paris." He was one of the first to recognize the unknown Hemingway as "one of the promising American writers in Paris." In 1927, with the help of his wife Maria MacDonald, Jolas was able to raise a modest fund and launch the very hospitable and catholic journal, *transition,* that formed a bridge between the new American men of letters and the European avant-garde. Jolas, a warm and generous man, worked hard, and functioned in three languages, translating French and German into English and vice versa.

When I revisited Paris in 1927, I found many thousands more Americans living there than in 1921. They were more knowledgeable than the earlier tourists, but Montparnasse as the "American quarter" had quite disappeared. Its cafés were refurbished; one of them, La Coupole, was enlarged to seat 500 patrons. A huge mixed population of artists from all parts of the world, with attendant *demi-mondaines,* filled the whole quarter, while the literary center of the city had moved a mile downtown to the old St. Germain district. Everything had become more chic, and the American residents were *embourgeoisés.* The literary gatherings were no longer free-for-alls in Montparnasse cafés, but sedate tea or cocktail affairs held at Ford Madox Ford's apartment or at the beautiful antique mansion of Natalie Clifford Barney, the "Amazon." It was there that I saw Gertrude Stein again, a woman of real prepotency; with her eagle eye and her proud, close-cropped head, she looked like some Roman orator of ancient times. In earlier years I used to read her *Tender Buttons* aloud to people with high enthusiasm; but when I knew her powerful personality I better appreciated her "automatic," often recalcitrant prose text. At that period the republic of letters in Paris was apparently divided between the camp of Gertrude Stein and the camp of James Joyce, neither of whom cared much for the other.

Economic forces intervened rudely: after the Crash of 1929 the remittances of Americans dwindled and they drifted home. Paris was more beautiful, more "impuritan" than ever, the city became less and less international and more and more French again.

W. H. Auden has written that the most painful problems for young writers and artists are created by the necessity of their earning a living by doing work they detest. What the young need above all, he urged, was time—time to grow up slowly and undergo their lengthy apprenticeship. The young Americans of the postwar generation who went to Paris, like the youth of today, were concerned for the *quality* of their life in the United States, and determined to improve themselves by living abroad. "Paris was our mistress," wrote Samuel Putnam after his long exile. Certainly Paris was good to us.

Matthew Josephson

Acknowledgments

In the past two years it has been my good fortune to become acquainted with many former *Tribune* staffers here and abroad. I am grateful to them for sharing with me their time, their recollections, and their support. In particular I should like to thank the following persons: Mr. Louis Atlas, Mr. Wambly Bald, Mr. Lawrence Blochman, Mr. John Clayton, Mr. David Darrah, Mr. Ralph Jules Frantz, Miss Florence Gilliam, Mr. Wolfe Kaufman, Mr. Alfred Perlès, Mr. Waverley Root, Mr. Irving Schwerké, and Mr. George Seldes.

In addition I wish to acknowledge the help given me by Mrs. Fanny Butcher Bokum, Miss Kay Boyle, Mr. Ramon Guthrie, Mrs. Maria Jolas, Mr. Lawrence Klingman, Miss Sigrid Schultz, and Mr. Vincent Sheean.

I am also most grateful to Mr. Clayton Kirkpatrick, editor of the *Chicago Tribune,* and to Mr. Harold Hutchings, his assistant, for their cooperation in making the files of the Paris *Tribune* available to me; and, in the *Tribune*'s London bureau, Mr. Arthur Veysey and his staff, particularly Miss Kay Jackson, for the generous assistance and kindness they extended to me during the summer of 1970. All articles from the *Chicago Tribune, European Edition* are reprinted courtesy of the *Chicago Tribune.*

To the American Council of Learned Societies and to the Research Committee of Trenton State College, I am greatly indebted for the grants which enabled me to undertake and complete this project.

Of the librarians who aided me I wish especially to thank Mr. David Mendenhall, *Chicago Tribune* librarian, and Mrs. Louise Fradkin and Miss Joyce Brodowski, of the Roscoe L. West Library, Trenton State College.

Finally, for much of the dirty work I am indebted to Mrs. Joyce Kaminski, Mrs. Natalie Knoll, Mrs. Inez McIlroy, Miss Janet Smith, and to my wife, Therese Ford.

Hugh Ford

Introduction

In some ways Jim Thurber was right when he quipped: "The Paris edition of the *Chicago Tribune* was a country newspaper published in a great city." Certainly it paid small-town wages, as staffers never tired of saying, and it was "clubby," and those who worked for it got used to doing jobs they had not been hired for, and although it purported to be America's voice in Europe from 1917 to 1934, and did faithfully print news from "back home," its real beat turned out to be Paris itself, and chiefly that legendary place called the Left Bank.

While the *Tribune*'s two American rivals in Paris, Commodore Bennett's *New York Herald* and, for a brief time, the *Paris Times,* catered to the "lobster palace Americans" on the Right Bank of the Seine, the *Tribune* began reporting the activities of the cultural adventurists from America, as well as Europe, who were turning the old Latin Quarter of Montparnasse into an artistic and social *pied-à-terre. Tribune* critics scrupulously reviewed their exhibits, concerts, and books (not always favorably however); they wrote endlessly about their little magazines of experimental verse and prose, particularly *transition,* and printed accurate listings of the limited editions announced by their little presses; *Tribune* reporters even noted when they arrived from the Riviera or sailed for New York, which prizes they received or refused to accept (very few), and gleefully reported their jibes at America; *Tribune* columnists mingled with them on the terraces of Left Bank cafés like the Dôme and the Sélect, alert for undiscovered idiosyncracies, signs of genius, or bits of gossip, mostly the latter. And although *Tribune* managing editors sometimes hired and fired them with monotonous regularity, they also tolerated their eccentric behavior—up to a point—and maintained amazing restraint in the face of their deplorable ignorance of, or more often, disregard for, basic newspaper routine. But long before the *Tribune* annexed (or was annexed by) the Left Bank, or Latin Quarter, or Montparnasse, as that region was alternately called, it had more in common with *Stars and Stripes* than, say, the *Boulevardier,* the smart, sophisticated, short-lived Paris version of the *New Yorker.*

It is doubtful if many in the throng that watched the first American troops march down the Champs-Elysées on 4 July 1917, in a display of pageantry that confirmed America's entry into the European struggle, noticed a new

1

arrival among the newspapers displayed on the boulevard kiosks, a small tabloid bearing in Gothic-typed letters the name Army Edition of *The Chicago Tribune*. But its appearance that day was a *succès d'estime* for the tiny staff that had struggled for weeks to surmount the problems and war restrictions which had plagued their efforts to publish an English-language newspaper in mobilized France, and which had reached a climax on the eve of publication when a zealous French censor had "killed" nearly a third of the first issue. The alternatives of printing a paper consisting of mostly blank columns or delaying publication until fresh stories could be composed were equally disagreeable to both Joseph Pierson, the editor of the Army Edition, and to Colonel Robert R. McCormick, the owner and publisher of the *Chicago Tribune*, who enthusiastically supported the overseas venture and had wired Pierson the day before to have the paper operating by Independence Day. Repairing the censor's ravages during the midnight hours was neither easy nor completely successful, but the patching at least gave the maiden edition the appearance of a newspaper, and guaranteed that Colonel McCormick's "gift to the American Expeditionary Force," as Aleck Woollcott called it, would reach the stands on schedule.

Two months after its appearance, the Army Edition changed from a tabloid of four pages to a newspaper of full size, a cable service from Chicago was started, and the original staff of three—Pierson, his assistant Pierre Barbou, a French army veteran who was remarkably expert at finding publishing facilities in Paris, and Germaine Berio, a member of the Italian family of printers in whose shop on the slope of Montmartre the Army Edition was born—more than doubled. As more Americans arrived in France, the *Tribune*'s circulation outgrew the Berio plant, and in November 1917 Pierson signed a contract with the prosperous *Le Petit Journal* to print and distribute the paper. Before the Armistice a year later the Army Edition was being read by nearly 2,000,000 doughboys who found their nostalgia for America whetted by the cartoons of "regulars" McCutcheon and Briggs, and their fighting ability praised in the reports of Floyd Gibbons and Ring Lardner.

When the war ended Colonel McCormick made good his promise to turn over the profits of the Army Edition to the American Expeditionary Forces, and in January 1919 the redoubtable Floyd Gibbons presented General Pershing a check for 112,000 francs, who thanked the publishers for their "signal service" and "generous and helpful attitude to officers and men." The event might have marked the *Tribune*'s final act of generosity and the end of its European service, but in fact the occasion heralded the beginning of the *Tribune*'s emergence as one of the leading English-language newspapers on the Continent. Whereas the Army Edition had been a friendly appendage of the AEF, fulfilling its patriotic purpose of enhancing the "morale of the battlers from the States" and "making life a little more pleasant for the brave fellows who are doing their bit . . . for the independence of the world," and covertly of bringing something of the spirit of the Middle West to France, the *Tribune*'s new Paris Edition quickly established its independence by drawing charges from military headquarters of being "ill-advised" when it began bannering across its front pages the demand: "Get the Boys Home Toot Sweet." This direct challenge to the AEF won noisy approval from camp-bound troops anxious to return home, and probably helped the paper's campaign succeed. In any event, 300,000 soldiers a month were soon leaving for the United States; and at the same time the *Tribune* launched a second campaign, this one against Wilson's peace treaty, which brought the newspaper, in its own words, "the scoop of the century"—the first full publication of the text of the Versailles Treaty. Revelation of the treaty enormously strengthened the anti-Wilson forces who intensified their attacks on the president's program and successfully campaigned for his defeat in the 1920 elections, a defeat in which the *Tribune* did not deny it had played a part.

The need to stay on in Europe to interpret America's attitude toward the League of Nations, the war debt, the occupation of Germany, the balance of trade, to explain and if necessary to defend matters vital to American growth and power, seemed all the more imperative as the country's might and international standing grew. The resolve brought the final change of designation when the Paris Edition became the European Edition. The *Tribune*'s rival, Commodore Bennett's veteran *New York Herald*, had no intention of quitting Paris after thirty years of publishing abroad, but the Colonel's views seldom jived with the Commodore's. "The *Tribune*," he said, would reflect "Americanism," its point of view would be "American and not European," and "pro-truth" in European controversies and impartial toward the "participants of the controversy." While the second part of this credo was usually observed, due to the efforts of correspondents like William L. Shirer, George Seldes, John Clayton, Henry Wales, Sigrid Schultz, and Vincent Sheean, whose cables often appeared in the Paris edition of the *Tribune* as well as in the parent newspaper in Chicago, its point of view, apart from politics, gradually became less American and more European, that is, French, and while the front page still carried reports from the United States, the inside pages often contained columns of rather negative criticism of America.

No one in Paris, from the managing editor down, wished to do battle with Colonel McCormick, particularly on the matter of "Americanism" and its labyrinthine meanings or the loyalty it was intended to evoke—and happily the matter never forced an issue—but by the early twenties most Tribuners were Americans who had come to Paris voluntarily, and not always with the intention of seeking a newspaper job. Though the reasons for their odysseys were obscure and as individualistic as they themselves were, they comprised a part of the burgeoning colony of American exiles who poured into Paris after the war, often disenchanted with their own country and intent upon finding their salvation in another. Even if in the unlikely event a *Tribune* staffer had arrived in Paris without any strong gripes against America, proximity to those who had quickly acquainted him with an endless assortment of ills. Moreover, there was one among his colleagues who had publicized exile from America as a way of survival. He was Harold Stearns, editor of *Civilization in the United States,* which reached the depressing conclusion that America was anathema to anyone but the most unregenerate materialist. Many a staffer joined Stearns in condemning (once again) the hypocrisy of prohibition, the puritanism of the Middle West, the rampaging materialism that threatened to make America's artistic sterility permanent, and a plethora of minor annoyances.

If America had failed them, at least temporarily, what did France have to offer? In the first place, a job. Stearns, who had reason to know, described Tribuners as a "sort of elastic-band staff which expanded in good days and contracted in bad." The minuscule pay staffers earned, which averaged around $50.00 a month paid in francs, did little to exact a sense of duty or loyalty, and nothing at all to prevent staffers from moving on whenever they wished. Absenteeism at times reached a crisis state but few except in rare instances (one involved Henry Miller who vacated his proofreading post for two weeks unannounced and was fired by managing editor Jules Frantz) ever lost their jobs, and even if they had, they could generally get hired on at one of the other American papers at approximately the same salary. Among this floating population of newsmen journalism was secondary, a necessary and for some an onerous way of making a living while waiting for their "real" talents as writers or artists to mature and be discovered and rewarded. Meanwhile, encouraged by the assumption that the *Tribune* evidently regarded employment in Paris sufficient compensation for a low salary or as something even better than money, many Tribuners inclined more toward sampling the available joys of the city than conforming to the daily routine of putting out a newspaper.

Balancing the itinerants was a small band of semi-professional and professional journalists, competent and dependable, whose education or training in the United States had prepared them for newspaper work, and who either remained with the *Tribune* in Paris until it closed, or who, like David Darrah, William L. Shirer, and Vincent Sheean, eventually joined the roaming staff of foreign correspondents. The enticements of money, travel, and prestige offered by the Foreign Service never stopped beckoning those who remained behind in Paris—when they succeeded in silencing its siren call they did so by convincing themselves they were already at the hub of artistic and intellectual activity. For was not Paris, after all, the natural and abiding mecca of every American resident, whether genuine expatriate or semipermanent exile? And did it not at least promise to satisfy their urgent searchings for freedom, diversion, beauty, adventure, and intelligence, or whatever; and for the aspiring literati, including some journalists, a chance to write and to be heard and perhaps even to be published? Whatever skepticism might accompany one's reaction to Ezra Pound's pronouncements, it is hard to deny the truth of his observation that Paris functioned as a "laboratory of ideas . . . where poisons [could] be tested, new modes of sanity discovered." And the characteristically cryptic remark of that other teacher-interpreter, Gertrude Stein, reinforced Pound's claim: "America is my country and Paris is my hometown," a statement which, among other things, meant that creativity could be stimulated by—in fact, depended upon—residence abroad.

It would be difficult to estimate how many Tribuners were nudged into writing poetry or fiction by the ambience of Paris, but it might be possible to conclude that nearly all were. Almost everyone, that is, intended to write something, some day, even if, when pressed, one was not quite certain what it would be. Intentions however sometimes failed to spawn productions. Not long after he turned up at the *Tribune,* word spread that Harold Stearns had just finished another book, which he announced would bear the rather incriminating title, *Studies in Stupidity.* Further, it was said he would deliver the book personally to a New York publisher, but when, following a lengthy interval, it did not appear, both book and author were gradually forgotten. However others did better, several benefiting from the help of Elliot Paul, the only published novelist on the staff in the early twenties, who directed the writing of Bravig Imb's first novel, *The Professor's Wife.* In addition Paul can be credited with at least providing the *Tribune*'s financial editor, Virgil Geddes, with a place to write—the quirky Hotel du Caveau which Paul memorialized in *The Last Time I Saw Paris*—and an introduction to his first play, *The Frog,* which had a successful run in Boston. Years later Gertrude Stein, in *The Autobiography of Alice B. Toklas,* praised Paul for his efforts to turn journalists into writers; she might also have thanked him for writing kind words about her in his *Tribune* column, as might Geddes, Imbs, and, for that matter, Hemingway, Cummings, and a multitude of others.

Paul also became an editor of *transition,* the little magazine specializing in experimental writing founded in 1927 by Eugene Jolas, a *Tribune* staffer who remained the magazine's guiding light until its demise in 1938. Even after he quit the *Tribune* Jolas maintained connections with members of the staff, who obligingly reviewed issues of *transition* and discussed the future of the magazine in their columns. In 1928 Robert Sage, a copy reader, joined Jolas as associate editor, and by then several Tribuners, including B. J. Kosposth, Waverley Root, Ned Calmer, Leigh Hoffman, and M. C. Blackman, were among *transition*'s contributors. *Transition* was not the only place however where *Tribune* journalists found a receptive welcome. Both Ford Madox Ford's *Transatlantic Review* and Ernest Walsh's *This Quarter* published work by Tribuners, and Samuel Putnam's *New Review* opened its third number to just about any *Tribune* staffer who had written something publishable, a situation created partly by Putnam's temporary absence and the installation of Henry Miller, one-time *Tribune* proofreader, as interim editor. The number appeared, much to Putnam's amazement, with contributions by staffers Don Brown, Bob Stern, Wambly Bald, Alfred Perlès, and of course, Henry Miller, who announced himself in print with the short story "Mademoiselle Claude." Miller and Bald also appeared in Peter Neagoe's anthology of American writing, *Americans Abroad,* as did Sage and Emily Holmes Coleman.

As reassuring as it may be to note that many Tribuners resisted the reputedly enfeebling pastimes of Paris long enough to write a fair amount of poetry and fiction, it is primarily their work as newsmen that must be recognized here, for in that capacity they erected in the pages of the Paris *Tribune* the one most comprehensive documentary history we possess of the Left Bank. Because Tribuners often lived in the Quarter or spent their off hours there and became acquainted with its inhabitants, there eventually developed between Quarterites and the newsmen a sort of familial relationship. Everyone expected the *Tribune* to report the doings and the gossip of Montparnasse. And expectations were seldom disappointed. But there were other expectations that were not gratified. Those creative Quarterites, genuine and specious, who tried to inveigle *Tribune* critics into reviewing (favorably, of course) their books, recitals, and exhibits were, with a few notable exceptions, either ignored or scorned. Some of the harshest criticism ever published about George Antheil, the meteoric American composer who enjoyed the support of several prominent exiles—notably Pound and Joyce—appeared in the columns of music critic Irving Schwerké, who, it must be added, before Antheil's European career tapered off in the early thirties, also wrote some of the most laudatory comments the composer ever received.

Standards at least as rigorous as Schwerké's also prevailed among the *Tribune*'s many book reviewers, notably Waverley Lewis Root, who at one time argued that the Nobel prize should have been awarded to Theodore Dreiser, not Sinclair Lewis. And art critic B. J. Kospoth, by nature gentle, had only to be slightly chary of praise to deflate a reputation, a technique also used by Kospoth's colleague Florence Gilliam in her reviews of the theater. *Tribune* critics could not be intimidated, not by aspiring Quarterites, not by Nobel prize winners, not even by Gertrude Stein. But they could be impressed, and when they were, that is, when they concluded their standards had been reasonably well satisfied, they said so, and sometimes enthusiastically.

And while their record suffered from occasional lapses in taste and hyperbole, more than compensated for by their thorough coverage and often shrewd estimates of expatriates' work, Americans still received more serious attention than they could have expected from critics at home, and considerably more than their European counterparts, a situation that led to charges of provincialism. Undoubtedly many Americans, untouched by Paris publications, learned from the *Tribune* that they lived among important European artists—not just the major figures like Gide and Colette but others like Raymond Radiguet and Paul Fort—and the same might be said for some Europeans to whom the *Tribune* served as an artistic directory. Without consciously trying to function as a clearing house for the arts on an international scale, or to stimulate increased European-American cultural cross-fertilization, the *Tribune* managed to do both, despite the near physical impossibility of reporting, not to mention examining, all the artistic experiments and manifestations of the period. In making Americans aware of the exciting, creative world they inhabited and Europeans conscious that among those Americans were serious artists, the *Tribune*'s influence was invaluable.

The coverage given the arts, however, reflected only part of the multifarious life of Paris which so intrigued Tribuners. Among the most fortunate in this regard was a handful of columnists who, free to write about almost anything, naturally lighted often on topics related to their surroundings and circumstances. In his column called "Of Fleeting Things," Alex Small, a Harvard graduate (*cum laude*) who joined the *Tribune* after a try at teaching, created a forum of brilliant controversy in which he pitted himself in opposition to nearly the entire expatriate colony. Small argued that the repressions of America prevented his fellow exiles from enjoying the freedoms of France, and that no matter how long they lived abroad they would never cease being the same depressing Americans they had always been. More than most others Small grappled with the questions his colleague and friend Harold Stearns had posed in *Civilization in the United States,* questions which directed him to an examination of the value of expatriation as the central episode in the pilgrimage so many confused Americans had made in quest of self-discovery and fulfillment. That his findings seldom satisfied Quarterites was no doubt due partly to the testiness with which they were delivered, and perhaps to a feeling that his observations supported his conclusions a bit too patently. Understandably, Small antagonized Left Bankers by reiterating that they still possessed the very faults they had come abroad to exorcise: naiveté and prudery. Querulous, opinionated, but always thoughtful, Small made a perfect devil's advocate; if he failed to shock expatriates into some new awareness, he at least provoked questions that could.

Far less acerbity and a good deal more jollity born of an appreciation of the absurd characterized Louis Atlas's column "Anything Can Happen," an entertaining and original feature in which Atlas made unpredictability an art. His puckish sketches of the life in the Quarter contrasted with the zany renderings of Wambly Bald, and the incisive reports of Edmond Taylor, who along with William L. Shirer and William Leon Smyser, often interviewed American visitors—arriving and departing in mighty battalions by mid-decade—and resident dignitaries, including the French, for the paper's "Who's Who" column. Of course Montparnassians could always be counted on to provide abundant copy for a long string of *Tribune* reporters and columnists, beginning in the mid-twenties with Eugene Jolas and Paul Shinkman and ending in the early thirties with Wambly Bald, a perennial bohemian who, Samuel Putnam contended, might be a "genius in disguise." Observant, quizzical, brusque, Bald patrolled the Quarter with a policeman's familiarity and insouciance. Everything he saw and heard went into a column he called "La Vie de Bohème" (As Lived on the Left Bank), which, as Putnam observed, was written in an idiom unintelligible to the tourist but "understood perfectly" by Left Bankers, "a truly uncanny amalgam of prose, the like of which was never seen before or since." Bald's column mirrored a noisy, bizarre world of fake and real bohemianism, where a divining rod might fail to distinguish one from the other and where such skilled self-publicizers as Greenwich Village bohemian Maxwell Bodenheim and Nobel prize winner Sinclair Lewis could be snubbed. No one, not even Elliot Paul or Harold Ettlinger, could quite catch the illuminating nuances which turned Bald's depiction of the Quarter into lively and artful entertainment.

The *Tribune* survived the financial collapse of 1929 that sent the first wave of exiles home, but it could not survive the depression that followed. As Managing Editor Ralph Jules Frantz has said in his account of the final years of the paper, the advertising revenue from which the *Tribune* derived most of its support dipped in the early thirties. In March 1932 the staff was forced to take a cut in pay as it was again a year later, while at the same time the paper increased its circulation. But advertising made the difference between profit and loss, and when it continued to decline men drifted away and were not replaced, leaving a small and, by necessity, versatile staff to put the paper out. Finally, abruptly and without explanation, came word from Colonel McCormick that the *Tribune* had been sold (for $50,000 it was rumored) to its rival, the *New York Herald,* and would close 30 November 1934. Instructions to settle "equitably" with the staff followed, and Tribuners, many of them stunned and angry over the long-rumored but still unexpected news, deliberated the gloomy prospect of serving out their time working for a doomed newspaper.

The final days of the *Tribune* and the surprising events that followed have been reconstructed by Ralph Jules Frantz and Waverley Lewis Root in the last chapter of this book, which includes other recollections by ex-Tribuners. On Friday 30 November after a farewell party the day before at Harry's New York bar—not a favorite of Tribuners but always a stopping place for news—the last edition of the *Chicago Tribune, European Edition* came off the presses. In it Louis Atlas once more marshalled the Rover Boys, for years butts of his satire, to give three last "hurrahs" for the "dear old Chicago Tribune military academy"; Lee Dickson, while agreeing with others it was "sad to quit" a sheet he had liked and separate from "colorful" and "friendly" colleagues, admitted he still could not work himself into a "Russian lather"; on the other hand, Herol Egan, sports columnist, confessed that it was just "too painful to think of leaving so many good friends"; Alex Small, in his usual measured prose, completed a long review of the expatriate experience and concluded that an "interesting experiment in international living" had ended, one "too good to last," and then chauvinistically added: "A man must live, fight and die with his own people." Jules Frantz bid goodbye to *Tribune* readers, thanking them for their support and farewell messages, which, he added, encouraged staffers to believe that their efforts, "often in the face of enormous difficulties," had not "gone unappreciated." No one knew better than Frantz how mighty some of those difficulties had been.

The next day Paris had one American newspaper, the inveterate *Herald.* That is, officially. For before the day ended a tabloid bearing the name *Paris Tribune,* "Europe's American Weekly," turned up in subscriber's mailboxes. Managed by Waverley Root and written by former *Tribune* staffers, it promised to provide subscribers, for as long as their support lasted, a dozen or more columns and features by Herol Egan, Alex Small, Lee Dickson, Louis Atlas, Carol Weld, and Bob Stern. But the events of this episode are much better told by Waverley Root, the man who created them.

By 1934 the Left Bank had already ceased to be America's "spiritual mistress." The year before Wambly Bald had decreed the Quarter finished in his final "La Vie" column; it had turned into Main Street, he wrote, practically indistinguishable from any other region of Paris. It had also become half deserted, as Bald and others sorrowfully noted whenever they ticked off the names of departed friends. Alex Small's contention—that it was well the end had come—for once brought forward no challengers. For it was apparent to those still in Paris that that once vibrant spiritual matrix of life and art, the Latin Quarter, had all but disappeared. Vanished was that time when Life and Art drew passionate souls together on café terraces and in shrill manifestos, when Life and Art seemed at last to be entwined (for how could one live without art?), and when both were so ardently savored and rhapsodized and recorded with originality and verve and dedication.

And since then (how long ago it seems) memorialists, novelists, and critics have trained shafts of light on that crepuscular era, seeking to illuminate what legend and time threaten to darken forever. And numbering among those who have searched their memories for the meaning of that epochal time in Paris and who have scattered some of the shadows that obscure it are former Tribuners Harold Stearns (*The Street I Know*), Bravig Imbs (*Confessions of Another Young Man*), Harold Ettlinger (*Fair, Fantastic Paris*), Elliot Paul (*The Last Time I Saw Paris*), Alfred Perlès (*My Friend Henry Miller*), Ned Calmer (*All the Summer Days*), and perhaps in some ways the greatest shadow-dispeller of all, Henry Miller (*Tropic of Cancer*). And now joining them in this book, in reminiscences that tell us how often Tribuners were the shapers as well as the recorders of the twenties and thirties, are Ralph Jules Frantz, Wambly Bald, Lawrence G. Blochman, Louis Atlas, Irving Schwerké, and Waverley Root. They also remind us that their legacy—theirs and that of dozens of their colleagues—the Paris *Tribune,* remains a rich personal document, as eclectic and spirited as its staff; a human record created by people who shared with Browning's irrepressible monk Fra Lippo Lippi the urge not "to let a truth slip," and whose word-odysseys can throw deep and broad beams which reveal still more of that mercurial life of Paris—so fascinatingly like the present—than we have been accustomed to see.

The selections from the Paris *Tribune* printed here have been placed in chronological order in each section, an arrangement intended to assist the reader to trace the evolution of opinion, the developments in the arts, and the changes in the life of the Left Bank, which the *Tribune* documented from the early twenties to the mid thirties.

Before embarking on a reading of the selections from the Paris *Tribune*, the reader interested in enlarging his familiarity with the period of the newspaper's existence as well as with some of the men who served on its staff is invited to turn to Chapter VI, where he will find retrospective articles written especially for this book by five former *Tribune* staffers and former Managing Editor Ralph Jules Frantz.

H. F.

I The Place

Most descriptions of the Left Bank dwell on the uninhibited conduct and the noisy and tedious efforts of expatriates to express themselves. The oft-repeated terrace brawls at the Dôme or Sélect, the boozy adventures, and the loud-voiced "literary" arguments which ended in swirls of charges and recriminations, all belong to the legendary picture of Montparnasse. It is both true and apocryphal. Tribuners like Harold Stearns and Elliot Paul however, themselves habitués of the Left Bank for many years, more often challenged than fed that legend; and even short-term Quarterites, like Maxwell Bodenheim, Sinclair Lewis, and the Reverend Cochran of the Right Bank American Church, seldom allowed the Quarter's popular reputation to influence their generally unfriendly views. Perhaps the most authentic descriptions of the place came from Alfred Perlès, who, with his proofreader companion, the peripatetic Henry Miller, explored the domain of Montparnasse and beyond with a scavenger's thoroughness and excitement; and columnist Alex Small, surely among the most perceptive of observers, whose penchant for ridiculing the Quarter's empty proclamations and thinly disguised provincialism seered many a bohemian neophyte.

Like retired generals, old Paris newsmen are inclined to recount their past adventures using superlatives, for as *Tribune* staffer Ned Calmer said in *All the Summer Days*, his novel about newspapermen in Paris, every generation lays claim to having enjoyed the "golden era." By the end of the twenties a few Tribunemen began describing Montparnasse as a "movable feast" that could not be moved, or had simply been devoured, a place with a past now dead, and the better for it. They wrote accounts of what Montparnasse had once been like, recalling the colorful and famous figures who had inhabited the Quarter at an earlier time, and contrasting their own halcyon days there with a tawdry and purposeless present. But debilitated or no—and there were Tribuners convinced it was— Montparnasse somehow continued to cast its spell, and only a few staffers deserted it before the *Tribune* closed.

The attractions of Montparnasse however never dampened a Tribuner's urge to wander, if only into a neighboring *arrondissement*. The joys of such perambulating became the subject of Alfred Perlès' articles, two of which, "Paris in Ut-Mineur" and "Gobelins Tapestries," were actually written by his friend Henry Miller. Other staffers, too, like Don Brown, the *Tribune*'s artist, and Louis Atlas, a reporter and columnist, roamed tirelessly in search of the unusual character or setting, both of which Paris supplied in abundance.

H. F.

Montparnasse Described

Dôme Jottings

This is not a description of the famous Montparnasse café. No one has ever really described the "Dôme." Probably because since that abode of international Bohemianism in Paris has attained maturity, the world has not produced a literary artist big enough to describe it. George Bernard Shaw might do it, of course, but the result would not be the "Dôme"; it would be a Montparnasse projection of the Shavian mind.

Besides, the "Dôme" is not a place: it is an atmosphere. And no one has ever succeeded in describing an atmosphere. It may be felt, it may be absorbed, and you may, with the aid of a sensitive ear and a surreptitious pencil, record some of its concrete if fleeting manifestations.

You sit ensconced in a corner, sipping an *apéritif*—or if editors have been unkind lately, a *café crême*. Tags of conversation reach you, floating down with the smoke of cigarettes, wafting to you with the draught caused by scurrying waiters. People pass by your table unconcerned, and a few words drop on your ears in their passing.

If all else fails, and your immediate vicinity is made up of witless dummies or chess-playing fiends, you go a-wandering yourself, drifting between the tables, ostensibly looking for a paper or a friend, culling bright thoughts as they sparkle around you. Some of these are recorded here. There are few that attain to the maturity of conversation: most of them are just snapshots, flashes caught on the wing.

Such as they are, here they are:

A voluble Italian woman is brandishing an enormous cloth doll in the face of a quiet, silver haired man, on whose lips lies a tolerant smile. A fantastic doll, like a nightmare Harlequin the face a black waste with a tiny red lozenge in the centre.

A tactless Young American has just blurted out:

"Say, what d'you always carry that thing about for? "

... "A woman must have something. I have no children and my *concierge* will not allow me a dog."

A gaunt man with a reddish Van Dyke beard, with emphasis:

"No, the best medium for painting is dung!"

A man passes by a table—an American table, young men all, with armfuls of unsold batiks.

"That's that French writing chap, Goodwedding."

"Funny name! Ought to have written a book called 'Divorce'."

A short laugh. One of them turns to a silent member of the party:

"Pity you weren't O. Henry. Would have looked well in the bookstores: 'The Goldbug' by Goldburg!"

Goldburg rises and leaves without a word.

"Yes," says the wit, "he always leaves the table whenever his name is mentioned in conversation."

An old man comes in, hatless, stumpy, with greyish hair and beard, fine eyes and a laughing mouth. He is wrapped in a clumsy overcoat although it is midsummer, and the ancient trousers hang in a fringe on the dishevelled boots.

"Who's that? "

"Don't know his name—only thing I do know is he hasn't had a room these last eight years."

"No room? Where does he sleep?"

"In cafés here and there. They all know him around here."

I look at him again.

I remember once catching a glimpse of one of the world's richest men; a little, crabbed, wizened old creature, sour discontent etched on his face. And this homeless old man is radiating with happiness and love.

Love . . . some one is talking about it at the next table. An American painter, of German origin, slight, darkhaired, with finely carved features and delicate hands.

"Love . . . " he is saying; ". . . that is what we all want, what we all need. The love that is made up of tolerance and charity. The love that will kiss a loathsome sore. We need it infinitely more than intellect. . . . That man who has just left us is an intellectual. A good man, an honest man, who has written one really great book, and about whom there is no pride. But he hankers after things beyond our reach. Very clever . . . spiritualism and all that. But he does not see the things that are here, at his side, on this earth, things that are merely waiting for Love to fructify them. So he will never, I fear, write another great book. . . ."

"Spheres . . . cubes . . . lozengers . . . angles. . . ."

One would think one was listening to a debate between young geometrical experts. They are painters. Some of them are passably good painters. A larger number imagine they are painters.

"That's nothing, my boy. I have been arrested twelve times in five different countries. I have been twice in jail, once in a fortress, once in an internment camp and once in a lunatic asylum."

The speaker is a journalist.

A languid Dutch girl at his table, playing with an orange scarf splashed with green, remarks:

"Not a bad record. One of the best I know. But then, nearly all my friends have been to prison some time or other. It's quite the thing! "

Two men, both of them fluttering on the outer edge of literature.

"There is a vast difference between the Ideal Woman and the Ideal Wife."

"In theory or in practice?"

He looked nonplussed for a minute, then, easily:

"My dear Rob, woman is theory and wife is practice. But to resume. Ideal Woman is a compound of romantic and imaginative memories. Ophelia and Roxane, Cleopatra and Rosalind—a being of infinite charm, beauty, liveliness and—yes—seductiveness, wreathed in smiles, with golden hair and silvery voice and lips like pomegranates. The Ideal Wife is perfectly different: calm and sympathetic, orderly and well managing, a useful household ornament, dispensing at your will spiritual companionship or domestic felicity."

The person addressed as Rob, an old young man with tired eyes and a flowing tie, pink with round white spots, interrupted:

"Your description sounds like a passage out of an advertisement of a Hire Purchase Furniture Store."

"Don't be flippant! I am trying to show you the inherent difference between. . . ."

"I know—Ideal Woman and the Ideal Wife. It's far shorter and less confusing to show the inherent likeness between them, which is that, being both of them ideal, they are both unattainable and therefore not worth discussing. *Garçon! Garçon!* . . . Confound that waiter! . . . Ah! *Un demi!* "

Two women, and no mere man can put a definite label on them.

"That shock of red straw on her head is real hair, you know. But it ought to be a wig—it really ought to. . . ."

Group of Scandinavians. One of them is pointed out to me as perhaps the acutest art critic in Sweden. Some one has just asked him what he found most beautiful in England.

He reflects for a moment, then flicks the ash off his cigarette:

"Two things—two cities—Oxford and . . . London! "

Thus the "Dôme."

In the corner some one with both hands to his mouth is imitating a gramophone. The black moustached waiter has just smashed his seventh syphon bottle tonight. Outside, a youth is shouting shrilly among the crowded tables: "Cacahouettes! Cacahouettes! ." As he goes out, a tall, golden haired American sweeps four chairs to the ground. . . .

Geoffrey Fraser
21 December 1924

Sinclair Lewis

Montparnasse Intellectual Resents
Sinclair Lewis' Attack on the Dôme

What promises to be the hottest literary feud among the present generation of American writers has just begun. The principals are Mr. Sinclair Lewis, the author of *Main Street* and *Babbitt,* and Mr. Harold E. Stearns, author of *America and the Young Intellectual* and principal editor of *Civilization in the United States.*

The row began with the publication in the October number of *The American Mercury* of Mr. Lewis's article on *Self-Conscious America* in which he attacked the geniuses and their disciples who frequent the Café du Dôme in Montparnasse. The main attack was on a person whom Mr. Lewis referred to as "very father and seer of the Dôme . . . authority on living without laboring." This person, it was insinuated, based his opinions of the intellectual capacity of people on the amount of money he could borrow from them.

To frequenters of the Dôme there was no doubt that the person meant was Mr. Stearns. Mr. Stearns himself was the first to acknowledge that he was the person at whom this hot shot had been fired.

Stearns' Opinion

Weighing his words carefully and speaking in the measured periods which he uses even in the most trivial conversation, Mr. Stearns, in an exclusive interview with the *Tribune,* has told the world, especially the intellectual world, which listens to him attentively, what he thinks of Mr. Lewis.

"I will not join Mr. Lewis in a competition of ignominy," began Mr. Stearns. "Just because Mr. Lewis, by his malicious personal attack, chooses to expose himself at last in public as a cad and bounder, he cannot expect me, in spite of my great admiration for his salesmanship talents, to imitate him.

"Discussing his article objectively, it is chaotic, cheap, inaccurate, and absurd. He missed both the good points and the bad ones of the American Montparnasse colony—the good points, because he couldn't understand them, and the bad ones, because he so perfectly exemplifies them.

"The chief good point, of course, is that remotely, somehow, somewhere, even the dumbest American expatriates have been touched by the spiritual forces of French life. The realization that there is something in France which he has missed was what finally drove Mr. Lewis back to a country where his publications have a dignity which, to Europeans, is simply incomprehensible."

Dômites Of Sorts

"Many of the eccentricities and absurdities which Mr. Lewis mentions are, of course, quite true. In fairness to the people mentioned, I ought to point out, as one of them, that they are only grouped together by Mr. Lewis's spite. With one or two exceptions, they are not social with one another, and in temperament and intellectual outlook are utterly antipathetic.

"However ridiculous may be the people he disparages, they were not so ridiculous as to take Mr. Lewis seriously. He has made the traditionally quaint error of confusing hurt pride with high perspicacity."

10 December 1925

Real Artists Don't Need to Imbibe
Inspiration at the Dôme, Says Bliven

Mr. Bruce Bliven, American political writer and critic who is stopping in Paris on his way back to New York after a tour of the Continent, supports the attitude taken by Sinclair Lewis, famous novelist, in attacking the habitués of the Latin Quarter.

"Of course," Mr. Bliven said in an interview, "it may well be the case that of ten Latin Quarter aesthetes, one genuine artist may be produced. It may also be true that this one artist has a real need for the sort of life the left bank offers. In that case, the nine who provide the milieu may well be excused for the sake of the tenth."

Mr. Bliven went on to suggest, however, that in all probability most of the serious work being done in the arts and literature today as in all periods, is being done by "the men who steal away from places like the Dôme and do their plugging in solitude."

"Sinclair Lewis is an example of the type of artist who not only does not need, but actually detests anything that smacks of a literary clique or a soi-disant esthetic milieu. He wrote most of his first novel during his hours of train-riding while commuting to and from New York where he was engaged in publicity work. He feels that to attempt serious writing in the Paris Quarter is to run the danger of ruining genius."

In this last, Mr. Bliven does not support the creator of Babbitt. "Any writer who is ruined, even by the Latin Quarter, probably would be ruined inevitably, and it might as well be the Quarter as anything else. If a man has real genius in him and is of a certain temperament, not that of Lewis, the Latin Quarter may help him to express himself. On the other hand, a good man probably runs little danger of corruption. He will see through the foolish aspects of Latin Quarter life soon enough, and continue to attend to his work.

2 December 1925

Dr. Cochran Flays Social-climbing, Pleasure-seeking U.S. Expatriates

Social climbing; an inordinate love of money, of popularity, of fashion; a perpetual round of pleasure; an incessant quest for spasms and sensations that resemble real life as much as a penny candle rivals the blaze of the noon-day sun—these are the disintegrating vices which afflict the American colony of Paris, as enumerated by Dr. Joseph Wilson Cochran in his sermon at the American church, Rue de Berri, yesterday.

"After three years of residence in Paris," said Dr. Cochran, "I am stupefied by the extreme indifference of the American expatriates in Paris to things religious. Spirituality has departed from their lives. Indeed, it seems as if these expatriates, before leaving New York, packed whatever religion they had in a suitcase, and then—left the suitcase behind. Love of money, of fashion, of pleasure, of social climbing dominates their lives, and ninety per cent of them have no interest in religion whatsoever. Perhaps the proportion is just as great in the United States, but I doubt it.

"Certain expatriates, having tasted certain physical thrills or experienced certain animal sensations, sing hilariously, 'This is the life! This is the life!' Fools! Imbeciles! What they have experienced has as much relation to life as the flickering of a penny candle to the warmth and light of the sun at midday. Jesus, strangely enough, also said, 'This is the life!' But it was a life of service, of decency, of wholesome pleasure, of constructive activity."

Dr. Cochran's topic was "The Abundant Life," and his attack on the social climbing, money-amassing, pleasure-seeking and fashion-loving expatriates was only incidental, but it helped to emphasize his theme. His sermon was an eloquent reasoned plea for an abundant life, not expressed in dollar marks, or golf scores, or midnight parties, but in the Christian virtues of hope, faith and love realized in practical fashion.

14 June 1926

Elliot H. Paul

From a Litterateur's Notebook

The Americans in Paris, and they are becoming so numerous that I expect some political party in the States will soon start a move to permit them to vote by mail, fall into various classes and each class receives its share of abuse.

Those who have money excite the envy of the natives of low-exchange countries and the penniless have an especially hard time with their French creditors because of the current belief that all citizens of the land of the free are wealthy. If Americans talk, the sound of their voices drowns out the conversation of their more copiously be-vowelled neighbors, and if they keep silent they are suspected of plotting against European prosperity.

Those who know the French language have the disadvantage of being able to understand uncomplimentary remarks and those who do not are uncomfortable because they suspect such remarks are worse than they really are. If they are temperate or moral, it is called bigotry, and the other ninety per cent are thought to be disorderly. To conform to American customs as to dress and deportment exposes one to the charge of being provincial, and if one wears a pinchback suit, a black necktie, and drinks sweet aperitifs, one is accused of aping the Latins.

The tourists, whose orbit swings with reference to the Opera by day and Montmartre by night, ride the big busses, tiptoe through cathedral aisles, stumble along the corridors of the more accessible museums, infest the shops, motor to the battlefields, and spend the balance of their time looking for ham and eggs and ice-cream.

The hardy annuals who go in for society inhabit the Etoile district and are considered snobs by their countrymen and climbers by the remnants of the European aristocracy. The business and professional men have to prey largely upon the tourists, and while away their leisure hours during the closed season by listening to pep talks at the Chamber of Commerce or the American Club.

Visiting politicians entertain Paris journalists with their recollections of prohibition and prosperity in the States in exchange for hints as to what they shall tell the New York journalists about liquor and poverty in Europe, and divide the rest of their stay between the Folies-Bergères, the Embassy, the neighborhood florist, and the tomb of the Unknown Soldier.

The students occupy themselves in trying to find familiar books in the unindexed French libraries, in painting narrow streets in oils, bridges or gardens in water colors, making drawings and woodcuts of hoboes on the Seine, or practicing Czerny's School of Velocity on a pension piano. On Sunday evenings, they gather at some American welfare organization to look at the street scenes, etc., on the walls, and hear one of their classmates play Rachmaninoff's "C-sharp-minor Prelude," ending with community singing of "Seeing Nellie Home" and "Sur le pont d'Avignon."

On both sides of the Atlantic, the ways and days of the afore-mentioned groups are known. They have their friends and admirers, all except the tourists, and the articles or books written at their expense or in their behalf are either avowedly humorous or humorously earnest.

There remains Montparnasse.

Montparnasse is more difficult to define and classify, and by its elusiveness commands either respect or vituperation.

The Montparnassians sleep in the morning and in the afternoon and spend the evening and the neo-evening, up to the rising hour for ashmen and concierges, upon the terrace of The Dôme, The Rotonde, The Sélect, and other neighboring cafés. They have dark circles under their eyes, have read parts of *Ulysses*, and are likely to be self-made Freudians. They speak most impressively when they are vague and most erratically when they seek to be specific. They hate to spend money for either food or clothes.

The fact that they lay themselves open to the conventional kind of ridicule leads me to suspect there is something profound about them, and while their positive qualities escape both quantitative and qualitative analysis, their negative ones are delightful.

First of all, they make no pretense to love work and they do nothing whatever which may be termed useful by any of the known standards, either practical or aesthetic. Although they have a world-wide reputation for Aphrodisian drollaries, actually they are less interested in sex than the average graduating class of a Michigan high school. Prices are too high to admit of drunkenness.

For hours at a time, they sit on the terraces talking of Heaven knows what or staring into space. But why should they be abused? Why should successful magazine writers and wall paper designers sniff at them, when they cannot understand them? If inscrutability is a virtue in La Joconde, Buddha, and the Sphinx, why not in a Montparnassian? If they have devised a mode of life which cannot be utilized even in this most efficient of civilizations, all honor to them. They are no funnier than the business men, the producing artists, or the politicians, and exist with much less exertion and gusto.

Elliot H. Paul
29 August 1926

Left Bank Notes

With the first of June, as every year, the season begins—and not merely for Parisians, but for the American and English Left Bank quarters. It is a common thing now to hear one say on the terrace of either the Dôme or Le Sélect, "The *Berengaria* gets in tomorrow at Cherbourg in the morning and the *Paris* at Havre in the afternoon—there will be a big crowd up here after dinner tomorrow night." And a big crowd there always is. Familiar faces are returning. When I stop to think of a few of them—Sinclair Lewis, Raymond Holland, "Sandy" Rome, Horace Kallen, Frank Frazier, Robert Chanler, "Barney" Gallant—that I have encountered either in Montparnasse, at the race-track, or "over town" in the more pretentious cafés, where prices are usually a bit too high for your continually indigent Left Banker, I realize how Paris and the Left Bank in the last five years have become almost a road-house suburb to New York. People pass through Montparnasse, even when they do not stay there long, and I fancy had anyone the temerity to sit for two years during the busy hours on the terrace of the Dôme, there would hardly be anybody of importance or interest whom he had not seen at least once. Except, of course, Lindbergh, who was so carefully guarded that he never had a chance to see Paris as a normal tourist would, that is, to have a good time and to take a peek at Montparnasse. But even then by straining one's neck last Saturday around one o'clock, he could have been seen where he properly belongs, in the sky. Montparnasse misses nothing—even occasional boredom.

But it will be difficult to be bored this month, the most glorious in the Paris calendar. The earnest schoolteachers and flip flappers on a vacation that will not improve their minds seldom have time to arrive before the very end of the month, when the Grand Prix has been run and it is all over.

Only the leisured, the idle, the independently curious, and the plain fantastic who, like God in Romantic poetry, arrive at the most unexpected moments [and] can be counted upon—which makes it more amusing and exciting. Anything, consequently, can happen during these four weeks in the Montparnasse ballyhoo, including nothing at all, as seems to be the case usually on Sunday evenings. For on Sunday evenings, with the celebration of that ancient Anglo-Saxon custom of "Saturday night," nearly every true Montparnassian is financially on his heels, and the favorite fairy story of the early Monday morning hours is commonly about "waiting for the banks to open." When Monday, too, happens to be a holiday, then desolation is complete. For it is a measure of the difference between the old Montparnasse and the new that in this year of grace, as contrasted with the more simple joys of 1920, 1921, and 1922, it is money rather than wit that sings, so that when there is no abundance of francs with which to tip unnecessary "chasseurs," to pay more for a simple glass of beer or port or champagne than even the most lavish of Frenchmen would do in his right mind, to take a taxicab back home to more bathroom-bedecked quarters on double rates, to buy expensive cigarettes because it is too much trouble to get them at a tobacco-shop, then the tone and temper of Montparnasse dwindles and dies. It is sometimes not the same in the other sections of the Left Bank, though there—as traditionally—the arrival of a good check was always the signal for a holiday. But it is true of Montparnasse, and I give fair warning to prospective tourists.

June, however, is different. Money magically becomes more plentiful. The weather is too fine ordinarily to do anything but put even the worst grouches in good temper. Everything is going on at full blast—art exhibitions, the best of the races, society functions that occasionally draw upon Montparnasse for their window-dressing freaks, the arrival of old friends, the blossoming of new flirtations simultaneously with a long list of "divorces granted," and above all the magic of these warm late-Spring Paris nights. It is easier to be happy in Paris, probably, than anywhere else in this modern machine world: it is very easy in June: with a little luck, it is easiest of all in Montparnasse, when—as now—it is in its old and best temper of good-humour, tolerance, and "laissez-faire." It is difficult in this mood to start controversies or to try to belabor certain of the intellectual and artistic pretensions that are strutting their little day now among some of the most aggressively modern of American writers and painters. I shall reserve this pleasure for a later date, when the weather has been bad, my favorite horse has been looking out the window and lost me my month's salary, and I have had a bad dinner.

Harold E. Stearns
2 June 1927

Montparnasse Glances

From twilight on, the "American Bars" in Montparnasse are crowded with raucous, virile, and alas, sometimes mundane gentlemen from the United States. From the viewpoint of understanding and idealism, one might hope that these gentlemen did not travel to Paris for the sole purpose of securing excellent, inexpensive, and legally sanctioned beverages, and yet, the rapidity with which they empty their glasses, and their reluctance toward leaving the havens in question, would seem to suggest that Paris, to them, consists of a gratified thirst, sometimes acquiescent and slightly mercenary ladies, and a chance to swagger in the roles of imaginary kings.

The *rodomontade* at Montparnasse tables and bars is a little amusing, a little pathetic, and never deserted. At this table we have a tall gentleman in a huge, high-crowned, black hat, with a gold watch-fob dangling from his vest and an air of bored, stolid importance. Two young ladies in pale blue hats invariably sit beside him and reveal an attitude of pouting complacency which can scarcely be based upon anything except the fact that they have pretty faces. A poet and novelist, wearing an old rose *béret*, takes a seat near them, and the trio regard him with supercilious smiles, stares, and whispered asides. Any departure from the ordinary in visual appearance is a silly weakness to such people. . . . Nearby, a stout lady with an aristocratic nickname, and a face where haughtiness and weariness are slightly more assumed than real, sits with a wooden-faced, sullen man. She will sit with at least seven or eight other men, in rotation, before dawn arrives, and the air of self-conscious superiority will never quite leave her face. The ancient Chinese had a proverb which applies perfectly to such ladies, and the proverb goes: "Rice-pickers are often insolent to their neighbors but *Mandarins* can always afford to be unassuming."

At another table we have a gentleman with a huge shock of brown hair and sideburns slanting down the middle of each cheek. He earns his living by wandering through the cafés and making semi-photographic sketches of men and women, who purchase them as souvenirs—to the happy purchasers art is only the second word in the phrase: "Thou art commanded to be commercial."

At still another table we have a group of young German artists and students, who exchange gossip about the people they know and look at passersby with a sneering and inimitable smugness. Since they can be seen sitting at the tables, on and off, from noon to midnight, a visitor from Mars might be tempted to wonder whether they ever worked, or whether it might be possible to discover some excuse for their existence. . . . At a table to the left we can spy a young English girl, who claims to be an artist—if you met anyone in Montparnasse who didn't claim to be one, you would never recover! —and is forever waiting for some man, or woman, with whom she will sit for hours and trade the most banal babbling possible to human beings. . . . At a table to the right a group of American artists and dawdlers gather and spend an hour in dilating upon the alleged stupidity, queerness, and silliness of some gentleman whom they know, with endless anecdotes followed by volleys of derisive laughter. After listening to their conversation for a while, one begins to wonder whether the man whom they are ridiculing may not be an exceptionally intelligent person!

Other figures rise in the background—a young Russian girl with thick lips, calcimined face, and an air of: "Amuse me, varlet!"—she might grow pale if she were ever assigned the task of amusing herself: an amateur actress sitting with a young Swede and assuming a mien of professional listlessness; an American lady in a green leather jacket, whose fingers are burdened with diamond rings, possibly from the fear that people might otherwise think that she was poverty-stricken.

Midnight comes but still they sit and chatter with scarcely a minute of silence, and drink, and burnish their little phantom thrones—the red and blue chairs where self-weary indolence pretends to be aristocracy.

Maxwell Bodenheim
14 April 1929

Is Art Center Cause, or Merely Scene, of Tragedies?

Not being a real sob-sister, I cannot assess the wickedness of Montparnasse. It is splitting hairs to argue whether or not such an environment is destructive to some people or not. Weaklings carry within them the seeds of their own disintegration, and Montparnasse is a place where such weaklings congregate. When the disintegration is complete, there is a tragedy, if the violent abridging of a life can be called tragedy.

Within the last four years, I have known of four suicides in Montparnasse, two of whom were Americans. All these people were gnawed by internal uneasiness. Montparnasse gave them something which they wanted, in opposition to other things, and then they found that they did not want Montparnasse. To live there requires (or rather used to, for I cannot speak of the present) a perverted courage.

People who all their lives have been taught the virtues of industry and of punctuality, find themselves in a place where those virtues are unknown. They can at last indulge themselves in the cravings of the unregenerate man—immense laziness and immense aimlessness. Days flit by in the unending undistinction of drinks and chatter, each one a perfect unpricked bubble on the sea of time.

Only the more robust or the more logical souls can stand so much indulgence in what all their lives they have dreamed of doing. They betray their uneasy consciences by the endless repetition of the Montparnasse litany "gotta getta work—starting tomorrow." Finally that uneasy conscience gets the better of everyone who has lived there, and then they see that the only thing to do is to go away. Some, deciding they can go no better place, go to their graves.

Alex Small
8 August 1929

Why This Montparnasse?

To the Editor of *The Tribune:*

Sir:

I visited Montparnasse the other day.

To many this name connotes Paris and all that in there is. For myself, I was rather disappointed. I do not say that there is anything radically wrong with the structural amenities of Montparnasse. It is the people who inhabit that delectable quarter—there is something queer about them.

I asked a friend of mine what was this amazing collection of amazing people that I found congregated on the café's terraces there. He solemnly assured me that there were to be found the great writers, artists and musicians of the coming generation. My first impression was that the majority suffered from the lack—absolute lack—of the veriest vestiges of tonsorial attention.

Still, I suppose that wild shocks of unkempt and uncared for hair and straggly growths of unpicturesque whisker are the necessary accompaniments of the real artistic temperament. What matters personal hygiene so long as the divine flame of inspiration burns within?

I believe also that a probationary period of starving in a garret is a *sine qua non* to the ultimate achievement of fame as a literary luminary, or the possession of a niche in the Valhalla of the great painters.

Well, none of the denizens of that quarter, impressed me as being particularly desirous of enduring the preliminary starving process, either in a garret or anywhere else.

Then we have the female of the species. Her hair, in contradistinction to that of the male, is worn in inverse ration. In fact, the feminine fashion of hairdressing would seem to be the sole justification for the existence of barbers in Montparnasse.

A very queer people indeed! Between periods of starving—that is to say, the painting of worthless pictures which no one will buy and the production of reams of piffling drivel which never reaches the hand of the compositor and which no normal person would read even if it did—they take their inspiration in glasses, generally a pale green liquid smelling like cough mixture.

I am not trying to fight the battles of the city of Paris. If the authorities care to tolerate this weird and worthless agglomeration of unwanted and unwashed humanity—well, the fault is Paris's.

I am, etc.

R. F. D.
22 February 1930

One Reason Why

To the Editor of *The Tribune:*

Sir:

R. F. D.'s (Rural Free Delivery?) scathing criticism of the futility of "This Montparnasse" may be readily refuted. His condemnation of the denizens of That Quarter as a horde of unshriven, unshaven effetes merely indicates that he fails to understand their highly organized sensitive artistic natures. Undaunted by his taunts and gibes, they will continue to hold aloft the dull diadem of Unattainment, the trident of Despair so long as vibrates the inner urge. For them it is a salutary struggle to strive to realize the ideal to which they pay such deep and rabid devotion. Even the vagrant few who clamber at the Portals of Dementia, a prey to inward gloom, experience such aspirations, joys and tender sorrows as he wots not of.

Montparnasse is set high upon a rock, and his supercilious and self-complacent attitude will not lessen the consumption of the saffron and bewitching kirshbaum, nor diminish the nectarious delight of a passionate love for Art. The terraces will continue to be encumbered by "this amazing collection of amazing people" who pass their time in watching the heavy clouds scud airily into the black chalice of another day, the while the green "i" and the red circumflex fasten keenly upon their idea of transfixed pride.

I am, etc.

Tristan Gervais
24 February 1930

Yesterday's Montparnasse

Phil Sawyer Mourns Passing of Old
Latin Quarter; Decides To Go Home

Old timers in the Latin Quarter say it is not a shadow of its former self for picturesque, medieval, inexpensive living. Before, the old Dôme was frequented by a little family of artists, whereas it has now become "a sort of open air post-graduate school for tourists to study life," as Phil Sawyer, the former art critic of *The Chicago Tribune,* wittily observed. He says also that he is a little fed up on the change and is sailing for home.

Shorty Lazar is still there as he was when the corner was built. Alexander Harrison drops in occasionally while Otto Gaenslen has gone across the street. Bi-Bi la Purée has gone into the great beyond and little Jeanne of the Crémerie has long since married. The Hole in the Wall went when Boulevard Raspail was pushed through.

In the old days, they talked of literature and painting at the Dôme; today, the only subject for discussion is the exchange. Sixteen men could sit around one drink and the waiters never kicked and said "merci beaucoup" for two sous.

A few of the stars in those days were Dickey Brooks, Lionel Walden, Alfie Maurer, Bill Noble, Pop Farrar, Augustus Thomas, Booth Tarkington, Edgar Mills, Edward Simmons, George Luks, Jimmy Preston, Pat Rumsey, Berkeley Smith, Tom Robbins, and Mickey Burns, the jockey. True, there were very few of the fair "Americaines" then and there was not "jovial Flossie."

Since coming over as a mate on a transport ship and serving in the French artillery, Mr. Sawyer has brought his work in portraiture up to a high standard as his annual exhibitions in the Salon have testified. He is now returning home for an exhibition of his work and to paint more portraits.

6 August 1925

Left Bank Notes

Begun by somebody who has been familiar with it—occasionally, perhaps, a bit too familiar—for several years, a new series of comments on the old subject of the Latin, or Montparnasse, quarter of Paris justifies a hint of the general attitude of the writer towards his theme. Particularly can it be endured, since with this introduction gladly goes a promise that variations on the same theme will not often be repeated. It is evident the writer keeps a certain affection for the Latin Quarter, even if in many ways it was jollier, more intimate and loyal, less commercialized and gaudy in the years gone by than one can find it nowadays. Otherwise he would not write about it at all, as it is well known that he is undauntedly lazy and has to be forced by bayonets to write about anything—except, possibly, horses and horse-races.

But though one laments the good old days when the Dôme was dingy and had a billiard room, when Le Sélect was an old furniture shop and The Dingo an ordinary bistro, when Parnass Bar, The Vikings, and the new La Grande Chaumière did not exist, when the American and English students and visitors actually talked French and those who didn't made serious effort to learn it, when there was camaraderie instead of exploitation, when it was possible without meditation and prayer to think of a dozen people in the Quarter with whom one might have an entertaining and intelligent conversation—though gone are those intellectual snows of yesterday under the desert blight of progress and too easy transportation, the Quarter remains.

Or, to be more accurate, the Left Bank remains. The little section clustering to the corner of the Boulevards Raspail and Montparnasse is, after all, only one part of the Left Bank of artists, dreamers, drinkers, students, and vagabonds, and not by any means the most important part. For example, if any youngster fresh from college were asked to name what sort of people he expected to see in the Latin Quarter in Paris, he would probably reply Santayana, if he was thinking in terms of the old tradition, and James Joyce, if he was thinking in terms of the new. I name these two, because both happen to be idols of the day as well as of the past, and by all groups. Now he would probably never see Santayana in the Quarter, though he has lived often on occasion near-by with a friend on the Avenue de l'Observatoire. When alone—and Santayana is usually alone—he lives in a little hotel in one of the noisest and busiest of Paris spots, the Place de la République. Like most hermits of great sensitiveness and intelligence, he likes the bustle and stir of humanity all around him, though not touching him, as bachelors usually believe in large families. Yet I have often seen him having dinner with his friend Professor Strong at Duval's, next to the Café des Deux Magots at Saint-Germain des Près, so that in one sense he is part of the life of the Left Bank, when in Paris. But our youngster would look in vain for him at either the Dôme or Le Sélect.

He would come nearer his quest with Joyce, but even then, he would have to wait a long number of months for him in the true American Montparnasse section of today. For a period—perhaps the habit continues—Joyce took his dinner at Les Trianons, a restaurant opposite the Gare Montparnasse, and of course he could be seen every now and then near the Odéon and Sylvia Beach's bookshop. But the Dôme saw him practically never. If not discouraged, and courageous in his quest to see the great persons of our modern culture, the American youth might catch a glimpse of a new literary idol, Ernest Hemingway, when the latter passes through the Quarter on his way to or from Spain, Switzerland, and Austria, or even New York. He might see Sinclair Lewis once in a blue moon, but it would be Sinclair in quest of this writer or of a good time, not Sinclair in a serious articulate mood. He might see Ludwig Lewisohn oftener, though not often. He would see certain of the better known French, European, and American painters, sculptors, and musicians from time to time, but once more not frequently. In a word, he would stand a better chance to see the real people that interested him by exploring other parts of the Left Bank—the real, i.e., the French, Latin Quarter near the Boulevard Saint Michel—than by remaining firmly in Montparnasse.

For it is the Left Bank, not Montparnasse, which endures. The old Montparnasse was a special thing, and it has almost vanished into a

memory. The new Montparnasse is a different thing and in many respects
not so pleasant and intelligent a thing as the old.

Harold E. Stearns
26 May 1927

Left Bank Notes

With the full rush of summer and the visiting vacationists from home,
sometimes it seems on the Left Bank nowadays—particularly in the
Saint-Germain-des-Prés and Montparnasse Quarters—as if a recapture of a
bit of the old spirit of 1913, 14, and 15 in the brief true Bohemia of New
York before the war submerged us all and changed us all were not
impossible. Those were the days when rents really were cheap in
Washington Square, and the real estate of the Greenwich Village section
had not been exploited for the benefit of stock-brokers looking for
"atmosphere" and relief from the boredom of respectability in those
monotonously same houses on Upper Riverside Drive.

Those were the days when Sinclair Lewis was not a best seller, and felt
himself lucky, if he could have a dinner at the old Brevoort: when Jack
Reed was writing for the old *Masses* and Max Eastman cared more about
poetry than Russia: when Bertelloti's, Castle Cave, and Billy The
Oysterman's served meals at a third of the price of today and were three
times better in quality; when *The New Republic* was young, uninstitu-
tionalized, almost diffident, and neither *The Freeman* nor the new *Dial*
existed: when Gilbert Seldes was unknown and not unhappy over it: when
the Washington Square and Provincetown Players were starting, fathers of
the present prosperous Theatre Guild; when the Algonquin Lunch Table
was unthought of and H. L. Mencken was still regarded as a rebel; when
writing was for something beside a check, red wine softened the palate
rather than as today when synthetic gin congeals it, when Van Loon had
not written *The Story of Mankind*, and Walter Weyle had the finest
moustache in New York.

How the names come, when I think of those days! Let me see: Helen
Westley, the Boni brothers (not then incorporated to capitalize the second
B), Cuthbert Wright, Walter Franzen, Harry Kemp, Mary Pyne, Djuna
Barnes, Frances Gifford, Griffin Barry, Hiram Moderwell, Kenneth
MacGowan, Van Loon, Mary Heaton Vorse, Bob Minor, Susan Glaspell,
Edward Massy, Eddie Goodman, Jimmie Smith, Philip MacMahon, lovely
Vyvian Donner, Edward Eyre Hunt—really I think I could go on for a page
of enumeration, and then leave half unaccounted for. A few of these
mentioned and thought of, like Walter Franzen and Mary Pyne, are no
longer with us, and it seems difficult to believe. Most of the others at one
time or another come to Paris regularly, with natural gravitation towards
the Left Bank. Some are perennial, and seem even to get younger as the
years pass, like Griffin Barry and Cuthbert Wright, the second of whom I

met the other day at the "Deux Magots" on my way to the races. Cuthbert is the eternal undergraduate, whom it is inconceivable to imagine as ever growing old, even though he has taken on the apparent dignity of maturity with the publication of what I understand is an extremely fair, entertaining, and yet sound history of the Catholic Church. But the quality of his mind, its pliancy and sensuous perceptiveness, seems never to become dulled by experiences. The world war made him a trifle more bitter perhaps, but then, it did that to most of us.

Djuna Barnes, too, I observed the other day at the "Deux Magots": she spends much of her time in Paris. Then, also, this week, I saw Philip MacMahon again after several years: he has abandoned advertising to become a professor of Spanish Art in New York University, rather a drastic change, when one thinks of it. Edward Massy likewise appeared on the scene, charming as ever and pre-occupied as ever with new plays he is writing and has written, as is never-failingly George Middleton. It is really astonishing how that general group, with its ramifications, which we may say began to be articulate and wag its tail in the five years between 1911 and 1916, has branched out into every sort of artistic, political, even business and industrial activity, and how much it has done to leave an impress on our time. It is still active and alive, too, and in spite of ourselves our lives are constantly interweaving, touching forgotten shreds of our personalities in the most unexpected situations and places, reacting back on ourselves and others of that group even when quarrels have divided us or petty jealousies made us suspicious. Whether we like it or not, we are all tarred with the same brush; we all understand each other; we come from the same background; we have all tasted the same bitter waters of disillusion and revolt.

Paris is the cross-roads of the world in an intellectual and artistic sense, even more than in a political one, and to it come at some time or other—for brief or long periods—everyone cursed with ideas, sensibility, political curiosity, or the passion for wandering and seeing the world. At some time or other they pass through the Quarters of the Left Bank, though it is rare for them to remain permanently—they are too restless. Paris thus naturally becomes a sort of cross-roads for this group of which I have spoken but hardly even attempted to describe.

The Left Bank is really the most natural place in the world for exchange of reminiscence and forgotten ambitions, a sort of clearing-house for those old memories. New forces are springing up, of course, revolt-driven as are most new forces with vitality and courage. Sometimes I wonder if they quite realize how much they owe [us] for their weapons of attack and defense from the stupid. . . . Perhaps one of these days it would not be uninteresting to point out one of two of the things that are directly due.

Harold E. Stearns
24 July 1927

Shadow of M.E. Church Hung Over
Montparnasse And Its Tawdry Bums

To understand the Montparnasse of a few years ago, one should first know the preconceived ideas with which people approached it. With most people, those ideas were mainly concerned with the outward and obvious sides of what was supposed to be the life there. One could dress as one pleased and one could get as drunk as one pleased, and one did not have to account to the neighbors for one's private life. It was, literally, another vie de bohème.

To those with higher aspirations, Montparnasse meant something more profound. It was what they had imagined Greenwich Village to be, before they had blown the foam off that, and become thoroughly disillusioned. It was the free city to which the weary eyes of the anarchistic part of humanity had been aspiring. Economic problems had been solved either by stodgy ancestors, about whom one did not care to be reminded, or by a sublime will to disregard the whole business. You did not have to put on side; you could be yourself.

And you would find yourself in a society of ideal sophistication, hardened to every possible vicissitude of fortune or every caprice of human nature. You could scale the heights of Olympus, if you wished; or you could systematically go to hell. No one would care. Delirium tremens was a joke, and death was a subject for a gale of laughter. Whatever the dull people of the world anywhere had cherished was to be the butt of the wisecracks. Out of this was to come the ideal life, in which the main concern was not mere existence, nor any of the silly casual occupations with which most people take up their time, but the arts which ennoble life, including the greatest of all the arts, that of life.

With these preconceived ideas, the panting pilgrim from Mansfield, Ohio, approached Montparnasse. Usually he was sadly disillusioned, if he ever came up for air long enough really to see the spectacle before him. What he saw was not a company of sublime and liberated companions of Lucifer, fallen though ever so enlightened, but a gang of tawdry bums, who did not even have the courage to be frank about their uselessness, but had to invent transparent excuses, such as going to "work" next week or month. Few had any native talent even in conversation, and still fewer had the breeding and cultivation to put up the facade which takes the place of real ability. What had brought them to Montparnasse was a vague discontent with their former environment. They had in common their inarticulate restlessness.

That is dead, now, that life in Montparnasse, and a decent respect should prompt me to say only good of it. Much that is good is really to be said of those wastrels who were my familiars for some years, but first the case should be taken at its worst. What was so absurd about the whole lot was not what shallow critics used to say, that they were accomplishing nothing. That is thoroughly untrue; they were loafing and drinking and palavering. What irked me, for one, was that few had the courage to be completely themselves, to be useless and to be proud of it. They wished desperately to be emancipated, but few knew how to achieve emancipation. They had to revolt against something definite, and that something definite was the ideas and prejudices of the people back home.

Over all Montparnasse hung the shadow of the First Methodist Sunday School. It was no accident that profanity and obscenity was the substance of all the talk there; every one had to outdo the other in profanity and obscenity to show how completely one had conquered the inherited and acquired inhibitions.

As for being free on the economic side, a bohemian, the American of the Montparnasse of a few years ago broke down completely. What with him passed for bookkeeping was, of course, fantastic, but never did he lose sight of essentials. Often he showed a superb indifference to solid nourishment, but he never forgot his drinking. He knew, too, that the hotel-keepers and bartenders of Montparnasse could be bluffed only so much. Sooner or later came the day when you had really to take something out of your pocket which looked like money, and really was money. Many a tradesman got rooked, of course, but the proportion of bills that really were paid was much higher than romanticists of Montparnasse think. I have yet to hear of more than one person (and I know that one) who got away with a first class swindle in that region.

The old American Montparnassian therefore was very cagey about ordering the drinks. The free and easy, communistic assumption about Montparnasse was to him so much literature. He did not buy the drinks liberally, and he usually sneaked off to dine alone. In any crisis, he showed a talent for check-fumbling which would make a visiting millionaire jealous. And he was assiduous about the pathetic cables home, which told how he had just broken a leg or had been sent to the hospital. Then he would get into a taxi, go over to what he disdainfully called the "right bank," as if it were a taint to live over there, and, once before the cashier of the bank which had his remittance, show all the acuteness of a pawnbroker in disputing about the exchange.

Alex Small
6 April 1929

No Inhibitions and No Work—
Such Was Montparnasse Formerly

The Montparnasse of a few years ago was not, so far as the Americans in it were concerned, a gathering place of free and distinguished spirits who were practising the arts. Most of them had no familiarity with the arts. They did not read, though some occasionally pretended that they kept up with all the latest books. Their thirst for knowledge was assuaged by the English-language newspapers of Paris. Few displayed any intellectual curiosity about France and the French. Whenever one did hear an opinion expressed about this country, it was usually condemnatory. The most summary judgments based on preconceived ideas sufficed.

It was, for one thing axiomatic that all Frenchmen were sou-pinchers, and that the intellectual and creative life of this country was dead. Few Americans in Montparnasse could read French with ease, and still fewer could speak more than enough to order their drinks. Any sincere attempt to master the language, or even just to get some honest impression of France by taking the trouble really to see what was going on in front of one's eyes, was a snobbish affectation. Of all the ill that can be said about the now dissolved American group of Montparnasse, this willful blindness to the culture and civilization of France is the worst count.

Chroniclers of the doings of the Left Bank have written, at least in newspapers, of the "discussion" that went on in the studios and cafés of Montparnasse. The implication was that highbrow badinage about literature and esthetics was the ordinary sort of conversations. I wish that just once I could have got into one of these feasts of wit and eloquence. Maybe I had bad luck, but I have seen just two sorts of studio-parties in Montparnasse—the serious sort where literature was really talked in the sense that people matched names and titles with each other, and the non-serious sort, which was just a plain drunken brawl, such as could have been staged back home on Main Street. Nor at any Montparnasse café have I ever heard any discussion of esthetic theories, nor indeed, could there have been any in that group of old Montparnasse, so few had knowledge of the most elementary terms which would have had to be used. Of the efforts made by any of the young painters, when they painted, the simplest words sufficed for critical eyepreciation, such as "original" or "strong." There was but one damning reproach; it was to have fallen into a mystic heresy known as being "conventional."

In compensation, there was one sort of conversation in which the Montparnassians excelled. That was gossip and personalities. It began usually with autobiographer, and the hapless victim of the monologue would be lucky if he could escape without hearing all about the amorous, intellectual, and spiritual life of the talker. It is unimaginable that anywhere in the world would relative strangers from widely separated regions of the United States, on no provocation, unbosom the most intimate secrets with no reticence whatever. Everyone who came to Montparnasse had the passion for explaining himself. It was a daily revelation of the number of unique and misunderstood people in the world.

As in Montparnasse, no one spared himself, neither did he spare others. Tourists who were looking for thrills could have got them aplenty out of one of those conversations. No one could quit a party of four or five drinkers without at once having his or her character torn to shreds. The subject's physical peculiarities, his opinions, his drinking, and his love-affairs—all were examined. Literally, every one was living in a glasshouse and everyone threw stones.

In most of this there was really no malice. It was just taken for granted that personalities were highly interesting, and each person was expected to contribute to the entertainment of the community a picture of his character, entirely nude. Whatever rules of conduct had been learned in earlier life about the sort of conversation which is the only one possible among civilized ladies and gentlemen, had been forgotten in Montparnasse.

Probably it was this complete absence of all reticence which gave Montparnassians the sense of living in a community unique in the world. To add to the gayety, and to the unreality of the atmosphere, no one in the crowd I am describing ever worked. There were serious painters in Montparnasse then, as there always had been, but they could not be distinguished, except for some negligence in dress, from a tourist. The fantoches who gave Montparnasse its reputation, though they sometimes vaguely hinted that soon they were going to "get down to work," knew that they were fooling no one, not even themselves. Fresh from America, new arrivals would really go and take a few lessons at Colarozzi's or at Julian's, but it did not take them long to discover that they could not drink all night and then paint all day. In all but a few cases of exceptional virtue, they chose to drop the painting.

Of course, even had they been so disposed, it was impossible for these Americans, being exiles, to get jobs at any of the ordinary occupations of the world. Hence the way in which many of them solved their economic problems was a perpetual mystery. His finances were the one subject on which the average Montparnassian kept a thorough discretion. The admission that you had any steady income of any kind would have marked you as the victim for all the panhandlers.

Far more than ever admitted it were getting allowances from the United States. Every one officially was broke, and many actually were, at different periods; yet this community of idlers lived in relative comfort with enough to eat, most of the time, and always plenty to drink. Every one borrowed from every one else, of course, as much as possible, but obviously that game was bound to come to an end some day. Fresh supplies had to come in from the outside world, in this case, from America. And it was apparent that, in spite of the regular pleas of complete poverty, especially if you were trying to make a touch, that the amount of that money was considerable.

The individuals of that crowd are now all scattered. A few are still in Paris or in the newer art colonies along the Riviera. The majority have gone back to the United States, where, from casual reports, they have accepted their destinies, after their one brief escape. That a Montparnassian community does not exist somewhere today, I should not deny, but it is not in Montparnasse. That is now too vast, too given over entirely to the business of being another Montmartre. No homogeneous group can gather in dance halls or in cafés as big as railway stations. Studios there still are aplenty in the Quarter, but they are a new and luxurious variety. People who pay that much rent do not go in for being ribald, fantastic, and thoroughly irresponsible.   Alex Small

7, 9 April 1929

Beyond the Quarter

Paris in Ut-Mineur

It is toward the outskirts of a big city that the stigmata of personality break down, grow blurred and confused. What individuality has Paris, for instance, 200 yards either side of the exterior boulevards? I asked myself this question last Thursday while I was taking a walk. I had just been to the Abattoir de Vaugirard.

I was walking along with my head down. Between the cobblestones were huge gobs of blood. Chemin de Perichaux was the street. Pleasant, too, despite the blood. Gardens and courts running back from the winding lane. A rooster crowed. The last time I had heard a rooster crow was in Le Chien Qui Fume, and it turned out later that it wasn't a rooster.

The houses were plain and substantial, like all French provincial houses, like French power houses, like French telephone and telegraph bureaus, like French slaughter-houses. A little girl sat in a window. She had golden hair and her face was grave and pensive. She belonged in a book by Du Maurier. More windows. Laborers with vacant faces, going pleasantly crazy with time on their hands. Peasant women with iron loins and busts of marble leaning idly over the balconies. Grown lop-sided with toil, their solid bulk poised in a luminous ambiance, they recalled to my mind the dreams of Lurcat, of Gromaire.

Now I am walking along the outer boulevards. The country begins to dip and roll, the houses are scrambled in the hills, smoke rises up from the factories, and between the telegraph poles is discernible the scar of the railway. "Cold and mournful perspective of the suburbs." Suburbs are everywhere the same. I think of Corona, Maspeth, Bayonne, of places I have never seen, of cemeteries and vacant lots, of dump heaps where the goats browse among empty ketchup bottles and tins of sardines, where the ozone becomes sewer gas and the clouds are filled with dishwater.

Ambling leisurely along the Rue de la Porte de Vanves. Stop. Where am I? Am I in Europe or in North Carolina? These miserable shacks that line the road—who lives in them? They tumble over one another like discarded rattle-traps in a Ford cemetery. Pieced together with tin, canvas, odd pieces of lumber, mattresses, empty-sacks. Poorer than poor whites. No joy in them, no music. Cold and mournful, without perspective, without future or past. Patches of farm and thrown together like old rags. Women with wooden shoes spading the ground, or pitching manure. Chicken coops and dog kennels. Plots of parsley and leeks. An old farmhouse with a great, untidy yard, such a yard as little Count Mölln once played in. Kai Mölln

who tried to make a man of Hanno Buddenbrooks. A gate of slats
barricades the entrance to the yard.

It is only a stone's throw from here that Emile Zola once lived. Emile
Zola Philosophe-Ecrivain: 1840–1902. Nobody around here remembers
him. He's a dead letter. So are the others: Gambetta, Renan, Hugo,
Voltaire, Béranger, Rouget de l'Isle ... Soon I will come to that other
back number, President Wilson. How long will Wilson's name linger in the
street directories of Europe?

I am strangely excited. Not the names, but the streets themselves, their
stagnant hues, their decrepitude, their pallor as of disease. It is this excites
me. They may be named after the wordmongers but the reality of them
belongs to the painter, to those especially who, like Goya, Daumier,
Utrillo, fevered in the streets. I pass a worker leaning against a lamppost,
his muscles relaxed, his thoughts opaque. It is on the Rue Victor-Hugo I
am walking. No, I am not walking. I have stopped. I am looking above a
colored awning, at a gilded sign which reads: BOUCHERIE HIPPO-
PHAGIQUE. It seems like a portent or an omen. Curious word—
hippophagique. A scion of that large family which gave to the world such
monsters as "anthrophagous," "phagomania," etc. Distantly related to this
family, as the bronco is to the jackass, is the *Ivorious* clan: herbivorous,
carnivorous, criniverous, to mention only the more outstanding members
of the family.

There is about this *bouchérie* the aura of the Exposition Hall. In the
show-window is an enormous paste-board horse spread open like a page
from the Apocrypha. It is decorated with plates and medals, with rosettes
and ribbons. The proprietor eyes me suspiciously while I make a sketch of
it in my notebook. How intelligent the horse looks by comparison! I
wonder how this butcher would look if he were split open like a saloon
door and hung from two iron pegs.

In Malakoff I whiled away a pleasant hour or so in a *guinguette*. Two
men in uniform were playing billiards. The cue ball refused to stay on the
table. After a time they grew tired of playing billiards and sat down to
play cards. The madame came from behind the bar and gave each of them
an affectionate kiss for which she received in exchange an affectionate pat
on the rump. Then she went back to the bar, took all the glasses and
bottles down from the shelves and gave them a Spring cleaning. The names
on the bottles put me in a pleasant reverie. I ordered a couple of Easter
eggs and thought of the posters in the windows of the Ligue Contre
l'Alcoolisme on the Boulevard Saint Germain. How can one expect to
wage war against the poetry of the bottle with charts and statistics?

Stepping outdoors I feel that I am emerging from a dream. There is
green ink in the gutter and the houses are dilapidated, lean against one
another like drunken sailors. Canaries are singing in their commodious jails
that oscillate with the wind. The cages flap gently against the damp,
cracked walls. And from the windows in the gloomy quadrangles iron
clothes-hangers extend rigidly, reminding me of the noisy triangles in a
Tschaikowsky symphony. The clothes are full of holes, like the *1812*

Overture. The gardens, in which there are no flowers have the melancholy aspect of abandoned cemeteries. The car track winds like a lizard through the sour streets.

"There are in Paris certain streets," wrote Balzac, "as dishonorable as can be any man convicted of infamy; there are murderous streets, streets older than the oldest possible dowagers . . . in short, the streets of Paris have human qualities and impress us by their physiognomy with certain ideas against which we are defenceless." These are the streets with character, but in the suburbs there is no character; the streets have names, but the names do not belong to them. There is a physiognomy, but it is one of despair. They yawn like empty vestibules.

Alfred Perlès
8 March 1931

Bloodstained and Boozy, Battered and Old, Soldier of Street Still Sticks to Colors

A good soldier is one who, no matter how badly wounded, does not forget that he is a soldier. I found that out on the Rue St. Jacques the other night.

It was about 3 o'clock in the morning and I was walking along thinking that the good people of Paris leave their streets at night to the Americans and the police. But that night I was not alone on the Rue St. Jacques. As I turned the bend between the Rue des Feuillantines and the Val de Grace, walking in the street because the sidewalk is too narrow even for one person, I saw a woman lurching along some yards ahead. Head and arms hanging, she moved in jerks, unconsciously trying to keep from falling and make a little progress at the same time. As if giving up, she stumbled against the wall, and leaned there motionless until I rushed up from behind her.

Before me was the dusty side of a bedraggled coat and a mat of black hair. Below were two dirty shoes, and one of her stockings had lost its dignity and was curled around the ankle. I took hold of her arm.

"May I help you? " I asked. No answer. I shook the arm slightly, but still no answer. I shook her arm again, and slowly the mat of hair moved and a face appeared. It was covered with dirt and blood. The round nose was scratched, and from over one eye a hideous red stream ran down a smudgy cheek.

She looked at me with bleary eyes, her head trying weakly to remain upright for a few moments.

"My heart—" she said, "It is beating very fast."

"Can I help you? " I asked again.

"It is beating very fast," she repeated. A hiccup shook her body. She slowly took stock of the front of her, taking her white, blood-covered scarf in her hand and then making a stab at brushing the front of her coat. She would have fallen had I not still held her arm tightly.

"You are all covered with blood," I ventured. She peered at me from between fringes of kinky hair while this remark penetrated. Her head shifted position, reclining now on the back of her neck, and the odor of liquor became more apparent.

"All evening it's been this way," she murmured. "My heart—it beats—it beats," she added, thumping her breast. Then the head gave up and went back to its position between the cat-fur lapels of her collar.

"Where do you live? " I asked. "I'll take you home."

"Right over here," said the collar.

"Where? " I insisted.

"Not far," it replied.

"All right," I said. "Let's go." Taking a firmer hold of the arm, I began to march her slowly toward the Val de Grace. The head sat up again, and to my surprise a smile tried to appear from beneath the bloody nose. But it did not succeed; it was only a grimace.

We had only walked a few steps when she stopped.

"Here it is," she said. We stood in front of one of the old, prerevolution buildings, a hotel. She leaned against the yellow, weather beaten door.

"You're sure you live here? " I asked.

"I live here," said the grimace. "My heart is beating very fast."

"Very well, then, ring the bell, and I'll wait until the door opens."

She pushed the buzzer, and in an instant the big door snapped open a few inches.

A feeble hand pushed back some of the mat from her face, and a labored grin made the blood on her cheek quiver.

She held out her hand.

"Voulez-vous venir avec moi ce soir, monsieur? " she asked.

Harold Ettlinger
25 March 1931

Gobelins Tapestries

The hour to visit the Gobelins district—that is to say, the 13th Arrondissement—is toward *le crépuscule*. It would be better still to go when you have a nightmare, but then you might forget your *carte d'identité* and your revolver. And you might walk into a hospital by mistake and have your insides removed before you woke up.

There may be quarters in Paris more hoary, but it would be difficult to find another more sinister, more terrifying. Around the Place Paul Verlaine there is perhaps only a consumptive melancholy aura, but when you come to the Place Nationale the life of the 13th Arrondissement burgeons into cancerous loveliness. If you have come by way of the Boulevard de la Gare, along the Rue Nationale, you will already have had a foretaste.

I have always noticed that where the hotels have the most high sounding names the streets are most dismal and decrepit. The hotels themselves are apt to be morgues or infirmaries. Take the Grand Hotel de la Paix, for example. Which Grand Hotel de la Paix? Any one. Nine times out of ten, the roof is collapsing, or the clients are standing in front of the door with bloody aprons, or there is a dead canary swinging from the window ledge.

But the Place Nationale! Well, in the first place, the Place Nationale is not Red—it is Surrealist! Part of it belongs to Paris, the rest has been filched from Poland, the Ruhr, Williamsburg, Monaco . . . The sky is made of zinc, the walls are burnt milk, the people are prisoners, the cats lie on the low roofs like houris after the bath. When the bus comes dashing around the corner, dragging its anchor, the urinal lurches like a drunken pedestrian.

There are caps in the windows that no man would wear unless he was about to commit a crime. The crimes here are Sundays and holidays. Children fetch top prices. They are tastier than rabbits, and you can wash them if they get dirty. Mannikins without arms dress and undress themselves. Some windows display flower pots, others are torn with rage. Green jalousies are all the mode, particularly those with a few slats missing. The awnings are red and white, like the Japanese flag.

About a stone's throw distant is the Eglise Jeanne d' Arc. This brings you back to mass, if you are blessed with myopia. It all depends upon how you approach the Place Jeanne d'Arc which the municipality spells without an apostrophe incidentally. If you come from the elevated, which is at the foot of a gentle slope, and if the atmospheric conditions are right, the church becomes tremendously elongated, looming up in the violet of distance like another Woolworth Tower. If you come upon it suddenly, from the Rue Lahire, the amplitude of the square dwarfs it, but at the same time solidifies it and lends it that New England quality of firmness and righteousness.

The Place Jeanne d'Arc is not precisely disappointing—it is simply different from what you expect it to be. It has an air of tranquillity, but it is a heavy tranquillity, as of turbines going to sleep. All about it is death, desolation and despair. Coming along the Rue Jeanne d'Arc, from the Boulevard de la Gare, you pass through a veritable Purgatory. The charred tenements, arranged like prison blocks, are almost terrifying; they are separated from one another by gloomy courts barred at each end by enormous iron gates. What you expect to happen happens. People emerge from their dwellings garbed in black, their shoulders stooped, their limbs bloated or broken, their voices raucous and malign; now and then you see a face with a nose missing, or an eye. Their gestures are heavy and repetitive, as if they were still attached to the machine. Wherever there are factories and mills, wherever there are ghettos and almshouses, wherever there are clinics and madhouses, you will see these sorrowful, bent figures, these worn coins that have circulated so long that they are beyond recognition.

On the Rue Charcot-Prolongée, right off the Square, stands a little pink house made of stucco. There is no reason for such a house to be here. Nobody ever saw such a house, except Lewis Carroll. But then did anybody ever see a wagon filled with silver horses? The wagon was going nowhere. It was moored to the curb. On the front seat were wooden negresses—all of them with the same expression, all of them grinning like Aunt Jemima. In the back of the wagon there was nothing but legs, silver legs, stiff and inextricable.

It was dark. Somebody named F. Genève was dropping his name in letters of fire along the street. It was the Rue du Château des Rentiers and there were people hurrying along it, and their shoes made a tremendous clatter. In the windows were old hags, paring their nails; the lamps were lit and there were no shades over the chimneys, so that the rooms seemed to burn with a phosphorous fire and the old hags looked evil. More hospitals and iron gates. Madmen speeding over the cobblestones on pneumatic tires. Subterranean bistrots filled with card-players—torpid, listless clients doped with *vin rouge* and pipe tobacco.

Finally the Rue Harvey, one block long, and packed with phantoms. When I think of the Rue Harvey I think of realism as it may develop some day in the French films. I think of that Zola who will lift the cinema out of the bogs of sentimentalism. It will have to be a myopic Zola who records this Paris. A perfect vision will yield nothing. It is not enough to come here with a pad and take notes. The Rue Harvey is a universe in which there are no stars, no trees, no rivers or lakes. The people who live here are dead. They manufacture dreams. They make chairs which other people sit on. They stagger in and out of the houses like drunken marionettes.

The 13th Arrondissement is as variegated as a tapestry. The Place d'Italie lies in its midst like a huge compass, pointing this way to the gallows, that way to the mosque. Down by the Seine, where the railroad yards obliterate everything human, the earth rises up in smoke and concrete.

Alfred Perlès
26 April 1931

II The People

While Gertrude Stein never tired of explaining why it was necessary to live in France rather than America, many exiles either lacked her certainty or doubted her explanations, and inclined more toward silence than expression of opinion. To say they regarded expatriation as too private a matter for public airing, or too complex even for the participant himself to understand, or even something that hardly mattered to him, at least at the moment, is to represent the beliefs of many who found their way to Paris in the twenties. Nonetheless such rejoinders usually belied the really crucial reasons for exile. Even the replies to the questionnaires drawn up and circulated by a few little magazines, which asked readers to state why they lived abroad, often sounded evasive or playful, but several *Tribune* writers, nagged no doubt by a sense of their own exile, wrote illuminating analyses of the motives of American émigrés which, unsurprisingly, differed considerably from the theories advanced by Gertrude Stein.

Though Miss Stein continues to hold a formidable place in accounts of the Paris years, and will obviously continue to do so, she was but one of many talented American exiles of her sex who collectively comprised an extraordinary group of entertainers, artists, and writers, a group to which Tribunemen gave at least as much attention as they granted to male residents, or to the distinguished visitors who descended on Paris each spring. Of course especially magnetic were the flamboyant Josephine Baker and the tragic Isadora Duncan. But just as appealing and providing reporters with abundant copy were more restrained figures like Sylvia Beach, the imaginative and energetic proprietor of the bookshop Shakespeare and Company, Natalie Clifford Barney, whose exotic refuge in the rue Jacob was the setting for her "Fridays," the day set aside for her celebrated gatherings, and Margaret Anderson, who arrived in Paris trailing her *Little Review* and a reputation for total dedication to all creative spirits.

In 1925 the *Tribune* started a "Who's Who" column and offered a few francs to any staffer interested in writing it, though as it turned out William L. Shirer, Alex Small, and Edmond Taylor signed most of them. They featured transients, of course, especially literary notables like Sherwood Anderson, F. Scott Fitzgerald, and Michael Arlen, who often agreed to discuss any subject except their writing; but permanent residents appeared too, and their profiles generally contained fresh information.

H. F.

We're in Paris Because . . .

A Feast of Reasons

Some weeks ago in these columns a number of reasons were assigned for the artist's living in Paris. Since then we have received a slipping avalanche of protests from our kindly-disposed friends and acquaintances who, while vociferously objecting to our rationale, have been good enough to submit their own more specific persuasions, which we have gleaned both by letter and from conversation.

When we last visited Mr. Marsden Hartley in his studio on the Left Bank, he was propped up in bed, suffering from a Paris cold due to the recent *purée de pois* or thick wet fog. It seemed a bit embarrassing to our shy sensibilities to ask him how he liked Paris at such an unpropitious moment. Nevertheless we screwed up enough pointed courage and posed the question just the same. Mr. Hartley, considering the annoying state of his health, responded most valorously and what he said, we append in capsular form here below:

"That is a poser at the present moment, as you realize. Offhand, however, I should not hesitate to say New York. But that does not, I see, answer the question as to why I do live here. Paris furnishes the least resistance, probably, for the artist than any other city in the world. Its position has changed, however, as a purveyor of impeccable taste. It does not furnish it any longer, from many points of view. It represents taste and judgment still, to be sure; it is probably more comfortable now than before the war because that formerly distressing though perhaps then energizing intellectualism is at a stand-still, quite out of vogue—and for the present at least thoroughly unnecessary.

"It is never the intellectuals in any case who represent the true charm of life anywhere—and certainly not in Paris. If there is always an engaging clarity in the French sensibility, there is also a discomfiting restlessness due to surface passion and a natural internal desire to withhold the real experience of the soul. It is the lovely manner of the French peasantry which please and draw one to the French way of living, and to France.

"Likewise it is more comfortable living in Paris now because the war has brought to it the larger vision of how to go on being essentially

French, retaining with this a larger comprehension of the outer world's way of living, in the presence always of the French spirit. Paris is probably lovelier, more engaging than ever it has been in the last fifteen years because its artists have been properly placed with relation to the general experience, and can no longer assume the prerogative to dictate to the outer world what must be accepted as the inevitable law in esthetics.

"In this sense the war was the saviour of esthetics—and the true saviour of Paris as a place for artists to live peaceably once more. Esthetics can no longer be enforced, any more than philosophy or religion, and for this reason alone Paris is happier, more peaceful in its own soul, and for this reason, too, more habitable than ever."

Miss Jessie Fauset, one of the best known negro writers in America, associate editor of *The Crisis* and author of the novel *There Is Confusion,* urged an altogether different reason for living in Paris.

Miss Fauset replied: "I like Paris because I find something here, something of integrity, which I seem to have strangely lost in my own country. It is simplest of all to say that I like to live among people and surroundings where I am not always conscious of 'thou shalt not.' I am colored and wish to be known as colored, but sometimes I have felt that my growth as a writer has been hampered in my own country. And so—but only temporarily—I have fled from it.

"I adore my own people and I like to be among them and of them, despite the race issue in America. In myself at times I deplore a certain departure from various accredited traits—I wish I danced more and had a truer ear for music. But I am, of course, a product of what I am—my parents, colored people with wide intellectual interests, Quakerism, instilled by Philadelphia where I was born, and a certain kind of creative living among people of all sorts in New York; nevertheless I will be forgiven, I am sure, for wanting to forget the color question just the same.

"I am not irked by it because of the discrimination alone, in theatres, restaurants, cafeterias and railway stations, or by the inability to purchase a home in a neighborhood to which my tastes and means incline me. I am somewhat tired, pardonably so, I think, by the unnatural restraint imposed when both races meet, and this restraint is mostly my own. It manifests itself in my personal behaviour because I am conscious of belonging to another race. In order to offset criticism, the refined colored woman must not laugh too loudly, she must not stare—in general she must stiffen her self-control even though she can no longer humanly contain herself.

"I believe the colored people are happiest among themselves, and I like best to be with my own people. But, you know, that sort of thing is impossible all the time for the artist. And I wish to regard myself purely and simply as an artist, without losing my essential identity with my own race. How is a negro to avoid mediocrity if he or she does not mingle with other creative spirits of the same temper and inclination? There is no more crushing criticism for a colored writer or painter than the words 'Well, it's not half bad considering she's colored.'

"So I am in Paris where nobody cares—not even Americans, it

seems—whether an artist is white, black or yellow or, as Forster says in *A Passage To India,* 'pink-gray.' Later on I shall return to Paris for other reasons—to meet, as I have done this time, members of my own craft in goodfellowship and to my own great advantage. I have met more members of my own guild here in four months than in New York in four years. It has pleased me to know them; they seem pleased to know me. Why did we have to come three thousand miles to achieve such a simple pleasure? "

Pierre Loving
1 February 1925

The Skyscraper Age and Harold Stearns

Harold Stearns, *enfant terrible* of American journalism, recently made a flying trip to his native shores, and since his return to Paris has written his impressions in such a pontifical fashion as to sow a tempest in the journalistic forests outre-mer. . . . "I had to go back home to discover that I was an American through and through," he writes in the Baltimore *Sun.* "Also I had to go back home to discover that it would be impossible ever again to live happily in America. . . . I realized that I was not an exceptional American in being dissatisfied with the local scene, wherever it might be, North or South, in the Riviera sunshine of Carmel, in California, or the bleak, frozen slush brilliance of New York; I was just the average American. Everybody was dissatisfied, everybody was hysterical.

"I found that the myth that New York did not represent America—that it was a kind of special skyscraper primitive miracle apart in its specious cosmopolitanism—was completely false; a myth I had myself always before loyally believed in. All of America was nothing but New York, or at least a feeble imitation of it. . . . New York was simply the whole country more concentrated and intensified. And in New York nobody was happy, not even when a new case of gin was delivered. Everybody was hectic, making money furiously, working at the game of pretending to work, shameless and audacious in their heterogeneous love-making to a point where I, a quiet and respectable citizen of Paris, was actually embarrassed. . . . With so many organizations and clubs and fraternal orders, I never saw people so tragically lonely. With so much sentimental and romantic tenderness of talk about love and the first blush of affection, I never found fewer people who realized that religion has no civilized appeal above and beyond its purely esthetic one. With so much and varied good food in the land, I haven't had worse meals for five years. . . ."

Eugene Jolas
3 May 1925

Tarkington Thinks Exile in Paris Is
Good for U. S. Writers "In Moderation"

To say that Booth Tarkington warns against anything would not be good reporting, for he isn't that kind of person.

However, he did soberly aver to *The Tribune* yesterday that he thought Paris for young American writers and artists all right—"if taken in moderation."

Considering the spectacle of a whopping percentage of America's youth who are sensitive enough to interpret her life sojourning abroad, he announced that he was sure that the exile business could be overdone.

For this American among Americans believes that our literature or any other will only retain significance as long as it is native.

"Paris," he said, "will do lots for our youth but they mustn't stay away too long. They shouldn't let their roots in their native soil shrivel up. I recall something that Zuloaga said in an interview the other day advising painters not French to leave France often enough to return to their own countries."

And he thinks, too, that there is something a little tragic in the person of the man who tries to get along without roots.

"I knew an artist in Italy," he said, "who had built himself a house at Capri. We went to his housewarming. And aside, he told me, 'Yes, I'm laughing and all that, but if you'd scratch me with a pin you'd uncover an ache. For I know now that I will be buried in Italy."

2 June 1925

17 Writers and Artists Explain
Why They Live Outside of U. S.

"America is the mother of the twentieth century civilization, but she is now early Victorian."

This is the opinion expressed by Gertrude Stein in an answer to a questionnaire sent out by *transition.*

"The United States is just now the oldest country in the world. There always is an oldest country and she is it; it is she who is the mother of the twentieth century civilization. She began to feel herself as it just after the Civil War. And so it is a country the right age to have been born in and the wrong age to live in. . . . America is now early Victorian, very early Victorian. She is a rich and well nourished home but not a place to work."

Sixteen other writers and artists answered the question, "Why do you prefer to live outside of America? George Antheil, the American composer, states:

"Musically, it is absolutely impossible to live in America. I am a musician, a composer, and this type of artist needs vast organizations such as opera companies and symphony orchestras to write for to produce his works. . . . My Polish origin means that I love the ground upon which I was born, New Jersey, with a love that is difficult to explain, or understand. . . ."

Robert McAlmon says he prefers Europe, "if you mean France, because there is less interference with private life here. There is interference, but to a foreigner, there is a fanciful freedom and grace of life not obtainable elsewhere. . . . If by Europe you mean England, Italy, or Germany, I think America an exciting, stimulating, imaginative country with the fresh imagination of youth and ignorance. . . ."

The fall number, in line with the international policy of the editor, contains work done by writers and artists of seven nations on both sides of the Atlantic.

26 October 1928

Thirst for Booze and for Liberty Sends Americans Abroad

The exile leaves America from what unsympathetically would be called pure laziness, though most remain true enough to the spirit of their own people never to use that word. They may assign themselves every sin and weakness which would horrify the pastor of the First Methodist Church back home, but they always maintain that they are here to "work." In justice it must be said that most of them do work very hard—at the Ritz bar, at Harry's, Luigi's, Zelli's, Lipp's, or on the terraces of Montparnasse. Whatever they do, they are relieved of that fearful tension which they knew at home, the treadmill struggle to keep pace with American life. Especially you do not here have to work to keep up your social station, on which we set more price than any other people in the world.

The Fathers did us but an indifferent service in abolishing titles of nobility. In its stead, we have the aristocracy and hierarchy of motor cars and country clubs and period decoration. Unless we would be disgraced, we must have all the indispensable paraphernalia. America knows what it means in work just to keep up appearances. Thus laziness has become the capital American sin. Myself I have had the disagreeable experience, in the United States, of passing for a moral leper because I made the mild remark that I saw no reason for "hustling." Of all that the exile is free. Whether he admits it or not, he is enjoying to the full the privilege of indulging his natural-born indolence and procrastination.

"I came over just to get a drink," says many an American, meaning to be devilish, and many a spinster foe of exiles maintains that nothing more than a depraved thirst for strong liquor is the motive which attaches her compatriots to Europe. Figuratively, that is true. Prohibition, in its moral implications, explains the presence of many exiles here. On this subject most of them are frank and talk sound sense. They know that they can get all the enamel dissolvent they desire in America, but they want to drink it in public before all the world, and without the risk of going to jail.

In other words, they want liberty. They may not be able to define the sort of liberty they desire, but they feel that they are deprived of it at home. Despite what some satirists may say, Americans are still a liberty-loving people, though they do not seem to know at present how to get it. It is really lucky for those who have taken their liberties away from them that Americans are so occupied with business and are, despite evidence to the contrary, essentially law-abiding. Otherwise they long ago would have made short work of the licensed murderers who enforce the prohibition law and of the sombre and cruel fanatics who protect them. Such already would have been done in France by a people more demonstrative than we and more jealous of their rights.

Finding himself unable to do anything about it, many an American who feels outraged at living under a government which treats its subjects like a set of naughty children, who shall be told what to drink, to read, to wear, and to see at the theatre, prefers to go into exile. If he had to become a citizen of France or of any other country, it might be another story. As it is, he can enjoy liberty such as is known to few people in the world. It is certainly unknown to all of his compatriots except those who are afflicted with a masochistic adoration of tyranny.

There are some reasons, then, why young Americans go into exile. This, I feel, is but skirting the subject, but thus far I have not found the clue to the enigma. Maybe some exists, and maybe it is not an enigma.

Alex Small
20 September 1929

Paul Morand Knocks Exiles Who Like Paris Better Than America

"I am a friend and an admirer of America," said Paul Morand, the writer, at the weekly luncheon of the American Club yesterday. "Before I went there, I thought all Americans lived in Paris; they don't. I have met such nice people over there who had never heard of Paris. We know why Americans live in Paris: for instance, because life is cheaper. 'I'd rather live in New York,' wrote an American friend of mine, 'but I can't afford it'; another said: 'I never had, at the same time, the desire to go back and the money to go back with.' Old-aged Americans like Europe; Europe is made for old people: at 70 a French statesman, a French writer begin their career.

"Europe is a white-haired lady; she expects people to call on her. Her pleasures are only fully appreciated after 50; I mean by pleasure, the knowledge and contempt of other people, scepticism, good cooking, in a word: society life. Snobs like Europe; and dainty exiles also; they say: 'My

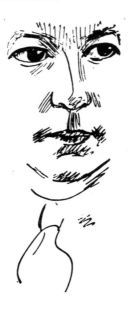

Paul Morand

country is where I feel at home,' instead of saying: 'I feel at home in my country.' Artists like Paris. As Stevenson wrote, when he was living at Fontainebleau: 'There is something in the air of France which communicates the love of style.'

"But an artist must work. Many Americans see Europe only during the vacations; so they are inclined to think that Europe is a continent of holidays. In America, everybody works and there are no idlers; it is shameful to be in New York without making money; so, when people want to give up work, they leave America. Dürer, the German painter, was asked once why he lived in Venice. 'Because I like doing nothing,' he said. 'When I do nothing in Venice, I am considered as a gentleman of leisure; but when I do nothing in my own country, I am looked down upon as a loafer.'

"Some people come over here, not to find Europe, but to avoid their homes. The exotic air of Europe stimulates them. 'The house where one is born is not a place to work in,' says Gertrude Stein. A charming friend said to me one day this very striking sentence: 'I live in Paris because nothing there reminds me of my childhood.'

"I think it is often very true; I like the prodigal son, not because he is a good son, but because he has traveled much; the other sons like their father; the prodigal son prefers him. He comes back because he is sick of the outside world; he is sick of gay Paree; he is sick of belonging to what Sinclair Lewis calls: 'The Salvation Army of Compulsory Sin.' ''

"Can They Stay Home? "

"Therefore, we know well enough why Americans like Paris and enjoy Europe; but, what I would like to examine with you briefly is this: 'Must Americans who want to enjoy a superior life come to Europe, or can they find it at home? '

"Let me tell you that artists and writers and all others who say that they can't live without leaving America get on my nerves. 'I have come to see Europe. I want to see all the great things and do what the best people do,' says Newman, in *The Ambassadors*. I have quite enough of these refined American characters that one meets in the novels of Henry James.

"I know that my friends Mencken and Sinclair Lewis feel that way, and I like them all the more for that.

"Some time ago, I was writing to Sinclair Lewis about his new novel *Dodsworth,* which is, so to say, the adventures of Babbitt in Europe. 'I shall never write again another story with a European background,' he answered. 'Europe spoils Americans. It unsettles them.'

"A superior life! Perhaps it was impossible to lead a life of the spirit in New York in the sixties, but now! By superior life, I mean science, which no book, no university teaches, which is, so to say, the exquisite essence of culture, and which we call in French: *L'art de vivre.* You all know what it is, this gentle art of living. It is a lot of things: good manners, picture galleries, English tailoring, Paris frocks, the knowledge of wines, the enjoyment of conversation, the attendance of plays or the strategy of love. Good manners?

"The greatest hindrance to refinement is the standardization of life; but I find that we have now in Europe all the drawbacks of standardization and none of its advantages. And, after all, are the United States so uniform all over? People believe it, but is it true?

"We talk of our art, of our great European masters, as if they still belonged to us. Where are they? They are in New York, and with the help of antique dealers, in fifty years, Europe will be a kind of Middle-West, and, no doubt, Salt Lake City will become a land of treasures, like Italy.

" 'Let's go to Paris and see nice plays,' say people in New York. What do they see when they get over here? *Broadway Melodie, Show Boat, The Trial of Mary Dugan,* or *What Price Glory.*

"Formerly, it took twenty-five years for a reputation to cross the Atlantic. Today it takes a week—and for bad reputations, even less. The new books of Maurois and Ludwig are published the same day in Europe and in New York. The great actors of the world, from the Guitrys to Ne-lan-fang, the Chinese, are famous on Broadway. Everywhere, in New York, you see beautiful libraries, full of the rarest editions; everywhere you meet cultured women. Everywhere you get the impression that America can do now without Europe and is actually doing without it. Immigration has practically ceased today, in America; yet without any fresh blood from Europe, we can see that it develops the most beautiful specimens of the white race. The same with culture. America during the rest of this century will possess a culture of its own. I am pretty certain that the day will come when our sons will say: 'One can only live by leaving Europe.' "

28 February 1930

Left vs. Right

To the Editor of *The Tribune:*

Sir:

Apart from the quibble re relative sensibilities of boobs and bar-flies, there was a sober intention in my last note.

We live in a plutocratic era, i.e., de facto governed by money, with a thin wash of democratic pretense. Honest men recognize the de facto condition, the honest ploot and the honest rentier accept things for what they are, and the good ones try to do their small bit to preserve the vestiges of civilization or to construct a bit more for posterity.

The point of my letter is that the "right bank" (a "section") is surprisingly contemptible in this respect. And its denizens have not the excuse of being lost in a geographic desert.

America occasionally produces a great collector or encourager of the "arts," for example a Barnes or a Quinn. America has produced also the Guggenheim brothers one of whom assists aviation by a direct and well proved system, the other by a less perfect mechanism but with unimpeachable intentions has attempted to help invention not only in science but in letters.

I cite these names because they are known. I might cite a score of more modest examples, men who have spent money, according to their means, in order to see a better grade of book printed, or in order that some living painter or sculptor should have means and leisure to continue his work.

But from the "right bank of the Seine" we have no indication of any such intelligence or will. We have on the contrary an astonishing lack of either good will or knowledge, and an almost unvarying stupidity.

The American Conservatory at Fontainebleau (a right bank institution) did not discover Mr. Antheil. Mr. Antheil on his own went to Vienna and was accepted by the "Universalverlag," the first American to be so honoured. His opera has been accepted at Frankfurt. The shame and degradation of the American Universities is that they are not centres of intellectual activity, but incubators for teachers, the law of that profession being that every disciple shall know less than the "great authority" who preceded him. Fontainebleau is a place of this type. Antheil has never been invited there for a concert or to speak to the unfortunate pupils.

The painting and sculpture bought by the Americans of the right bank is of a quality to discourage any set of heroes less hard-headed than the painters and sculptors of Montparnasse (a SECTION).

The haute bourgeoisie is not in our day greatly honoured. It is not the stuff of the old Strasbourger *"qui portait sa bourgeoisie comme un marquisat,"* but the *haute bourgeoisie américaine* of the right bank is very low in the scale of even the *haute bourgeoisie.*

And on that count, indifferent as I am to several habitués of the several assorted cafés of Montparnasse, I am ready, in so far as I am able to defend even the less brilliant Montparnos, devotees perhaps of the contemplative life, perhaps lacking that cogency of contemplation recommended by Richard St. Victor. Despite the failure of undergraduates from Nevada to discover the "spirit of Montparnasse" in ten days it is a damn sight better to fail in an endeavour to construct something than to sit about feeding pug dogs.

Ezra Pound
Rapallo, 13 March

16 March 1930

Why Americans Leave Home and Settle Down Permanently in Europe

"An American who comes to love and understand France" writes M. Paul Morand, who apparently talks sense whenever he does not think that he has to please Americans, "is so profoundly stirred that he finds himself forced to stay there always."

Obviously then he loves France by contrast with things as he knows them at home. This brings up once more the reasons for expatriation. The crop of expatriates of the year 1930 is certainly obedient to other motives than the ones of 1890. Few today give up their American citizenship or even attempt in any thorough way to go native. Still, they are firm about not wanting to live in their own country. It is, if you will, a negative preference. Below I enumerate and explain, as I see them, the main reasons for expatriation.

I. Henry Jamesianism. This is a hangover from an earlier age, but it is still potent. In some slight degree, and often unconsciously, it is to be found in all expatriates. Henry Jamesianism is the desire to see and associate with people who have easy and dignified manners and who move against a rich, highly colored background, like an English country estate or a French chateau. It is disappearing as the truth spreads that the War has left few Europeans of this sort, and the few left generally want to use Americans.

A humbler form of Henry Jamesianism is the desire to be in the presence of monuments and ruins, the evidences of a rich past, evoking the ghosts of a long and stirring history. The American afflicted with romantic antiquarianism will be unhappy among skyscrapers, Federal postoffices, state capitals, and even fake Gothic churches, with which the industry and genius of Mr. Ralph Adams Cram are dotting the American landscape.

II. The desire for social success, or better, the desire to be a part of a deracinated, cosmopolitan society. With a little money, it is easier to be both conspicuous and respected in Paris, or even in London, than in Framingham, Mass., or in Burlington, Iowa. It is much more fun and people do not ask embarrassing questions.

III. The relations of the sexes in the United States. This usually affects men. They dread gold-diggers. They are in revolt against the accepted American attitude that a husband must support a wife in the style to which she would like to become accustomed. In Europe the protesting American male may not be much better off than he was at home, but at least he is not under social pressure.

To be sure, many a modern American girl, especially in the big cities, has dropped the traditional attitude. She pays her share at parties and would disdain to be supported in marriage. But there are other complications—imbecile laws like the Mann Act and the general inability of the American public to take natural things naturally. We invented sex and have made far too much fuss over our invention. Passion is still considered a disease and pure comradeship an ideal. The French take no such false attitudes.

IV. The inordinate influence in American life of public spirited women. Of course, the individual who is not poor and helpless may escape their pernicious benevolence, but the spectacle is always there and it is sickening. It is to be dreaded, too, for no one ever knows what forms it is going to take. These managing women (who may be of any sex) have no respect for liberty. They defend their tyrannies with the claim that all living in society is a restriction on liberty, which is perfectly true, but is a sophistical excuse for their mischief making.

V. Prosperity, pep, and advertising. These need no comment.

VI. The national hunt for culture, with its elaborate apparatus—public libraries, radio talks, book clubs, lectures, and hundreds of so-called colleges and universities. This performance is the most obscene of all the triumphs of American democracy; out of it are bred the most obnoxious types humanity has ever produced.

Chief among them are the fake scientists, the statisticians, the sociologists, the sapless professors, shallow of mind and vulgar of soul, whether their specialities be international law, literature, or economics. For all their supposed facts and their figures, they remain profoundly ignorant of everything. Less obnoxious are the amateur pedants who wear their culture lightly, who are versed in interior decoration, figurines, heraldry, ancestors, antiques, period architecture.

The whole business is not only loathsome in its degradation of things that are fine; it is dishonest. It deludes the majority of the people into thinking that they can have rational lives and noble sentiments on cheap terms. It poisons private leisure by keeping people in a constant fever for improvement, when no improvement is possible or desirable; it makes social life an ordeal where every individual is terrified lest he appear not so refined, learned, and sophisticated as his neighbors.

VII. Religion. It is a national obsession, and cannot be escaped, no matter what you do. To a free spirit even its venerable and intellectually respectable forms, like fundamentalism, are annoying. It is too much trouble warding off their assaults.

Still worse is the pullulation of freak, fancy, and highbrow religions, ranging from disintegrated Protestantism of the Fosdick type on into the infinite. They fill the land with their gabble about unity, idealism, the higher nature, vibration, right thoughts and new thoughts. Generally they are grafted on the most intolerant Puritanism, which they both practice and promote.

Even one degree lower I should put the enlightened sceptics, who have found out that the Christian epic is not literally true, and must let the world know about it. They are intellectual clowns, as the others are frauds. From fundamentalists to atheists, all are alike in using a jargon fit for idiotic savages.

A sane man is driven to France, where people do not touch the question. If he cannot do that, he had better go into a monastery.

VIII. Absence of friendship. Americans, of course, are as capable of friendship as any other people, but the circumstances of their life are against the cultivation of this finest flower of civilized living. It cannot flourish amid tension and a constant conflict of ambitions. It needs disinterestedness and leisure. In America a caricature usually takes the place of the real thing.

The average American thinks he is being friendly with another man when he plays golf with him or when he smiles affably as he picks his pocket.

Alex Small
10 July 1930

Some Women Quarterites

American Girl Conducts Novel Bookstore Here

One of the most interesting and successful literary ventures in Paris is "Shakespeare and Company," a little library of English books started by an American girl, Sylvia Beach, at 8 rue Dupuytren.

It is perhaps most in the public eye at the moment because of the courageous undertaking of its proprietors to publish *"Ulysses"* by James Joyce. This book was suppressed in America when it was about to be brought out by the *"Little Review"* and attracted sensational attention at the time among the ardent followers of James Joyce. It is said that its present publication may mean that Miss Beach will not be allowed to return to America.

Shakespeare and Company was founded more than a year ago. Miss Beach returned from Serbia after doing Red Cross work and suddenly conceived the idea of starting her original little book shop. Her effort was to get French people in touch with the best and newest American work, particularly the American authors of today, to bring to them for the first time our modern group.

The "Specialité de la Maison" is perhaps its loan library which for a small sum offers its shelves to the cosmopolitan group which are Miss Beach's customers, French, American, English, Chinese, Spanish, all the variety of the varied quarter near the Sorbonne.

An interesting group of authors has gradually made this little shop its center and almost all the literary celebrities of the day are Miss Beach's friends. Their pictures are on her walls and scarcely a day passes that some stray poet or novelist does not drop in to browse at her crowded shelves.

The shop itself is attractive. Outside is a quaint painted sign, showing Shakespeare himself, done by Charles Winzer, and on one of the corner shelves is a tiny porcelain model of the poet's home. There are open bookshelves and rugs and hangings in soft vivid colors that came from Serbia. The final romantic touch to the little shop which is in a very old building, is that it was formerly a "Blanchisserie."

A year ago it had an official christening, and was fortunate enough to have as its godfather Valery Larbaud, the well known French author, who, instead of the traditional silver cup, the gift of all correct godfathers, gave it his influence and support and has made it a center for the French literary group.

Perhaps the strongest factor in the success of the shop is the personality of its owner. Miss Beach is one of the three daughters of the minister of

Sylvia Beach

the First Presbyterian Church at Princeton, Woodrow Wilson's old church. They are a pioneering family. One daughter, Cyprian, is now in Paris, doing work in moving pictures, having made a considerable success in many films in America. The other, Holly, is in Italy doing Red Cross work, and Sylvia finds her time quite filled with running Shakespeare and Company. She is an attractive as well as a successful pioneer.

28 May 1921

"He's Crazy," Is Isadora's Verdict on Runaway Poet

"Everybody knows he's crazy."

That Serge Esenin, her young poet husband is more deserving of tears than laughter was Isadora Duncan's statement to *The Tribune* yesterday when interviewed at the Hotel Reservoirs in Versailles, where she fled after last week's domestic fracas in Paris.

"He wanted to go back so I sent him," she explained tiredly, "he will be better off in Russia where they love him even if he is foolish. He can smash things up in Moscow and no one will care because he is a poet."

The famous esthetic dancer was draped in a flowing robe of royal purple trimmed with gold. As she talked she shuffled moodily around the room, wearing a pair of heelless gold mules.

"How could he have taken any of my money as he declares he did? " she asked. "I gave it away to the starving mujiks along the Volga when I was there."

Miss Duncan, as she is registered at the Versailles hotel, has been greatly upset by her erratic husband's behavior. A doctor was in attendance at her boudoir yesterday and her brother, Raymond Duncan, who goes about Paris barefooted and in Greek robes, was expected any minute.

"Serge has always been mad since the war," she declared pointing to her own handsome head and rolling back her eyes, "he also has epileptic fits and alcoholic poisoning."

She was just as bitter against the United States as was her Russian mate. Declaring that Esenin is one of the victims of prohibition laws bearing death, blindness and insanity in their wake, she related stories telling how he had bootleg whiskey offered him in every city and on the boat by which they returned to Europe.

"America's poison whiskey finished him," she sighed feelingly, "the last time we were in Paris we dined with Mlle. Cecile Sorel where good French wines only inspired him to happy thoughts of culture and beauty."

Although unwilling to comment much on the hasty departure of the youthful bard, she attributed all his idiosyncracies to moonshine and a few passing brainstorms. She was certain that in his normal state he has a most beautiful spirit.

Lorimer Hammond
19 February 1923

Isadora Duncan Writes *Tribune* Her Own Version

The Chicago Tribune, European Edition, has just received from Madame Isadora Duncan, through her attorneys, a request to print the following communication from her on an article in *The Tribune* a few days ago recounting the circumstances of the departure of Madam Duncan's husband, Serge Esenin.

Miss Duncan's communication to *The Tribune* follows:

> Dear Sir:
>
> In the course of the last week there have appeared in *The Chicago Tribune* three front page articles in which my name has been used in large disrespectful headlines and in which my character has been put in an extremely false light before the public. As the incident which is the supposed subject of these articles was of so slight a nature as in no way to be of interest to the public, I conclude that these articles were inserted on your front page simply with the object of injuring me, and I insist upon my right,

according to the laws of France, to your publishing my reply in the same column and same page as the articles in question.

In your article of Feb. 16 you declare that there was between my husband, Serge Alexandrovich Esenin, and myself "another domestic row," whereas if you had taken the trouble to learn the truth you would have known that the explanation of the incident of the Hotel de Crillon was that Esenin was seized by a fit of deliriums, that there had been no quarrel of any sort between us, as my friend, Mrs. Howard Perch, who was with us all afternoon and evening, can testify, and that at the moment of Esenin's fit of madness, I was not in the hotel, having presaged what was coming.

I had left with my friend, Mrs. Perch, to call a doctor.

All this was explained to your reporter, Mr. Lorimer Hammond, by Dr. Aszoule, chevalier of the legion of honor, but Mr. Hammond preferring to write, and only looking for a scandalous and defamatory article, paid no attention to this information.

The exact truth that Serge Esenin is the unfortunate victim of momentary fits of madness, at which moments he is no longer responsible for his actions or his words, was too simple a solution for your reporter who was looking for scandal.

Two days after, this same Mr. Hammond penetrated my retreat at Versailles, where I lay in bed ill under the care of the doctor. The doctor forbade me to see him. Mrs. Perch told him this, to which he replied that the article coming would be "worse if I did not see him."

Hearing this, and wishing so far as I could to protect the character of Serge Esenin from further harmful writings, I rose and putting on a dressing gown went into the next room. I saw at once from the attitude of Mr. Hammond that he had come with hostile intentions to continue his attacks on me and my unfortunate husband.

I explained to him as gently as I could the truth of the case and that I was very tired and in great sorrow. Of all this the next day he was pleased to make a huge joke in a most unpleasant article. If this sort of journalism continues, we will have your reporters coming into no matter what house of misfortune or grief and making a joke at the tears of the mourners. They will be opening the coffin lids and describing in humorous fashion the expressions of the dead. No one will be safe from their malice, and the poor public will be the continual dupes of their gross and uncomprehending vulgarity.

Hoping that your paper will in the future refrain from this unworthy policy, I remain,

(Signed) Isadora Duncan
23 February 1923

28 February 1923

Natalie Clifford Barney

Mlle. Natalie Clifford Barney, to whom Remy de Gourmont addressed his "Letters to the Amazone," has just issued a protest against the "sometimes impertinent requests for biographies" addressed to her on the occasion of the recent anniversary of Remy de Gourmont's death. "I shall continue to live Remy de Gourmont, not to re-live him," she says in part. "When I have prepared such and such an episode—delivered such and such a letter—will you be more advanced? You had better seek it in the best part—his books."

8 June 1924

A Literary Portrait of the Amazone

The portrait of Miss Natalie Clifford Barney, "L'Amazone," is sketched by Mme. Aurel in the last number of *Le Monde Nouveau*. This American woman, whose mind has totally absorbed the French genius, is represented with a touch of almost rhapsodic understanding. . . . "When the demon of letters breathed to me: 'Considering that this foreign woman has the strongest and most biting trait of the great moralists and immoralists of France—that she has done you the honor of writing in your language, the homage to her country alone would demand that you define her,' I awkwardly replied to myself: 'It must be done' . . ." Mme. Aurel says later: "Natalie Clifford Barney has invented grace without love. You live in that halo of ardor where nothing rests heavily on us, but we must consent to the burdens in order to live. Your art, therefore, is too fine, too pretty, too artistic for me, but it has a consummate intelligence. . . What a miracle of balance you are, you who fled your roots! . . . But where have you learned, dear anarchist, that rectitude of countenance, that discipline of the word, and above all else that divine negligence which makes you so easy to read, when you write words like these: '*La dame, une femme expurgée*' . . ." Mme. Aurel quotes a word of Miss Barney's on men: "All those penguins who do not know how to wear their clothes. Dispatch them, if not into the flames, at least into the cold."

Eugene Jolas
22 March 1925

Olga Rudge

This young American violinist, who has made Paris her home for the greater part of the past eight years, has a greater claim to musical fame than mere virtuosity. Although as an executant she has achieved high rank, she has done even greater work in the creative line. She does not compose, but she innovates.

Miss Rudge has specialized in modern violin music, which has as yet very few prominent interpreters on the concert stage. Her readiness to play, in public, work of new composers, demanding a new violin technique which other executants are unwilling to essay, has been the inspiration of at least two composers who, but for her, would not have written violin music.

One of these is George Antheil, whose two sonatas for violin Miss Rudge has already played at different concerts in Paris. The other is Ezra Pound. Miss Rudge created Mr. Pound's first fiddle music at the French Conservatory in 1923, and late this month she will appear again as a creator of Pound's new opera, "François Villon," of which vocal and instrumental selections will be given.

Olga Rudge, who is 25 years old, is the daughter of Mr. and Mrs. Henry Rudge, of Youngstown, Ohio. Her mother was Julia O'Connell, an American singer of note, who took Olga to Europe at the age of three to begin her musical education. She made many trips to Europe during her girlhood, studying chiefly with the French teacher Carambat. She in 1918 definitely took up European residence, and had her first concert triumphs in London at the age of 17, giving the first performance of Paray's violin sonata while Paray was a prisoner in Germany.

Her revolutionary career began in 1923, when she took up the works of Antheil and Pound. Subsequently she carried the violin music of Erik Satie to Italy, giving the first performance in that country of *"Choses vues à droite et à gauche"* in Rome only a month ago.

Miss Rudge has developed an entirely new violin technique for the interpretation of the tempestuous and, as classical players would say, "anti-violinistic," music of to-day. In order to do this she has been obliged to run the risk of damaging her classical technique, acquired by so many years of earnest effort. Yet, so much does Miss Rudge believe in the experimental side of her work, this sacrifice has been made without regret.

Miss Rudge is of the unpretentious brunette type. There is nothing of the poser or high-brow about her. Her experiments in the newer music spring from inner conviction, not from an ambition to achieve notoriety.

Her one ambition, indeed, is to possess a fine violin. The instrument she now uses would satisfy anybody but an extremely fine critic, but Olga has her heart set on a Stradivarius which she saw at Milan last winter. Failing to get that, she has in view an Amati.

Ezra Pound classes her as the foremost woman violinist of the day. Whether or not this estimation is hyperbolic, there is no doubt about her rank as the chief among the innovators.

15 June 1926

Isadora Duncan's Temple of Dance
on Auction Today; Friends To Buy It

Isadora Duncan's Temple of Dance is in a fair way of becoming a reality and her beautiful home in Neuilly, for years a gathering place of artists and those others who saw in art an escape from the rigors of politics and professional life, has been saved from the encroachment of commercial exploitation.

It will be sold tomorrow at public auction at the Palais de Justice but unless unforeseen events develop it will be bought by friends who yesterday took steps to form an association which will sponsor the proposed Isadora Duncan school which is to be established at her former Neuilly residence.

"We are ready to make the necessary bid in order to regain the property," a spokesman for the association told *The Tribune* last night, following an informal reception at Miss Duncan's apartment on the Left Bank.

The merchant who bought the property at the auction held on last Thanksgiving Day has left Paris and will not be represented in the bidding.

The Duncan home brought a sale price of 310,000 francs at the auction sale and, according to French law, the lowest price with which it can be repurchased is that price plus the amount of the *surenchere,* which was put up by the friends of the dancer in order to bring about another sale and which amounted to 50,000 francs. The opening bid at tomorrow's sale therefore must be 360,000 francs and it is for approximately this amount that friends hope to effect the purchase. The *surenchere* on the house was put in the name of M. Alfredo Sides and the negotiations tomorrow will be handled under his name.

After the house is re-bought tomorrow there will still remain the task of raising complete funds to pay for it and to take care of the installations necessary to provide facilities for the proposed school. Aside from her primary purpose to build up a school where children may be taught not only dancing but appreciation of the other arts as well, Miss Duncan intends to fit up studios and an auditorium for the use of artists and dramatic producers, who may find themselves without adequate funds or who desire to institute works which do not find a reception in the commercial theatre.

A fair start already has been made in the campaign. A statue, donated by Bourdelle, is expected to bring between 35,000 and 50,000 francs. Yesterday Mrs. Ogilvy-Druce presented Miss Duncan with a painting by Edmund Van Saint-Algi which will be sold, and she also started a new subscription list with a gift of 1,000 francs.

While most of the money is to be raised in Paris a campaign for subscriptions also will be opened in America, it was announced.

William L. Shirer
16 February 1927

Isadora Duncan Will be Buried in Paris Grave

After being held up yesterday by the refusal of a Nice police commissaire to authorize its removal the body of Isadora Duncan, world-famous dancer who was killed in an automobile accident in the Riviera city, was released and will be brought to Paris for burial.

The police commissaire, who appeared on the scene following the accident, found a Russian passport on the person of the dancer. He immediately announced that the body could not be removed before the arrival of the Russian consul from Marseilles.

At the last minute this difficulty was eliminated, and the body will be placed on a bier today and brought to Paris by the artist brother, Raymond, of Paris, and Victor Seroff, Russian pianist, who went down to Nice yesterday.

Miss Duncan, who worked faithfully on her memoirs for the last eighteen months, finished them a few days ago, it was learned yesterday. They will be published in the United States shortly, although the dancer has frequently expressed the fear that the authorities would seize the book as immoral.

The whole Paris press yesterday devoted columns to eulogy of the great danseuse and the Latin quarter, of which she was one of the most picturesque figures, is in mourning.

"She was the renovator of the dance," says Fernand Divoire in the *Intransigeant*. "She delivered it from everything which was not human, rid it of its unnecessary accessories. Thousands of men and women who have seen her, from Baku to Buenos Aires, and who have wept with enthusiasm, know this. Today there is a void in the hearts of thousands. They saw for an instant the most beautiful representation of Joy that our century has known . . ."

"Isadora Duncan dead," says Raymond Cogniat, "is a bit of beauty less in the world and above all a great inspiration vanished. . . ."

16 September 1927

Edna Ferber Hates This and That, Likes a Few Things, But Never Talks Any More—As You Can See for Yourself Below

Edna Ferber hates writing, small rooms, florid wallpaper, Americans who write like Englishmen, Americans who write like Russians, typewriters with a heavy touch, St. Louis, Mo., British passengers on trans-Atlantic liners and interviews.

She loves writing, America, unusual frontnames, fresh literary sources and interviews.

Her great ambition is to take a bath without hearing the phone ring.

She never had a story rejected and feels very apologetic about it.

These are the impressions gathered and the expressions recorded during an interview at the Hotel George V yesterday afternoon with the woman who is one of America's most popular female writers.

Miss Ferber surprises you because she looks almost too much like a lady novelist to be one. Her hair, which is black, is bobbed, naturally. She has smouldering eyes. Her voice sounds almost hysterical.

Read over without stopping the first four paragraphs above and it will give a suggestion of the way she talks. It isn't that her talk is merely jerky and disconnected. There is the contrast—maybe the most striking thing about her—between her rigidly controlled movements and the unruly force of her nascent ideas erupting in little phrase-fragments and propelling themselves by a series of internal explosions, like a rocketcar.

You can't imitate her speech on paper. This little excerpt—not quite verbatim—is about as close as you can come:

"Writing is the most loathsome drudgery in the world. You have only little moments of exhilaration when you write a sentence or a paragraph that you feel is good, you know, you stop and say to yourself, 'That's not so bad.' I don't know why I write except that I have something I want to say, and I love to do that. What do you think of Remington typewriters?

"I was in newspaper work from the time I was 17 until I was 23. I suppose that's why when I started to write I never had anything refused. Where do you come from? St. Louis? I hate that town. You can only write about what interests you.

"It's a good thing American writers are going native. For a while they tried to imitate the Russians. The country was flooded with near-Dostoyefsky stories. Ugh! Then the English. That was worse. 'The first thing he could remember was the sunlight shining on the floor of his nursery.' Wrooogh! How did you happen to come to Paris?

"I used to like to talk and give interviews. I never talk any more. I don't know why. Something horrible and Freudian I suppose. This room is too small to work in. I'm going to change it. I'm writing a new novel.

"No, I won't tell you anything about it. That would spoil it. I would get tired of it. What is your first name: (To a girl reporter) Arthur? What an odd name for a girl. How interesting. Doesn't it complicate your life terribly? You say it was a family name? How awful. Just think of that terrible urge that parents have for impressing their personality upon their children, even to giving them their names. (To the writer) I gave you a special ash tray all for yourself on the table over there. Don't you see it? I hate people who spill ashes on the floor."

There was nothing very interesting about Miss Ferber except herself. She didn't say anything striking. Some of her remarks, however, were interesting for the light they threw on her own personality and life.

She believes, for instance, that being a sob-sister and feature writer on a sensational evening paper, helped to develop her talent as a writer.

During the years she was in newspaper work she said she had no idea of writing. Her ambition was to be an actress.

She really seemed to think she didn't like to talk and stated seriously she had not been interviewed for a long time.

She much prefers America to Europe and thinks the latter is dead.

"America is so tremendously vital," she declared, "that you almost can't live in it. It's like a human with a personality so strong you can't bear to have him around you much."

Somehow that last sentence stuck in the memory, long after the interview was over.

Edmond L. Taylor
4 May 1929

Kiki

Kiki as seen by Tono Salazar

Samuel Putnam is the father of a new Kiki. He prays that God and Kiki forgive him but what he did was necessary for the good of Montparnasse. Before Putnam, Kiki was rapidly spreading into a legend. Now, after his experience, she belongs to the ages. Let's say 29.

All we know is this. After a brief acquaintance, Putnam decided to translate Kiki's *Memoirs* into English. It was only fair to her. In his introduction, he said: "The problem is not to translate Kiki's text, but to translate Kiki. To be able to do this, one must have the feel of Kiki." Others have felt this macrocosmic personality and been glad. Putnam put English on it, as they say, and here is what happened.

Everyone is discussing the English version of Kiki's *Memoirs*. They tell me it is the most daring event of the year. There is no subtraction from the

French version. In fact, twenty leaves were added to the mulberry bush. Small wonder then that this book is creating an unparalleled sensation.

In his lusty introduction Ernest Hemingway says: "If you ever tire of books written by present day lady writers of all sexes, you have a book here written by a woman who was never a lady at any time." Again he says: "She certainly dominated that era of Montparnasse more than Queen Victoria ever dominated the Victorian era." They say it is impossible to sit all afternoon on the terrace of the Dôme without seeing Kiki or hearing mention of her name.

And yet Kiki, the focal interest of Montparnasse, was becoming unreal. Tourists sitting in the crowd would stare at the lady (or woman) and play guessing games as to her past. Putnam came along and whispered in her ear. She consented to have her book translated providing it be unclipped. Unclipped it is, and while some Americans are shocked, others are whistling like school-boys, for the book reveals a world wherein life is as simple as breathing. Above all, it is a document of Montparnasse. It suggests to orderly people new possibilities.

"Kiki's style," says the translator's introduction, "is the most subtle that I know. At rare moments, you think of a remote sort of Anita Loos flapper, but the next moment, you banish the thought as sacrilege. I know of no other prose so hiddenly delicate, so deceptively nuanced—not even *Fanny Hill.*"

The real value of the book, however, is its searching penetration into the character of Montparnasse. The intuitive reactions of Kiki to the individuals and crowds of this world are more revealing than the thundering and fictionized word-excursions of the literary gentry. Her experiences as a model, ammunition worker, house maid, bar maid, and other professions are told without emotion or exaggeration. The chapter entitled *Love Wakes* is of universal interest.

Kiki has met them all. Foujita, Broca, Kisling, Pascin, Man Ray and other astral bodies are her playmates. Years ago the Vedettes crowned her Queen of Montparnasse. Like Catherine of Russia, her lovers were frequent. But I never had a hand in it. Never was she daunted by the magnitude of her courtiers.

Here is an account of her first contact with Jean Cocteau. "He came to have his photograph made. He had put on a pair of woolen gloves colored red, white and black. I thought at first that he must have come to have his gloves photographed! "

A number of Kiki's paintings decorate the bookshop of Edward W. Titus. It was Titus who decided to publish the translation of her book. In his introductory note, he says, "It was from me that Kiki received the first suggestion to write them. Generous enough with promises, she always stopped short of performance." Thus Titus stopped short of persuasion, but Henri Broca gave her a push and she went to work.

Putnam's job was not easy. Yet this litterateur who wrote that "all translation is a miracle," has rendered in English a translation that has them sounding gongs in Montparnasse. Kiki is so satisfied that she has offered to learn English in order to translate anything Putnam writes. It is no easy task to give Kiki to the American public. She was too fond of artists who loved her and proved it. Perhaps now the Americans will.

Wambly Bald
7 July 1930

Anderson's War of Independence

The artist is an exceptional person: being an exceptional person, he has something exceptional to say: having something exceptional to say, he will say it in an exceptional way. Such is the rather simple theory of Margaret Anderson, founder and editor of *The Little Review*. As is apt to be the case with simple theories, there is nothing particularly wrong with this one as far as it goes, but it doesn't go very far. It does go far enough, however, to furnish a raison d'être for Miss Anderson's autobiography, *My Thirty Years' War*. And her book is a proof that she is an exceptional person, has something exceptional to say, and is capable of saying it in a way that, if not entirely exceptional, is at least fresh, interesting, direct and very much to the point.

Besides being exceptional, Miss Anderson believes that she has never felt very much like a human being. This, I fear, is a pleasant illusion, for her autobiography reveals her as experiencing feelings much the same as other human beings. It would appear, indeed, that her motivation is about six parts of sound conviction to two parts of feminine uncertainty and two parts of pose—which I think is not an uncommon proportion.

The fact is, although she would be the last to admit it, that she might serve admirably as the Model Modern American Girl. Where she is exceptional is that she has had the courage (or, less elegantly but more exactly, the guts) to go ahead and do the things the Average Modern American Girl only dreams about doing. Not that she has made whoopee, in the traditional sense. (This book is not the place to look for any love affairs, nor is there a single reference to alcohol.) Her whoopee is, rather, of the intellectual variety. But her impulse and that of the A.M.A.G. are the same—they both want to be "free" and to "lead their own lives." To do this, it is necessary to get rid of family influence and become indifferent to "what people say." Miss Anderson accomplished both these things early in life.

That the desire to "lead her own life" was stronger than the family ties should be sufficient evidence that she is "modern." That she is thoroughly American is demonstrated by her ideas, attitudes, and actions, all of which bear the "Made in the U.S.A." stamp. Her unfailing self-confidence, her unshakable faith in the possibility of doing things which she has been told are impossible, her refusal to be frightened by lack of money, her impatience with foreign methods—these are typical American traits. It is impossible to imagine a European girl talking a piano agent into renting her an expensive piano for nothing, or convincing a landlord that it would be to his advantage to bestow an unoccupied house upon her. Who but an American girl would, after she had spent her last cent, walk into a drug store, explain to the cashier that she had forgotten her bus fare, borrow a dime from him—and then buy a sack of candy? Again, like the majority of Americans, she is ashamed of entertaining a strictly American idea. It seems, for example, that she had for some reason thought that she was obliged to "stand everything"; but, in France, she learned that such an attitude was American and "that she could discard it"—which she promptly did. Yes, beyond a doubt, Miss Anderson is thoroughly American, even to the point of being sensitive about being an American.

Moreover, despite her periodic claim that she never felt much like a human being, she shows that she has frequently felt, not only like a human being, but like a woman. (Lest I be misunderstood, I do not take the supercilious stand that women are inferior to men: they express themselves differently, that is all.) Throughout her career she has remained not only a romantic woman but a rather sentimental one as well. She has a quite human love of nature, about which she frequently rhapsodizes; a quite human fondness for interiors arranged after her own taste; a quite human weakness for chocolate candy, and a quite human affection for cats. She has romantic ideas about leading a "beautiful life"; it was as a romantic that she first saw Chicago and New York; first attended the theatre and concert hall; she was an eager convert to Emma Goldman's anarchism in the romantic hope that it would enable people to live more "beautiful" lives, and when she founded *The Little Review* she thought of calling it *The Sea-Gull* after her romantic conception of art as soaring like a gull. It was a decidedly sentimental Margaret Anderson who paid out a part of her meagre salary for a daily yellow rose and who went to such lengths each year in order to have a Christmas tree and presents for her friends. And it is a very human Miss Anderson who has enough sense of humor to realize that her younger self must have been a very unpleasant person.

I mention the fact that Miss Anderson is American, human, feminine, romantic and sentimental, not to disparage her, but to demonstrate that her claim to be un-human is an innocent but pointless pose. These qualities are nothing to be ashamed of, and, once granted, I am quite willing to grant her pretension to be an exceptional person. That is why I am rather impatient at finding her trying to justify her pose by arguing with Emma Goldman that it is permissible to be sentimental about flowers, kittens and chocolates but that it is puerile to be sentimental about people. Such an idea has a strong aroma of poppycock.

But Miss Anderson is not very strong in the field of ideas. Her strength is in her personality, and in her conversation. There is something of an admission of this in her impatience with people who oppose her often fantastically impracticable ideas. She detests explanations; she feels that people should gladly and immediately accept her ideas. When they don't—she finds them stupid. Personally, I find her ideas frequently confused, frequently impractical, nearly always original. It is this striking, original quality that excuses many weaknesses in logic. It is what makes her role fundamentally that of a conversationalist rather than of an artist or critic.

Her critical faculty, registered in cold, printed words, is mostly superficial. Her criticisms usually make good spoken conversation but poor written judgments. It is in this confusion of the functions of talk and literature that lies her weakness.

Miss Anderson, from her own account, has always loved conversation. It is not unnatural, then, that her original aim in starting *The Little Review* was to print "the best conversation the world has to offer." But this is a curious aim for a literary magazine, for, it must be repeated, good conversation rarely makes good literature, just as good literature seldom makes good conversation. It is evident that the early numbers of her magazine suffered considerably from this confusion, as well as the uncertainty of her judgment and her changing ideas (for example, she became a confirmed anarchist a few hours before the third number went to press and until she got tired of the Goldman Utopia, the magazine was rabidly anarchist). She, apparently, relied too thoroughly on her exceptional-people-have-something-exceptional-to-say idea, and the result was a review of very mixed standards.

Then Ezra Pound stepped in as European editor and his influence seems to have given *The Little Review* a sort of a direction for the time being. He brought with him most of the first-class writers who have contributed to the magazine. It was he who secured the manuscript of *Ulysses,* the publication and successive suppressions of which were *The Little Review*'s chief claims to fame.

Miss Anderson and her friend, Jane Heap, displayed a splendid courage and spirit in defending Mr. Joyce's extraordinary work. They went to court in its behalf, and they tartly replied to the scores of asinine letters they inevitably received from outraged puritans. In view of their loyal defense, it seems rather pathetic that, in their farewell editorial, they could find nothing more to say about it than that it was "an intense and elaborate expression of Mr. Joyce's dislike for this time." One wonders—in spite of Miss Anderson's implication that she recognized it as a masterpiece—if they ever really understood it.

Robert Sage
18 January 1931

Gertrude Stein Pinch Hits for Fay, Who Stands Up U.S. Women's Club

There was a party a party was a party at the American Women's Club last night but guest of honor Bernard Fay guest of honor professor at Princeton a while while wasn't guest of honor because guest of honor didn't show up wasn't there didn't come so guest of honor Gertrude Stein stepped manfully into the breach and spoke spoke to American Women's Club clubbily about modern Roosevelt modern art creative artist.

Mme. Jacques de Morinni, chairman of the Book Hour committee, said, "Professor Fay hasn't come. I imagine he was snowbound—you know, he went to Copenhagen—or else he just forgot us. But Miss Gertrude Stein, whom you all know, has consented to speak to us. She hasn't prepared anything, so I suggest we all just ask her questions."

Gertrude Stein smiled sharply gayly alertly. Alice B. Toklas, alter ego ego of Gertrude Stein was at her side. Gertrude Stein began to talk obligingly, obligingly about Roosevelt and Democrats.

Republicans are natural rulers of the United States, said she, and Democrats only get in when they are singularly seductive. Roosevelt isn't singularly seductive so he will not have a second term.

"Roosevelt was elected honestly—for the first time since the Civil War," said Miss Stein, and that statement might have prepared her gentle listeners for what was coming.

Soon the talk went to modern art and Miss Stein explained why she kept her paintings some of then changing others around while ordinary

Gertrude Stein

people live in contemporary things too lazy too unthinking unthinking to take interest in modern art.

Back Numbers Miss It

She told how she had published herself self her first book and six kids six had read it. All young boys kids come to her else they are back numbers back, said she, and now Macy's has sold 1,300 copies of her first book in a single month.

Spoke up a member: "Old art came from within, all modern art seems sort of to come from without."

"Don't be silly! All creative art comes from within," said Miss Stein steinishly. "Have you read my book? "

"No, I haven't had the chance."

"You'd better go do it."

Spoke up the member undauntily undaunted: "Are modern painters sane? "

"Us who create live in the epoch," said Miss Stein. "Sure they are."

"I do too," said the member. "But when I saw a painting by Picasso with two buttons sewn on the canvas it didn't mean anything. And when I asked Picasso about it he said something vague."

"That's what creative artists always answer to people who don't understand," said Miss Stein.

Function of Artist

On went went on, and Miss Stein who at last has got recognition after years years effort misunderstood most people told taught told women's club about the creative artist's functions in life.

The fundamentals don't change in the world, but the scene shifts, she explained, the creative artist senses the change and senses his generation and tries to express it to the world.

"He catches what's taking place. The rest of the people, the outsiders, don't bother. Their world was made for them. But the creative artist . . . the creative artist creates what is to exist."

"He's a prophet, isn't he? " asked the fearless member.

"No, he's not a prophet! That's what people always say."

"But modern art is—"

"A great many people don't understand modern art!"

Bang bang bang bing.

Rose is a rose is a rose is Gertrude Stein's motto motto for her *Autobiography of Alice B. Toklas* and Gertrude Stein Gertrude Stein is. Club is club and 60-odd Fay-less members learned about life life books life art life is art is life and Gertrude Stein says she never says anything she doesn't mean everything she says.

A party was a party was a party was a party. Was a party!

9 December 1933

Who's Who

Frank Harris

You ask me how long I have been in France, and you want a short resume of my career here:

I came to the Riviera from a holiday spent in Rome in '85, and I had not been a week in Nice before I used to go about saying "They tell me I was born in Galway, Ireland, but the real place I was born in and love is Nice—an Earthly Paradise—lovely scenes bathed in golden sunshine!"

Ever since, I have spent the winters in France. Even editing *The Fortnightly Review* and *The Saturday Review,* in London, I used to go to the Riviera every winter for the climate of England gave me bronchitis and perpetual colds.

Then you want to know my "major interests here." My chief interest for the last thirty-five years has been to write as well as I can, and I find much stimulus in Nice. Here I have met distinguished men, such as Barbusse, a great writer, Maeterlinck, too, and my friend Maurevert, and the painters Matisse, Anquetin and Barry Greene, the American.

Only last night Maurevert and I had a long talk over old acquaintances, such as Jean Lorrain, one of the wittiest of writers, and Henri Rochefort. . . .

Here at the club, the Artistique, one meets all sorts of people of importance, such as Yvette Guilbert, who always seems to me the best *diseuse* in the world, and Colette Willy, one of the greatest of women.

My chief recreation is driving through this beautiful country, finding continually new scenic wonders, and little villages of astounding archaeological interest.

You ask me about my part in the War activities! Now, even more than when I was a New York editor, I loathe all war, and all preparations for war: It should be put an end to, as duelling was put an end to, a practice surely more defensible than war, and it would be so easy.

The United States is the most powerful country in the world, more powerful today than all the other Powers put together. Why does not Coolidge propose to Great Britain and Japan to give up their Navies, and establish a joint naval police force to guard the seas against piracies? That would relieve many countries of an enormous, futile waste. And if Coolidge could be induced to disband the American army, he would be setting a great example. As I told his predecessor, Harding, the American Army and Navy were only sets of false teeth: in case of war you would have to take them out and put them in your pocket. What decided the last

Frank Harris

war? Nothing known at the beginning of it, but poisonous gases and tanks. And England should know that the next war will be decided not by the obsolete cruisers and battleships she is building at such huge cost; but by airplanes and electric machines; by scientists and not by sailors.

I think I have fairly answered your questions, and as Volume III of "My Life" calls me, I remain.

Yours sincerely,

Frank Harris

The Tribune wrote the author of *The Man Shakespeare* questing facts about him for this column. He answered as above and requested that it be run as he, after all the most competent person to do so, had written it.

6 November 1925

Sacha Guitry

Probably the person who best embodies all the qualities which can be summed up in the word "Parisian" is M. Sacha Guitry. In his work, both as a playwright and as an actor, there is all the polish and finish, the lightness and sureness of touch, the scintillating wit, and the ripe urbanity which are the qualities that come into almost anyone's mind at the mention of this city. And the Parisian public has shown that it recognizes this, that M. Guitry is not only one of them, but the one who appears to them as the type of what each Parisian feels is the best in him, by the enthusiasm with which each new play of his is welcomed, and by the sustained approbation which they have given to him all through his long career.

Guitry may be said to have been born into the theater, for he is the son of the great actor, Lucien Guitry, whose death this year was mourned by the entire playgoing public of the capital. For many years, the one production of every winter about whose success there was never the slightest doubt, was a play by Sacha Guitry in which the principal male role would be played by his father and the principal woman's part by his wife, Mlle. Yvonne Printemps. The untimely death of Lucien broke up this famous trio; but after a period of retirement Sacha Guitry and his wife have returned once more to the footlights.

M. Guitry went directly into the theater on leaving school, and to the theater alone he has for over twenty years now given unstintedly his energy and his splendid talents. What is amazing in his work is its combined abundance and excellence. He seems to compose with facility; at the age of forty he is already author of over twenty plays. Merely to have written this much would be sufficient accomplishment for any man; the really astounding feature of Guitry's work is its uniform high level of excellence.

Every Guitry play is characterized by the firmness and suppleness of its structure, as well as by the brilliance and naturalness of the dialogue. The plots, when analyzed, often seem insubstantial enough. The miracle of Guitry's work is the skill with which he uses trivial situations. And nothing in these plays ever seems forced; masterly and sure as is his technique, probably no dramatist has ever done work which is less "stagey." This, one feels, is the way things happen in real life. The dialogue, too, is always fresh, spontaneous, and perfectly natural; it takes some moments of voluntary reflection to realize that people in real life could never talk so well. The characters in the Guitry plays speak as we should all like to in our most civilized moments. Here is no pedantry, straining for effect, or artifice; it is the quintessence of urbanity.

Sacha Guitry is not a playwright with a message. He does not solve "problems"; in fact, he may be said to be almost unaware of their existence. The only problem which he touches is the eternal one of human existence. In the best sense of the word, his sole aim is to amuse.

It must not be thought, however, that his work is undiluted comedy. He is fully aware of the pathos of life, and is well capable of presenting it. His pathetic scenes, too, never descend to melodrama or bathos; Guitry's good taste is unfailing. He is also capable of creating characters of great nobility. Undoubtedly the finest of these is that of Pasteur, in the play of the same name. This is beyond question the best thing he has done. Probably no one but he could have seen the possibilities for the stage in the life-story of the great scientist. Of a subject which most dramatists would have rejected as impossible, he made the greatest success of his career.

He has written two other studies of great men; one of which, *Mozart,* he is now acting in at the Theatre Edouard VII. The other, presented some years ago, is based on the life of Berenger, the song-writer who in the first half of the nineteenth century was the idol of the Parisian population.

28 December 1925

Michael Arlen

Michael Arlen

Mr. Michael Arlen is now in Paris, which he finds a good place for work, writing another novel, and he plans staying here till its completion.

Probably it is no more than recalling things already known when one tells a few salient facts about him. He is an Armenian who has never been in Armenia; he was born in Bulgaria; he came to England at the age of four; has been there most of the time since; and is now a British subject.

His real name is Dikran Kouyoumdjian. He denies that he picked his assumed name of Michael Arlen out of the London telephone book. He says that he made it up, and that, so far as he knows, no one else has a legal claim to the same name.

Mr. Arlen is now twenty-nine years old. He has been writing ever since he was seventeen, at which age he came to London from Malvern College and launched into journalism. During his lean years he claims to have written every sort of article—sob stories, musical criticism, women's fashions, even poetry. During all this time he was writing stories, but he found it difficult to get the public used to his style.

His first published work of any length was *The London Venture*, a confession, written when he was nineteen. For it he got £30, and later $15 came from the United States. His second venture was a collection of short stories called *The Romantic Lady*. In 1922 he had a third try at capturing popular favor with a novel called *Piracy*. This time he succeeded.

Then began the series of astounding successes which made Mr. Arlen the champion of the world in hammock literature. The short stories in *These Charming People* had all been refused separately by American editors; when the book appeared it sold 56,000 copies in a few weeks. As for *The Green Hat*—probably only in France has any other novel had such a sale, and its stage version, which Mr. Arlen wrote himself, has been a Broadway success. In his policy of alternating a novel with a book of short stories, he followed *The Green Hat* with the collection called *Mayfair*.

The Green Hat has been the greatest of Mr. Arlen's successes. It has been translated into French, German, Swedish, Danish, and Armenian. As a play it is to appear in a few months in Germany, Sweden, and Hungary.

Some reason must exist for Mr. Arlen's phenomenal popularity. So many readers with ordinary intelligence find him fascinating, that he cannot be dismissed with the facile remark that he has a tricky style. For that matter, it is no small achievement to have created a style of such superb ease.

He has had the happy chance of being entirely in tune with his age; if he does not represent the post-war generation, he represents what they should like to be. He deals with the people who a world gone mad with money thinks are its aristocrats; it is that enchanted realm of those whom an abundant supply of gold lifts above the petty cares of life.

It is significant that he should have great popularity in America. There a sudden plethora of wealth has set the whole world to imitating the ways of those considered grand and elegant. We are recovering from our cruder stage, and going in for the "finer" side of life, with tapestry-brick and culture clubs and polo and even ancestors. Mr. Arlen seems to describe the life of those who have arrived at the stage of wearing these trappings easily. So he has become the Harold Bell Wright of the flapper and the lounge-lizard and of the pathetic elders who bemoan their ways while they feverishly try to imitate them.

Alex Small
3 May 1926

Louis Bromfield

At the early age of 29, Mr. Louis Bromfield has in a double sense arrived. He has arrived in Paris, and he has arrived at relative success.

Mr. Bromfield is the author of two novels already, and he is now working on another or others. Those two, *The Green Bay Tree*, and *Possession* have each sold from 35,000 to 40,000 copies. So the work of Mr. Bromfield, if it has not attained the phenomenal figures of that of Mr. Michael Arlen or Mr. Sinclair Lewis or Mrs. John Emerson, still deserves to be classed among the best sellers.

The sort of thing Mr. Bromfield does is not likely to run wildfire. For he tries no tricks, and he does not have a style which gives one a jolt. It is straight, competent novel writing. He himself describes it as "the Victorian novel with trimmings." It is possibly a bit more honest than most Victorian writing was, and more filled with the sense of wonder.

Still, in America at least, this sort of work would have been impossible as lately as fifteen years ago. When Mr. Bromfield undertakes to write the history of a family, in all its ramifications, from the 1890's on, the angle which he takes is more objective than that taken by a novelist like Howells. But, superficially at least, the technique approaches that of an older day; the canvas is as broad as life, with forty or fifty characters (seven or eight leading ones), and all of them seen in three dimensions. He has the sustaining power to carry them on through several books, which, however, are not sequels.

Mr. Bromfield is a typical product of the America of our day. He is one of the yearners from the hinterland who felt uneasy in youth, and, at least so far as individuals are concerned, wanted to do something about it. Mansfield, Ohio, and a farm, gave little nourishment to a youth avid for the picturesque. He belongs to the class of young American who is naturally citified. A year of learning to farm at Cornell and a year more of really doing it at Mansfield, apparently meant little to him.

So this young man drifted to New York, and, with a chronological proximity which had something fatal about it, was called on to take part in that greatest of all invasions which was called the American Expeditionary Force. Greatest, at any rate, in its consequences for young men like Mr. Bromfield, for, without it, how long might have elapsed before they came to Europe and to the critical consciousness born of comparisons?

After the war, Mr. Bromfield got back to New York and went straight after what he felt to be his career, writing. He did incidentals in the meantime—bus-boy work—such as assisting a man named Pemberton in a theater and being an advertising manager for a publishing firm. But he, so he claims, wrote three novels before he tried to get one published. Which may account for the extraordinary success of that first effort.

Mr. Bromfield is now getting the reward of his hard work. He finds that writing pays, and, like many young Americans, is still aghast with wonder at the feeling of being rich and successful. Let those who always or never have been both scoff at this attitude. It is entirely justified. It is an achievement to swim up to the surface from Mansfield; and, in the stress that American life puts on the pocketbook, it is amazing for anyone to be able to keep his own carcass, not to mention that of others, above the ground.

He is a man of great communicative charm. On a casual view, he may seem slightly soft, but that is merely a sign of his sensitiveness to the impacts of life. If he really had been soft, he would have become, as many young men of his sort did, who took part in the great migration, merely a postbellum beachcomber. But he had enough sense to leave dreams where they belong.

When he was a soldier, Mr. Bromfield spoke at one time of becoming an innkeeper at Compiègne. It seems a pity that he did not; he would have been a charming host and stood out as a genius in a trade which counts few geniuses. And even if he is a very good novelist, the world could easily get along without one of the number, or even several.

Alex Small
13 June 1926

Elmer Rice

Recently there came to the office of this newspaper a copy of one of the latest enterprises of certain members of the great American literati. It was called, if we remember correctly, *The American Parade*. It purported to be a quarterly magazine in book form. It also boasted a slogan, flung from the cover page, and as slogans go it was as good as the next one.

Also, there was an editorial in this magazine in book form. And it dealt in no uncertain terms with those who had left the fold and were now at the business of exalting American letters from every *mansard* of Paris. When Rome was rising to eminence certain members of the writing craft betook themselves to Athens. And while they were basking in the memories of the Golden Age, certain of the brethren back home were really producing the literature which has been called Roman. So the escaped American members of the trade were duly warned to take a moment off to ponder about the historical precedent.

Today's subject of these lines lives in Paris. He does not however belong to that group whose adherents thumbed their noses at the Statue of Liberty after cutting all traces in the homeland.

He makes Europe his home for the good reason among others, that here he finds time to work and some peace and quiet in which to do it. In America, he complains, there was little time and no quiet. So having already achieved position in the dramatic world by such plays as *For the Defense* and *The Adding Machine*, written in the hubbub of Gotham, he slipped away for a little respite. Which of course is not exactly why others have left, or at least not all of the story.

Mr. Rice is a full-fledged attorney, an honorable member of the New York bar. Just why he slid into such a ponderous profession neither he nor anyone else knows. He has long since left its dreary circles. But for a time it afforded him a living and was no more unpleasant than being a university instructor or a newspaper copyreader.

He was born in New York City in 1892, quit high school at 14, floundered into a law office and finally graduated from the New York School of Law with *cum laude* honors in 1912.

While still in the law office he had dabbled in playwriting and in 1914 he succeeded in getting his first play *On Trial* produced. It struck the fancy of New York, ran a whole year and resulted in young Rice forsaking the legal profession.

Then followed numerous plays, most of which are well known to the American theatre goer. There was *Iron Cross,* then *For The Defense,* in which Richard Bennett starred, and *Wake Up Jonathan,* which was done in collaboration with Hughes.

Mr. Rice's most important play up to date of course has been *The Adding Machine,* produced first in 1923, and which, as *The Tribune* announced yesterday, is soon to appear in Paris. It is among the best of the expressionistic American plays and already it has received attention in Europe.

Mr. Rice, it seems, like certain of his fellow countrymen is prolific enough. Despite his host of plays he found time to spend two years with the motion picture industry, being on the staff of the Goldwyn Company. He also did a story for Will Rogers entitled *Doubling for Romeo.* This winter The Theatre Guild is to produce his *Life Is Real.*

A few days ago he finished his latest play. It is to deal with marriage, he says. Let it be hoped that it is not the result of too much contact with the French theatre.

William L. Shirer
15 December 1926

Sherwood Anderson

"I am just the mixture, the cold moral of the Northwest into whose body has come the warm pagan blood of the South. . . . Behold in me the American man striving to become an artist, to become conscious of himself, filled with wonder concerning himself and others, trying to have a good time and not take a good time.

"I am not English Italian Jew German Frenchman Russian. What am I?"

—A Story Teller's Story.

On that afternoon in the up and coming town of Elyria, Ohio, when Mr. Sherwood Anderson, prominent manufacturer of house paint, stopped in the middle of dictating a hot sales-letter, offered the place to his stenographer, bid her good-by and shuffled out as happy as a kid getting out of school the above lines may have buzzed through his mind.

That night he got a train to Chicago, went in for advertising in lieu of selling house paint, and thereafter the world, if it had been observing him, might have noted the American man striving to become an artist in a raging hot-bed where about everything else abounds but art.

The strife, of course, did not date from there. An Anderson working before a pegging machine, in a Chicago factory, or trucking freight in a

Sherwood Anderson

Chicago ware-house or selling whatnot for one of Chicago's hustling, bustling, progressive business houses probably had days when he would have chucked the whole bristling business into the slimy Chicago river.

Being unable to do that he chucked himself. So he roved around from one job to another in a manner which would have alarmed the Apostles of Success who perhaps at that time were not shouting so loudly to the young of the land.

It was an age of Vision then. Any barber or mechanic with a few dollars in his pocket was going into business, erecting a factory, becoming a capitalist. So Anderson got into the game and the merry pastime brought him out to Elyria as the head of one of the town's increasing number of manufacturing establishments.

Which is the point at which this hasty sketch begins. Back there in Elyria he had stolen time from house paint. And he had spent it in story-telling. When he began writing advertising in Chicago, three or four novels lay in the bottom of his trunk. One of them was *Windy McPherson's Son.* The other was *Marching Men.*

One day Carl Anderson, his brother, took them to Floyd Dell, then literary editor of the *Post,* and to Theodore Dreiser who also was living in Chicago. They succeeded in interesting John Lane, a New York publisher, and the books were brought out in 1916 and 1917 respectively.

Winesburg, Ohio was published by Huebsch in 1919, though not until considerable pressure had been brought to bear. It revealed a mature Anderson where the former had been a groping, shifting person. Here at last was a man who fathomed the American scene. Who saw through the dull, drab victims of life in small Middle-Western manufacturing towns and knew how to depict them. He didn't deplore them or the peculiar quirk of civilization which produced them. As he told another representative of this newspaper the other day, he can not interest himself in the business of the salvation of mankind. In Winesburg humans lived, had aspirations, had them crushed and died. It was but the old story in a different setting. Chekhov adapted it to Russia, Anderson to America.

A Story Teller's Story was more or less of an autobiographical account, full of fancy, it is true, but a highly illuminating commentary on our great land. *Dark Laughter* was published last year. It established Anderson definitely as one of the three or four best American novelists.

Tar, his latest novel, is just off the presses and *The Testament,* which is to be published this month, will mark Anderson's second excursion into the form of poetry as a means of expression, *Chants,* a book of poems, appearing in 1918.

Anderson, it may be of interest to know, continued at the advertising business up until three years ago. Many talked about him, even read his books. Not so many bought them. *Winesburg,* for all of the hullabaloo about it, sold but a few thousand copies, the *Story Teller's Story* but 8,000.

"There is no danger of Americans becoming cultured," he said the other day.

Neither is there danger, then, of his becoming rich.

William L. Shirer
19 December 1926

Berenice Abbott

One of the outstanding creators of camera portraits in Paris is Berenice Abbott. She has explored and experimented in the realm of photography until she has achieved a reputation for genuine creation of art. In her studio on the Rue du Bac, she has photographed some of the outstanding persons in the capital.

Miss Abbott has reached this field of expression by a slow development which led her through a background of designing, painting and sculpturing. That, perhaps, is the explanation of her work with the camera. For, after a glance at her portraits, it is obvious that she is a skillful worker in black and white, using these two extremes with careful precision.

She molds and shadows with the experience of an artist and the effects derived are what might be called "camera-drawn studies."

She was graduated from the Cleveland high school, remained for one year at Ohio State University and then came to New York to study art. Three years were spent as a student resident of the then thriving Greenwich Village and then she was given an opportunity to come to Berlin to continue her work in that capital.

The patron who inspired her to this voyage abroad was negligent and Miss Abbott soon had to shift for herself. She came to Paris and obtained work as an assistant in the laboratory of a photographic establishment here, thinking that she would return to her art studies at a more opportune time.

The work with the camera interested her to the extent that she devoted all her time to experimenting with it. Last year she exhibited her first set of portraits at the Galerie Sacré du Printemps. The simplicity of her studies was something new in photography.

In her work is manifested an extreme opposition to all traditional ideals and methods. In that respect, she might be called the first of the impressionists in the art. Like the painters of the impressionistic school, she finds it necessary to represent her sensitive impression of the person apart from any analysis or study of character. Her portraits are characterized by their broad simplicity and their lack of attention to detail.

Her work has appeared in the leading magazines of France, Germany and America. At the same time, she has illustrated several books of French authors with her camera.

20 May 1927

Sisley Huddleston

There is something in the dominating situation of Mr. Huddleston's studio which symbolizes the man's whole position: he looks out over Paris. Not only the immediate heights of Montparnasse fall under the observer's eye, but older and more classical Paris, historic Paris, clerical Paris, and, with the distant Luxemburg, the Paris of politics and art. For two decades this English author has followed every complex mood of the capital at his feet. Today numerous editors and publishers regard him as one of the best informed men who devote themselves to maintaining a liaison between the Anglo-Saxon countries and France.

The secret of Mr. Huddleston's success is three-fold, lying not only in the information which he has acquired through long residence and study in Paris, but also on his ability to present this knowledge, and in his personality. Not a stylist in the sense that Landor or Pater are stylists, Sisley Huddleston is nevertheless a master of words in that he always succeeds in his effect. The Victorians worked for mood and melody. He works for lucidity and concision. He has learned the effect of simplicity.

Mr. Huddleston has always known France. His mother was of French descent, while his own education had lain in Paris as well as Manchester. After zoology and design and government employ, he came back to Paris and continued his work in literature at a time when George Moore and

Yeats were familiar figures. Gradually the French scene took possession of him. He broadened to include politics, music and antiquities among his other interests. The man who was to write about every aspect of French life was fully prepared.

With the war came the need of expert information. It was then that Mr. Huddleston began to write for the *Christian Science Monitor,* and it was shortly after the war that he abandoned his early policy of independence to become chief correspondent of the London *Times.* From the first prewar days till the present, Mr. Huddleston has contributed to over a score of papers, and written ten books . . . besides pamphlets and published speeches.

Peace-Making at Paris, Mr. Huddleston's first book, was also the first book about the conference published by one who had followed every phase of the discussions. Then came the general work, *France and the French,* where every aspect of that complex after-the-war phenomenon, victorious France, was analysed. Within the past few months, *In and About Paris* has appeared, but already he is at work on a local sketch of Normandy. Few men could have more to write on such subjects.

William Leon Smyser
1 November 1927

Lincoln Gillespie, Jr.

What about the pioneers?

I breathe hard whenever I think of those literary hermits who struggle in the south of France. Beyond the reach of glory, they live in solitude and slave their days away. For the love of creation, they ride their convictions through clouds of pink and do not complain. And such is the kingdom of heaven.

I am thinking of Lincoln Gillespie, Jr. His history reads like a Pindaric ode. Years ago he gave up a good job as a timekeeper in a million-dollar railroad company, where he was earning $22 a week with the promise of a bonus every fall. But dollars meant nothing. One day he told his boss:

"A new word is as good as an old dollar."

That is the story of his life. Now this literary Gauguin lives on the brow of a bluff overlooking the Mediterranean. He writes poetry when the spirit pushes him, and nothing pleases him more than to whack the bushes of beauty for an elusive symbol. He likes to be employed about those regions which are never quite understood.

The following is an extract from one of his more recent achievements:

> *Truth circumstance*
> *'salways a gripe relish acefetidy*
> *antitharmorplate*

> *to breath strinct-scoriate one's*
>   *fellociate*
> *in public*
> *And awksquirms?*

Enter: Beard of Cullipodus.

A few days ago, the poet arrived in Paris with a chin string which he called "the beard of Cullipodus." Several hours later, while Link was asleep at the Dôme, a girl friend played a trick on him. With a nail file and a hairpin, she nipped the beard, and he no longer looks like Richelieu.

Said Link to his friends:

"That woman is only a social rodent, a criniverous manapstasia. She used to rawk with sandatalama!" No one believed him, however.

They say about Link that he is capable of melting five words into an oath. He is reported to have stated that he can use seven images without the aid of grammar. The meanings are not always clear. Once he said:

"My meanings are just around the corner." Link never talks; he lectures. The boys and girls at the Dôme hang on to his words with grim smiles. Listening would be less difficult if he didn't have a habit of reaching in his vest pocket every minute or so for a chunk of cheese. Nibbling cheese is Link's favorite soother. Years ago he said:

Joyceophalicosity

"There are two great moderns and Joyce is getting old."

Yesterday afternoon, the word-maker was asleep at the Couple. I grabbed his shoulders and shook him until he closed his mouth. I said:

"Wake up, Link. I want to interview you." He opened his eyes, stared and fell back into the subconscious. I squirted some seltzer down his neck and then shouted:

"Pull yourself together, Link. This is an interview." Two garçons standing behind me were smiling at my efforts. Neither they nor Link appreciated the dignity of an interview. At last he woke up. A piece of cheese did it. I pulled it out of his pocket and held it to his face a full minute.

"I never give out interviews," said Link. A few minutes later he added: "Montparnasse writers are too loose! Why don't they tighten up their prose? What do you know about Dutch architecture or the geometric application of Sanscrit? I like the melodic lines of Epstein's work. The trouble with English and American women is that they have a strawy odor, because they don't eat enough vegetables. Order another *fine a l'eau.*"

Again he fell asleep. I picked him off the floor and set him on a chair.

About 7 o'clock I saw Link asleep at the Sélect. I woke him up and said: "Answer a few questions." He said, "Shall I be banal or would you like to hear a few Pizzikaks?" I said, "Mix them up." He said, "All right." Then it was my turn.

"What do you think of Beethoven? "
"Froghide croakboom legs for dinner."
"How do you react to Ravel? "
"Diamond dice thrown high."
"What is a Pizzivol? "
"Kissqueak fingplek daddleback."
"Will you ansamander one more questackaquaff? "
"Poefix may ultraprovide anything! "
"Tellabel me this: Can you let me take 30 francs until tomorrow? "

Ambiblitheriticous

"I haven't any money on me, but stick around and we'll borrow some together."

A little after midnight, Link was fast asleep in Jimmy's bar. I didn't have the heart to disturb him. As he lay there, whistling to himself, I thought of his psychological separation. To him words and word unions are like crawling animals. They are microscopic and fertile. "A new word is as good as an old dollar" and sometimes they are just around the corner.

I walked over to the recumbent figure and studied it. Protruding from one of its pockets was a sheet of paper. I drew it out and read *A Poem from Puzlit*. The last lines clarified everything:

> sardonically towers
> ghoubrel
> i shing my ostracization
> come back!
> come back, I implore you
> no—stay away
> here
> i am ecstaticly.

Those lines will go down in the history of Montparnasse poets. They hold a cry and a weapon. Poor Link! As he lay there, asleep on the shelf, I wondered if his words slept too. What does he think about? Does anyone know? Does he know? Does anyone care?

Before my tears wash the ink off this copy, I shall close our panegyric with a love story. That story is old, but most of the stuff I write about is old. Link had a girl. She loved him. He didn't mind. Came a day when he decided to have two women. He added a young peasant woman. . . . His girl was furious.

"Dismiss that woman," she said.

"My needs have increased," said the author of *Amerikaka*. "One and one make two."

Subadditorialization

That night the vengeful paramour departed and took the rival with her. They went to Paris. Link was left alone. He found the following note pinned to the kitchen wall:

"You thought that one and one make two. Well, one minus two make zero."

The deserted poet wired back:

"One minus two rid me of you. Anyway, I was beginning to tire of your synthetic olfactory reprehensibility. Asyndic desertita yowlacat scrap finalapurgatude chainbind pettabibbletory. And I am glad of it."

Wambly Bald
5 May 1931

III Montparnasse through the Years

In 1924 the *Tribune* started printing a column by Eugene Jolas called "Rambles through Literary Paris," a mélange of book news, reviews, and gossip, mostly about French and American writers who interested Jolas, which was the first serious effort to provide news of the Montparnasse literati. With Jolas's departure for America in 1925, the assignment fell to Paul Shinkman, whose "Latin Quarter Notes" generally featured gossipy bits about prominent (at least at the time) Quarterites. Occasionally Shinkman's column was written by Bravig Imbs, a proofreader with literary aspirations, but more often by the acerbic Alex Small, whose sardonic views of most Latin Quarter habitués flowed over into his commentaries.

By the late twenties the *Tribune* usually gave full coverage to any major or bizarre event that affected Montparnasse—the suicides of Harry Crosby and Hart Crane, Raymond Duncan's latest experiment in communal living, Aleister Crowley's expulsion from France—and kept several staffers busy writing about the Quarter, the main ones being Louis Atlas, whose column "Almost Anything Can Happen" continued until 1934; Harold Ettlinger, who wrote a series in 1931 called "What Writers Are Doing"; Edmond Taylor, Leigh Hoffman, Richard LeGallienne, and "Montparno," an omnibus pseudonym some staffers preferred.

But the liveliest and probably the most artful column the *Tribune* published about Montparnasse was "La Vie de Bohème." Its creator, a proofreader named Wambly Bald, a master of deft and hilarious characterizations and situations which often conveyed, in not too subtle terms, unpleasant truths about Quarterites, became the Left Bank's ubiquitous Boswell, one more often feted than ignored, and praised than damned, and undeniably the one *Tribune* writer, in the opinion of Janet Flanner, Quarterites never failed to read. When he voluntarily ended his column, because, as he said, Montparnasse had ceased to exist, Sisley Huddleston's letter to the *Tribune* must have expressed the opinion of many a Constant Reader: "The Montparnasse of Wambly Bald is worthy to be set beside Erewhon and Utopia, and Atlantis and Laputa and all the other legendary kingdoms and republics which are far more living than, say, America."

H. F.

91

1924

Through Paris Bookland

We recently went to visit that temple of Modern French literature—the house of *La Nouvelle Revue Française*. Here, where postwar currents of contemporary letters flow together, the atmosphere of the N.R.F. books was most pleasant. Huge piles of books labelled "Equipage," "Le Lin," etc., were stacked on the floor. The walls were decoratively plastered with book-titles printed on strangely colored paper. During a chat we had with M. Jacques Riviere, the young director of the magazine, the famous critic told us that Marcel Proust represented the summit of contemporary French literature. We asked his opinion about the younger men, and he was most enthusiastic about Jacques Lacretelle, the author of "Siberman," Jacques Sindral, Raymond Radiguet (who received the New World prize for his novel "Le Diable au Corps" a year ago), Jean Giraudoux, a former Harvard student, Drieu La Rochelle, Henri Montherlant, Jean Cocteau and others. M. Riviere spoke very highly of Carl Sandburg and Waldo Frank, the two Americans who seemed to have made a profound impression on *les jeunes* here. He feels that, while the background against which Sandburg paints his pictures differs, of course, from the French, the technical process used by the modern Americans is not vitally different from that used by the young French poets.

We met in one day Miss Gertrude Stein, Mr. Ernest Hemingway, and Mr. Ogden Donald Stewart, recently. Mr. Hemingway explained to us his esthetic theories, although he is the least theoretical of writers. His "Three Stories" (of which "My Old Man" has just been re-published in O'Brian's *Best Short Stories of 1923*) have a dynamic directness and go straight to life, without being "literary" at all. Watching him engage in a friendly boxing bout, as we did, gives a definite index as to his method. He told us he had never read Zola, and we were wondering how many writers still read the great experimenter of the scientific novel.

Eugene Jolas
1 June 1924

Rita Studientica

How many dollars does it take to live comfortably in Paris? No, not francs—dollars. *Moi,* I have never found out at first hand, for since that immemorial day at Cherbourg when I stepped into the special train and gave an obliging porter twenty francs for sending a telegram to an expectant friend in Paris, since that day, I have been living close to both ends of an inadequate but hard-earned French salary. *Soit!*

Oh, I have managed to pick up a few useful French words here and there. And a generous mead of experience. There indeed my stars have not been niggardly. Rather have they been both lavish and unique. Above all, unique. Too inimitable it often seems for clumsy words and printers' ink. Some things there are that defy expression.

This, then, is not autobiography. It treats not of myself but of Mary-Helen-Alice-Jane-Rose-Marie Studientica. Though her name in this case was Rita. I collided with her one day last spring near the Opera, in one of those seething, pinch-beck rendezvous which I braved to get out of the rain—one of those sudden, unlooked-for, always-to-be-expected Parisian showers. It was months since I had been there. She went every day to call for mail and look for new names in the register. Bus fares and taxi bills meant nothing to her. Rita wasn't counting francs. We fell on each other's necks, and for a moment or so provided a little distraction for the bored aliens.

"How long have you been here? "

"How long have you? "

"Where are you staying? "

"Come and have tea."

"Isn't it wonderful? "

We had both been in Paris since the early winter, both in the Latin Quarter. But—I worked and walked, read a bit, wrote a bit, ate a bit, slept a bit. Rita—Rita was fulfilling my dream of a father back home, a monthly check, a course at the Sorbonne, high life with nary a care in the world.

Rita Studientica. We had been sorores at college in olden days, intimate enough for practical purposes, between us an incipient friendship nipped in the bud. Driven by a chronic wanderers' urge and a fear of impending failure I had abandoned the east in favor of one of our great western Halls of Learning. I heard vaguely that Rita galloped through college with characteristic brilliance, and was going abroad to be finished, polished and properly labelled. Rita's father is a foreign language professor, a sincere scholar of another day, with an enviable knowledge of that legendary Europe *avant la guerre.* There were other mouths to be fed out of the professorial stipend, but if Rita was to carry on the intellectual tradition of the family, to Europe she must go for an intensive field course in ancient culture, comparative literature and contemporary civilization.

We sat in the smoke and smell of a notorious café at the intersection of the boulevards Raspail and Montparnasse, while Rita drew a sketchy outline of her two years in Germany. Presently came a few of her friends, and we drank some more, gossiped animatedly, and reminisced with excited or sentimental do-you-remembers. We spent long hours together after that, met after her evening class at the Alliance Française, rushing each other with perhaps something of desperation in our souls. What she may have searched for in me I know not, though now after a year's separation I can guess and admit that I must have meant little more than a symbol of the old familiar faces. But she, she had so much that I coveted—leisure, independence, study, travel, friends. . . . I devoured her eagerly.

She had gone to Berlin first, in those immediately post-war days when one could live in Germany comfortably not to say luxuriously on ten dollars a month, or some such trifle. Through friends of her father's, she had access to everything, and with her almost perfect German she escaped most of the unpleasantnesses encountered by most foreigners. She skipped through the University much the way she had done in the States, with her quick, receptive mind. Her holidays she spent traveling in Germany, in Austria, in Italy, in Switzerland, in Denmark, in Norway.

A year at the Sorbonne was to round out and wind up the process, but an accidental twist to her ankle kept her in Heidelberg last Fall, so that she had only one semester in Paris. Here too there were friends of her father's waiting to take her in, introduce her to people and places, grease the way lest petty annoyances intervene between Rita and cultural refinement. She made friends on her own also, habitués of her pet café, students, artists.

Never in the two or three months during which we saw each other constantly (I was no longer working, for reasons irrelevant to the subject) did she refuse an attractive social invitation on the plea of study. Never to my knowledge did she spend even a meagre hour at the library. Seldom did she miss an afternoon or evening at the café. I went with her to one of her classes, and when the lecture was over, ventured a humble question. Rita: "Oh! Did you notice the tall spiffy girl who walked in so late? She's the daughter of the great cold cream king! "

"So? "

She trotted forth such terms as I thought to have left behind me. Cram, cut (bolt, we used to say), pipe course, grind. The campus transplanted! The Undergraduate Attitude!

But no! The American student's scorn of the studious may be sincere, but this is pretence, a mere superficial hangover. One doesn't come to Europe for years of postgraduate work without developing a genuine thirst for knowledge and imbibing a bit accordingly. I struggled to deny that I was finding Rita sadly like unto the Rita of freshman days.

"Have you been reading lately? What do you read? " I was going to clear the air.

"Read? Oh, I don't have much time, you know. But I have been reading Leonard Merrick. I can't resist him—buy all his books. I have a whole collection."

An advanced student in contemporary and comparative literature.

Mais enfin, she's living at any rate. Thank heaven the life of the spirit

doesn't depend on books and academic study. These people for instance—
new contacts, new vistas, new philosophies—these people, her new friends,
were giving her more of concentrated life than she could gather from a
whole force of canned courses and priggish professors. So I set myself to
probing them, looking vainly for more than a pound of flesh.

They have no prejudices, Rita boasted to me. Genuine Bohemians they
are, with an expansive sardonic tolerance towards vice. Ye gods! What do
they call vice? What evil? What immoral? Are their standards different
from those of their witch-burning forebears or their Main Street
compatriots? *Tolerance* towards *vice!* Where then are those passionate
Bohemians who know no tolerance because they see no vice? Where—
where—

But they get excited. Rita was nibbling delicately at the spicy-coated
sugarplums of the café. They were mild but they satisfied. She found life
fascinating and exhilarating *pour le moment,* and confided to me that she
would probably commit suicide on her thirtieth birthday. Meanwhile there
were balls to dance at, coffee to idle over, and, unhappily, exams to
contend with. She left the café at about ten-thirty one evening in order to
get an early start at her cramming. On the way home however she
encountered one of the artists who had joined us that first day. He is an
etcher, well known and quite genuinely talented. Older than Rita by a
goodly number of years, and surely, surely, amused at her naive
immaturity. They sat on the doorstep of Rita's dormitory (she roomed
with a French family) and talked until dawn. Mostly about sex and other
things. Can it be that our modern educational systems and social
inhibitions are tending towards a prolongation of adolescence? I ask in all
seriousness.

For a week then Rita closeted herself with her books and her
lamp-light, and a determination bred of the fear of meeting her father face
to face. It was a brief period of hectic energy and valiant frustration,
confounded by the confusion of preparations for departure on the last day
of June.

We saw her off at the Gare St. Lazare that hot Saturday afternoon. To
date the exam results had been moderately encouraging. One of her
student friends was to obtain the final report that evening, wire the news
to Cherbourg, and see to the eventual forwarding of the diploma and other
formal credentials. Rita went with fearful reluctance. She hated and
dreaded going back to the States, she had grown too fond of the
continental way of living. She would miss her friends and the life of the
boulevards, the freedom, the joyous irresponsibility.

"I'll be back in September," she called as the train jerked out.

Next morning I saw her school-mate and learned that Rita had failed.
Failed.

How sorry they all felt. Not for Rita, of course—she wouldn't mind
much. But her poor father. What a disappointing blow for him.

Why all this unholy sentiment? Why sorry? Rita hadn't failed. It
seemed to me the most logical conclusion conceivable. Anything else

would have been failure indeed. I make no doubt that her father's influence secured her a fairly desirable post as foreign language teacher *quand même.* She didn't come back in September, and as for me I never heard from her. *Sic transit.*

But I comfort myself with the reflection that they can't all be like that. *N'est-ce pas?*

R. W. Guthrie
1 June 1924

Rambles through Literary Paris

Paris today is doubtless the cerebral crucible of the world. Nowhere does the visitor from America face such a plethora of ideas, revolutionary concepts, boldly destructive philosophies, ferociously new esthetic principles. . . . And the role of the spectator is the more interesting as the flux of ideas and the interchange of ideologies produce a constant war of the spirit which finds its expression in literary and artistic brawls of the most violent kind. Thus we take great pleasure in announcing a new fight which promises to surpass all of the preceding struggles in intensity and interest. This time the protagonists are M. André Gide and M. Henri Beraud. And the war is being fought in the *Mercure de France,* where M. Gide has massed his heavy battery and in the *Paris Journal,* where M. Beraud has dug his trenches. This little war has its genesis in the now well-known controversy between M. Jacques Riviere of the *Nouvelle Revue Française* and M. Beraud, which . . . ended almost in a delightful little duel.

How James Joyce spends his hours in Paris is being revealed by Valery Larbaud, brilliant French poet and romancier, and "European." Frederic Lefevre gives a scintillating causerie with Larbaud, in which the latter . . . chats about the great Irishman with remarkable frankness. "The last time I met Larbaud," says Lefevre, "was in that American bar in the Latin Quarter, whither his friend James Joyce calls him whenever he wants to read a new work to him. 'We come here,' states Larbaud, smilingly, 'because we are very quiet from nine o'clock in the evening until one o'clock in the morning. The little dancers arise late.' " Valery Larbaud, according to the writer, is at present supervising the translation of Joyce's *Ulysses,* although the work is to be given to the French public only in fragments, as it would take a life-time to translate it.

"I met James Joyce towards the end of 1919 in the studio of a friend in the Rue Dupuytran," Valery Larbaud related. "Miss Sylvia Beach introduced us. Joyce is a man who does not speak; he is a man—*tout a fait en bois.* When I went away, Miss Sylvia Beach gave me the numbers of *The Little Review* in which fragments of *Ulysses* had appeared. On my arrival at home, I began to read them, thinking it would be an excellent preparation for sleep. I had a happy surprise, when I finished the last number, it was early morning. Dedalus—the portrait of the artist as a young man—is one of the greatest books I have ever read, and Joyce at this moment represents the entire English literature. . . . My admiration for Joyce is such that I am sure he is, of all contemporaries, the only one who will pass into posterity."

Eugene Jolas
8 June 1924

About Creative Work

In this age of mechanical over-production and standardized esthetics, it is a real delight to meet a writer who works with almost Stoic slowness. Miss Mina Loy, author of that strangely cryptic *Lunar Baedeker*, gave us an idea of her work the other day and incidentally told us the story of that famous poem of hers on Brancusi's Golden Bird, which, we remember, made a profound impression when it was first published. When she wrote this poem, she had never met the Romanian genius of sculpture and the poem represents a real intuitional appreciation. "One must have lived ten years to write a poem," she said.

Who are the American futurists? M. Marinetti, the father of the destroyers of the past, insists they are: Stella, Man Ray, Sandburg, Lindsay, Edgar Lee Masters, Amy Lowell, and Ezra Pound. If he had left out Amy Lowell, we might think the list was perfect; for her art is essentially a static art, we believe.

Eugene Jolas
20 July 1924

Books and Bookmen

The *Paris* is a grand ship, and her cuisine is the finest on the sea. Indeed, one dines and wines with such a Lucullian frequence and completeness that there is small time for reading. However, a certain amount of reading seems to go on. Ambassador Herrick and his family sit in a row of deck chairs, engrossed in three copies of Michael Arlen's new novel, *The Green Hat*, which we devoutly hope will be published in America this autumn. From an Armenian boy with a name that could not be pronounced by any one with the adenoids, Michael Arlen has (in a few years) become a distinct literary personage, a master of the light style, sharing the billing only with Aldous Huxley. He is hailed in London as "Dick" Arlen, and is no end of a dandy, to be seen any day lunching in elegance at Claridge's or the Berkeley. Which only goes to prove an old theory of ours that the wearing of spats shows in one's literary style—just as Sherwood Anderson's unshorn locks and thick soled shoes influence his writing, or the waist line of Mr. Dreiser, his.

Gene Markey
21 September 1924

Rambles through Literary Paris

It does one good in these depressing days of sur-realisme, literary insincerities and artistic intrigues to come across a poet to whom his art is not a means for fantastic perversions of the spirit. In meeting Mr. Arthur Davison Ficke for the first time one is impressed with the youthful élan of his Weltanschauung. The author of *Sonnets of a Portrait Painter, Out of Silence,* and other books, who has been intimately associated with the great literary Renaissance in America before the war, who has written some of the finest lyrics in the English language, and who, with Witter Bynner, dealt a death blow to the fanatic passion for creating literary "schools" in the States through the "Spectrist" hoax, is back in Paris, with Mrs. Ficke, after both have wandered about France on horseback. He told us about those Chicago days, when Floyd Dell first began to gather around him some of the young rebels, and Margaret Anderson, with her *Little Review,* irritated the old fogies of literature. He talked about those days with a certain sadness, as if modern literature in America had nothing like it to offer. Perhaps he is right. . . .

Eugene Jolas
28 September 1924

Rambles through Literary Paris

The one thing almost every European writer expresses about American art and letters is scepticism. Condescendingly they refer to the artistic endeavours of our tradition-less youth. They know little save Poe and Whitman, who undoubtedly wielded an immense influence on Continental evolution. Waldo Frank and possibly Theodore Dreiser among the moderns represent the extent of their horizon. But they always insist that America will eventually produce the art for which this age of epigones is waiting. It is so much more facile for them to write about America, the cubes of its visionary skyscrapers, the roar of the Chicago pit, the sing song of Jazz, which Milhaud discovered for them. The real America they do not know.

They are ignorant of the groping psyche of the nation as manifested throughout its limitless spaces. Ivan Goll publishes a World Anthology and gives a cross-cut of the Poetic Renaissance, featuring Sandburg, Edgar Lee Masters, Amy Lowell, Sherwood Anderson (the poet), Orrick Johns, Ezra Pound, James Oppenheim and Vachel Lindsay. Novels, probably because of the technical difficulty of translation—are practically unknown. The work of Eugene O'Neill is not understood, simply because the premises are unknown. To be sure, the realistic—or regionalistic—movement, as exemplified by the writers of the Middle West, has no real analogy in France. Rather it is a movement which owes its impulse to the Central European Heimatskunst of 1908–1913. It is, therefore, comprehensible that its period of greatest production fell in the years during and after the war. Sinclair Lewis, Sherwood Anderson (who is, however, also a mystic), and also Homer Croy! Dreiser, being a naturalist, does not belong in this group. As Homer Croy is now in France and has just finished his latest book—*R.F.D. No. 3*—we were happy to chat with him the other day.

Mr. Croy told us his reason for coming to France to write about the Middle West. "I did not come to France for the reason you imagine," he said, "because I had all I wanted back home.... There was merely a change in price. The reason is that the farther you get away from the scenes you are writing about, the better you are apt to do them. I live in a place, absorb all I can, and then go off and incubate. I would never write stories of the Latin Quarter while living there. I'd probably write 'em in the Middle West, and when living in the Latin Quarter, I'd write about the corn rows. I go on the theory that if you can't remember a thing, it isn't worth writing about. The novel I wrote here ... is *R.F.D. No. 3* and it has just been published. I wrote some of it in Paris, some of it in Nice and finished it in Sainte Maxime."

Eugene Jolas
19 October 1924

Open Letter to Ernest Hemingway

Dear Hemingway. We discussed you the other day with some American writers and we expressed to them our conviction that you have one of the most genuinely epic talents of any youngster writing in English today. In fact, we said that, in our opinion, you were destined to create a new literature on the American continent. We have never hesitated in expressing this view, in spite of some contradictions from men who disagreed with us. When we met you for the first time at Dave O'Neil's hospitable home here, we felt an aura of masculine strength about you that we like to connect with our dreams of America.... You have the root of the matter in you.... You have created in stark, acid accents the medium which is symptomatic of a great deal of modern hopelessness....

To be brief, we like most of your stories . . . they have power and often a beauty that leaves one with a sense of the terror of life. . . . Now, we just picked up *Der Querschnitt* and noticed your two poems in them. . . . We ain't able to follow you there. . . . We simply give up. . . . We believe you're on the wrong tack. . . . If you don't watch out, Dr. Summer will give you a raft of free publicity and then what's going to happen to you. . . . Please give us another "My Old Man" and let it go at that. . . .

Eugene Jolas
16 November 1924

Claude McKay Describes Struggles

Claude McKay required a European background to realize a dream he had had for describing the struggles of his life. This sympathetic interpreter of his people's lonely fight has injected an element into American literature of a beautiful exoticism which it needs. Against the harsh, Biblical rhythms of most of contemporary American writers he set the colorfulness of a Southern mind drenched in sun. The dream he had which he is about to realize on this continent is the fictional presentation of a segment from his life. The book, he told us, will be called *Jim Crow*. It gives in strong, realistic, and sometimes even eschatological accents the history of his early struggles in America, after he had arrived there from his native Jamaica. Days of misery will be resuscitated. . . . He is also thinking of giving the atmosphere of his West Indies in a group of short stories on which he is now working. And we cannot think of anyone who is better equipped for this job, for although we confess to a great admiration for Firbank's *Prancing Nigger*, we frequently had the painful impression that Firbank had not seen the colorful, bizarre spectacle of these characters from the inside.

Eugene Jolas
7 December 1924

1925

Rambles through Literary Paris

They have a Poet's Union in Soviet Russia, according to Mr. Max Eastman, poet, political economist, and philosopher, whom we recently met after his arrival in Paris following a year's stay in Moscow. . . . Moscow is apparently the poets' paradise. They have a club where they get their meals and where they can work without the hateful intrusion and fanatic madness of the modern world of trade and commerce. Mr. Eastman told us he was putting the finishing touches to his book, *Psychology and Marxism,* and that he is also writing a biography of Trotzky, in the creation of which the former Soviet War Lord helped considerably.

There are few manifestations of the modern mind as far as the arts and science are concerned that escape the attention of *L'Esprit Nouveau.* In the last issue we find Fernand Léger's esthetic guide-lines for the *Ballet Méchanique* he is preparing together with Dudley Murphy and George Antheil. Among the things he says about the film are: "There is no scenario—nothing but reactions of rhythmed images. The film is constructed on two coefficients of interest: the variation of the speed of the projection; the rhythm of this speed. The film is divided into seven vertical parts which go from slow to rapid. . . . Each of these parts possesses its proper unity due to the similitude of the groupings of image objects that resemble each other. This is done for the purpose of construction and to avoid the breaking-up of the film." Looking at the cinematographic picture of machines whirring at that rate of speed is not calculated for tender nerves evidently.

Eugene Jolas
1 March 1925

Latin Quarter Notes

There is one more vacant chair on the Boulevard Montparnasse these days and Broadway is feting the return of her prodigal prodigy . . . young Mr. Norman Bel Geddes, *enfant terrible* of the American theater.

Paris, it will be remembered, was rendered virtually *hors du combat* last month by the Geddes production of the de Acosta play, *Jehanne d'Arc.* Pulsating mobs sweeping across the stage with all the colorful harmony of

Norman Bel Geddes

a Florentine canvas, was something of a new thrill . . . and the wiseacres agreed that the Geddes settings and *décors* were the individual triumph of the entire venture.

An obstreperous mob, innumerable costume designs, and a colossal production, however, were not too much for the young producer. At any rate, he could usually be found of an afternoon dreamily surveying the passing show of Montparnasse over a *café crème* or *apéritif.* As to who will succeed to the chair, nobody knows. Elmer Rice, the young American playwright and a Quarterite for the nonce, has been suggested.

Before sailing, Geddes left a little souvenir of himself on the Left Bank in the shape of a sketch by D. F. Meziki.

Paul Shinkman
24 July 1925

Latin Quarter Notes

And still they are begging for copies of *Ulysses.* Sylvia Beach of Shakespeare and Co. tells us the sixth edition of the Joyce opus is due off the presses tomorrow. Meanwhile, his health being somewhat improved, the author is occasionally seen on the Left Bank. . . . Sylvia herself believes she is entitled to a well-earned rest and is leaving for the Savoie, not to write a book, she says.

Elmer Rice found the Left Bank so attractive that he took an apartment for himself, Mrs. Rice, and the children, and remained most of the spring. Now he is leaving for Switzerland to spend the rest of the summer, until he is called back to Broadway this fall to assist in the staging of his new play, *The Subway*.

Paul Shinkman
31 July 1925

Latin Quarter Notes

Marsden Hartley, after repeated rumors of a coming marriage, fled to the Riviera where he intends to take up his landscape painting again. Bob McAlmon dashed over from London and stayed a few days. He visited Sylvia Beach for one thing. Another book? When Donald Ogden Stewart isn't at the Ritz he's at Zelli's—most convenient for his friends! He's just returned from Hollywood, where he was an understudy for Reckless Rudolph. We surmise, very under. Blomshield is painting his portrait to prove the resemblance to his incredulous friends. After this is done, Stewart is going down to Antibes to finish his new book, or whatever it is they do at Antibes.

Bravig Imbs
9 August 1925

Latin Quarter Notes

Paul Robeson was a celebrated visitor to the Quarter this week. The actor was the honored guest at a tea given by Sylvia Beach and Adrienne Monnier. Robeson sang several of his beloved negro spirituals which he is to sing for America on a trans-continental tour this winter. He says he will then likely return to the stage.

Paul Shinkman
13 November 1925

Latin Quarter Notes

Having weathered the stormy censorial seas of America and England, as well as an occasional type-setters' walkout, Mr. Joyce's *Ulysses* is ready for a French cruise, where, it is safe to say, the sailing will be much smoother.

Auguste Morel, the French writer, informed us yesterday that his translation of the book, already well underway, will be completed in about one year. The French *Ulysses* is to be brought out by Adrienne Monnier of *La Maison des Amis des Livres,* who hopes to do for France what her neighbor, Sylvia Beach, did for America and England.

Paul Shinkman
4 December 1925

1926

Latin Quarter Notes

> Ideas exist
> As bleak, conceited hopes within the mind.
> The will to cast themselves
> Upon the outer visage of some form
> Gives way to talk of semblance,
> Or of friends.

Thus sings Virgil Geddes, the American poet, in the prologue to his new book of *Forty Poems.* Geddes, one suspects from no more than a casual survey of his works, is a wanderer, one of those wanderers in the realm of fancy who senses poignantly the tremors of emotional experience, who now smiles faintly at its whirligigs and arabesques, now cries out at the rumblings of its divine tympani.

Geddes is in Paris for the moment. The volume which is just appearing is made up of poems which were written over a period of two years and many of which have already appeared in American literary reviews. There is a revealing preface . . . written by Elliot H. Paul.

Paul Shinkman
7 May 1926

Latin Quarter Notes

Nathan Asch, a well-known Quarterite who is now in New York, is represented in the current number of *The Nation* by a review of the memoirs of Frank Harris (another familiar figure in the Quarter). Asch is none too easy on the veteran reminiscer and seems to resent a certain self-consciousness which he finds. He finds Harris neither a "Pepys writing to amuse only himself nor a Casanova trying to pass the time away in dull surroundings." It is the last chapter, which forms a sort of apologia, that Asch finds the best.

Speaking of Walt Whitman, the exposition devoted to the Bard of Camden is still in progress at Shakespeare & Company in the rue de l'Odéon. It includes original manuscripts, autographed portraits, and a collection of interesting first editions and autographed letters. The proceeds of the exposition are to go towards the erection of the Whitman monument which they are planning across the ocean.

Paul Shinkman
19 May 1926

Latin Quarter Notes

The reader of this column is asked to note that its editor, Mr. Paul Shinkman, has joined the vacationists for the next two months. No more, for a time to come, will he be seen scurrying around the Cameleon and the other haunts where he picks up his piquant items. In his place, this subdued and distant spectator of the puppets who gyrate about in the bright pool of light at the intersection of the boulevards Montparnasse and Raspail every night, will put out in this column any casual gossip about the Latin Quarter, whatever that may be, which he can shark up.

Summer seems to have come to Montparnasse as to everywhere else. Just what mutations are taking place among the old denizens, I find it hard to determine, for the small group of familiar faces make but an occasional speck in the mobs on the terraces of the Dôme and the Sélect. In fact, I see none of them at the Dôme any more; they all seem to have taken the diagonal trek across the street. The café which has become so famous that its name has travelled to the remote hamlets of the American hinterland is now inundated with the invaders from that hinterland, not to mention those whose ruddy faces show they have just come out of the pottery orchards of Staffordshire and the ever-increasing flaxen-haired horde from the fjords.

Anonymity has fallen on Montparnasse. No longer is it a happy family party of more or less sober fantoches, mutually diverting and boring each other. The only bond which all have in common is that each and every one at some time or other shakes Fernand for the drinks or the cigarettes.

Otherwise the groups seem to be mutually exclusive, and new ones have clustered together in which are never to be seen any of the old familiar faces.

Still, the former Montparnassian, returning to the scene, will by diligent search, find some one he knows, and may get a few moments of interesting conversation. In the wide-open spaces of the Sélect terrace it is now possible to talk by modulating one's voice to a gentle shout. I have noticed there recently Jo Bennett and Cheever Dunning and Ivan Opfer and Djuna Barnes and Thelma Wood and Myron Jacobson and Sybil Vane and a number of others who have been around for the last four or more years. Flossie is still there, even more so. And Harold Stearns, who, if one is lucky enough to get a few moments of conversation with him, will demonstrate that the spark of wit and intelligence still flickers in Montparnasse.

Ere I forget it in these lugubrious reflections, there is a real news item. The crypt of the Hotel de Caveau saw a very Latin-quartery dinner the other night. George Antheil was the guest of honor, and Miss Betty Robbins acted as hostess. Mrs. Antheil was there and Allan Tanner and Pavel Tchelitchew and Irving Schwerké and Elliot Paul. A homogeneous time should have been had by all.

To return to the source of these our woes, the annual summer inundation. I for one regret it not one whit. I see no reason why Montparnasse should not be turned into an amusement park. Such has been, since the war, its inherent and inevitable destiny. When, this winter, a whole forest of tall pines moved in from the fjords, the transformation was complete. And it has compensations. No visitor now can have any illusions about the place. The gossip, which is all was ever talked about there anyway, has lost some of its villagey venom.

Alex Small
2 July 1926

Latin Quarter Notes

This one got one prompt response to his appeal for news of celebrities. It comes from Juan-les-Pins, from a person who calls himself Alison Keyes. It is apparently becoming the thing for American and other artists to stay there all during summer. We offer some of the items for what they are worth, and even more than that.

First, it seems that the F. Scott Fitzgeralds are there. That is as far as they got on that rumored trip around the world. He is said to be doing a new novel, which is no great news, for he usually is, when he isn't doing something else. Still, if he can make it as good as *The Great Gatsby* it will be worth the wait. One is informed that FSF's place is to be found by the Stars and Stripes on his two-seater in front of the door. So that probably the wave of xenophobia has not got down there. It is, however, something not to be expected of Mr. F. I wonder what fantastic activities are now making up his real life?

Anita Loos is there with her husband, and we understand that all the others have made a great to-do about her, and that she now "is running in an English magazine a very serious treatise upon the importance of prenatal influence." Serious? We don't doubt; we've never read any of the work of Miss Loos; but we have had it rumored around us that she was an authority on mining and vacuum-cleaning, mostly the latter. I mean to search this work out and read it; maybe Miss Loos, by prenatal influence, will be able to account for the production among the human race of sharks, octopi, and other fauna.

Alex Small
1 August 1926

Latin Quarter Notes

A visit to the Anglo-American bookshops of the Left Bank gives one some interesting bits of information on current literary production. For instance, we said a little while ago that a Hemingway cult was in a fair way to being founded. Confirmation of this comes in a review which appeared in one of the lofty New York periodicals. There Mr. Hemingway is called an inevitable best-seller. That seems now to be settled; a little more repetition and the state will be achieved. Incidentally, the review in question puts Mr. Hemingway, or at least, his last novel, on the pan—even insinuates that he is writing facile caricatures of real people. Mr. H. should worry; the review takes him seriously and gives him plenty of publicity.

We got our first intimation of the death, in a motor accident, of Edward Cummings. His renown did not travel beyond the circle of Boston, where he was one of the last of the line which had its halcyon days about fifty years ago. Anemic they seemed in comparison with their ancestors, and without influence on contemporary thought. Cummings had a sort of left-hand connection with modern literature, however; he was the father of Mr. E. E. Cummings. His son's career as a literary man must have been a constant source of surprise to the dignified old clergyman.

Alex Small
28 December 1926

1927

Latin Quarter Notes

Reviews of one sort or another are soon to bless us aplenty. On top of *transition,* which Mr. Jolas lets on is to be the object of his labors, and Mr. Paul's also, Mr. Pound's is on the way or ways. There were rumors that the person was about to return to the United States after many years of absence, but no such intention is indicated in a long letter which he has just sent to one of the booksellers of the Left Bank (either one will do).

Mr. Pound's new effort is to appear but three times a year. We may then confidently expect that all the stuff in it will be good; it should have long enough to simmer. And it will be only thirty francs a year in price—hence accessible. He has confided (to the press, I believe) that the main item in number one is not a "mastodon of the size of *Ulysses,*" but that he is fond of it just the same. Make whatever you wish out of that.

The surrealists are at it again, this time in painting. Two days ago they opened an exhibition at their gallery in the Rue Jacques-Callot. Those on view are a judicious mixture of known and unknown names. There are André Masson and Braque and Picasso, and Picabia and the American, Man Ray. Others whose names have impinged are Yves Tanguy, Miró, Arp, Max Ernst (now famous for his picture in the Independants), Giorgio di Chirico and Malkine.

Alex Small
1 February 1927

Mrs. Ernest Hemingway, Author's Wife,
Gets Divorce in Paris

Certain American literary circles in Paris were not surprised yesterday to learn of the divorce decree which a Paris court has just granted to Mrs. Ernest M. Hemingway, wife of the well-known writer, who has made his headquarters here for the past several years. To the large following which the young author has attracted on the Continent, however, the news comes as a decided shock since the couple were believed to have been living happily together since their marriage Sept. 3, 1921 at Horton's Bay, near Charlevoix, Mich. The separation was amicably arranged and Mrs. Hemingway is expected to leave for America next month with their three year old child, of which she has been given custody.

Mr. Hemingway, whose Paris address is given as 69 Rue Froidevaux, has come into literary prominence comparatively recently with the publication of *In Our Time, Torrents of Spring,* and *The Sun Also Rises.* . . . He is expected to reach Paris today coming from Switzerland. Mrs. Hemingway is living in Paris at 35 Rue de Fleurus.

11 March 1927

Louis Bromfield Plans to Accept Pulitzer Prize for Best 1926 Novel

"Yes, I believe that I have been awarded the Pulitizer prize. At any rate, I had a telegram of congratulation this morning from my publishers," said Mr. Louis Bromfield, young American novelist now living in Paris, when questioned by *The Tribune* yesterday as to the rumor that the prize-award committee had chosen his novel *Early Autumn* for the $1,000 annually given for a novel written by an American which best meets the conditions of excellence laid down in the will of the late Joseph Pulitzer. "And I intend to accept it," continued Mr. Bromfield, when asked whether there was any chance of him following an illustrious example and refusing the award. "I am not looking for sensationalism, not at any rate in that way."

4 May 1927

Notes of Montparnasse

I seldom meet the divae of the Left Bank, but chance yesterday brought me directly before Mr. Ernest Hemingway, as the latter was toying with some books in the shop of the Rue de l'Odéon, and he made some amusing and casual comments on recent books and the denizens of Montparnasse, some of whom he advertised, you may remember, in a celebrated novel. We happened to be noticing that new so-much-praised novel by a Mr. Wescott, called *Grandmothers,* of which Mr. Hemingway remarked (which remark I transmit faithfully to the gentle reader, it being a mania of mine not to conceal from the public any remark of the literary huskies which I can get into print), "There are only two troubles with that book. One is that every work word of it was written for immortality." Here, alas, I must stop, truncate Mr. H.'s aphorism, and leave you in gaping wonder.

This one just recently returned to Montparnasse, after some months of wandering in the outer darkness. I am glad to note that the place is just as fantastic as ever, and I was agreeably surprised to note a supply of new and hardworking drunkards, all of them as excellent screamers as ever seen in the region. And the familiar barkeeps are still there, I note with pleasure, and a few of the old fantoches, whose gyrations have always interested me more than those of the "artists."

I regret that I have accumulated little gossip of Quarterites, but I offer the little I have.

Alex Small
12 October 1927

1928

Left Bank Notes

The open season seems already to have begun in Montparnasse. Already the caressing dampness of approaching spring has drawn to the terraces all those who do that habitually—those who come to drink, and those who want to look at artists. But for notes and personals of those who are practising or hanging on to the arts, I regret that I have none to give you. More and more I doubt if there be many there worth much serious attention. The only writer I have met in Montparnasse whose collected works I feel I might read with pleasure is Jed Kiley, and the only artist who seemed to me to be juggling with some real ideas is Hiler. Otherwise I hear of many a factitious reputation, but of little real accomplishment. Maybe as many as two books which are worth notice have come out of that region in the last six years, but, if one except *transition*, which is only incidentally and casually of the left bank, all the experimentation done looks pretty barren and amateurish.

Ergo, as I have so often repeated, the real occupation of Montparnasse is to drink and be fantastic. To be sure, I have lately seen, from that region, one book in manuscript which struck me as having the real authentic fire. But whatever I was going to say about that will keep.

Alex Small
8 March 1928

Tunny Quaffs a *Distingué*, Wilder a *Demi*, Battling Bookworm Discusses Newspapers

Gene Tunny sitting at a table with a great *distingué* of beer in front of him and Thornton Wilder, the famous novelist, beside him—that was the sight that met my eyes last night when I strolled into a café on the Boulevard St. Germain.

Under the circumstances there seemed only one thing to do. I did it. As I approached the table Mr. Tunny abruptly broke off a sentence he had been addressing to Mr. Wilder. He was already scowling up at me as the phrase "inimitable style" died out on his lips.

"Pardon me," I began. "Aren't you Mr. Tunny? "

"No, I'm not."

"And that isn't Mr. Wilder sitting next to you? "

"No."

At this moment my eye fell upon a little engraved calling card, bearing the name "Thornton Wilder," which lay face up on the table in front of the author's beer glass. I indicated it with my finger. Mr. Tunny scowled even more ferociously.

"Forget it," said Mr. Wilder, "go back and drink some beer."

I stayed, hoping for a chance to get in a few questions.

"Well, what do you want?" Mr. Tunny demanded with some truculence.

"I'm a reporter from *The Chicago Tribune*. I just thought perhaps. . . ."

"I suppose it will be in the paper tomorrow that Gene Tunny was drinking beer in Lipp's Café last night. Why can't you fellows ever let me alone? I am tired of publicity. I want to be able to come and go as I please without being spied upon at every moment."

"Well, Mr. Tunny, if you are anxious to avoid publicity you have come to a bad place. This is a haunt of newspapermen in Paris. You have walked right into the lion's den."

Mr. Wilder at this point apparently decided to ease the tension a little.

"Why do newspapermen come here? " he asked.

"On account of the beer."

At this magic word the scowl vanished from Mr. Tunny's face—a noticeable improvement. When he isn't frowning the boxer's face is sympathetic and charming.

"You know," he confided, "This is good beer. It's the first time I have ever tasted any really good beer. Before Prohibition I was too young and I have a prejudice against home-brew."

He emphasized the remark by quaffing off most of the contents of the *distingué*. Mr. Wilder sniffed the foam on a fresh *demi*. The conversation was approaching something like a friendly basis and when I slipped into a handy chair there was no protest.

"Are you writing a novel? " Mr. Wilder suddenly asked me.

I blushed and did not answer for a minute. Mr. Tunny saw my embarrassment and came to my rescue.

"I suppose you have some sort of literary aspirations; most newspapermen have. I hope you won't make the mistake of staying too long in journalism. I should think it would be very bad for your style."

"You don't approve of American newspapers, then? "

"Oh, I wouldn't say that. Naturally they are not good from a strictly literary standpoint, but I have the highest respect for sound, accurate, constructive journalism. I can't think of anything in the world finer for a man to do than to work on a paper that adheres to those principles."

"What is your favorite paper? "

"The *New York Times. The Chicago Tribune* is all right, too, but I'm afraid I can't say anything good for the New York *Daily News.* It is probably the least objectionable of the tabloids, but even that is no very high praise."

"You wouldn't enjoy work on a tabloid," Mr. Tunny said to me very earnestly, "a reporter on a tabloid newspaper is obliged to do very many things no gentleman would do. I have known some tabloid reporters that were decent fellows to start off but they ended up blackguards."

All this conversation had been very interesting to me but I was anxious for an opportunity to ask the famous friends other questions. I turned to Mr. Wilder, who had not taken much part in the conversation.

"When are you and Mr. Tunny going on your walking trip? " I inquired innocently.

Mr. Wilder laughed. A look of alarm came over Mr. Tunny's face. He jumped to his feet.

"It's late," he told his companion, "nearly twelve o'clock. We must be going. Excuse us please. I hope you aren't going to put anything in the papers about me."

Together the great author and the great pugilist hurried out of the café, casting fearful looks to right and left as if they expected a newspaper reporter to spring out at them from behind each table they passed.

Edmond L. Taylor
10 September 1928

Latin Quarter Notes

Returned Quarterites from St. Tropez bring stories of a historic luncheon shared by Emma Goldman, Bernard Shaw and Frank Harris. According to some versions it was Shaw who came off best conversationally, having held his two companions spellbound through an entire afternoon. Others claim that Miss Goldman had a word or two to say, and still others insist that the redoubtable Frank Harris was not outdone by either of his gifted companions.

Miss Goldman is still at work on a volume of her memoirs and will spend several months at St. Tropez where she has passed the summer.

Shaw's summer headquarters have been at Antibes, and Frank Harris lives permanently near Nice.

3 October 1928

Latin Quarter Notes

Although it lies somewhat beyond the *purlieus* of the Latin Quarter the Bal Colonial of the Rue Blomet attracts much of its patronage from that source, and those who claim to be the original discoverers of this haunt are numerous. We believe, however, that this honor belongs to Janet Flanner, author of *The Cubicle City* and Paris editor of the *New Yorker*. Miss Flanner was enthusiastic about the Bal Colonial more than a year ago; it was she who introduced Miguel Covarrubbias to it, and Covarubbias in turn introduced the readers of *Vanity Fair* to his version. Those experts on negro manifestations, Mr. and Mrs. Carl Van Vechten, recently visited the Bal Colonial and assert, their local pride touched on a serious point, that it cannot be compared in wildness and eccentricity to Small's in Harlem. But the Bal Colonial is quite wild enough for mild Montparnassians. It gathers together on three nights a week the negroes and half castes from the French colonies, and primitive dancing combined with sophisticated jazz produces a warm thick atmosphere, much appreciated on these chilly fall evenings.

Mr. and Mrs. Harold Loeb are stopping in Paris for a few days en route from Palestine to New York. They have spent the summer looking over the Zionist experiment in Palestine and touring through the Levant. Mr. Loeb has finished a new novel during the year.

9 October 1928

Latin Quarter Notes

For the American painter, Joseph Stella, whose *Brooklyn Bridge* has been always regarded as a masterly work, the combination would probably read New York-Paris-Rome. Rome is Mr. Stella's favorite city, but New York is his favorite workshop, and Paris his congenial eating-ground, so to speak. Mr. Stella is frankly a gourmet. He scarcely ever recalls the names of the restaurants where he dines, but he remembers vividly the taste and scent and savor of the food served. After a single trial, it is comparatively easy for him to find his way back to them.

30 October 1928

Proust Characters Come to Life at Mass for Writer

More than one character from Marcel Proust's monumental *A la Recherche du Temps Perdu* was present in flesh and blood at the little church of St. Pierre de Chaillot yesterday morning when a mass was said on the occasion of the sixth anniversary of the famous writer's death.

To many of those present the Chaillot church evoked that of Combray, destroyed during the war but immortalized in *Du Côté de Chez Swann*. Among those attending the ceremony was Mme. de Chevigny, for whom Proust always had the greatest admiration and respect and whom he is believed to have taken for the original of his Duchesse de Guermantes, Mme. Cocteau, the mother of Jean Cocteau, Paul Morand, and Paul Brach. Dr. Robert Proust, brother of the writer and himself a renowned surgeon, received those who came to the service.

A number of persons standing inconspicuously at the side of the church formed another reminder of that gallery of mysterious personages, suggesting various characters who played more or less important parts in the 5000 pages of Proust's sixteen volumes.

15 November 1928

1929

Suspended Judgments

From the Riviera comes word that Frank Harris is lying dangerously ill with bronchial pneumonia at Nice, where for the last few years he has made his home. Probably no other man living today has met and intimately known as many great men as Harris has in his lifetime, and there is surely no one who has animated and given life to these great men more than Harris by the personal touch of intimacy in his series of word portraits of them.

As a prominent editor and social figure in London during the last decade of the past century, Harris came into contact and made friends with all the celebrated men of his day, as well as with many who were destined to achieve greatness later. Through his works run such famous names as George Bernard Shaw, Anatole France, Thomas Hardy, Oscar Wilde, Remy de Gourmont, George Moore, Thomas Carlyle, and hosts of others.

In his life of Oscar Wilde, Harris has given us one of the finest biographies ever written in the English language. Not only was he an intimate friend of Wilde's, but he was one of the few persons who stuck by the brilliant writer in his downfall and gave him encouragement and help. . . . Harris's life of Wilde is a sad and revealing document, a veritable indictment of our civilization. . . . It was Harris who opened the columns of the *Fortnightly Review,* which he was then editing, to Bernard Shaw to write with unrestricted freedom . . . and it was he who hired Max Beerbohm to succeed Shaw as dramatic critic. . . . It was Harris, who, as editor, accepted some of Kipling's early stories shortly after the writer came to England. It was he who met Dowson and predicted that *Cynara* would eventually be accepted as a masterpiece.

Leigh Hoffman
17 March 1929

Fitzgerald Back from Riviera; Is Working on Novel

Describing the French Riviera as "the most fascinating amalgamation of wealth, luxury and general uselessness in the world," Scott Fitzgerald has returned to Paris after a short sojourn in Nice.

"That's the why of my new novel," said Mr. Fitzgerald. "It's about the Riviera, and that's all I can say about it today." The young author . . . didn't give the reporter a chance to ask questions. "As I said on leaving Nice," he continued, "I have nothing to say about the Hoover Administration, the I'm Alone case, Prohibition in America, Col. Lindbergh, or why I live abroad."

He consented, however, to confide a bit of Riviera scandal. "The American artists' colony at Cagnes-sur-Mer is having a lot of trouble with the town postmaster," he laughed. "Their cheques from home haven't been arriving fast enough, and you know what life is for Bohemians when cheques stop coming from home. Anyway, I hear they're going to have the postmaster fired for holding up their letters."

9 April 1929

Aleister Crowley Leaves France on Invitation of French Police Who Have No Sympathy for Black Magic

Aleister Crowley quit France yesterday, obeying the order of the French police that he get out within 48 hours. At 10 A.M. he took a train for

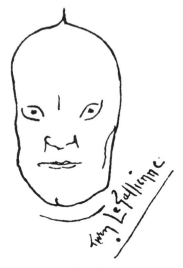

Aleister Crowley

Brussels. There he will join his sweetheart and marry her, he says. Following that, he will ask the French police to allow him to return and refute the charges against him.

He was ordered out for practising the black mass, or black magic, or otherwise comporting himself in such strange ways as to shock even the tolerant French police. It did not help his case that he is alleged to have been a spy for Germany in the United States during the war.

His departure rallied several reputable persons to his defense. They allege that whatever sinister quality there may have been about him was largely in his unusual piercing eye and in his manner, both of which items he employed in an exaggerated fashion to give the impression of mystic powers. But at the very outside he was only a "genial charlatan."

18 April 1929

Latin Quarter Notes

Perhaps the most well known book in which the Café du Dôme figures is Hemingway's *The Sun Also Rises*. But it is by no means the only one; indeed according to Lucien Aressy (*Les Nuits et les Ennuis du Montparnasse*) there are no less than fifty books, embracing about fifteen different languages, in which this café-tabac of the Carrefour Vavin plays a role.

Much in evidence around the Quarter lately is Maxwell Bodenheim. He arrived here recently for an indefinite stay and intends to do some writing while in Paris.

23 April 1929

Latin Quarter Notes

Sandy Calder, one of the gayest of a gay Left Bank group whose common bond is that its members have all at one time or another exposed at the Sacré du Printemps Gallery in the Rue du Cherche-Midi, is back from Germany. He comes by cycle and looks fitter than ever. Incidentally his "wire-sculpture"—not to speak of his brass horses, wooden cows, clockwork mice and toy kangaroos that can be made to behave exactly like their prototypes in the zoo—seems to have created quite a sensation in the German capital where he sold a number of works. He will now remain in the "dear old Quarter" for the summer, he says.

23 May 1929

"Cop Fighting" on July 4 Was Hot Stuff—
But Poet Crane Is Still Cooling Off in Jail

Social item—Mr. Harold Hart Crane, prominent young intellectual of Garretsville, O., Paterson, N. J., and the Boulevard St. Germain, and contributor to various advanced periodicals, has been spending the weekend as a guest of the City of Paris. Mr. Crane is being entertained by officials of the police force and a public affair in his honor is planned for the near future. He is making an indefinite stay.

The above paragraph, which somehow wandered out of *The Tribune*'s Social World column, refers to a story that appeared in the news section of the paper last Saturday, under the heading, "July 4th Celebrants Stage Car Barricade in Montparnasse But Lose Fight to Police."

Mr. Crane and some of his friends had been celebrating the Fourth in a well-known Montparnasse café. They had been celebrating it by playing a game which is very popular in these parts and which is known as "building castles." The purpose of the game is to erect towers and battlements out of the little white saucers which the café furnishes. When the game was over Mr. Crane looked at his castle and decided that it was too big for him to have built by himself, that someone must have been helping him on the sly. Accordingly when the *garçon* came around to make him pay for his fun, Mr. Crane replied that he hadn't had as much fun as all that and refused to pay the full amount of the bill.

The *garçon* called a policeman and the policeman after remonstrating with Mr. Crane offered him the hospitality of one of the city's handsomest hoosegows. Mr. Crane refused the offer. He loaded down the policeman with a charge of what was described as astonishingly proficient French invective, and wound up his harangue by leaping at the man's throat.

In due time he was subdued but even then his friends helped to complicate things by forming a barricade of autos across the Rue Vavin and trying to prevent the police from carrying off their prisoner. Everyone in Montparnasse thought it was a wonderful party and asked the police to drop in again soon, but the next morning Mr. Crane did not think it was so funny. Instead of letting him go with a warning or a small fine as is usually done they held him in jail for another day — then another one.

He was still there up to a late hour yesterday. He may remain there for some time. The public prosecutor is considering lodging a formal charge of resisting arrest against him and if this is done he will probably be tried shortly and doubtless given a stiff fine, if not a jail sentence.

Edmond L. Taylor
10 July 1929

Arlen Prefers to Work in Paris on his Book for 1930

Babes in the Woods, that delightfully old fashioned tale that has served to lull countless children to sleep for many generations will soon be refurbished for modern consumption to help keep the bright sophisticated young people awake nights. Michael Arlen, author of *The Green Hat,* is the author of the twentieth century version.

"Of course, there is no connection, except in name, between the original bedtime story and mine," Mr. Arlen told *The Tribune* yesterday. "It represents my annual literary output of one book a year. It will be off the press next month."

Mr. Arlen was reticent about the subject of his new work but explained that it was a study of five young English and American women who are members of the inner circle of London's ultra fashionable society.

Speaking of American writers, Mr. Arlen said they had developed an interesting school or expression of their own. "American authors seem to go through phases. At present they are nearly all occupying themselves with a phase of criticism, of showing up a person, a custom or an essentially American trait of character or habit of mind. It is what I call a depressing sort of literature, because, you see, it is rather fault finding."

17 September 1929

Crosby, Poet of Suicide Pact, Gave Promise of World Fame, Says Paris-American Editor

News of the death of Harry Crosby, young poet and publisher, who committed suicide in New York in a love pact with Mrs. Josephine Bigelow, shocked Paris literary and artistic circles yesterday. The wealthy writer and his wife, who was in Boston at the time of the suicide, had a place at Ermenonville and were prominent here.

"His death means a tragic loss to the younger generation of American writers," Eugene Jolas . . . said yesterday. "His writing showed a promise which in another five years would have made him world-famous."

The bodies were found outstretched on a bed in the Hotel des Artistes apartment of Stanley Mortimer, portrait painter, who had to break into his own suite. Crosby's arm encircled Mrs. Bigelow's neck and their hands were clasped tightly. An empty bottle of whiskey was on the table beside them.

Mr. Jolas said that when Mr. and Mrs. Crosby left Paris Nov. 24 the poet seemed in the best of humor. A letter from Crosby . . . declared: "Boston is the city of dreadful night. America is demented, but I like it. My parents are very good to me. They have just given me an airplane."

"He was always thinking of death, and always talking of it," one of his friends, a woman, told a *Tribune* reporter. "He said to me once that it was the greatest adventure, the greatest thrill. And at other times you would feel that nobody loved life more than he. His temperament was like that—at one moment a fit of deep depression; the next, exultant love of life."

Crosby's pathologic moods are believed to have resulted from the World War, in which he won the Croix de Guerre and distinguished himself several times by valorous conduct. Crosby's affair with Mrs. Bigelow, it was intimated, was also known to several of his close friends. Mrs. Caresse Crosby, his wife, it is believed, will continue with the directorship of the Black Sun Press, which Crosby established in the Rue Cardinale for publication of rare literary works in de luxe format. "Their married life was not always happy," a friend admitted.

13 December 1929

1930

Songs and Sonnets, Horses and Weather
Make Morn Merry as Left Bank Sees Dawn

Montparnasse turned over a new leaf during the early hours of yesterday and a few resolutions were silently cast about by some of the more prominent members of the big congregation which was gathered there. Promptly at midnight, Mme. Select, perched in her pew to the right of the bar, announced with her usual charm: "As for me, I wish the gentleman over in the corner would change his song. I've heard him repeat that refrain 40 times. *Et ça recommence!* "

Fernand, genial leader of the prayers at the bar, shook up a Martini sec. "I wish you all lots of luck." Then in the same breath, "What will it be, Mr. Stearns? " To this remark our esteemed confrère Harold Stearns said in his usual dogmatic fashion, *"Coupe de champagne."* Then, turning to the gentleman at his side, "If you have anything to say, say it and say it quickly. I've picked Champagne II to win."

"What," said Mr. Allan Updegraff, "are the seven best sonnets? "

"Don't know," we said quietly.

"You wouldn't know a sonnet from a lyrical drama," said a voice which sounded familiar. We turned in the direction from which the voice came. It proved to be a gentleman we had not seen in three years.

"Paris is Paris and Vienna is Vienna," said the man we had not seen in three years. "Ah, you must come to Vienna. I have just come from New York. But in Vienna life is different. *Se habla Espanol?* There, in Vienna, is a joy and a delight of living. And Spain, you understand, my friend? All is despair, despair, despair. I have forsaken my philosophy."

The gentleman we had not seen in three years left the bar for a few moments.

Eugene Jolas, editor of *transition,* strolled in. "That's all bunk," he said. "Happy New Year. Where's the rest of the gang? "

We suddenly found ourselves in front of a table at which we recognized Emma Goldman and Alexander Berkman.

"They make so much noise, my dear," said Emma. "I wonder how long this will last? "

"Forever," said Alexander Berkman.

"It is very warm outside for a New Year's Day," said Sisley Huddleston.

Two hours later somebody announced that it was 7 o'clock.

"Why, it's 8 o'clock and daylight has come. The roofs are like scribblings on the horizon. I shall not sleep today for I slept last night. Let us go home," said she.

"Don't you want to hear me recite Keats? " asked our friend on the left.

"I wish that man would stop his singing," said Mme. Select.

Louis Atlas
2 January 1930

On the Left Bank

The pulse of the Inner Circle of Montparnasse is beating much faster now that Nancy Cunard has decided to pack up and come back after a year and a half spent entirely, save for short visits to the Left Bank, down in the country. She returned after Christmas to arrange for space to set up her printing press, and then went back to Chapelle-Réanville to loosen things in readiness for transportation. The Hours Press, of which she is the mistress, will be established soon in quarters at 15 rue Guenegaud near the Seine. The presses are to be set up the last of this week. For the opening, the Inner Circle will no doubt witness a typical Cunard party with everyone who counts in the field of Montparnasse letters.

Ernest Hemingway left Paris behind for a long spell off the coasts of the Americas. Before embarking, he made a round of farewells. It appears that this voyage will be a long one and that Paris will not see the writer for what may stretch into years. He deposited a MS at the Black Manikin Press as his last act, his introduction to the English translation of *Kiki*, which that press is on the verge of publishing. It is hardly necessary to say that the introduction will be as amusing as is the book.

Montparno
10 January 1930

Left Bankers Believe Bob Brown's Pill Box Book Reading Machine Will Help Them Absorb Dozen Gertrude Stein Novels in Afternoon

Bob Brown came to the Left Bank not so long ago, but since his arrival he has had the Inner Circle pumped full of hope. He has an idea which he thinks, and the Inner Circle thinks, will advance what they are doing a generation or two.

His idea is a mechanical reading machine which will move so swiftly that only major words will assault the mind and leave their impressions. Commas, capital letters, periods, the the's, but's, and's—all punctuation marks and articles—will be minimized, slaughtered, made entirely useless.

And with the public accustomed to such reading, surrealism will be more understandable.

"Reading," says Brown, "is about the only thing left in our day which has not been subjected to mechanical processes. A mechanical reading apparatus for unreadable type would mean enormous economic savings in the matter of paper, ink and other materials and it would mean—and this is more important from my viewpoint—that modernist writers will have some praise in their own day."

Here is a fine topic for a café conversation on a rainy afternoon. But Brown has done more than talk about it. He has the manuscript for a book which will be printed in London on a British patented machine in type so small that the human eye cannot read it. This book he proposes to be the first one ever printed for a reading machine. As for the machine itself, he has definite schemes for that, too. Only the general outline can be given. It is to resemble a typewriter in shape, but will be much smaller. The printing will be done on a ribbon of tough impressionable material and it will unravel, electrically, much as a typewriter ribbon progresses. The book or newspaper or whatever the printed material may be, will thus be in the form of a pill box, vest pocket size. The machine may be used anywhere there is an electricity plug. In the center of the machine, where, on a typewriter, the key arms strike the paper, the actual reading will be done through a magnifying glass. The speed at which the ribbon will unravel can be regulated to the velocity desired by pressing buttons. The ribbon can be reversed at will—a line re-read, a chapter perused anew, a thought re-gathered.

Montparno
13 January 1930

On the Left Bank

The state of James Joyce's eyes is now attracting a great deal of attention abroad, where alarming stories stating that the Irish author was on the brink of total blindness have been circulated. That Joyce's eyes are not in any way as strong as a literary man's should be is not denied by his friends. But they are unwilling to say that their hero's ocular sense is about to be lost. The writer is taking a new treatment which everyone is hoping will turn affairs for the better. He visits his oculist daily and has submitted to eight different operations on the orb which troubles him particularly.

For seven years Joyce has fought against failing sight in an attempt to finish the most ambitious work he has ever planned. Unlike other authors, he is unable to dictate. He finds it necessary to write every word with a great pencil on huge sheets of paper. He cannot read a line of his manuscript without a powerful magnifying glass.

He works from 10 to 14 hours daily, but writes only a few hundred

James Joyce

words each day. A great part of the day is taken up in revising his manuscript which he does in a most thorough manner, often rewriting pages in proof. He declares that he can only write when dressed entirely in white, which he says is pleasant for his eyes. This crisis in Joyce's physical weakness, if it be a crisis, comes as he is in the midst of the third fragment of *Work in Progress,* which is to be published soon in Paris.

James Stevens, another writer from Dublin, has come back to the Left Bank after a stay in London. Stevens, in a way, is Joyce's twin. The two were born in Dublin on the same day, and both are writers. Aldous Huxley is at present drinking from the old wooden pail at the Left Bank well. He came over from London for an indefinite stay.

Montparno
26 February 1930

Raymond Duncan Tells of New City Founded by Dropping Corner Stone in Ocean and of Passports Good for Discount Some Places

"I have founded a new city," Raymond Duncan, dramatic apostle of simplicity, disclosed yesterday afternoon at a tea in honor of his return from the United States recently. "It is called New Paris York and will unite the inhabitants of New York and Paris.

"To the undisguised amazement of the captain, officers and passengers of the liner, I laid the foundation stone of the city's city hall, by dropping it overboard in mid-Atlantic, halfway between the United States and France.

"Already many prominent New Yorkers and Parisians have flocked to this new city, which is taxless, lawless and without obligations. Each and every one of these new citizens," Raymond Duncan declared, "will drop a brick or stone into the sea in mid-Atlantic when he crosses to or from America. Thus, in time, will the new city hall rear its glorious head above the waves."

Duncan stated that he was endeavoring to get the governments of France and the United States to recognize the new city and told those assembled that he was issuing passports to citizens. "Although not yet good for traversing boundaries and frontiers," he stated, "they have one valuable asset. They represent a slight discount in most of the leading stores here and in the American metropolis."

13 June 1930

Waiting Death, Cheever Dunning Carried on through Life Wrapped in Buddha-like Aura

The death of Cheever Dunning, famous Montparnasse poet, is a shock but not a surprise to the literary world. The solitary figure who had lived for more than a generation in a tiny cubicle in the Rue Notre-Dame-des-Champs had frequently remarked that "death is the last dream."

At the age of 14 he had been told by the family physician that he was destined for an early death, due to congenital tuberculosis. Since then, he had been obsessed by the terror and wonder of death. His poetry reveals a fluid preoccupation which had been hidden by a sphynx-like silence in daily life. To him death had been the final experience carefully prepared for by 40 years of contemplation.

This slow descent was often blurred by real poverty but the poet shunned assistance as he shunned all compromises with the material world. In the ordinary sense, his life was uneventful. After leaving Harvard he spent two years in Mexico, then followed a chartless course in odd corners of the world. Twenty-one years ago he came to Montparnasse and engaged the shelf-like single room that overlooks a tiny garden. It was in this garden that Dunning would sit wrapped in contemplation, indifferent to the usual exigencies of existence. In this garden, at the foot of a huge chestnut tree, the poet composed lyrics and sonnets whose metric beauty and marble solidity have long won the admiration of leading critics.

In Montparnasse the poet was known as the "Buddha." His friends had often declared that although his blood was a mixture of Scotch, Irish, Greek and American Indian, his temperament was definitely Oriental. He

Cheever Dunning

spoke little and was happiest when alone. Yet Cheever Dunning's extraordinarily sensitive face was a language in itself, a saga read by all who met him. Only he was unaware of his own subtle power. He was too preoccupied. He moved in an aura of peace and sympathy. And in slow relaxation he prepared for the final dream. To him only death was real, death after a row of dreams.

Wambly Bald
5 July 1930

1931

What the Writers Are Doing

Most of the American writers who spent the last few months on the Riviera did more writing than resting. Ludwig Lewisohn, who got back to Paris recently, tells me that the atmosphere was too conducive to writing for idling, and Lewisohn, for one, returned from the south with a 30,000 word novelette in his portfolio. The product of his vacation, which will appear shortly, is called *The Golden Vase*.

Alfred Kreymborg took a cottage between Nice and Villefranche in which to do just nothing for a few months, and a book of verse soon made its appearance. It has not been published as yet, but I understand it will be a long philosophical poem.

Another man who couldn't keep away from his typewriter was Joseph Wood Krutch. This month's *Harper's* contains the fruits of his rest on the Riviera, called *Still Innocent* and *Still Abroad*. He is due in Paris in June and back to work on *The Nation* in the fall.

Ernest Hemingway writes, in a letter to Edward W. Titus, the publisher, that he got into an argument with a tree while driving a car through Montana. Result: one broken arm and considerable shattered confidence in Hemingway's driving on the part of John Dos Passos, who was accompanying him. Hemingway reports, however, that the arm is healing rapidly and that within a short time he will be able to use a typewriter again. Titus has just acquired the English rights on *The Philosophy of Art,* a scholarly work by Giovanni Gentile.

Harold Ettlinger
10 April 1931

What the Writers Are Doing

While I visited with William Van Wyck at his place on the Boulevard Montparnasse the other afternoon, he brought out his newest published work to show me. It's a poem in free verse called *On the Terrasse*. The scene is the Dôme and the characters are Babbitt—the one and only Babbitt—and a Montparnassian. If Babbitt is frank, the other fellow is candor itself, and the result is an interesting exchange of wallops. Here's the way Babbitt describes his neighbors at the Dôme—

> ". . . these Dôme dumbells, sitting talking art
> And swilling booze and spilling bunko stuff,
> And slumming out their lives. . . ."

And part of the reply:

> "So you are Babbitt! Anything you say
> About the Dôme or Paris adds a bit
> To the world's book of total ignorance."

Eugene O'Neill will shortly leave his château at Tours for America. His *The Hairy Ape,* I am told, is to be produced in London by James Light, and Paul Robeson will play the lead. It may also be given in Paris.

With the aid of a picture book donated by a kind friend and assorted grammars, E. E. Cummings, whose *The Enormous Room* is rated as one of the topnotchers among books on the war, is studying Russian while waiting in Paris for the Soviets to okay his visa. Cummings is very modest about his progress with Russian, but I understand that the picture book method is bringing great success.

Work on a play is also occupying some of his time while in Paris. . . . His poetry, incidentally, was the object of an attack in the last issue of *Hound and Horn*. His theory that the poet should simply express as best he can what he sees and feels was criticized, it being claimed that moderns like him were neglecting the heritage of knowledge which classic writers used to advantage.

Harold Ettlinger
17 April 1931

What the Writers Are Doing

James Stevens, the Irish poet, is going to America for another lecture tour. I heard a good story about his last visit to the land of Prohibition.

It happened in Cincinnati shortly after the Volstead Act gave rise to the bootlegging industry. Stevens was invited to address a big St. Patrick's Day dinner, and many of the leading citizens were there to hear what an authentic Irishman had to say. There was much liquor. Stevens was well along in his speech and the leading citizens were listening behind their comfortable cigars when suddenly the main door to the banquet hall opened and a squad of policemen filed in. It was a raid.

But the policemen did not shout, "All right, you guys, let's go to the station." They were courteous policemen, and they stood quietly in a row against the wall to wait until Stevens had finished. The leading citizens were nervous, but the poet did not swerve off the track of his oratory. There was much applause when he closed his address, and before he sat down the hard boiled sergeant walked up to him and held out his hand.

"You've sure given me a whiff of old Ireland," he said, and he motioned to his underlings to retreat quietly.

Nancy Cunard is editing a book on the Negro. The book will include a study of the contemporary Negro and a discussion of outstanding Negro personalities. There will be a section on music with reproductions of Negro jazz, spirituals, blues and such African tribal music as is obtainable, edited by George Antheil. Reproductions of African art, sculpture and ivory carvings will be included as well as explorers' data, and another section will deal with the political and sociological aspects of the subject.

Harold Ettlinger
1 May 1931

What the Writers Are Doing

E. E. Cummings has already left Russia. Cummings went to the land of the Soviets about a month ago, with the announced intention of staying there for many weeks, months or even years. The question which is now bouncing from the Dôme to the Coupole and back to the Dôme again is: What hit E. E. Cummings in Russia? As far as the Left Bankers know, he has not been kicked out. Why, then, did he leave so soon? Is the supply of inspiration smaller than he foresaw? Mrs. Cummings is not returning directly to Montparnasse, but is going to America by way of Constantinople and points East.

James T. Farrell, whose short stories have already been observed in intellectual circles of the Home Country, is among the newer arrivals in the colony here. Farrell has taken up residence in Sceaux, the place to which the put-put goes which sends its smoke up through holes in the pavement of the Rue Denfert-Rochereau. He specializes in the language of the Chicago stockyards, and one of the local American publications plans to publish some of his stuff unexpurgated in the hope of getting it suppressed in the United States.

Ezra Pound is back from Rapallo after a long rest, if you can call it that, in Paris. His new cantos will appear in the July issue of *Pagany*, a magazine which Pound considers hot stuff. "Its spring issue reads like a manifesto of the best modernist literature," he says.

Gene Tunny's friend, Thornton Wilder, told a German newspaperman that Europeans know nothing of the best features of American life. Sinclair Lewis has done much to mislead them, he intimated.

Aldous Huxley is working on a new novel in his handsome villa, resplendent with fresh paint, at Bandol, on the Côte d'Azur.

Matthews Eliot
14 June 1931

Russians Love to Suffer, They're Suffering, So It's a Great System, Says E. E. Cummings

"Are the Russian people happy? They struck me like this: they just love to suffer and they're suffering like hell, so they must be happy. You know, Dostoievsky."

E. E. Cummings expressed the above impression of the Russian experiment to *The Tribune* last night.

"They couldn't seem to understand my visit," Cummings continued.

"They said, 'Why are you here? '"

"I said, 'I don't know.' "

"They are very serious. According to their point of view they are engaged in the greatest work of all time.

"They asked: 'What do you want to see?' I didn't know exactly. They suggested the theater; I said, 'Fine.' They suggested five or six other things. I said, 'Fine.' They said: 'You won't have time to see them all in three weeks.' I said, 'Fine.'

"I kept a regular old-fashioned diary. Getting it through was just a matter of graft. Just like in the United States. Only in the United States it would be a matter of dropping $200 here or there while in Russia it was small graft.

"You can't compare Russia with anything else. There is nothing sufficiently like it. I wouldn't dream of making any thesis. Nobody should shoot his face off about Russia. They themselves admit the present state of affairs is temporary. According to their own formula Russia is like a beleaguered city: traitors within and besieged without. This is no time to form any judgment of them.

"There are three worlds in Russia. The first world consists in the tourists for whom everything is fixed up. The second world is composed of sympathetic pilgrims from abroad. Naive bozos go roaring in there and see nude bathing carried on in complete modesty and think it is due to the system. It's not. It's just the character and temperament of the people. They are marvelous people. These people are the third world.

"People talk about the strain and tension of life in the United States. It is nothing to that in Moscow. If you said 'boo' to some of those people they might drop dead. If they are supposed to work 24 hours a day, they try to work 25. If it's 36 they try to make it 37. They are in a peculiarly nervous condition."

Cummings is going to make a book of his impressions. He is sailing today for New York.

Don Brown
20 June 1931

Hemingway Back in Paris; Sails for New York

Ernest Hemingway and Mrs. Hemingway are back in Paris from Spain on their way to New York and will sail next week aboard the *Ile de France*. At the hotel he talked yesterday of Sidney Franklin, the Brooklyn bullfighter who has made himself famous in Spain, and who is going into the arena at Madrid today for the first time in several months.

"Sidney is a marvelous fighter," he said. "He is absolutely courageous and keenly intelligent. He knows what it's all about. He's better than many of those boys who grow up in the tradition. They learn to go through the motions gracefully, but they don't know how to use their heads, as Sidney does. He's a regular Christy Matthewson."

Hemingway talked for about half an hour while he was posing for a sketch, but did not mention literature nor himself, except to explain that he is ten pounds overweight because his arm was broken in an automobile accident and hasn't yet sufficiently healed. This keeps him from boxing.

When he signed the sketch which was made of him, his wife remarked that the signature was hardly legible.

"Yes, I know, I wrote it that way purposely," he replied. "This town is full of chiselers. If I put a legible signature on this drawing and *The Tribune* prints it, there may be a half dozen bad checks at the bank by Monday morning. I'm taking no chances."

Don Brown
20 September 1931

1932

Laurence Vail and Kay Boyle Wed in Simple Ceremony

There were no wedding bells when Laurence Vail and Kay Boyle, American authors and for many years residents of Montparnasse and the Riviera, were married at the city hall in Nice this afternoon, but the knot was tied just the same. Moreover, the principals in the matrimonial venture were accompanied at the wedding by a ready-made family of four children.

However, Peggy Guggenheim, Vail's former wife, failed to show up.

After the witnesses, Carlton Brown and Clotilde Vail, had affixed their signatures to the register and the assistant mayor had given the couple the usual inside dope, the party—including a small delegation from the wild tribe of Cagnes-sur-Mer—proceeded to the couple's home at Col-de-Villefranche for refreshments. Among those present were Alexander Berkman, Abe Rattner, Bettina Bedwell, Dorothy Coleman, John Holmes, Caresse Crosby, Mrs. Frank Harris, Hilaire Hiler. A conspicuous absentee was Link Gillespie, once dean of the Cagnes colony, who recently sailed for home.

3 April 1932

Ludwig Lewisohn

Lewisohn Admits He Fled America Because of Book

Arriving in Paris yesterday after a six week's flying visit to Africa, Ludwig Lewisohn declared that he ran away to escape the repercussions of the recent publication of his latest book, *Expressions in America*. The book is an unconventional history of literature in the United States.

"I simply didn't want to go through the nervous strain of waiting to see just what results might follow the publication of my book," he said. "I told my publisher I would answer no correspondence during that period and the African trip was a success. I feel as though my mind had had a good washing."

The author of *The Case of Mr. Crump* also admitted that he is pleased with the critical reception of his new book.

9 April 1932

Sinclair Lewis, Noted Novelist, Writing a Novel

Sinclair Lewis has been fired from three newspapers, he revealed here yesterday. "I never have been able to get any newspapers to print that but it is a fact that I was canned by the leading paper in Waterloo, Iowa, by the San Francisco *Bulletin* and by the San Francisco Office of the Associated Press," he continued. "I don't know what they fired me for—I guess maybe it was for incompetence. As you know I am a novelist, and curiously enough for a novelist I am engaged in writing a novel. It is about an American business woman. The title is *Anne Vickers*.

"I'd like to give you an interview worthy of a Nobel Prize winner, but hell, I am just not up to it. I didn't have but three hours' sleep last night and if you don't hurry up with this interview I am going to pass out on you. . . . No, I don't mind posing for a sketch, but please make it snappy.

"Let me see it. Hell, Don, you can't draw! Give me the pencil and pad. Now this is what I look like and I'm signing it too. Good night, old timer. I'll be seeing you again."

Don Brown
25 April 1932

Sinclair Lewis drawn by himself

Sinclair Lewis' Many Friends Delay His Dinner; Wife Is Slightly Annoyed

Sinclair Lewis is so careless about making casual friendships with people he meets here and there that his wife, the former Dorothy Thompson, a high-powered newspaper woman, has quite a time with him.

Lewis, who is friendly and open-hearted toward strangers, had made a good many engagements . . . for yesterday afternoon at the Hotel Palais d'Orsay. People started calling a few minutes after the pair returned from the boat train and continued until late in the afternoon.

Mr. and Mrs. Lewis had planned to dine out and Mrs. Lewis was ready to depart before 7 o'clock. Sinclair, however, was still sprawled on a chair talking to a late reporter. Just then the phone rang.

"Oh hello, Father," Lewis said. "Come right up, I'll be glad to see you. That's Father Blank from Iowa. He's a fine fellow; I met him on the boat coming over."

The priest appeared a few moments later. "Meet my old friend here," Lewis said, introducing him to the reporter. "You'll find Father Blank a charming character. You know, sometimes I think these––priests get something out of life the rest of us miss. How about that, Father?"

Father Blank put the tips of the fingers of his hands together and, with lowered eyes, smiled slightly. "People get out of life just what they put into it," Father Blank observed.

"Oh, hell, Father, you don't have to pull that stuff here," Lewis protested. "Don't spill those old bromides. We think you're a good guy all right. Just save those truisms for Iowa! In the meantime, have another drink."

Calm as Buddha, the good Father replied, "Here's Health," and lifted his glass.

Just then, Mrs. Lewis walked in upon the happy scene.

"Meet some of my dear old friends," said Sinclair.

"I should be pleased to see some of your dear old friends clear out of here so we might go to dinner," remarked Mrs. Lewis.

"Now darling," said the Nobel Prize winner. He and Mrs. Lewis went into another room to talk it over. When he came back, he regretfully suggested that the Father and the reporter continue their interview at a nearby station of hospitality.

"It's no joke being married to a celebrity," he added.

Don Brown
26 April 1932

Hart Crane Lost from Liner, Suicide Hinted

Hart Crane, who last year won a Guggenheim fellowship enabling him to study Mexican poetry and legends, was lost overboard from the steamship *Orizaba* on its way to New York from Mexico. The possibility of suicide is strengthened by dispatches from Mexico City stating that Crane had grieved over the recent death of his father, and had told friends that he intended to kill himself. One of his best friends was accompanying him on the present voyage, expressly to prevent such an attempt.

Hart Crane's death will be deeply mourned by American literary and artistic circles in Paris, wherein he was well known. He had spent some time here, and many of his poems had appeared in *transition*. During his stay in Paris, he was frequently seen in Montparnasse and in other centers in the Latin Quarter.

29 April 1932

Friends in Paris Mourn Death of Crane

The report that Hart Crane was lost overboard has deeply grieved his many friends in Paris. One of the last letters written by Crane, from Mexico, dated March 31, and received here by Caresse Crosby contains nothing but good cheer. This letter does not indicate that the young poet was contemplating suicide, and yet dispatches have been received from Mexico City stating that Crane had grieved over the death of his father and had told friends he intended to kill himself. "My Guggenheim fellowship terminates today," wrote Crane to Mrs. Crosby, "but I am remaining a while longer in Mexico . . . Mexico, with its volcanoes, endless ranges, countless flowers, dances, villages, lovely brown-skinned Indians, with simple courtesies, and constant sunlight—it enthralls me more than any other spot I have ever known.

"It is—and isn't an easy place to live. Altogether more strange to us than even the Orient. . . . But it would take volumes to even hint at all I have seen and felt. Have rung bells and beaten pre-Conquistadorial drums in fire-lit circles at ancient ceremonies, while rockets went zooming into the dawn into Tepoztlan; have picked up obsidian arrows and terra-cotta idols from the furrows of corn fields in far valleys; bathed with creatures more beautiful than inhabitants of Bali in mountain streams, and been in the friendliest jails that ever man got thrown in. There is never an end to dancing, singing, rockets and the rather lurking and suave dangers that give the same edge to life here that the mountains give the horizon. I should like to stay indefinitely. Of the Epic—I have not written a line. Only a few lyrics. . . ."

Mrs. Crosby said yesterday: "Crane was a very good friend of mine and was present with me the night my husband Harry died. I was surprised to hear that he did what he did. I haven't the slightest idea why he would do such a thing. He had a happy and lovable disposition and his letter seems to reflect that all was well."

30 April 1932

Ralph Jules Frantz in the editorial room of the Paris *Tribune*.

Alex Small leaving Berlin for the Russian front, 1939.

Eugene Jolas, Paris, 1931.

George Antheil, age 20, Bernardsville, N. J., 1920.

Leigh Hoffman, Normandy, 1933 or 1934.

Sophie Tucker and Irving Schwerké outside the Paris Opera, 1931.

Waverley Root speaking at a meeting of the Overseas Press Club in the Ford Motor Pavilion at the New York World's Fair, 1939.

1933

Viola Rodgers, Paris American, Tells of Friendship with George Moore

Three weeks before his death, George Moore, Irish author who expired at his home in London last Saturday, had a premonition that the end was near, it was revealed to *The Tribune* yesterday by Viola Rodgers, American chatelaine of Lardy, who was an intimate friend of Moore's for a quarter century.

In his last letter to her, dated Dec. 30 last, he wrote:

"Dearest Viola: I was glad to hear from you. I think of you constantly, for you have been a good friend to me. The past was pleasant but I am afraid there is no returning to it. It is very probable that I shall never see you again, for I do not seem to recover from my infirmity. . . . This is the best letter that I can write through a secretary. I am waiting for a surgeon. Goodbye, dear friend. I do not press you to tell me why you never come to England."

Miss Rodgers, at whose lovely estate, Le Coin-sur-Juine in Lardy, he was a frequent guest, found the famous writer a "mystical Irishman, romantic and enthusiastic as a schoolboy, an entertaining story-teller, a meticulous dresser and a very finicky gourmet." He often told Miss Rodgers his plots for stories and was a brilliant conversationalist on art and music. . . . "English to the last, poor old man," Miss Rodgers reflected dolefully. He always wore blue shirts and though everything else he bought was of the best, he used very ordinary cotton handkerchiefs with cheap initials.

26 January 1933

Raymond Duncan Offers Asylum Here to All Who Are Beset with Privation

Raymond Duncan, apostle of beauty and action and brother of the late Isadora, who has thrown open his yellow and blue painted house to the world, says that suicide is caused by lack of companionship.

In his intimate studio in the Rue de Seine yesterday he told *The Tribune* that the world's creed of giving value only to certain humans and not to others was the cause of one man starving while another worked.

Duncan's belief is that everyone has value for the world, and on this basis he takes any who want to come into his family.

"If young people come to Paris to accomplish great things and cannot remain because they have no money, it's because the social system is all wrong," he said.

Garbed in his Greek robes which have made him conspicuous, the *Maitre*, as his adoring followers often call him, talked of his credo. "There are no geniuses in the world," he said. "Every man has talents, but they must be developed." Asked how his home was managed, Duncan said there were no rules, but everybody had dormant ambitions which in the Duncan domicile were developed. "My doctrine of philosophy is action. Our cult is that of human companionship, and we commit moral suicide—we kill old-fashioned habits which have been carried on merely in imitation. We live originally. We don't have rules, because nobody does anything he doesn't want to. We don't smoke or drink and we don't eat meat, because we feel they are a lack of refinement, and by that in not doing these things, we become the most refined people."

16 April 1933

Wambly Bald's "La Vie de Bohème"

Summer on the Left Bank

The face of the Left Bank wears a mask during the summer months. It is only with the advent of the autumn chill and the ensuing colder weather that the Quarter is revealed in all its mellow glory. They say the district hibernates not in winter, but in the summer time. Perhaps the impersonality of the crowded terraces, with their distracting sights and sounds, is responsible. But they are commencing to go inside now, where one doesn't have to shout and where cliques and groups may dream or talk without the sweetened Coney Island flavor.

21 October 1929

Countee Cullen

Hot off the press comes *The Black Christ,* Countee Cullen's third volume of poetry. Cullen is seldom seen on the Happy Highway. He prefers the seclusion and detachment of his studio out Montsouris way, where he has been living for the past year, as the guest of Julian Green. Cullen hails from Harlem and is generally acknowledged as one of her most brilliant progeny. He's a fine fellow, this poet, with none of the grating peccadillos that usually mark a man of letters. He is extremely modest in manner and speech, yet he has every reason to think well of himself, for ever since his first poem, "To A Brown Girl," appeared in *Bookman* years ago, his grip on recognition has become increasingly secure, culminating in his being granted the Guggenheim Fellowship, which is a rare distinction in America.

Eric Walrond, another Guggenheim scholar, is living with Countee Cullen. He is hard at work on his next novel, which we hope will be as interesting as *Tropic Death.*

4 November 1929

Ford Madox Ford

Ford Madox Ford

One gigantic figure who understands and condones the peccadillos of the "wastrels" who spend most of their time on the terraces, is Ford Madox Ford. The aimless tribe whom Gertrude Stein called "The Lost Generation" has always been considered by the British author a social force, a regiment from whose ranks occasionally springs a giant big enough to take the world by the ears and spank new rhythms into the dull mass. Ford is leaving for New York after a brief stay on the Riviera. He will be missed especially by the younger literati who haunted his apartment on Rue Vaugirard for guidance and encouragement. He never tired of pointing from his window to the innumerable houses in which great masterpieces were written or painted. He has often asserted that from his window might be seen 116 chimney-pots beneath each of which a great work had been written.

Many of us recall the long walks we took in groups through the Bois de Boulogne on moonlit June nights, with Ford leading the way, talking, always talking about everything imaginable and especially about himself. We would listen to his quiet discourses about what he told Henry James, what he told Conrad, how he cooks a fancy dish, how he began his career, the speeches he made during the war, the athlete he was in his younger days before he had asthma, the number of authors he had befriended, and all other manners of topics which were of especial interest to Ford.

And the memorable dances at some *bal musette*. Ford would hire a hall and invite his friends to dance their literary cares away. He was a graceful dancer himself and his huge, bland bulk would wander over the smooth floor while some young poetess half his size would dance with him, perspiring and happy when it was over. When the accordian would screech its strongest notes, Ford's jaw would woggle amiably in time with the music. He was a great figure.

Ford's library is not large, but one was always impressed when he brought out volume after volume inscribed to him. Many of the best living writers of today have dedicated their work to this great monitor of letters. He values them so highly that most of the literature has been safely stowed away in a private vault. On the fly-leaf of each of the books, one reads words of affectionate regard for the man who has been called the "Leviathan of Montparnasse." They are all significant, but there is one that has so impressed itself on my susceptible nature that in my last delirious moments, it shall be conjured up with the force of an oath but with the fragrance of a daisy. Here it is: "To Ford Madox Ford, who has often said he is a great author and critic and thanking him for both."

3 March 1930

Gwen LeGallienne and Radclyffe Hall

Naturally, I don't know what is meant by the term "real" Quarter or "real" Montparnasse, but if there were such a spot, Gwen LeGallienne would doubtless be sitting in the center. Very few people would know it, because Gwen would be sitting quietly and alone. Her utter indifference would mark her, as it does every night when she comes to the Sélect, or during the day, when she lopes with more than reasonable speed through Montparnasse traffic.

Gwen LeGallienne

Richard LeGallienne

This emotional condition, often attributed to inmates of Montparnasse, is not an attitude in Gwen's case. Too many people are lightly accused of attitudes. The very few who know her—and some of them are especially interesting—insist that she is incapable of insincerity. In speech, she is direct and frank, and she never talks unless she has something to say. One sentence ordinarily suffices for the dull, curious, or garrulous. After that, they stay away. Her curves, too, are interesting. They are all in her voice. Listen to it five minutes and you'll like her.

Gwen's temperament rests on chaos. She is fascinated by the intangible routes of her own career. For that reason, probably, she looks poetic, as does her father, Richard. The youngest LeGallienne is the most chaotic looking, which, in my careless opinion, is indeed a blessing, for what is poetry but chaos carefully handled?

Radclyffe Hall used to be a frequenter of the Deux Magots and the Sélect. She is a very blonde woman and wears her hair smack back over a determined head. Two curls drop over her forehead. She was always seen with Lady Trowbridge. Both wore monocles and both used long cigarette holders. The crisp-looking Miss Hall is said to have a practical sense quite developed and is reputed to hate the idea of promiscuity. She always traveled in a limousine. One of the literati has written a parody on *The Well of Loneliness* called *The Fish Pond*. There are mockers in Montparnasse.

16 September 1930

Kiki as seen by Mayo

Kiki

Kiki is the Queen of Montparnasse. She was elected by her friends a few years ago at a blowout at the Bobino. Kiki has been a model, café singer and movie actress. You may hear her sing any night at the Oceanic Bar in the Edgar Quinet district.

Kiki is still popular after her fashion, despite the usual battle with heft. She is still the life of the party. For many years Kiki and Broca, the caricaturist, were excellent friends. Neither of them has missed anything, but Kiki had less imagination and more vitality. Kiki is still Kiki, but Broca has collapsed and is obliged to rest in a local sanitorium.

31 March 1931

Samuel Beckett; Tea with Gertrude Stein

Another Irish poet now among us is Samuel Beckett, instructor at the University of Dublin. His book on Proust has just been published in London. One more Irish poet who is rising fast is Thomas McGreevy, whose book on Eliot, previously reviewed in *The Tribune,* is causing a stir. We understand that 600 copies were sold the first day.

We drank tea with Gertrude Stein a few days ago. She lives quietly with another woman in the Rue de Fleurus, about ten jumps from the Dôme.

For the past 25 years, Gertrude Stein has been saving the English language from that studio.

The walls are covered with Picasso. One of them is a portrait of Gertrude herself, for which she sat 91 times. That portrait and the actual Gertrude immediately put the visitor in his place. But John, who was with me, said:

"Your prose, I think, is obscure."

"My prose," said she who looks like Caesar, "is obscure only to the lazy-minded. It is like a deep well."

"Some people," said John, "are inclined to believe that it is a bottomless well or one with a false bottom."

John was a bit cruel. After all, Gertrude had been a star pupil of William James. She had graduated with high honors from Johns Hopkins. She has mastered the run of the sciences and her knowledge of literature is oceanic.

"I'll give you," said the writer, "a lesson in American history." Her eye is clear and her voice is incisive. Gertrude does not stutter when she talks. Here is what she said:

"America made the 20th Century just as England made the 19th. We have given Europe everything. The natural line of descent is the big four: Poe to Whitman to James to myself. I am the last."

"You are the last? " said John.

"Of course. My reputation is international and is spreading all the time."

"There is James Joyce," said John.

Gertrude smiled. "You would, of course, Joyce is *good*. He is a *good* writer. Let's not say anything about that. But who started the whole thing? My first great book, *The Making of Americans,* was published in 1905. That was long before the birth of *Ulysses.* But Joyce has done something even if his influence is local. John Synge, another Irish writer, has had his day. Have some more tea."

This fellow John is implacable. He followed with:

"I understand that Wyndham Lewis drops you into the Anita Loos category. The naive approach. . . ."

"Wyndham wrote that, of course. But all that is British propaganda against great American writers." John almost dropped his spoon. Gertrude went on: "You might learn that American writing is signalized by the consistent tendency towards abstraction without mysticism. There is no mysticism in my work."

John had nothing more to say. We went back to the Dôme.

7 April 1931

Djuna Barnes

Djuna Barnes, author of *Ryder,* returned to Montparnasse for a glimpse and fled to Vienna. She laughed at the Carey tale. "Montparnasse," she said, "has ceased to exist. There is nothing left but a big crowd."

"Don't put it that way," I said. "I love the Quarter."

Then we rested our heads on each other's shoulders and wept for a minute. Djuna is well built and has a rich, red ocean of hair. We swapped anecdotes and had tea.

"Do you remember—? " she said.

"Yes. And how about—? "

That went on for about an hour.

Djuna took an apartment in the Rue St. Romain, far from the present bluster. She told me it was all over. "Montparnasse is all over. And Greenwich Village is all over. It's all all over."

I protested. "You're teasing me," I said.

"It's all over in New York," she added. "Two weeks before the end of the *World*, I was spreading a high class Winchell. For what? That is all over now."

Everything is all over. Djuna heard me with frigidity. Everybody knows that that was all over before it started. We had more tea.

A girl I once knew in Chicago came into the room. "Is this interview all over? " she said.

Then the three of us had more tea and we talked about the post-war days when Bohemians pranced in circles and no one cared. I looked upon Djuna as a recovered hope. We agreed that it was all over.

2 September 1931

Wambly Bald Meets Henry Miller

Even in this barren age with its economic problems, romance is just around the corner. Indeed, adventure waits at night in the dark streets of Paris. Night before last all the stars were out and I was walking very slowly to appreciate their beauty. Occasionally a painter smiled and tried to block my way, but I wandered on and on under the big stars. And looking at a full moon often gives me an emotion.

Near the shadows of the Louvre a lone figure began to follow me and tapped me on the shoulder after a short chase. He was dressed in corduroy, a gray jacket and thick spectacles. His hat was carelessly jammed on one side of his head and the uncovered side was quite bald. It was Henry Miller, the novelist.

"Hello," I said. We talked about this and that and smoked a few cigarettes. Then I said:

"Where are you going? "

He replied: "Nowhere in particular."

That's just like Miller. He is never definite. Miller has been out of a job for some time and he hasn't a cent. But he's lucky. He has friends. They always take care of him. A couple of days ago he woke up on a bench

Elliot H. Paul, New York, late 1930s.

Wambly Bald, Paris, 1933.

William L. Shirer, Central European Representative and *Tribune* contributor, broadcasting the news of the 1939 papal coronation from St. Peter's Square, Rome.

Harold E. Stearns, New York, 1938.

Florence Gilliam, Paris, 1940.

Kay Boyle, Nice, 1930.

Louis B. Atlas, Paris, 1927.

Portrait of Ford Madox Ford by Georg T. Hartmann, New York, 1926 or 1927.

Henry Val Miller

outside the Closerie des Lilas. The only thing that bothered him, he said, was that he didn't have a toothbrush. "Being on the bum is all right if you can clean your teeth occasionally—say, every third day. Otherwise you feel bad."

But he doesn't worry. His friends are always backing him up. The other day he met Kann the sculptor, who has just landed a fat contract from America. They dined at Ciro's. During the meal Miller reached in his pocket for a handkerchief and pulled out a pair of socks. At Ciro's! In the evening he met another friend, Joe Chock. Joe has just broken into Broadway with a burlesque on heaven. It's a radio play. The hero goes around through five acts with a microphone concealed in his *caleçons*. Miller likes friend Joe because the latter drinks champagne and smokes Coronas. Miller showed me a few of the butts he had collected. Succulent snipes. He smokes only the best butts when he is with Joe.

"Then what? " I asked in a loud voice because Miller was falling asleep on his feet. He hadn't slept for two nights.

"I don't have to worry about a job. In Montparnasse no one has to work. The next day I met another friend of mine. You know, Ludwig Truss, the butter and egg producer. At four in the morning after a long discussion about life and travel, he took me for a long drive in his Suiza to Fontainebleau. The mist was rising from the lake and the ducks were very white. We sat on a terrace overlooking the palace of François Ier. Then we argued about how many horses one could drive abreast up the crazy stairs of the palace. But we both got bored and began to drive back to Paris. We had a big breakfast at the Dôme.

"What a wonderful life! " I said.

"That's how it is," said Miller. "Other friends came up. They look high and low for me. There's Osman the banker, who always treats me to sparkling *Mousseux*. I shake hands with people all day long. Even Link Gillespie once bought me a drink. Montparnasse is a great place. Everyone likes to help a fellow who is broke. A couple of days ago, a girl I hardly knew stopped me on the street. I told her about my status, so she took me home with her and sewed a couple of buttons on my coat and trousers. People are swell, do you see what I mean? They worry about you."

I am reporting our conversation very faithfully. Miller is not a son of badinage. He is a legitimate child of Montparnasse, the salt of the Quarter. He represents its classic color that has not faded since Murger and other optimists. A good word is *esprit*. I told him that.

"You have *esprit*," I said, lighting his cigar butt. Then he said:

"Can you give me an alarm clock? "

"What for? "

"Well, you see, Joe,"—(he always called me Joe. He calls everybody Joe)—"I am having such a good time that I hate to miss any of it. I like to get up early to enjoy every available hour."

Suddenly Miller staggered and fell back against the wall of a building. "What's the matter? " I said. His voice was frail and I could read between the lines of his face.

"What you need is food," I said, reaching in my pocket. "I'm your friend, too. Get yourself some food," I said, and handed him a franc. Montparnasse is that way.

14 October 1931

Harold Stearns Departs

The last blow to Montparnasse is the departure of Harold Stearns. He went to California where the warm sun revives tired people. He was tired of the monotony of his role. Harold was a cerebral solitary who lived pleasantly in a passive world, and he used to sit at the Sélect and dream of old episodes. Once there was great promise, but there is something epic about great resignation. The latter is an enticing achievement, and Harold will always be regarded as a legendary figure, a good compensation.

Before leaving, all his teeth were extracted, it having been discovered that bad teeth was the only thing wrong with him physically. It is hoped that this operation will radically alter his viewpoint and make him forget the appeal of great resignation. The deans of the Quarter have not lost faith in one of the most promising young men of America. The passing of Harold Stearns from Montparnasse is pointed to as one more symptom of its end. But new blood continues to pour in. New faces brighten the streets.

23 February 1932

Aldous Huxley

One or two letters have come in asking for an explanation of last Tuesday's note that Aldous Huxley has taken to painting. The implication was that Huxley is interested in painting only as a hobby. The literary work goes on, for better or worse. In fact, he has just finished writing an introduction to *Letters of D. H. Lawrence.*

Huxley's new pet is characteristic of the man. One may almost venture the statement that he is interested in everything. He is one of the most mentally active persons I have ever come across and conversation with him is an excursion through every conceivable field of fortified data, with Huxley, of course, leading the way. It may begin with Bach's fugues and end with Russian politics.

His occasional appearance at the Dôme always brings a stare. He is almost six and one half feet of angles, measuring from his large black hat to the floor. Although only 38 he looks like a person who has been concentrating for 75 years. Maria is generally taking books out of his pocket because he reads too much. He wears very thick glasses, and he gives the impression of being very shy and not quite aware of anyone, not even himself. He is very modest.

One afternoon last year Huxley was leaning against the old zinc bar with a leaf of poems in his hand. A local poet wanted his opinion. So absorbed was he that, in a clear and enthusiastic voice, he began to read aloud, dramatic pauses, and everything. The milling crowd stopped their clamoring, something like a hush unfolded and even the *garçons* looked up. At last he handed them back. From his great height he smiled patiently at the poet. "They are very, very bad." he said slowly. Then he walked out.

6 September 1932

Man Ray and Lee Miller

Man Ray thinks New York would look much better if all the skyscrapers were laid on their sides. Don't ask him why. An artist never gives reasons.

Another idea of his is the virtue of gold. "I'd like a golden automobile," he said, "a golden motorcycle or bicycle. Imagine Geneva on a gold foundation and golden bullets in time of war! "

Man Ray is a visionary, but all art is a wish. He says he likes the metal for its esthetic rather than its exchange value. It is a good light reflector and it doesn't rust. Imitation-gold background, says our Montparnasse modernist, is the latest thing in painting.

Man Ray is really a photographer. Twelve years ago he gave up painting and arrived in Montparnasse to experiment with the camera. He still paints now and then. "Photography," said Man Ray, "is the shorthand of painting. In another 50 or 100 years, the camera will entirely supplant the brush, and painters will have to get other jobs or become photographers."

Every argument I managed to interpose was overruled.

"The camera," said the photographer, "employs light and shade, not the illusion of light and shade. And the use of color will be accessible in our *métier*."

Lee Miller, platinum blonde photographer, who left Montparnasse to crash America, has just set up shop there. Lee told a smart girl reporter, who interviewed her recently, that "the American head has a better bone structure than the European." It is reported that American society women have been extremely flattered, and want their pictures taken by Lee.

29 November 1932

Depression Hits Montparnasse

The crisis hits Montparnasse. At last the ravages of the economic depression are felt in the Carrefour. Artists and their friends, once rich in dreams, are now reduced to drinking small beers and black coffee. At last the soul-starved are actually hungry.

It looks bad here. Painters of still lifes are eating their models—pears, oranges, grapes—before they are copied on canvas. This explains why Montparnasse artists are going in for abstract painting. Times are tough. On every street there are cases where four or five men and women are compelled by circumstances to live in a single room, a situation which may be classified as dangerous to the moral tone of our Quarter. *C'est la crise!* I am told that some of the men are obliged to give themselves to wealthy women. It is no longer easy to sponge meals. Artists are going hungry. One fellow became so vicious that he bit his girl friend, but they say he was always that way.

28 February 1933

A Farewell to Montparnasse

Let's say Montparnasse is a handkerchief. You crumple it up and put in it your pocket. When you go away, you take it out and wave it at your friends. It makes a pretty spot of color on the thinning air. Montparnasse, with which I have been occupied too long, is not a sanitary bit of linen with which to wave farewell. It is a filthy rag one drops into the nearest garbage can.

There was a time when it was a painters' rag. Then Cezanne and Modigliani and Zak and Picasso used it to wipe their brushes on. Even though a rag, it was clean enough at first. Cezanne wiped a blue brush on it. And Modigliani a green. Picasso preferred it for his rainbow brush, while Zak delicately tinged it with mysterious colors.

Was it a glad rag?

It was, and the flash of its tints enticed the world. In the whole world, people began to see the light. They wondered whence it came, they investigated, they were conquered. The spiritual gold rush was on.

But adepts are never so good as their masters, and those who followed in the tracks of Cezanne began to wipe their brushes on the same rag. Their colors weren't clean; the rag became dirtier and dirtier. But more and more adepts were drawn Montparnasse-wards. They were dilettantes, fakes. The true artists fled.

And then came the tourists.

Montparnasse became the supernal roost of the unclean and the wide-eyed. A few artists occasionally wandered in to sniff masochistically its degradation, and then they wandered out again. The rag was wearing out; not even a handkerchief lasts forever. Now that I am leaving it, that I am saying farewell to it, I insist that it has become so thin, so brittle, so precarious that one more good blow into it by an ambitious beetle—and *pouf!* It will fall into dust.

I've had a good time. I've seen them all; Derain and Braque and Chirico and Lillian Fisk and Fujita and Joe the barman. I've seen James Stephens and Huxley and Norman Douglas and Colette and Marie Laurencin and Brancusi and Paul Fort and—but this could go on and on; I no longer wish it to go on and on. I've seen the Coupole expand over the Quarter like a mushroom or like a weightlifter's chest, the Sélect go Oscar Wilde, and the Rotonde Nordic. I've seen the Dôme, that palace of cheap bliss, that ugly wart on the face of the earth, turn into an American Bar. I've seen all that—but it's all over now. I'm not deserting a sinking ship; it's been sunk for ages. You get something out of Montparnasse, and then it gets something out of you—just like bad liquor.

The writers—they took Montparnasse for a pen-wiper. Their ink is mixed with bile and venom, as only writers who cannot get into *Vanity Fair* know how to mix it. They don't use pens—they use machines, do they? Well, they took Montparnasse for a typewriter ribbon, and the frenetic smack of the keys against the roller gave them exercise, if little else.

Though not otherwise severing my connections with *The Tribune* I have decided to relinquish this column, and in so doing I am giving up my sympathetic ties with certain types and groups whom I've always admired. Farewell to my Montparnasse friends, who may be listed:

Modest intellectual artists.

Poets of the machine age, who ransack Sears Roebuck catalogues.

Poets of the night language, the chthonian plungers barking on the terrain of impressive obscurantism.

Sculptors, chiselers of time-space statues with concave breasts, and not only real hair, but dandruff.

Modern artists who do their tricks with wire and chewing gum, and don't call them Picasso.

Ex-Butter Merchants, gone literary, who compose esoteric dithyrambs on The New Economic Soul in between heavy meals.

Self-styled leaders of poets, who dispatch shrieking squibs from the sunken rim of the world to battle obscurity, who invent new spellings to remain afloat.

Benevolent old men who try to muscle in on literary circles by encouraging celebrities and by buying their work.

Literary females of yesterday, Montparnasse deserters, who choose to add decor to the Carrefour Saint-Germain with their arch and aging presences.

Disappointed wives who pretend they're masculine because it's smart and because they have given up all else.

Forty-year-old maids just beginning to live, who wear berets and are over-gay. Why can't a woman grow old like a man? Why must she battle every wrinkle of the way? I wish Samuel Johnson were here.

Nice people who drop into the Sphinx after dinner for dessert.

The trees in front of the Dôme, nourished by dead cigarette butts.

As I write this valediction I see the parade of silhouettes. What became of Flossie Martin, Harold Stearns, Homer Bevans, the Countess Eileen? What became of Samuel Putnam, who brought forth on this continent *The New Review*, conceived in liberty and dedicated to the proposition that almost anyone is literary? Where is Jolas now? Where is Link Gillespie, the unconquerable poet who fought so valiantly that words might escape their spelling? Whither hath fled flummery and mummery? Oh!

There were others: Gilbert White, the jocular nonpareil; Louise Bryant, who survives the rest; Harry McElhone, Scotch on the Right Bank and Bohemian on the Left; Ernest Hemingway, who is doing for a clumsy animal what Ziegfeld did for the American Girl; George Antheil, cherubic but gifted; Rona Benzie, who escaped to London; Michonze, the great Russian Surrealist, whose cartoons you have seen here now and then; Gwen LeGallienne, with her Siamese cat and Blakeian trance; Howell Cresswell, saintly, psychic and simply a grand conversationalist; Erskine Gwynne, the boulevardier; June Mansfield, the girl with the golden face; Hilaire Hiler, a dean of American painters; Richard Thoma, the blossoming poet, whose capacity for black coffee has turned his orbit into green chaos; Maris Wassilieff, with her rag dolls and mysterious son.

They have had their period of ordination.

The eccentrics of Montparnasse? The poverty? The loose morals? The drunkenness? The anxious idealists? The crusaders? What a tradition! The only difference between a Left Bank bum and a Right Bank bum is a few francs. The Left Bank bums aren't trying to hide.

The world is leveled off. Montparnasse is Main Street, and the "plastic" moderns have won their battle against cliché. Even automobiles and furniture are going Picasso. The staunch army may disband. Gertrude Stein has crashed (of all things) *The Atlantic Monthly*, and her autobiography is accepted for publication by the Book-of-the-Month Club (meaning 90,000 copies virtually guaranteed). I'll bet anyone my new suit she cops the Pulitzer Prize.

I think art should be put in its place; art is a solace, but no solution. Montparnasse might wait a while, because the world now is interesting. When the world ceases to be interesting, Montparnasse will have a nice new handkerchief, something to cover a new face. At present it covers a corpse. I am tired of jiggling a corpse.

Wambly Bald
25 July 1933

IV The Problem is America

The grand doyen of Americans in Paris, Harold Stearns, the compiler of *Civilization in the United States,* often cited (wrongly) as the book that started the exodus to Montparnasse, began his bizarre career with the *Tribune,* a career that cast Stearns as "Peter Pickem," the Tribune's racing tout, by dissecting France and America and concluding that the former had learned that the "art of contentment and happiness" depended upon recognizing that "the end of life [was] not how much but how." That America had been "sold" on the idea that "number and extent of possessions" constituted a worthy and desirable end of life was a major conclusion of *Civilization in the United States.* Its overriding message, however, was that life in the United States was hardly worth living, and to dramatize the point Stearns set sail for France soon after he delivered his manuscript to the publisher, thus forever fixing the belief that he was a man who acted on his convictions.

It would be wrong to claim that Harold Stearns influenced a generation of exiles, particularly *Tribune* colleagues who dubbed him the "Hippo Budda" and marveled more at his alcoholic consumption or his strange ability to remain silent throughout entire evenings at Montparnasse cafés. Nevertheless they generally shared his disenchantment with America and satisfaction with France, and his respect for a society that emphasized the "how" more than the "how much," and many of them added their complaints to the chorus of "anti-Americanism" Stearns helped foster, or amplified it in their interviews with hostile critics like Clarence Darrow and H. L. Mencken.

But criticism of America amounted to more than a recitation of ills; certainly among *Tribune* writers, who, after all, worked for a newspaper dedicated to explaining, if not quite defending, Americanism abroad, something close to a symposium existed. Besides tempering the negative opinions with optimistic reports (even Theodore Dreiser once told a *Tribune* reporter he had hope for America), the views of French observers familiar with the United States were printed and helped dispel the feeling that hostility toward America was an obsession of a few disgruntled expatriates.

By far the most vociferous and quarrelsome foe of the United States was Ezra Pound, who from his retreat in Rapallo regularly discharged a battery of seering missiles to the *Tribune,* and similar letters went to the Paris *Herald.* Pound's objections ranged from personal gripes about how U. S. censors had mishandled his books, to claims that passports for United States citizens were a massive swindle. Sometimes he advanced his economic theories, or warned of the dangerous competition among munitions makers, but most charges were directed against Republican administrations, top-heavy bureaucracies, and their leaders. Like Pound, many exiles looked ruefully to America, not just to confirm their objections, which may or may not have led to their expatriation, but for signs of change that might some day make repatriation an inviting possibility.

H. F.

Americans on America

Artists, Bohemians, to Climb Butte

Poets, painters, writers, models, sculptors, talkers, thinkers, actors and emancipators will join Harry Kemp's parade at the Café du Dôme, Boulevard Montparnasse, on Sunday morning at eleven o'clock to march to Montmartre where the self appointed ambassador from America's Bohemian colonies will go through the solemn ceremony of presenting his credentials to President Lucien Boyer of the free Commune of Montmartre.

Then there will be a luncheon in honor of the occasion and much will be done towards the establishment of the international league of kindred souls bound together by mutual oaths to art and ideals.

The marchers promise to be many . . . the spirits promise to be high and the day to be a determined rally of the chosen.

"America is seeing little colonies of liberal thinkers springing up in every big city, north, south, east and west," the one and only real tramp poet of the North American continent declares, "and all these groups have behind their ideas of freedom the desire for a philosophy and a culture like that we find and love in France."

"Young America wants to be Latinized," Ambassador Kemp asserts. "We'll put over the idea behind all this . . . the idea that young America wants to be latinized. It is towards France that the youth of the United States is turning for its inspiration. France stands for individual freedom; and that's what America's coming generation is going to yell and fight for. I realize that more and more every day. We do not know exactly what it is we want perhaps," he said, "but I am convinced since my visit here that it is just the wartime-education of the youth of our country yelling for that special joy of life so many of our best fellows and girls became familiar with in this land of honest-to-God people."

22 March 1923

Dear Pard

Café Bonvin,
Around the Corner
Paris
11 May 1924

Dear Pard:

A Drink in America is a whole intrigue, in France an incident. In America, once secured, it is an Obligation, in France a Recreation. Back there it is drunk fer the Kick, and here fer the Drink itself.

And that explains all the differences there is between Licker at home and Licker in France. At home it is made to be sold, in France it is made to be drunk. And that's the only Excuse I can see fer Prohibishion. It's also the reason why you're gettin rich, but I'll betcha that mine's the best satisfied Custom.

In France yuh don't have to hunt out a high class expensive bar to get Good Stuff . . . it's there on sale at the Corner Bistrot. And the bistrot, lemme say, is the Bulwark uv the Nation. There's no place like it in America and never was. Instead uv bein the Place where yuh start on a Tear, it's the place where yuh go for a Quiet Evenin. The Workin Man's little Daughter instead uv comin into the bar to get Father to come home, runs out to meet him and says: "Father, don't go home, cause Mother's waitin at the Bistrot."

After that the Whole Family sits down to eat and spends the evenin sippin Wine and talkin with their Friends and Neighbers. There ain't no noisy shoutin' and no guzzlin. The Madame knows them all and chats with them. Everybody's smilin, good-nachured and friendly. And Pardner, believe me, the Wine is responsible.

How much enjoyment, I ask yuh, do you get from sittin around with a Bottle of Ginger Pop? The conversashun is about as interestin as a Empty Bottle. And on the other hand, how long do yuh keep nicely sociable on Whisty Straights?

The Wine's the only lubricant! I never used to think so there back home. I used to think that there was only two Real Drinks, and those were Beer and Wisky. I still think there are only two . . . and both uv em are wine. Burgundy and Bordeaux, I mean. They're good fer yer Temper and good fer yer Soul, and they're the secret why the Latin Tempramunt's so gay. I used to half believe the propaganda that a drink was bad fer yuh, but now I know there's reason in the sayin, "To yer Health."

Pardner, they say that Pinard won the war. I think it did. And lemme say, if anything can do it, Wine will keep the Peace.

Leastways it would fer

Clancey Coogan.

Lansing Warren
11 May 1924

Goldman Scoffs at U. S. Morals

"I shall never return to America except on my own terms, although I should like to revisit the land where I spent so many years of my life. I will not promise the American government to be good."

Such was the statement of Miss Emma Goldman, who has been known to Americans for a generation as an anarchist and a lecturer on social questions, when interviewed by *The Tribune* yesterday. Miss Goldman, it will be remembered was deported from America to Russia in 1919. After staying long enough in Russia to discover that Bolsheviks have no sympathy with anarchists, Miss Goldman returned to the occident, and is now studying social problems in London. At the present moment she is on a brief visit to Paris, which she is leaving today.

"The Cathcart case is an outrage," continued Miss Goldman. "It is just another instance of the wave of ferocious morality which has been sweeping over the United States. The position of American women here is curious. They have protested for the countess; but it is not because they love liberty. They have simply seen a case of sex discrimination; they want both the man and the woman to be deported. Otherwise, they remain just as narrowly moral as ever. Some people were stupid enough to believe that woman suffrage would be a great liberalizing influence in American politics; as a matter of fact, women are the most determinedly reactionary body in America."

Radicals Blind

"This case is a fine instance of the absurdity to which American laws can be driven. I have always maintained that American liberals and radicals are the most short-sighted people in the world. They never see an attack on American liberty until it is too late. Then they start to howl, when, usually, either through their efforts or their inertia, some reactionary measure has been passed.

"Such was the case for prohibition. All the liberals were originally for this measure; they even helped the forces of darkness to pass it. Now, when it is too late, they oppose it. They see that an attack on one liberty may well end by taking away all of them. I saw the danger years ago;

before the prohibition movement had gathered strength, I was an anti-prohibition speaker.

"It is the illiberal forces of the south and the middle west which are the great menace to American life. The church shows no sign of relaxing its hold in those rural strongholds."

Whatever may have been the fire and violence of Miss Goldman's youth, all that has gone now. She wears the frumpy clothes and talks in the placid, almost pedantic, tone of a New England schoolmistress. Long experience of men, and disillusionment, has apparently worn the sharp edge off her ideas. Today she seems quite tame, perhaps because she was in the vanguard, and what seemed volcanic twenty years ago has become the commonplace of the young intellectuals of this day.

27 February 1926

Theodore Dreiser

Dreiser Is Hopeful about U. S.; Sees America Turning from Materialism

Mr. Theodore Dreiser, American novelist, who for twenty years has been harassed by Puritanical critics, side-tracked by timid publishers, and abused by the entire hierarchy of Pollyannas who control American reading matter from coast to coast, and who, because of the persistent support of such critics as Burton Rascoe, H. L. Mencken, and others, has at last become generally recognized as a great realist and a permanent figure in the country's literary development, showed himself to be quite hopeful for the future of his native land in an interview with Simonne Ratel, published yesterday in *Comoedia*.

The American business man, Mr. Dreiser said, is developing a taste for books, pictures, poems, paintings and plays, and the publishers and theatrical managers, drawing from the best European materials as well as the native talent, are trying to nourish this germ of culture in the land of pep and service.

"America is following an evolution opposite in direction to that of Europe," he said. "You have passed from idealism to materialism. We are passing from materialism to idealism."

His thoughts about European materialism were influenced somewhat, he admitted, by the fact that he got into the wrong kind of a restaurant recently, and being dressed in grey flannels and a softcollared shirt, like so many of his fellow-countrymen, had to pay about $4.00 for two cups of chocolate.

"The movement is proceeding rapidly and with surprising intensity," he continued. "Public taste is becoming cultivated, is gradually refining itself, is turning toward real beauty in literature, painting and music.

"Our editors and directors are constantly in touch with European productions and take advantage of your masterpieces in order to educate the American masses."

Speaking of French literature, Mr. Dreiser said that, in so far as America is concerned, it seems to have stopped with the death of Anatole France. The moderns are not being translated.

Questioned about Paris, Mr. Dreiser, who has not been here since 1912, said that at present it is more materialistic than New York. Whether or not, in his next novel, he intends to portray the budding idealist whose existence he has discerned in the American scene, Mr. Dreiser did not say.

23 September 1926

Sherwood Anderson Sees No Danger of America Ever Becoming Cultured

"There is no danger of Americans becoming cultured," said Mr. Sherwood Anderson, the American novelist, in an interview with *The Tribune* yesterday afternoon. He had been discussing the possible effect on American mores and the American outlook of such movements as the Book-a-Month Club. "Such things," said Mr. Anderson, "will, I believe, not make a dent on the spongy mass of general unintelligence."

Mr. Anderson let it be understood that he considered the cerebral density of the American people no greater than that of any other. In fact, he seemed little interested in any schemes for the spiritual salvation of mankind.

In the course of an hour, the novelist who has forged to the front rank in contemporary American letters, wandered discursively over many topics, such as prohibition, the place of the artist in American life, and the general spiritual unrest of the common American.

"Our greatest curse is industrialism," said Mr. Anderson, "with its deadly concomitant, standardization. What is desirable is that there be a direct relation between the man and his work. How is a man in a Ford factory to be interested in his work? Even the writer of short-stories is a factory hand. I have heard of purely mechanical writers of short detective stories who make as much as $75,000 a year. I've never done standardized work of that kind yet, but I'm not sure that I'm not going to."

The place of culture in American life drew some reflections from Mr. Anderson. "It is the latest mode," he said, "and shows what a naive people we are. What sensible person would go to hear a writer lecture? And yet, when I am broke, I can always get an engagement lecturing before women's clubs. The Book-a-Month club is a manifestation of the same naivete. There isn't a good book a month; we are lucky to have a good novelist every ten years."

Prohibition, according to Mr. Anderson, shocks the nature of every artist. "All Americans are bitten by the microbe of regulating other people's lives. Even the artists are not content to let the realtors and salesmen be what they are; they want to make them into a set of posing esthetes, and nothing is more dreadful than to see a tenth-rate mind wrestling with a conception of the arts. I am myself guilty of the general passion of my compatriots, but I hate myself every time I catch myself at it."

As for the row now going on in our United States about the wildness of youth, Mr. Anderson professed himself more or less ignorant. "Youth really does not interest me," said he. "I am interested in maturity, not in greenness and the thin dreams of adolescence. I wrote a story called "Tarr" about an eighteen-year-old, but I really lost interest in him before the story was finished."

Puritan Base Stands

"For the alleged wildness—I wonder if it is any worse than in the horse-and-buggy days. Of course, the girls of our day are probably in a hurry to get sophisticated. They may, with the same naivete, want sex experience as a short cut to culture. It is on a par with the Book-a-Month club.

"The Puritan foundation of the training of our youth stands. They have the idea of duty inculcated in them. The only way in which our girls could be corrupted into general immorality is to be convinced that it was their duty. Maybe immorality will become a new form of Puritanism."

18 December 1926

"Vive Sacco-Vanzetti," Cries Isadora Duncan;
"Bunk," Says Judge

Judge J. H. Hopkins, of the Superior Court of Illinois, who has just completed his year's work presiding over the criminal court, and who has twice sentenced prisoners to be hung, wandered yesterday evening through Montparnasse to hear the opinions of the many radicals who live in that section. Taking a seat on the terrace of the Sélect, he ordered a quart of Vichy, and lent an attentive ear to the conversations about him.

At the next table sat a red-haired woman with a party of five. Their talk was bitterly radical, and he understood from it that they had just returned from the American meeting to protest against the death sentence. It was not until after she had turned to the Judge and asked, "What do you think of the Sacco-Vanzetti case? " that he discovered that she was Isadora Duncan.

"I was under the impression that it had been definitely decided," said Judge Hopkins.

"The Sacco-Vanzetti case is a blot on American justice," said Miss Duncan. "It will bring down a lasting curse on the United States, a curse deserved by American hypocrisy. Fuller's name will go down in history with that of Pontius Pilate."

"Judicial processes in the United States," Judge Hopkins returned, "are superior to the criticism and condemnation of international politics, and it is a well-known and accepted fact internationally that the defendant before an American court of justice is guaranteed more safeguards in his defense than in any other court in the world. It is my firm conviction," he continued, "based upon my knowledge of the judicial systems of all the European countries that if the original sentence of death had been pronounced against Sacco and Vanzetti in any European country, the two condemned men would have been executed and buried six years ago."

"The extreme cruelty of American so-called justice," Miss Duncan said, "is responsible for the prolongation of the intense torture to which these men have been subjected for six or seven years."

To that Judge Hopkins answered. "The delays of American justice are not invoked by the prosecution but by the defense, and solely in the interest of the defense, so that the delays so bitterly complained of in this case were brought about by the defendants themselves."

A number of radicals joined in, and the argument became general, but neither side convinced the other. The only outcome of the dispute was Judge Hopkins' invitation to Miss Duncan to dine with him Saturday night and meet his very good friends, Mr. and Mrs. Clarence Darrow, who are arriving this week.

During the conversation, a bearded man, unknown to any of the party, asked the Judge where he was stopping. Upon being told that Judge Hopkins was at the Continental, he said, "Prepare to receive visitors tomorrow. The radicals of Paris will be glad to have the opportunity to see a representative of the American judicial system and show him what they think of it."

10 August 1927

Max Reinhardt, Sailing on *New York*, Praises America as Home of Newer Culture; Approves Modern Dancing

Professor Max Reinhardt, founder and greatest practitioner of the modern drama, who sailed yesterday for the United States on the *New York,* has dealt another cruel blow to the tea-table intelligentzia.

It was American life and American art that aroused Prof. Reinhardt's enthusiasm. America is today originating art, he declared, and has already given the world three notable contributions. These are American jazz, American architecture, and American dancing. Dancing in particular was praised.

"In the dance America has absolutely originated a new and wonderful form of art. I am speaking not only of what is called esthetic dancing but of all forms of the dance evolved in America. The young people in the dance-halls are only expressing in a cruder way the same thing that is expressed by the great artists of the concert stage and the ballet."

"Don't you think life is too mechanical in America to develop a really great art? " Prof. Reinhardt was asked.

"Oh no, no. How perfectly absurd! Why it is just the contrary. Machines in America are the greatest liberators the people have. Because Americans are freed from the dull toil and worries we have in Europe, they feel a greater need for spiritual and artistic things. The more highly industrialized the country becomes, the greater will be the interest in art. What is more, America demands a higher type of art than Europe; it is free from our petty hatreds and material sufferings. Europe now leads America in art; the time will come and soon when America will lead Europe. Indeed I sometimes think that our highest destiny over here should be to nourish the new culture that is awakening in America and will one day submerge our culture. For the present there is a free exchange of ideas and influence between the two Continents. A proof of this is that Arthur Hopkins' *Burlesque* was produced by me in Berlin and Vienna. In America I am going to produce O'Neill's *Strange Interlude.*

16 December 1928

First Impressions and Contrasts

To an American poet, Paris is a city difficult to fathom—a huge paradox divided into smaller ones: a city mercenary and yet effusively sentimental, liberal; gay on the surface and morbid underneath; bitter-sweet in the taste of its days and nights; coquettish in its emotions and stolid in its thoughts, with the two forever warring against each other.

The generalities narrow down to specific cases—a man is killed by one of the insanely darting taxi-cabs of Paris. In America, a crowd would promptly block the street and press around the prone victim; policemen would appear from nowhere, bellowing questions, shoving people back, reveling in officiousness; expressions of awestricken sorrow would fill the air. In Paris, a few quietly staring people gather; a single gendarme handles the tragedy with cool dispatch; the victim is hurried off in a few minutes. It is the difference between childlike histrionics on one side and quiet fatalism, resignation, on the other.

Or again, you are riding in a taxi and it collides with another machine, not severely but enough to push your machine to the curbstone. In America both men would descend to the pavement; accusations and invections would rend the air; each man would take the name and license number of the other; and an Irish policeman would rush up to complicate matters. In Paris, the driver who was to blame smiles sheepishly; the driver who was innocent remains at the wheel and contents himself with one sentence of reproach; and both speed away in a few seconds, as though they were anxious to forget the occurrence. It is the difference between an ungraceful aggressiveness bestowed upon the most minor details of living, on one side, and a more practical poise and acceptance on the other.

Again, two average men are sitting in a French café, wrapped in a terrific argument, since one proclaims himself a Royalist while the other flaunts his Communistic beliefs. In nine cases out of ten, in America, an average conservative and communist would come to physical blows as a climax to the verbal tilt, or would be on the verge of a physical tilt, but the two Frenchmen in the café thrash the matter out for hours, always vehement but never vicious. Most Frenchmen seem to realize that fists are futile, are at the bottom of the controversial scale, while large numbers of Americans have not yet acquired this passive sophistication.

Another example presents itself in the Bois de Boulogne, where a svelt, sloe-eyed French girl is perched upon the lap of her swarthy, grinning escort and exchanging kisses and hugs with him. Their bench is as removed as a walled-in room to them, and although the time is 3 p. m. on a sunny afternoon and the bench fully exposed to view, they act with a charmingly direct and childlike spontaneity. The endless file of passersby scarcely glance at the amorous pair, or regard them with envious admiration. In an American public park, such a rare happening as ardent, persistent, and unashamed embraces in the full glare of a crowded afternoon would bring snickers, staring watchers, derision, and finally a roughly interrupting policeman. Americans are apt to desire privacy for their more intimate and intense emotions whereas French people—the most conservative and elegant excepted—pin their hearts to their right sleeves for all to see.

Again, a French girl is weeping in a café, with her blonde head bowed and her precious drink neglected. Several women immediately hasten to her side and try to calm her without resorting to prying questions. Finally she brightens up, tosses her head, and begins to banter with the waiter, with a proud concealment equally as intense as the abasement of grief which preceded it. In America, in eight cases out of ten—a judicious estimate! —the surrounding women would have eyed the weeping girl uneasily, embarrassedly, and then, after a lapse of several minutes, one or two of them might have approached her with offers of help accompanied by curious and detailed questions. It is the difference between hearty and instant sympathy on one side and sympathy a little cautious, a little constrained, on the other.

Paris is a city of paradoxes while New York is a series of one-colored essences, as prearranged as the squares on a checker-board.

Maxwell Bodenheim
21 April 1929

Anita Loos, Here To Escape U. S. "Culture," Says Her Flapper Tirade Was Misunderstood

"I love going back to United States about once a year to get a good laugh. But after I've had my fun, and see the standards of life people are cultivating back there—"

Anita Loos, the girl who rose overnight from Hollywood hack writer to world fame with that terrific indictment of the American flapper, *Gentlemen Prefer Blondes,* emerged from hiding in Paris long enough to tell that to *The Tribune* yesterday afternoon.

"Prohibition is a pest," she added. "It is ruining America. There is no excuse for such an absurd system restricting a man's most elementary liberty—the right to drink what he wants. Prohibiting drink as a matter of principal; why, it's the most absurd and ridiculous idea in the history of our so-called self-government.

"Please don't imagine from that that I am not a patriotic American. I am; it is just because I have an acute sense of patriotism, and because I love my country, that I feel so sensitive about our present troubles in America."

George Nelson Page
2 May 1929

Speaking Mildly, Darrow Thinks U. S. Is Crazy;
Came Here for Drink That Wouldn't Paralyse

"If I were to say all I think about America I probably couldn't go back, but putting it moderately, kindly and honestly, I think Americans are crazy."

That was only one of the many scintillating aphorisms with which Mr. Clarence Darrow, famous lawyer, free-thinker and anti-prohibitionist, dazzled his hearers and evoked storms of cheers and laughter at the weekly luncheon of the American Club of Paris at Langer's Restaurant yesterday. Mr. Darrow's address flashed and sparkled with brilliant paradoxes of this sort.

With trenchant wit and sarcasm, he destroyed the great American fetish Efficiency, whose worship brings everything except enjoyment of life, and set up in its place Inefficiency and Happiness. Denouncing what he termed the present puritanical trend in America, he proclaimed the right of every human being to regulate his life as he sees fit.

Here are some of the maxims and confessions of faith that illuminated Mr. Darrow's speech:

"All my life I have been trying to get to a point where I don't have to be efficient—at last I have arrived.

"I am interested in liquor because it tends to inefficiency, and I am very sorry at what we are learning in America; we are not learning to live, we are learning to make things and sell them if we can find somebody who is not making them—induce them to buy a million and then attempt to civilize heathens so that they can buy them. People in the South Sea Islands and other parts of the Pacific, who have never been 'efficientized' and don't wear clothes, are told that it is immoral not to wear clothes, and when they learn that it is immoral, they buy the clothes. That is all right. For my part I would just as soon they did not wear them. It saves the trouble of undressing."

Regretted Long Hours of Work

"But I am interested in living—not that I am going to live so long. I have regretted some long hours in which I have worked, but I never have regretted those in which I have played, and I never expect to.

"I like France because they don't get up so early in the morning and they stay up later at night. The first time I came here I was with Cook's Tours, so as to be sure not to get lost. I found I could not do any business between 12 and 2 o'clock because the tourist office was not only closed but they had taken the key and the handle away with them—and I got to like it! None of them preached to me; none of them told me to go to any church; none of them told me what I ought to drink; none of them lectured me when I went to the Moulin Rouge and other places of interest and of importance. I really liked it. I still like it.

"I think there is something to be said for just plain living. I may miss many good things that I would realize in 'Kingdom Come,' but suppose I never get to 'Kingdom Come.' I would like to see people come to the idea which I have come to that life consists in getting as much pleasure and as little pain as possible; that anything that does not mean pleasure is not worth having; anything that means pain should be avoided. No question can be settled regarding life, unless one has some aim in life, some purpose. My purpose is not to make machines, or even to plead cases, my pleasure is in all pleasurable emotions and I try to help them as best I can.

"In America, I think—pardon me for criticizing our own country—I will not be very severe or I might not be able to go home—but just moderately, kindly and honestly, I think we are crazy! Otherwise we are all right.

"I like America. I like it better than any other country in the world. There is one reason: I know what they are talking about and can answer them back. I don't know in France. . . . I have a glimmering of it in England, and not very much more.

"I like America because I am used to it. I am acquainted with my bathroom, and with my books, and with my neighbors—those who will associate with me—and I feel at home.

"I witnessed various Americans coming home on the ship that I have gone home on, and as we were approaching New York, near the Statue of Liberty, which still stands there, but now does not stand for anything, they said: 'America is good enough for me.' Of course I don't know whether they were just glad to get back to the bathroom and to the old girl, or just because they were used to it."

Patriotism Largely Habit

"A large part of our patriotism is habit; a large part of anything and everything is habit. No one in the world would be able, if they tried, to figure just what country is best and what is the best for one people and another; it depends largely on our habit.

"If I have a mission in life—which I have not, except to get all I can out of it—it is to preach the gospel of tolerance and freedom, that every man may work out his own life, in his own way."

21 June 1929

Mencken Seeks a Naval Holiday in London— for Himself—and Purple Spats for Paris

A little group of ship news reporters, armed with an extra supply of pencils and reams of copy paper, assembled yesterday afternoon to meet the jovial, waggish, bad boy of Baltimore, Henry L. Mencken, upon his arrival at the Gare St. Lazare from Cherbourg, where he disembarked from the North German Lloyd liner *Columbus* after crossing from New York.

Snorting, fuming, bellowing, and spluttering, Saint Henry of Hollins Street—for he has already been canonized by the Young American *révoltés*, although he is still very much alive—hopped off the boat train fully three leaps before it came to a standstill in the station. Thus the *enfant terrible* of American literature, the nemesis of all right-thinkers, forward-lookers, boob-bumpers, and reformers, the everlasting foe of puritanism, prohibition, and democracy, and the editor of *American Mercury*, arrived in Paris for a brief visit before proceeding to London to attend the coming Naval Disarmament Conference and write special articles about it for the *Baltimore Evening Sun*.

Whatnell?

"What the hell's happened to France? " he snorted, in a series of staccato explosions sounding like the discharge of a rapid-fire gun. "Happened? Why between Cherbourg and here there's nothing but a hideous, obnoxious, obscene stretch of billboards. The beautiful Norman country-side, once the glory of France, and formerly one of the most exquisite, fertile, sumptuous, and restful landscapes to be found in the entire world, is being polluted with an endless, uninterrupted chain of cheap, tawdry billboards and gaudy advertising signs. What an eyesore! A real tragedy. An unmitigated swindle perpetrated to rob and cheat the land out of the lavish dowry that nature bestowed upon it! "

Bang! Boom! Bangity-boom-boom-boom.

"The scoundrels who perpetrated such an outrage ought to be shot," snorted the author of *Prejudices,* puffing on a cigar more vigorously than puffed the panting, throbbing engine beside which he stood.

"But this is no place to talk. Can't you come to my hotel in an hour and then I'll tell you something."

And he did.

Unofficially, Mr. Mencken is on a holiday. Officially he is going to London to write up the naval pow-wow.

"I'm on my way to London for the 5-Power Naval Conference," he said. "I wouldn't miss it for anything. I look forward to it as being one of the most delicious and spectacular sort of things ever staged in the history of the human race. What could be a more sublime and noteworthy sight than a group of politicians solemnly quibbling with each other over the size of their navies. But I am optimistic," he added, with a sly chuckle, "I don't think that England will come out of it with more than twice as big a navy as the United States."

When speaking seriously about the outcome of the conference, if Mr. Mencken can ever be serious, his clear blue eyes lit up and he leaned back on the sofa, puffing on his inevitable cigar, and said: "Well, who knows? I don't think that anything has ever been held on such a grand scale before. Where, exactly, does Hoover himself stand on the question? Has anybody yet found out whether he is British or American? If he is not a downright Anglophile, then it is because he has been so wonderfully successful in America. He could never have gotten where he has if he had stayed in

H. L. Mencken

England. Only now, perhaps by making him the king of England, could you entice him to turn on America. Obviously, nobody knows just how he stands."

Literary Blah!

"But anyhow it ought to be a good show," he added.

Some one suggested that the weather was terrible at this time of the year in London.

"But the bars are always cosy," Saint Henry dryly replied.

A pause.

"What a huge delegation America is sending to the conference! " he said. How many are there, exactly? Sixty some, I believe, including the stenographers, secretaries, under-secretaries, and spies. There are always a couple of gum-shoe men taken along on such momentous occasions. I hope I'm not arrested as a Japanese spy. During the war I was accused of being in the pay of the Kaiser." And his eyes lit up again as he started recalling old times. Such reminiscences. The walls had never and will never again hear such talk.

"What do I think about the present state of letters? " he responded to a question. "Not much. In America there is a young group, a quite hopeful group, but they cannot be put beside their elders. I don't profess to know much about France, but it seems that the country, literarily speaking, is at a standstill. And I can't forgive the French for not having a consulate in Baltimore. I had to send my passport to Washington for a visa. Took three days to get it back."

Purple Spat Market

"In Germany there are the same old men constantly rehashing the same old themes. It is my opinion that the novel, as a form of expression, is no longer adequate. Hence such men as Joyce, Anderson and Hemingway are seeking to find new methods of expression. Of the younger Americans, Hemingway stands out by far the most prominently. But he doesn't ring convincingly all the time. Dreiser has just brought out a book about women that's good.

"Well, I'm going to buy myself a beautiful pair of purple spats, a checkered waistcoat, and a batwing tie to wear while I am in Paris. Say that I have great hopes in the coming conference, providing, of course, it doesn't end in actual hostilities breaking out among the powers. I've heard the beer is still bad in Paris. That's a shame. English beer is no good either. Thanks for calling on me."

And the Bad Boy from Baltimore stood in the doorway, graciously shaking hands, a mischievous twinkle in his clear blue eyes.

Leigh Hoffman
5 January 1930

The American Mind: In Defense of a New Philosophy

I venture to take up the cudgels in behalf of American mentality after several years of comparison between the thinking of Europeans and that of my own compatriots.

The native critic of American thought makes the initial fallacy of comparing two non-analogous strata of society. When he thinks of the American mind he is thinking of the great mass of people—the average or even the sub-average American. He has come into daily contact with the American mass and he rightly considers the small intellectual class as the exception. In Europe, however, he never learns anything about the average man at all. His meetings with Europeans are necessarily restricted to the cosmopolitan section of European society, a carefully selected and exceptional group. He does not discuss politics with the "Bistrot" keeper, as he cannot help doing with the barber at home, nor does his "concierge" regale him with her opinions on art, which he might be enabled to compare with dissertations on literature which he has very probably endured from high pressure advertising salesmen in the United States.

Divination On Women

Indeed, even if the American visitor were equipped to talk with this "concierge," or, better still, with the "commerçants" of a provincial town and the peasants of the farm districts, he could not discuss literature with them, for they would know nothing about it. Americans are an over-educated nation (not necessarily an evil), and hence are equipped with the vocabularies and the confidence to talk glibly about subjects which they do not understand. The male American who as a rule would, left to himself, have intelligence enough to stick to the subjects that interest him, is only too often, in our woman-dominated country, corrupted into mouthing phrases about arts which have no appeal to him but of which he believes the admission of ignorance would be tantamount to acknowledging some defect in himself, females in all ages and countries having manifested a characteristic penchant for dabbling in matters about which they were hardly qualified to learn anything. This is a dangerous pastime for the male, who has nothing more brilliant than comprehension to oppose to female intuition, and who thus invariably finds himself on the losing side of any argument conducted with a woman.

If we compare, then, the American elite with the European elite (and these comparatively small classes are the only groups who count in the comparison of the thought of different cultures, the great masses being always some centuries behind the time), we shall find that the American mentality has nothing to apologize for. The European may be enabled to present his philosophy more smoothly, for he has behind him a long tradition which has presented him with a technique of thinking, while the American must hew his idea out of the rough matter of a still uncodified philosophy. But by the same token, the European mind finds it harder to deviate very far from the accepted way of thinking that centuries of habit have imposed upon him. The individuality of the European, the regimentation of the American, are myths. European individuality is a matter of deviation in small details. The individuality of single Americans is swallowed up in the unique individuality of an entire nation, whose great divergence from European ideals minimizes the minor divergences of its units at the same time that the greater force of a newer and stronger philosophy imposes superficial details of sameness on its individual members.

A Nascent Philosophy

That something new is actually arising out of America is sufficiently evidenced by the great interest that Europe has lately begun to take in the New World. Many of the authors of the flood of foreign books on America find our civilization ugly or discordant; but they find it impossible to ignore it. It is not a mere question of higher buildings or better telephone systems. A philosophy, a new way of thinking is developing in America. It is hardly out of the womb yet, but I think it is not impossible to prophesy already the direction that it is taking. That, however, would require a great deal of space, and I therefore renounce any attempt to suggest, in this article, the direction.

In the meantime America is not doing so badly. A number of American cities can provide companionship for any American who wants to lead an intellectual life. My own experience has been confined to the northeastern part of the country, but I can vouch for the fact that both Boston and New York provide plenty of opportunity for sharpening the mind. Baltimore also has its elite, but I noticed no signs of any great mental awakening in Philadelphia which, however, I must confess, I fled after no more than two weeks' residence, despite the consoling presence of the Philadelphia Symphony Orchestra. From what I have heard of other American cities, I am sure that San Francisco and New Orleans must also possess their circles of intelligentsia (the word is used without any derogatory connotation), and Chicago and Detroit, newer and rawer, seem to show a strength and vitality that augurs well for the future. The great central region from the Alleghenies to the Rockies still appears to be intellectually nonexistent.

Praise for the States

As for the present state of the arts, America is in an enviable situation. No capital has better music than New York; nor has any capital better theatre. Despite the large amount of trash that appears on the New York stage, there still remain a large number of theatres free for good plays. No important production occurs abroad that does not eventually find its way to New York. As for England, the comparison is pitiful. A good theatrical season in London now is one in which American plays predominate. The native crop is painfully weak. The same is true of literature. The English product is weakening; the American writers are gaining strength. American museums, despite their late start, can be compared without shame to many of those in Europe, excepting, of course, such exceptional collections as that of the Vatican. And nowhere is access to libraries less complicated.

All this, of course, is because America, regardless of stock market crashes, is wealthy. Artists, particularly interpretative artists, flock to the countries that have the money to support their art. The creative artists seldom get a large share of the money, but they get enough to live and work on. Nor is American wealth always employed unintelligently in its application to art. What European of wealth has ever brought together any collection of paintings comparable to that acquired by John Quinn, whose modern canvases were mostly purchased while their painters were still comparatively obscure and who, therefore, had no other guide in making his purchases than taste and comprehension?

The art patron is, of course, a rare bird in modern America. The artist is supported there by democratic dollars. The first-rate author may sell thousands of his books in America, and be understood by no more than a few score readers; but I see no objection to allowing those who have no oversupply of intelligence to contribute to the support of artists who delight the few, even if their motive is a type of snobbism, or literary social climbing, which makes them want to appear to be appreciative of what the critics tell them they should like. Incidentally it should be noted that though many artists work in a rarefied atmosphere which necessarily limits their audience, a great artist may very well have a wide appeal in his own day and time; that is more or less of an accident. The urge to express one's self strikes in unexpected places. The mantle of greatness descends upon those who speak a language that all may understand as well as upon those whose speech is restricted almost to themselves alone.

The American mentality is worthy of respect. It will become more so in the next century. You may not sympathize with it, you may not like the way it works, but it is there and cannot be argued aside. It will last longer than you will.

Waverley Lewis Root
5 January 1931

Negro Writer Assails Race Prejudice
Harlem Has Shown for Nancy Cunard

Moral pressure brought to bear against Nancy Cunard by the proprietor of a Negro hotel in New York's Harlem district which forced her to leave the place drew an ironic protest here yesterday from Eric Walrond, Negro novelist and Guggenheim scholarship winner, who wrote *Tropic Death*. The pretty, intelligent, wealthy, and altruistic young English woman, who had made no secret in Paris of her friendship with Henry Crowder, Negro musician, found a warm defender in Walrond.

"The action of the hotel manager who indicated to Miss Cunard that she was no longer welcome was cowardly and sycophantic," Walrond said when shown cabled reports of the Cunard incident in Harlem on Wednesday.

"It is too bad that the hotel manager had to stoop to the same race prejudice which has made life so miserable for thousands of his people," Walrond continued.

"Nancy Cunard has moral and intellectual courage. She has an understanding of the psychology of the Negro which has been equalled by no other person. It is a disgraceful thing that she had to be subjected to such treatment.

"She has had the courage to take up a problem which is vital today, especially in the United States. I mean by that, relations between Negroes and Whites. She deserves better treatment than she was accorded by the proprietor of the hotel.

"Have we taken . . . the worst things from the ideology of the people with whom we live in the United States? "

6 May 1932

Frenchmen on America

As France Sees America

"America cannot act speedily to extricate us (Europeans) from our difficulties, but she will certainly act, and she will do it some day with all her heart, with the greatest generosity, as she made war. That hour is drawing near. We ought to be ready to take advantage of it even though we can do nothing, or almost nothing, to hasten its arrival. If in the moment when the United States undertakes to reorganize Europe we are the most unpopular nation with the New World, despite our merits and our incontestable rights, it will cost us dear."

This is the warning addressed to France by Bernard Fay, a French observer recently in America.

One of the most striking things this French visitor discovers about the United States is the sameness of its economic life all over the country, so that houses, motors, shops, are alike everywhere; from socks to works on theology, anything that makes a hit in one corner of the country is soon found everywhere in it. Ideas and theories have their countrywide market also; the whole country talks at the one time about Einstein, Madame Curie, Freud, the New Brunswick murders, Valentino, Clemenceau, each topic having exclusive attention until it is dropped for another. Hence also the American habit of concentrating for weeks on various causes.

But with all its economic unity, M. Fay finds three distinct geographical and social zones in the country. There is the East, not very different from western Europe, attracted toward Europe by tradition, interest and desire, seafaring and seeking European markets; the Middle West, nationalistic and interested only in the American Continent, ignorant of Europe and despising it; and the Far West, yet in its infancy, drawn toward the sea, but whose distant Pacific overseas seems not the abode of sister nations but a land to dream about, to hunt in and to exploit.

The social zones are those of the non-Caucasian races, black, yellow and red, together with the immigrants who speak English not at all or badly; the middle classes, from the factory worker up to Edison, who speak English, make money and vote. The American bourgeoisie, he finds, is ignorant, moral, good looking, healthy, and limited, clever in politics, shrewd in economics, expert in baseball, more comfortable and generally more polite than the mass of Europeans. Above it is the university world, with its graduates. This dominated in the Administrations of Roosevelt, Taft and Wilson; the middle class in that of Harding, while the masses of the humble and discontented are behind Borah.

America is ignorant not of what is going on in Europe, for its press keeps it well informed, but of what Europe is. The American cannot conceive that a Continent hardly bigger than the Union can contain five distinct civilizations and twenty different nations, each intensely conscious of its differences from the others.

The only American solution for the ills of the world, according to M. Fay, is unification through federation.

3 March 1923

French Writer Thrills at Wonder of New York; City of Efficiency, "Forest of Giant Cubes"

New York is to a European city as a modern Picasso is to an old Rembrandt.

You may love Rembrandt. But you don't take your first look at a Picasso and cry out, "Horrible! There's no Rembrandt in that! " You are just so astounded that you don't even try to explain, define, or defend.

That is a thumbnail abridgement of a long and laudatory article by Georgette Leblanc, French writer, in the Paris *Comoedia,* giving her impression of the American metropolis.

"It is a Cubist city," she exclaims. "It was constructed by a new pleiad of artists—architect-engineers. It will remain as the representative of an epoch which turned the laws of art upside down.

"When I left for New York, I didn't go there in order to see Athens, or Constantinople, or Bagdad. I love Rembrandt, but when I saw a Picasso for the first time, I didn't say, 'Terrible! Nothing like Rembrandt! '

"I cried, 'What beauty! ' "

Americans Are Modest

"My guide, a New York newspaperman, apologized at every turn. He thought I ought to be surprised by so much ugliness! It was he who surprised me. Later I became accustomed to the ignorant modesty of Americans.

"After all, to understand is not the business of the average folk; it is the business of the elite and of the artists. These latter have, in general, seen enough things and enough countries to be free from the tyranny of comparisons.

"I found in New York nothing of what I had seen in any of the capitals of Europe. New city, new conception, new air (the air over there is bracing). A city which borrows nothing from the others and which does not worry about making imitations, if you except certain older buildings whose neo-Gothic quality shocks you somewhat. . . .

"You hear criticisms of the hardness of the city, of its being cut up like a checkerboard, cut at right angles, forming endless, enormous blocks. No ornament, nothing to amuse and attract the eye to its interminable walls, and never a tree. . . . That last is one of the most prevalent criticisms of New York.

Trees Out Of Place

"But, imagine what a figure would be cut alongside these skyscrapers by trees that would be charming along our boulevards! Useless to expose them to such a humiliation. A tree with its romantic curves is not in place in this forest of giant cubes."

Special reference is made in the article to the synchronized traffic movement of Fifth Avenue, where policemen in towers by means of colored discs and lights, without even a thin whistle, cause the whole motor mass to move up the street in long, well-spaced pulsations.

The last part, "City of Light," deals mainly with the Great White Way.

"Broadway is a luminous bridge," says the writer, "which reaches from dusk to dawn! " The dazzling, magnificent mass of window lights from the great sky-scrapers also has caught her imagination.

"The speeded-up life of New York," she concludes, "does not weigh heavily. You play with it. It jumps, bounds, falls, and rebounds, like a ball. Some day it will fall 'the other way,' but there isn't any time to think about that."

30 January 1929

Women Dominate American Civilization, Maître Honegger Discovers—Men Are Too Busy Working To Pay the Bills

America's civilization is dominated by women. The women make up the audiences in the concert halls, they patronize all the arts and they rule the country by meddling with its laws. The men pass their time working in order to pay the bills.

That is the picture of America obtained by Maître Arthur Honegger, the famous French composer, during a three months' concert tour of the country. Maître Honegger, creator of "Le Roi David" and other brilliant symphonic works, arrived in Paris Sunday after crossing on the French liner *Rochambeau*.

Seated at his working table in his apartment on the Rue Duperré, Maître Honegger smilingly told a *Tribune* representative that America's civilization was "really something difficult to understand." He admitted that he had been well received wherever he gave a concert—but only by women.

"Women," said Maître Honegger with great emphasis, "are leading the American civilization somewhere. I don't know where. In every concert hall, I found that the audience was dominated largely by women. Of course, they are only interested superficially. I suppose that the men are so busy working away that they have no time for music. I was received in homes of several prominent persons—by women. A few times, I was introduced to the men of the family. 'How do you do, pleased to meet you,' these gentlemen would say. That was all. I never saw them again."

Maître Honegger tapped his fingers nervously on the blue blotter in front of him. He opened and closed a volume containing his dramatic psalm "Judith." He turned down the collar of his heavy, red and black dressing robe.

"C'est grave," he said. "This civilization which is dominated by women. Nevertheless, your country is really remarkable. It performs in a big way. America has some remarkable symphony orchestras. I found the Boston and Chicago orchestras the best. Your people give these orchestras good support. You are generous about such things. You don't impose the heavy, burdensome tax which the French Government imposes on our concert halls. The public rallies to the support of these orchestras but they are not so appreciative of good music as a French audience."

Maître Honegger said he would not understand the attitude of the American critics toward European musicians.

"They asked me if I liked jazz. I told them I was fond of syncopated music but they thought I was joking with them. I think they expected me to play the snob.

"I don't like the silly, sentimental songs that come out of tin pan alley," sighed the Maître. "It's awful. Along Broadway, there are fifty immense loud speakers screeching out the latest trash. They wake you up in the morning and they keep you from sleeping at night. *Çà, c'est assommant, vous savez, c'est assommant."*

Maître Honegger hummed a few of the dreadful tunes which he described as "boring and silly."

He said he was fond of the talkie movies, although he found the American movies to be made up of canned sentiment which was handed out indiscreetly. The music in the movie palaces was even more sentimental than the movies, he declared.

"I think the talkie films are great. Imagine making a permanent document of a Chaliapin concert," he said.

4 April 1929

French Critics Find Americans Take Intellectual Quantity for Quality

Speaking of the intellectual progress of Americans, it is said that "number and quantity give to this people the illusion of quality." Further, "the American is powerless to create in the intellectual field. His philosophies do not direct, they follow the crowds."

It is clear enough what our French critics have in mind. They mean that the purveyors of wisdom in the United States, more than anywhere else simply reflect back the simple moral notions of the ordinary man. They are regimented, and help in turn to regiment others. The French clearly have the advantage on us, if thinking differently be a good. They positively encourage mental eccentricity, or are not shocked by it, whereas the United States has become the classic country of thinking by contagion.

We reap advantage from this thinking by contagion which, I imagine, will never be known in France. If a sound idea be really made a subject of propaganda, especially among a people susceptible to it, it may make its way through all strata of society and stick. Thus, because a scientific attitude toward health, sanitation and child-raising has been accepted in America, we have got rid of more physical superstitions than any other people. It is a fair conjecture that the infant death-rate would fall in France, if the American attitude could take the place of old granny notions.

On the moral side, the French may with justice say that we are extraordinarily sheepish, though I wonder if candor could say that we are more hidebound than are French provincials. The stock of notions by which we live is small, but satisfactory for us—optimism, faith in "clean" living and in work, faith in democracy of rather simple organization. The academic leaders of youth are touchingly unanimous about spreading the prevailing gospel, as any one can see by just following the commencement addresses. Never does any one of them venture to suggest that life is a mystery, full of sorrow and deception.

The intellectual leaders of the non-academic life say the same, if more vigorously; hence the vogue of books to prove that Christ was a business, or an advertising man, or a realtor. Such easy popular philosophy naturally seems superficial to the cultivated Frenchman.

In regimented intellectual life, or the business of education, we and the French may be said to stand at the opposite poles in theory. We have, as they say, gone in for quantity. The case with which the whole population in the United States can have access to higher scales of learning has done undoubted good; it has brought forth talent which, in France, would be stifled from the lack of funds to get an adequate start.

One last observation, made by M. Régis Michaud, is worthy of attention: that in great part Americans are a people of "the worn out and the neurotic." No figures are given, and I have none available, nor do I see how any are possible except for those extreme cases of nervousness which we call insanity. It is then a matter of impression, gathered possibly from our craze for jazz, the inhuman nervous tension of our business and industrial life, from the air of uneasy boredom which so many of our compatriots exhibit.

If M. Michaud be right, it is interesting but hardly alarming. Presumably our constitutions will in 50 years get adjusted to the exigencies of the machine age. It remains curious, however, as I have had chances for observing among the youth whom at one time I was charged to instruct, how many of the children of our rich people were nervous wrecks. These quivering weaklings were the descendants of the pioneers who conquered a continent. There is a startling paradox for Europeans, but then they know that we are the people of paradoxes.

Alex Small
10 October 1929

American Puritans

Most of us have always believed that all good Americans "go to Paris when they die," that is to say they love the French capital and France above all else in the world. Now Paul Morand, author of *New York* and other clever books of a cosmopolitan nature, tells us that there are two sorts of Americans, and that while one sort loves Paris the other loathes and abhors it. He bases this theory on his impressions of the United States and its inhabitants gained while collecting material for *New York* and his new novel of American life.

There are, according to Paul Morand, writing in *Le Journal,* Americans who have a native dread of Parisian influences and resist them with all their power. These are what he calls the "Puritans of America," whose moral sense is offended by the freedom of French life. Their refusal to succumb finally develops into genuine hatred.

Personally, we admit that we have never met any of these Americans who hate Paris. Plenty of American "Puritans" come over to France every year, but their moral indignation is generally tempered with secret delight. To M. Morand belongs the glory of having discovered them in his new book.

"There are two reactions of the average American towards France," he says. "There is the American who sets himself to love and understand France and is so profoundly stirred that he cannot live anywhere else any more. He is lost forever to his native country; the individual has triumphed over his race; the joy of living has killed the Puritan. But there are other Americans who defend themselves against this danger, who repress tendencies which conflict with what they believe to be their duty, who pull themselves together and become our irreconcilable enemies. This is the explanation of the hostility which certain American senators manifest regarding France."

All real Americans, according to M. Morand, are Puritans at heart. There was a moment in the 16th century, he points out, when France might have succumbed to Puritanism. Even today there exists a certain Puritan rigor in such French cities as Lyons. But France in general happily surmounted this menace.

"In general," he remarks, "we have not that religious fanaticism, that fervor of work in common preceded and followed by prayer, that unhealthy horror of sex and pleasure that distinguishes the Just. It is true that the upheavals of the last few years have created a certain tolerance between the peoples; but nevertheless Frenchmen will like Barcelona, New Orleans, Lisbon, San Francisco and Buenos Aires, which are rationalist cities, better than London, Boston, Moscow or modern Rome, which are Puritanical towns.

"In France, every real American must feel himself on foreign soil. Paris café terraces, French wine drunk openly, love that does not seek concealment, all this marvelous excess of personal liberty of which there is scarcely today another example in Europe, must amaze and trouble the mind of the American Puritan. And although there are Americans who are not Puritans, they are not real Americans, and in any case they are not the Americans who made America what it is."

6 July 1930

Americans Need Philosophy of Older, Sadder Nations To Confront Crisis

It has been a general sentiment of humanity that the miseries of those who have always been poor and unfortunate are worthy of little interest. The best that can be accorded them is contemptuous pity—charity in the worst sense of the word.

Real pity, indulgent tenderness, is reserved for those who have fallen from the seats of the mighty, for dethroned princes and impoverished magnates. The latter, we feel, and probably quite rightly, have the harder lot. What difference does a little more misery make to those who have never known anything else?

Regarding Americans, as compared with other peoples, amid the troubles of our times, this old idea has recently been expressed by the brilliant French economist, M. Lucien Romier. Americans have in one way, he says in effect, been harder to hit than any of the others. To understand how, he gives Frenchmen a brief analysis of the American soul, which seems to me at least as good as most analyses of a like nature.

The United States, writes M. Romier, is above all "an economic agglomeration." The social bond and the economic bond coincide; all individuals and groups are interdependent in the pursuit of one ambition—riches. The American, in fact, has no conception of social relations except as they have something to do with business.

The American woman, too, is immured in this economic circle. "She, even more than the man, submits to the prestige of money, the attraction and intoxication of getting rich. The American marriage forces the husband ever to 'produce' more to cover the expenditures of a wife who is ever consuming more."

American patriotism likewise is economic in its basis. The American's pride in his country is largely a consciousness of the practical advantages in being a citizen of the United States. At least a third of the population is attached to America by gratitude for an improved economic situation.

"Hence," is the conclusion, "the profound disarray of a special nature which an economic and financial crisis of exceptional duration has provoked in the American imagination and soul. That also explains the almost mystic hope of the American crowd in a brusque reversal of the situation, and their simple belief that it would be sufficient to find some device, a boom, or some juggling trick, to set prosperity in motion again. It is as if a young automobilist whose sole pleasure is in speed should try his motor and still persist in stepping on the starter."

It seems to me a valid explanation of the panic state of mind into which so many of our compatriots have fallen. An injury to the pocketbook is never fatal, says French popular wisdom. That may be true enough for the French but it certainly does not apply to many individuals, and even to some peoples.

When a pocketbook, and all that goes with it—pleasure, power, and prestige—is irretrievably ruined, they find that their honor has been touched and that there is nothing more worth living for. Even in France do not ruined millionaires sometimes shoot themselves?

It is easy to imagine that today millions of Americans are suffering far more acutely from something other than the thought of the unpaid grocer's bills. Each has been humiliated, diminished in his self-respect, by this inhuman concatenation of circumstances which will not allow him to live in the style he has been accustomed to within the last decade.

Slower and sadder peoples do not take such crises so tragically. When you no longer can live handsomely, you just live poorly, but you go on living and making the best of it. Above all, you take such troubles as being in the nature of things, like stomach-aches and disappointments in love. The average American of our day is probably only too inclined to think of them as something abnormal, monstrous, and outrageous.

What, it may be wondered, has become of the national heroine, Pollyanna? Now, if ever, is the time for her, as we say, to be doing her stuff. She should be teaching our compatriots not to shake their fists in barren rage at the immortal gods. Life is pretty good anyway, Pollyanna should be whispering in their ears; there is plenty of fun to be had on the cheap, and it is silly to be crying because some of your toys have been taken away from you.

That is a big trouble, too, that people have lost their toys. It should be a revelation of how much the American spirit was occupied with games and gadgets. The biggest and most exciting game was chasing the dollar, and now millions cannot play at it. Incidentally, there is revealed how much of the vaunted culture of Americans was pure window-dressing, a mere function of power and prestige.

If it had been real, now is the time when it would be a consolation to everyone. But as a people we were not yet ready to store up treasures in heaven.

Alex Small
26 October 1931

The Man from Rapallo

Ezra Pound and Passports

To the Editor of *The Tribune:*

Sir:

"850,000 Enter U.S. Illegally." Good. If anybody wanted proof of the idiotic hypocrisy of our officials re passports, here it is. It cannot be too clearly understood that the sole reason why we have short time passports at high rates is to pour money into the pockets of the state department in order that that small clique of mastoid and malevolent office holders can be independent of congress; i.e., have a boodle purse, the strings of which are under no legislative control.

The drivelling inefficiency of measures alleged to be useful is definitely proved. The people who suffer are the orderly travelers going about their lawful occasions for business or study. The crooks either have faked passports, or they find a nice bit of frontier and walk over it.

The annoyance began under Wilson, the most tyrannous ideologue whom the American people ever elected. It continued under Harding, of whom the less said the better for the international respectability of our country. It is a very nice little test case. We have a very good opportunity to see now and at once whether little Cal can do anything but keep quiet.

Ezra Pound
4 December 1924

Ezra Pound

Pound Denounces Idiocy of U.S. Mail Act

Ezra Pound still retains a healthy "disrespect for the misdirection of our unfortunate nation," particularly as regards the federal statute against sending obscene material through the mail. He believes that Section 211 of the U. S. Criminal code affords conclusive evidence against the doctrine of evolution.

Pound was provoked into making these remarks by reading a recent editorial in *The Tribune* on "Reform Laws in Practice." The editorial told how a section of the Mann act had been misused to settle a personal grudge and contended that this incident . . . showed the impossibility and stupidity of trying to reform individuals by law. And "this little editorial," remarked Pound, "is quite to the point, but again omits one factor of the case, i.e., the actual text of the legislation. Until they see the actual words, the people will never understand the nature of these laws."

1 November 1927

Ezra Pound's $50 Book Ruled out of U.S. Mail by P.O. Moral Critics

Ezra Pound is grumbling. He doesn't think much of American postal officials or for that matter any American officials, and this particular grievance is that those postal authorities have just confiscated a copy of his *Sixteen Cantos* and are threatening to prosecute the bookseller to whom it was addressed. This was one of an edition of 94 published in Paris by the Three Mountains Press in 1925 and valued at $50. The complaint of the postal persons is that Pound used words and ideas in his poetry which are not quite fit for the *jeune fille* to see right out in print.

This is the first time that any of Pound's writings have gotten into trouble in America, although literary America is well acquainted with these *Cantos*. . . . Pound himself is surprised that the authorities should have found anything wrong with them. There is this also to be said for the poems: that even if the charges are true, one is forced to understand not only the modern languages but also Latin and Greek to understand their subtleties, and Pound suspects that in that case the *jeune fille* is quite safe from shock.

8 June 1929

Montparnasse Forever!

To the Editor of *The Tribune:*

Sir:

Since your letter box is so full of wails from the Butter and Eggs men who don't like Montparnasse, perhaps we might say that there are two banks of the Seine. Montparnasse is inhabited by a few thousand people who are engaged in making the little trifles that the big bellies and profiteers will in time be buying at *Record Prices* such as they now pay for Tiepolos and Rafaels. After 4 p.m. it is also inhabited by a few thousand boobs and butter and eggs men who have heard that art is nice but naughty and who go away with a grouch because they haven't got something for nothing.

The other bank of the Seine harbours the detrimental part of the American colony, rich illiterates still looking for Marie Antoinette's bed slippers, or for Louis Philippe whom they confuse with Louis XIV. These people are still hunting for French Society. They never buy or read a book. They are no better and not much more ignorant than the what-used-to-think-itself "society" in Philadelphia or Boston. Occasionally one of the more obese tries to break into French society by petting a few gallic lame ducks or debilitated novelists. They have no sense of art or civilization, though they occasionally approve of someone's putting a roof on a french national monument. No idea is further from their occiputs than that of participating in any form of intellectual life. No all-seeing journalist has ever yet discovered any one of them in an intelligent act, though a conscientious journalist might waste his time trying, and the tabulation of his results wd. be of interest to determined students of pathology. These people have not even the virtues supposed to have inhered in plutocracies of the slightly better plutocratic epochs. They represent the scum of all the demoded snobisms of the past 230 years. In comparison with them the lower ranks of Montparnasse, the least successful of the Montparnos who once wanted to write or paint, shine out as human beings wd. among animals or as a civilized man wd. shine in halls of congress.

Vive le Carrefour
Ezra Pound
11 March 1930

Pound Paints Peccadilloes of Pedants in Money Murdered Marts of Learning

Ezra Pound sits upon his sun terrace at Rapallo, with the deep blue waters of the Tigullian Gulf reflected in his blue eyes; the classic ilex on the mountains lifts a green garland against the azure skies. Men always have done and always will do things with their pens because of the soul's urge. Mr. Pound's soul looks straight out of his deep blue eyes.

"Washington, Thomas Jefferson, Quincy Adams tried hard to lay a foundation for the civilization of America," says Mr. Pound. "Are their successors, Borah, Smoot—Smoot, an insult to every literate American, or are they men with real, i.e. financial power? How many combine with their economic power a sense of responsibility? Taft had been advocating the education of diplomats and politicians. Taft said he approved of sending Wilson to Europe, thinking to educate Wilson in the European situation. Unfortunately Taft supported Harding's rural simplicity, doubtless from party loyalty. Filling up Government with inferior men is expensive.

"You can choose between the elected politician and a financier. Carnegie is one of the best recent examples of a man who sincerely desired to civilize America. He left enormous endowments. But what happens? These endowments fall into hands of men of the academic type impervious to the present. Take the men directing the Carnegie Peace Foundation. Nothing will persuade those people to study the causes of war. They study writers who wrote 300 years ago, or the effects of the war, for example, on Chile. Carnegie's Foundations were made with definitely declared intentions. The libraries are useful. They mostly supply mediocre novels to the masses, ten per cent of the 'possible efficiency.' They lack the mechanism for stimulating the publication of just those books which most truly constitute the intellectual life of Europe, or even of such translations as should be published in English for the use of the serious reader who is trying to live a contemporary intellectual life. Why should not a man in Texas or in Montana lead as actively contemporary a life as a man in Toulouse or Perugia? Why not?"

American Universities

"It is appalling to think that our universities today are in the same state as the Conservatory of Fontainebleau, though Fontainebleau has less excuse. It is geographically nearer the center of action. The Fontainebleau Conservatory is here pretending to exist. It ignores George Antheil's existence. Were Antheil a German or a Swede even his Ambassador would know he existed. The German Ambassador knew he existed even four years ago. Not America today but Vienna and the Frankfort Music Festival must acknowledge and honor George Antheil of New Jersey. And Fontainebleau is run for hide-bound professors.

"With the radio and the gramophone, music today, as in the Elizabethan period, is an accomplishment. Personal performance of music offers a livelihood to a decreasing number of players. The serious student of 1930 would in 1940 consider that he had been fortunate if he had come into contact with the great contemporary composers, as he perfectly well could at Fontainebleau. . . . A Texas University professor might have an excuse for not recognizing Antheil."

And Mr. Pound continued, with that half-melancholy gentleness of manner habitual to him. "But in America there are no institutions functioning at maximum efficiency, except the banks. The banks do add to the amenities of life. At least they do what they can to mitigate the manias of the Washington bureaucracy. We do not have to spend hours cashing a check. Actual society is feudal. The fortunate freeman is the feudatory of a bank. His enemy is the official bureaucrat. The less fortunate not free man is the feudatory of Mr. Ford.

"Democracy of the alleged government is to some extent camouflage. It has a mania for interfering with the normal and useful activities of the citizen. It loathes the amenities.

"Twenty years ago there were three potential energies that could have been used for the civilizing of wilderness—newspapers, universities and people doing advanced work in literature. Since then there has been a definite *rapprochement* between newspapers and literature. The universities do not join. The Carnegie Peace foundation is represented largely by academic persons. Our big endowments are often sabotaged by bureaucrats, by non-productive parasites. They could distribute the results of such research as they consent to do at less cost and to a greater number of people, if they would employ an A-1 journalist to make a report every year or every four months. By an A-1 journalist, I mean men like Lincoln Steffens, or Albert Londres. They fill me with more respect than the second and tenth-rate novelists and *gens de lettres*.

"Of the University of Pennsylvania fellowships, a professor there wrote me 'the University is not here for the unusual man! ' Then your university system is dead. The American professor or librarian dislikes buying books by contemporaries when they are first published. They prefer to wait twenty years and then buy unimportant letters of celebrities from second-hand dealers.

"Another impediment is college spirit. In a mediaeval university a professor expounded his opinion, if he had one. I don't advocate having in a lot of uncontrolled cranks to pervert the minds of the young. I think we could in a limited way and with advantage let in a few contemporary minds; let them talk. Johns Hopkins started something. There should be five or six universities that could deal with literature and general ideas as Johns Hopkins deals with science: be centers of activity and not archives. The institutions founded professedly to foster the arts are in great measure nullified by a gang of professors or selection committees who know nothing about art or how it is produced. I believe one might improve the system by having a largish board of electors who at least professed an interest in the subject and let the candidates for directorship contend for paid jobs, the pay going to the directors with the most active programs. There ought to be a provision for the ideal university, for the publication of serious works and freedom from censorship for serious literature."

Mary Howell
19 April 1930

Europe Rearms

To the Editor of *The Tribune:*

Sir:

Your two eds. remind one that America had a president as recently as 1908 or thereabouts. Further deductions might confirm the solid belief of at least one reader that Wilson was both a fool and a scoundrel. Whatever Theodore's limitations were, he would have made his presence felt the day Belgium was invaded or possibly three days before. It might have saved a good deal of trouble. The other president mentioned in the same column (Hoover) had an idea that the U.S.A. should keep OUT of European affairs. So far as America's foreign policy is concerned I doubt if this idea can be improved on. As Europe only wants to be let off its debts in order to buy more guns, perhaps debt reductions could be based on agreement that Europeans should murder only each other.

The political divisions in Germany might be clearer if each of the German parties would tell us plainly WHICH firm of munition makers they wish to get the stores from.

Ezra Pound
29 November 1932

Rearmament

To the Editor of *The Tribune:*

Sir:

The damned and driveling hypocrisy of the League of Nations shows up neatly in the simultaneous rebuke to Nippon and the full steam ahead order for selling guns. The real righteousness shining in primal purity. Can't you follow the lead of some of the old home papers and print a few comparative figures showing at least which sections of the international *mitrailleuse* combine are getting which gobs of graviee?

The embargo just sure would lift at this moment when the "need" (O blessed word) for powder is rising.

Ezra Pound
27 February 1933

England and America

To the Editor of *The Tribune:*

Sir:

I see by *La Stampa* that "Garwin" of the London *Observer* is asking Mr. Roosevelt not to stop with saving America but to save the world. If this is the Garwin whose death I hoped I had read of, it might be well to remind him and the rest of Britain that one American President was made more of a fool of than was strictly necessary by responding to such appeals. As the *Observer* has contributed in no little degree to the suppression of economic discussion in England it might be well to ask that particular component of the British hierarchy to begin a little house cleaning on its own before bothering Frankie who has enough to do for the moment, and hasn't yet got round to examining Herbie's and Andy's past.

As long as England continues to violate and ignore every principle of sound domestic economy the U.S. will do well to attend to her own affairs FIRST.

Ezra Pound
13 March 1933

V The Arts

Even local French periodicals in the twenties ran hard to keep up with what was actually happening, or seemed to be happening, in Parisian salons, garrets, and ateliers. And *Tribune* critics, despite the availability of the French coverage, fairly lost their breath, too, trying to describe an international art community, alive and surging with ideas and creations. That they failed can hardly detract from their record. Often practitioners of the arts they surveyed—Elliot Paul, Irving Schwerké, Don Brown and Eugene Jolas stand out—they mingled easily with traditionalists and avant-gardists, listening, observing, discussing, evaluating, and ultimately judging. Their estimates, concise and unequivocal and never dull, rested on standards rigorous enough to demolish some works and enhance others, and to earn for themselves only little opprobrium and considerable respect.

The dean of all the *Tribune* critics was Irving Schwerké, an honor justly bestowed upon this inveterate music critic, who between 1921 and 1934 attended an incalculable number of operas, concerts and recitals, in and out of Paris. His musical knowledge and reputation grew tremendously as he locomoted tirelessly over the Continent, conducting an Italian jazz band at Casenatico in the presence of Il Duce, organizing in Germany the first festival of American music ever given in Europe, and back in Paris sponsoring the first radio concert performed by American artists living abroad. His taste was unerring, his standards firm, particularly when he scrutinized Americans. Besides George Antheil, Schwerké scolded Copland, he praised Menuhin, he ridiculed Ezra Pound's compositions, he acclaimed Paul Whiteman, and he warned Americans in Paris against tooting their nationality as a means of gaining entry into the European musical world.

Serving the paper nearly as long as Schwerké and with equal distinction was art critic B. J. Kospoth, who, along with Eugene Jolas and Louis Gay, contributed articles to the *Tribune*'s "Sunday Magazine Section," a supplement devoted mainly to the arts, which Roscoe Ashworth edited for several months in the mid-twenties. Kospoth's domain, physically smaller than his colleague's, was nonetheless as rich. Fond of making meticulous examinations of a painter's style and life, he formed a preference for contemporary artists who had lived or were living on the Left Bank, among them Modigliani, Picabia, Kisling, Van Dongen, Alexander Calder, Jo Davidson, Hilaire Hiler, Man Ray, his *Tribune* colleague Don Brown, and Robert Hallowell. It was the last who, in an interview with Kospoth, so impressed the critic with his remarks on the expatriated artist that Hallowell's words might stand for Kospoth's own position: an "artist is like a field plowed and harrowed, and prepared for the sowing. Whatever environment puts the seed of inspiration into that ground is the best environment for the artist to work in. The plowed field, so to speak, is

American whether, for the moment, it has transplanted itself to France or to Zululand."

Theater coverage, though somewhat less extensive, was capably done by several Tribuners, particularly Florence Gilliam and Irving Schwerké. Miss Gilliam, arriving in Paris in 1921, began her career abroad by founding with her husband, Arthur Moss, an occasional contributor to the *Tribune,* the first English-language publication of arts and letters on the Continent. They named it *Gargoyle,* and for it Miss Gilliam did all the theatrical criticism, in addition to serving as Paris correspondent for New York's *Theatre Magazine,* and in the late twenties, for Erskine Gwynne's *Boulevardier.*

From the start book reviewing, including abundant news of little magazines and presses which in the twenties and thirties lived and died like moths, assumed a prominent place in the *Tribune,* and during Ashworth's tenure as editor of the "Sunday Magazine" the roster of reviewers included Louis Gay, Eugene Jolas, and Ford Madox Ford, whom Ashworth signed to write a dozen "Literary Causeries," which to no one's surprise ranged from esoteric discourses on Conrad to explanations of Tristan Tzara's catalytic value. And as the Latin Quarter became more populous, and reputedly more literary, the *Tribune*'s coverage expanded, due largely to the efforts of its new reviewer, Elliot Paul, until it was by far the most comprehensive offered by any of the English-language newspapers in Paris. Besides reviews, the book page usually carried a listing of best sellers in America, a "literary letter" from London and another from New York, written by Sidney Dark, Gene Markey, or Frank Swinnerton; several regular columns of book news, such as Paul's "From a Litterateur's Notebook" and Jolas' "Leaves from A Paris Diary"; H. L. Mencken's syndicated column; and, after Waverley Root became editor of the book page, a lively department called the "Voice of Book Page Readers," managed by Root in masterly fashion, as, indeed, he conducted the whole page. Root made the *Tribune*'s book page the envy of the Paris *Herald,* which failed miserably when it tried to copy it. And even after Root became news editor and had to write the book page while supervising the flow of copy on the night desk, it retained its reputation for comprehensive and perceptive reviews.

H. F.

Painting

Dadaists War on "Tactilism," Latest Art Form

The dadaists and futurists, who have been brother enemies ever since the inception of the former, have come to open war. What it is all about only they themselves know, for no outsider, even if he does pretend to understand futurism and Signor Marinetti, can ever understand dadaism. Even the dadaists don't.

They, however, have taken the offensive in their war against the futurists, and, apparently jealous of their place as the very newest of all the new movements, they have banded together to brand as utter foolishness all the works of the futurists and especially "tactilism," the latest form of art discovered by the futurist leader, Signor Marinetti.

In the opinion of the dadaists, "tactilism" is just rot, and in true futurist fashion, for they are descendants in direct line of the futurist movement, they scoff at all allegiance to their former leaders. They poured scorn on Marinetti when he tried to expound his great discovery before them.

"Tactilism" is the art of touch, which according to the futurist leader has been sadly neglected by mankind. Marinetti arranges objects which, when touched in succession, tell a whole story, just as a poem or a sonata unfolds itself. Thus he has written with square inches of different kinds of cloth, paper, feathers, and other odds and ends a poem for his fingers to read. This poem he calls "Paris."

The feathers, he explained to the audience, represent the lightness and gaiety of the French people, conveyed to the senses and the brain by the touch. When one comes to a strip of silver paper, one knows one is crossing the Seine. And a score of other places and impressions in the capital, including the bustle of traffic are supposed to be conveyed by the brush of fingers over cloths of different texture, at least to those whose nervous systems are supposed to be properly organized.

17 January 1921

An Evening of Dadaism

In the United States "nothing" is defined as not anything; in Paris it is "Dada." That is, it is nothing but pure nonsense, although the Dadas or Dadaists believe they have a serious mission in life, in protesting against everything that is recognized in art, science, music, religion and what not. They are the *ne plus ultra* in artistic anarchy.

There is no better way for one who is bored to be brought back to normalcy than to attend a soiree Dada; nor is there a better way for a sane person to lose his mind, easily and painlessly, than by attending the same soiree.

Being simply bored Friday evening we wandered into the Galerie Montaigne. At first glance we thought we had made a mistake and were in the private salon of an asile d'alienes. For, despite the fact that good-looking and well-dressed people sat about quietly, and therefore, intelligently, the decorations of the room bespoke what, to be charitable, we shall call a complete disregard even for the most advanced theories of cubist and futurist art.

And it was to be a musical evening. The stage was set. At the left of the room was a small elevated platform and a full length mirror; in the center of the room a buff-colored tent covered something which later proved to be, from the sounds that issued forth, a piano and at the left was the apotheosis of Dada—nothing.

Shortly after nine the concert began. Mme. E. Bujaud, at the piano, sang "La Chanson du Catalogue de l'Exposition" which, so far as tone and harmony went, was most satisfactory; and it served the purpose of giving us a much-needed lesson in counting in French. As the last note was vibrating through the Galerie, many noises were heard from the rear of the hall. The Dada idea of the president of the republic of Liberia, clothed in black and with his face to match, strolled in, escorted by several of the most prominent Dadaists. He examined the pictures on the walls, all the creations of Dada artists urged on by Dada notions, and "très Charmanted" everyone, without exception, proving that he is a loyal Dada himself. As a token of the esteem in which he held the emancipated skill of the Dadas, he presented each of the receiving committee with a candle, which he lighted, and which he as quickly extinguished and repocketed.

M. Louis Aragon next appeared on the balcony in his rendition of "A l'Evangile." M. Aragon should make a good successor to Billy Sunday, for his voice has depth and power, and while he did not indulge in slang so profusely as does the Reverend Billy, he read entertainingly from some French book not the Bible. At the conclusion of his Dada exorcism, M. Aragon disappeared to make room for Valentin Parnak, who descended from the balcony to the stage, via a ladder which everyone had been wondering about. M. Parnak has divested himself of his coat, and had strapped on his arm a large silver foot, such as one is accustomed to see in the States outside parlors of chiropody. With the aid of the foot on his arms, M. Parnak executed an admirable interpretation of "La Volaille

Miraculeuse," in a style that, with proper training and control, should bring him fame and fortune as an exponent of the classic terpsichorean art.

Georges Ribemont-Dessaignes, whose work of Dada art "L'Arbre a Violin" occupies a prominent place in the exhibition, next read "Le Livre des Rois" and declared that he was, in turn, an angel, Jeanne d'Arc and Mme. Sans-Gene. His skit was slangly, amusing, for American consumption, but needed soap in spots. But the French audience was enchanted.

During the entr'acte, we inquired of M. Joliboit, who is the conductor of the orchestra when he is not repairing china, whether the balance of the program, if there was a balance, would be given. He replied that it would depend on the audience entirely.

Truly, a novel protest against art and music and accepted standards of things in general, was the Dada evening. It should go big in Greenwich Village where hair is long and art, even as the Dadas admit, is short. It is quite the smartest state of mind at present, anyway, this Dadaism.

13 June 1921

The Problem of Fujita

In an age that has witnessed Japanese statesmen presiding over the councils of the European nations, it seems only natural to see a Japanese artist occupying a place in the front rank of modern French painters. Some discern in this diplomatic and intellectual penetration of the West by the East a symptom of Europe's decadence, others hail it as welcome evidence that Kipling's famous axiom is invalidated and that East and West are meeting at last. However that may be, it is from this portentous viewpoint that it seems necessary to examine the work of Fujita, the Japanese painter, who has won fame and recognition more rapidly than any of his Western comrades in Montparnasse or Montmartre within the last few years.

The haunting problem of East and West, which has become since the war the dominant cultural and political problem of the world, is ever present in Fujita's paintings, and this mystery—though most beholders, and perhaps even the artist himself, may not be conscious of it—is the secret of their attraction.

Fujita is not an isolated figure—if he were his achievement would be less significant. They are already legion, the Japanese, Russians, Armenians, Levantines, who are imposing the fascination of their strange artistic personality on Europe and America, in painting, in letters, in music, and on the stage. Fujita is but one of these Oriental conquistadors, and the fact that he has conquered Paris, so long regarded as the international capital of art gives his victory peculiar significance.

The same mysterious force that has compelled Japan to take such a prominent part in Western affairs since the war would seem to have made

Fujita come to Montparnasse and become a French painter. This artistic imagination alone is curious. One would think that an artist privileged to record the ineffable beauties of Japanese landscape and life would not feel attracted towards the hideous vulgarity of modern Western cities. And yet Fujita has felt this impulse, and left the wonderful pyramid of the Fuji to paint the factory chimneys of the Parisian suburbs. . . .

The Japanese, we are told, regard Fujita as an absolutely Westernized painter, who has severed all bonds linking him with the East's artistic traditions. That may or may not be a sincere expression of the Japanese attitude towards Fujita, but it is at best a very superficial judgment. Fujita paints the same subjects as the modern painters of the West, in a manner that shows their technical influence, but he sees them through Eastern eyes. All the intellectual element in his work—and Fujita is a very intellectual painter—is purely Japanese. And for us the fascination of his paintings lies in their revelation of how the Western world of ours, its cities, its women, its civilisation, appear today to the ancient and reawakening races of the East.

That hitherto impenetrable secret: what is back of the Oriental mind contemplating Western life—is disclosed, fitfully at least, and most often involuntarily, in Fujita's paintings, as in the works of all the strange men of the East, who have come to live in our midst since the war, professing themselves humble converts to the superiority of our art and civilisation. Dark glimpses of it are unveiled in his pictures of the proletarian streets and suburbs of the great city, in his curious attempts to penetrate Christian religious mysticism, above all in his painting of women. Only his animals and flower pieces, significantly enough, are free from this underlying note of concealed criticism.

Like Kuniyoshi, the Japanese painter who has made his home in America, and whose work is, in some respects, even more interesting than his Parisian compatriot's, Fujita is a problematical personality. The East has always been a problem to the West, and since it has begun ostentatiously to assimilate Western civilisation it has become a more complicated problem than ever. Fujita ceases to be a problem only when, with the sureness of line of the greatest Japanese artists, he paints trained dogs and cuddling pussy-cats, or slim blossoming twigs in a slender vase—in a word, when for a moment he allows himself to become a pure Oriental once more, heedless of the Western life about him.

B. J. Kosposth
8 February 1925

The Tragedy of Modigliani

When Amedeo Modigliani, just five years ago, had coughed out the last drops of his lifeblood at the Charité hospital, his former Bohemian comrades, and some of the connoisseurs and dealers who were soon to realize small fortunes through his paintings, made a collection to give him a splendid funeral. Three thousand francs' worth of Riviera flowers covered the bier, and as the procession passed along the streets the policemen—the same policemen who had many a time dragged the half-clothed painter out of the gutter and locked him in filthy cells—stood to attention and saluted, impressed by so much magnificence. And Picasso, walking behind the hearse with Max Jacob, Vlaminck, Francis Carco, and the rest, most of whom had already succeeded in making good their escape from Bohemia, turned and muttered: "He is avenged."

That same day Modigliani's wife, on the eve of giving birth to her first baby, ended her life—a gruesome sensation that largely contributed to cause an immediate increase in the value of the paintings he had peddled about from door to door and been content to sell for a few francs. . . .

Such was the end of the ill-fated painter, whom the artists of his generation today call "the last Bohemian," because they themselves, having achieved fame and fortune, have become prosperous "bourgeois." Modigliani is not the last Bohemian, for as long as artists are born there will be miserable and tragic lives, but his story contains the latest revelation of the sordid destitution and despair lurking behind the falsely romantic facade erected by Murger—who himself died broken in a pauper's hospital—for the edification of the public that likes to read about the wild pranks and merry impecuniosity of these happy-go-lucky Parisian painters and writers. *La Vie de Bohème* has never been anything but an euphemism, and the present rate of world progress renders it highly probable that the kind of existence it represents will be more sombre still in the future.

There have been artists who cultivated what the French call their legend in order to exploit it commercially, advertising their eccentricities and even their misery with the design of exciting the sluggish imagination of the public. Modigliani, the Italian Jew from Leghorn, is above this suspicion, for he consecrated his legend by his miserable death, and it only profited those who had exploited him. His passing, at the age of thirty-five, bereft the world of a great painter, but it established, once and for all, his artistic sincerity. It was sheer desperation, not one of those inimitable Bohemian larks people love to hear about, that impelled Modigliani to offer one of his loveliest portraits—not long afterwards sold to an American collector for eleven thousand francs—on the café terraces of Montparnasse for ten francs. A few months later he was dead, his wife was dead, and the whole tragedy which not a few had been inclined to regard as a comedy, was definitely over.

Modigliani had only a few hectic years of life left when he entered this circle. He was consumptive and not equal to the pace set by his sturdier and perhaps less sincere comrades. He seems to have been too passionately in earnest about Bohemia, and he failed to escape in time like the others. The current anecdotes about him, most of them, needless to say, greatly exaggerated, it is useless to repeat. I am quite willing to believe that, when he lay dying at the Charité, he persuaded his wife to smuggle liquor in tiny bottles, which he hid in his bed. So did, long before him, Verlaine. Modigliani's vagaries and vices have no more to do with his art than the frescoes he painted on the wall at Rosalie's, in return for a few dishes of spaghetti. The tragedy in the rue Vercingetorix sounded the death-knell of the old Montparnasse, whose Bohemians are today prosperous figures in contemporary French art and letters. Doubtless, there is a Parisian *Bohème* today, but its whereabouts is still a mystery, and we shall hear of its exaltations and tragedies only when it has ceased to exist.

B. J. Kospoth
8 March 1925

M. Van Dongen

Van Dongen and the Social World

No contemporary artist has awakened greater expectations of becoming the supreme caricaturist of our grotesque age than Van Dongen, the acute satirist of the international post-war "social world" of Paris, Deauville and the Riviera, and fashionable portrait painter adored by beautiful women. There was a time, not so long ago, when the wild hope seemed justified that he was destined to be, if not another Daumier, at least a modern Constantin Guys, and that the curiously fascinating and distorted world in which we are at present living would find in him the great chronicler to whose brush it offers such unlimited and unprecedented opportunities of diversion.

To this marvelous occasion, let it be confessed at once, Van Dongen has not quite succeeded in rising, but the work he has done, apart from its pictorial virtuosity, is important enough to justify the prediction that it will endure as documentary evidence of at least one aspect of our extraordinary times. Future historians of the life and manners of the first quarter of the twentieth century will find invaluable documents of its psychology, so far as the world of wealth and fashion is concerned, in this singularly gifted artist's paintings and drawings. They will learn, as we do from Gavarni and Guys, in what strange manner the world of pleasure and idleness diverted itself, how it danced and made love, what clothes it wore, and where it dined and supped. This alone, it will be admitted, is no slight achievement on the part of an artist, and while we may be disappointed that Van Dongen, with his exceptional powers of observation and ability to record them, fails to realize a complete and definite vision of modern society, in all its bizarre and occult manifestations, no one can deny that he has established a strong claim to enduring fame by fixing that part of it which he chose to picture.

All these reflections, of course, concern Van Dongen's art only in its literary aspect. In his case, however, the word involves no disparagement. He would be no satirist at all, nothing but a painter with a peculiar virtuosity in rendering the colors and substance of fair women's costly gowns, if the literary element did not predominate in his work. It is as a recorder of social life, an often pitiless, sometimes cynical, but never very bitter observer, almost a moralist, that he claims our attention, and with his portraits, however notable or notorious the originals may be, and however well the *crêpe de Chine* or the velvet may be painted, we have no great concern. There can be no idle talk of "pure painting" where Van Dongen is concerned, but, I repeat, in his case, the restriction implies no criticism.

Van Dongen's social satire, of course, is not caricature in the sense that his pictures depend for their interest on captions. These our imagination must supply. Nor is it often at fault, for Van Dongen has, to a supreme degree, the real caricaturist's gift of stirring the most sluggish fancy. His women—and it is one of his limitations that his satiric world is inhabited almost exclusively by women, whereas Guys, a greater artist, was equally interested in the fashions and follies of men—are full of the suggestive mystery of modern decadence. Their words and thoughts are written in their painted eyes, in their studied gestures, as they walk along the "Croisette" at Cannes or sip drinks at the "Potinière" in Deauville, or dance in the casinos with their paid partners. There is a picture of Van Dongen called "The Return to the Fields," which is typical of the predominance of this literary element in his art. It shows a young woman, simply but very stylishly dressed, standing with her hands behind her back leaning upon a long slim stick, in front of a beautiful meadow with a row of trees and a little, country church in the distance. Her attitude, the expression on her powdered face, her garb despite its ostentatious simplicity, communicate to the beholder an impression of unutterable vacuity and boredom, all the barbaric incomprehension of a mortally materialistic age for rustic enjoyments, which appealed even to the artificial eighteenth century. In this case, indeed, the title of the picture is almost a caption; it is as suggestive in its way, though untainted by eroticism, as Rops' famous etching "Les Adieux d'Auteuil."

It is in the registration of the special aspect of the modern world, its materialism, its incurable boredom, its superficial glamor, that Van Dongen excels. He lacks the universality which made Constantin Guys, in the words of Baudelaire, "the painter of modern life"; perhaps, also, he is not quite cruel enough to be a really great satirist, although I know, of course, that most critics, when speaking of him, are in the habit of expatiating on his "brutality." Van Dongen's "brutality," I rather think, is expended chiefly on his fair and fashionable models, whom he treats very cavalierly, and it startles and charms them, but it gets into his work only in a strongly diluted form.

Van Dongen has been tremendously successful, and there again, I imagine, we have an explanation why he has failed to rise to the supreme heights of social satire. His pictures sell, and have sold for years, for high prices: even the vulgar are capable of admiring his marvellous facility in painting the costly fabrics of fashion; princesses and stage stars compete with each other for the favor of having their portraits painted by his expert hand. He has not merely made money—he has himself become a member of the brilliant circle whose pleasure and follies he pictures. It would be strange indeed if he were to lash too cruelly a world that has treated him so well.

B. J. Kospoth
14 March 1926

A Talk with An American Painter

"American art lovers who are discouraged because America has not produced a Matisse ought to be discouraged if it had. The value and significance of a work by Matisse is that it is a Matisse, and by virtue of that fact, French. If we could bring ourselves to think of works of art simply as children of the hand and brain that produced them we would be by way of achieving the rudiments of what the highbrows call a national aesthetic."

A problem that confronts all painters at some period in their career, and American painters abroad in particular, was thus ably exposed by Robert Hallowell, the American artist, in the course of an interview the other day. Mr. Hallowell, whose pictures hang in many collections in America and who has already shown distinctive work in Paris, is one of the rare artists who can both paint and talk about painting.

"All this raises the currently burning question of nationality in art," he continued. "Stay home, young man, the big-wigs are saying to those of us who find the French atmosphere congenial. Stay home, and help create an

American art; and if you must go to France, don't paint there, but spend your time studying the masters in the Louvre.

"This advice, like the foregoing Matisse complaint, arises from the mistaken notion that art can be viewed scientifically. It presupposes that, hidden away in the masters' works, there are absolute rules, detachable, assortable, classifiable, that can be lifted out, packed in a suit case, and transported to the American scene; and that, applied there, an American art will automatically result. It presupposes, too, that subject matter has something to do with the nationality of a work of art. Neither assumption is justified, however much each and both wear the aspect of plausibility. They are unjustified because they miss the point, elementary and fundamental once more, that art is not science, that the creation process is subjective and synthetic, not objective and analytic.

"An artist is like a field plowed and harrowed, and prepared for the sowing. Whatever environment puts the seed of inspiration into that ground—and I admit that that environment may as readily be the Louvre as Kalamazoo, Michigan—is the best environment for that artist to work in. The plowed field, so to speak, is American whether, for the moment, it has transported itself to France or to Zululand. Is a Gauguin less French because it was painted in Tahiti? "

The case has never before, I think, been stated with greater clarity. And what Robert Hallowell has to say about modern art in general is equally illuminating though all of us may not always be in absolute agreement with his every statement.

B. J. Kospoth
18 September 1927

Francis Picabia

If the word "dandy" were still current, Francis Picabia might be called the "dandy of modern French painting." He has all the qualifications which our ancestors connected with the term in days when artists played and aspired to play a bigger role in "society" than is generally the case in our business age. He has the reputation of vast wealth, elevating him beyond the necessity of working for money, a sprightly and satirical turn of mind, and a knack for producing pictures that often please and amuse, and always mystify, the uninitiated public. As one of the creators of Dadaism, he has sought, temporarily not without success, to outdo his ingenious countryman Picasso, and if today he has returned to more traditional conceptions of art it only proves that in his case also Latin common sense has triumphed over nebulous theories.

Not everybody knows that America was the birthplace of Dadaism. Of course, it was merely by chance that Picabia happened to be traveling in America when he had the first revelation of the doctrine that was destined to create such a stir in art circles after the war and that was doomed to such speedy and complete eclipse as soon as the fantastic confusion caused by that catastrophic interlude ceased and the mad world reverted to "law and order." Picabia, Marcel Duchamp and de Zayas constituted the triumvirate that set up the initial principles of what Tzara later christened Dadaism. A magazine was founded in Paris under the mysterious name "391," and the new creed spread over Europe with the devastating swiftness of the "grippe," then likewise at its zenith. In order to appreciate Francis Picabia's very real talent, one cannot do better than turn over the pages of "391," to which he contributed drawings, and particularly verses of a highly characteristic nature. These contributions are witty, paradoxical and frequently full of truth, and they represent Dadaism at its best. However incomprehensible, they are almost invariably pleasing to look at. It is this faculty of being always attractive despite obscurity that distinguished Picabia as a Dadaist from the rest of his comrades.

French critics are fond of referring to Francis Picabia as the *enfant gâté de la peinture.* It seems a little late to call him that today, for he is fifty years old—old enough, in fact, to know better, and he has demonstrated that he *does* know better. He was, at the outset, what is called a "child prodigy," astonishing his fond parents so greatly by artistic precocity that they insisted on his showing his work at the *Salon des Artistes Français,* the real, traditional *Salon,* at the age of seventeen. Perhaps it was this adventure that generated in the youthful painter the spirit of revolt that eventually conducted him, *via* the detour of Impressionism and Cubism, to the Dadaistic discovery. For it is a fact, although it may seem strange, that Picabia began with imitations of Sisley and Pisarro, imitations very good in their way and indicative of genuine talent. Naturally, Impressionism, already moribund at the time he underwent its domination, could not satisfy him, and when Cubism was invented on the Butte he was one of its first adherents. At the "Section d'Or" of 1912, in company with Juan Gris, Metzinger, Gleizes, Segonzac, Moreau and Marcel Duchamp, he exhibited huge canvases in which a keen sense for the rhythm of color triumphed over mere problems of composition and drawing.

Picabia is a "master" in the sense that he has a "school." His ideas have been developed by Jean Crotti, Suzanne Duchamp, Ribemont-Dessaigne and others. He himself, like a true "dandy," has quickly tired of his own inventions. His sceptical and paradoxical nature has reverted in recent years to traditional composition, to portraits and figures which afford him an opportunity to exercise his powers as a draughtsman. In this he has been but following the common trend of modern French painters, who have rediscovered, after many fascinating experiments, the existence of certain, immutable laws governing art throughout the ages.

B. J. Kospoth
12 August 1928

Paul Colin's "Black Tumult"

The invasion of Parisian nightlife by negro dancers, singers and jazz bands dates from the appearance in the French capital of Josephine Baker whose personality was hailed by the world of pleasure and the world of art as a revelation. Americans may have looked askance at all this excitement, but to Parisians it was all new and fascinating and their enthusiasm was unbounded. Thus there was a period in the life of modern Paris which was dubbed *Le Tumulte Noir*—the Black Tumult—and Paul Colin, noted poster artist, has thus entitled an album of lithographs which has just been issued by the Editions Succès, in order to perpetuate its grotesque and fleeting aspect.

Paul Colin's posters are the delight of wanderers through the Paris streets; he is a worthy modern successor of Steinlen and Lautrec. The pages of his album are equal in conception and execution to his most celebrated posters. Gifted with a masterly technique, he has drawn directly on the stone, according to his excellent habit, and the result is a fine freedom and incredible vivacity of movement. It is really a "black tumult," dancing, gesticulating, grimacing, which he has succeeded in perpetuating for the amazement of future ages.

Josephine Baker herself is responsible for a preface to Paul Colin's album, where it is reproduced in her own inimitable handwriting and style. It begins: "I'll say its getting darker and darker in Paris. In a little while it shall be so dark until one shall light a match then light another to see if the first is lit or not."

It is, indeed, as Josephine says, getting darker in Paris, if by darker one means that the Americanization of the "Ville Lumière" is making irresistible progress. But it is, of course, futile to wax pessimistic over this inevitable development, and it is by far the best thing to take it philosophically and humorously like Paul Colin and to turn its picturesque features to artistic account. Fashions pass, more swiftly in Paris perhaps than anywhere else, and the epoch of the "black tumult" will probably be no more than a memory in a few years. That, in fact, is exactly why Paul Colin has hastened to fix its features on stone.

B. J. Kospoth
20 January 1929

Hilaire Hiler's Paintings

It was while examining the works of Hilaire Hiler at the Galerie Zborowski, the other day, that we were suddenly struck by the esprit with which the modern generation of artists do their painting. Hiler, despite his Philadelphia upbringing, happens to be possessed of a rare Gaelic wit as his paintings indicate.

Hiler as seen by Louis Atlas

The works of this artist possess a delightful spontaneity which is understandable, when one knows the artist. He is fortunate to be able to paint his landscape, his people and his surroundings as he sees them—with good humor. One does not find solemn inspiration or professional sentimentality in his work.

Hiler came to France ten years ago. The change from his native country to France overwhelmed him. He was (judging from his paintings) very much amused by the great French scene. The little *bistrots* and their clients, the life in the French seaports, the funny little streets, the wine and wood merchants, all appealed to him.

He was not seeking to inspire anybody with his paintings. He did, however, wish to describe the joyous side of French life as he saw it. And he seems to have succeeded exceptionally well. He achieves unusual effects with his colors. One of his works, *L'Homme au Chat,* is a good example of how skillfully he handles his pigments. *Oporto,* and *Près de la Frontière Portugaise,* are the fruits of a trip to the Iberian peninsula last summer. His *14 Juillet* is as good a canvas of French life as we have seen in a long time.

Hiler is not a "school" artist, which may explain his freedom from any accepted style. Following three years' attendance at the University of Pennsylvania, he entered the Philadelphia Academy but he left after three days. And he has been doing lithographs, paintings, gouaches and drawings ever since—after his own fashion.

During the past few years, Hiler has been amusing himself decorating some of the little night clubs about Paris. The novel interiors of the

College Inn, the Jungle and the Jockey are his. And in his spare time, he is writing and illustrating a comprehensive history of costumes.

Louis Atlas
8 December 1927

Yasushi Tanaka

From one angle, Montparnasse is like Charlie Chaplin—the imp hides the artist. The circus on the *carrefour* is interesting but misleading. The cafés are crowded with individuals living in the past tense and dramatizing their weariness with amusing costumes and confessions, but here and there a few artists are hard at work and occasionally a new meteor prances around the artistic world.

The foregoing is fearfully said, for such banal wisdom is usually rewarded with a barrage of atmospheric eggs or the milder punishment of burning indifference. This tabulator will probably have to protect himself with an asbestos armour having an egg-proof lining. Or he might wear galoshes to keep his feet warm. Such banality! "The real artist stays home and creates." Everyone is aware of that. Then why even mention it? I don't know.

How the name of Charlie Chaplin became involved in this argument is a complete mystery to me. Of course, it is generally agreed that Charlie Chaplin has a soul. So have dogs and horses if one were to read the minutes of the famous Jack London Club of Seattle, founded to protect the bodies and establish the souls of all animals. One of the charter members of the club was a Japanese painter, Yasushi Tanaka, born near Tokio, matured in Seattle, and a resident of Montparnasse for the past ten years.

The movie comedian and Tanaka look so much alike that the latter's wife sometimes refers to him as "C. C." There may be something in the theory that human beings run in grooves, for not only do they both resemble each other, but are equipped with the same style of soul. Tanaka's pantomimic powers are at times even funnier than the other's. Friends sitting with him at the Coupole have watched his facial muscles copy the expressions parading along the aisle. Who but Tanaka would rush half-dressed into the chilly night, accost the first *agent,* hand him 50 francs, and then run after having caught a fleeting glimpse of the flatfoot's face? It wasn't drama: it was work. He often paints an impression from memory.

Tanaka's early days in Seattle were hard. He worked as farmer, peanut-vendor, cook, and fruit dealer. Once he sold a portrait for the price of a bowl of noodles. Before he left for Paris in 1920, his studio was the rendezvous of the elite. At his last exhibit at the Fine Arts Society, 5,000 visitors went to his show. One of them was Joaquin Miller, the "good, grey poet," who gave him the queer-looking felt hat he wears in his studio today. The hat was made in Belgium and belonged originally to Maeterlinck. Another visitor was the mystic Tagore who had been attracted by the painter's personality and ability. When the painter got as far as Chicago, he wanted to return but how could he after that memorable parting with his friends? He came to Montparnasse, was recognized almost immediately and was made a member of the Salon d'Automne, Société Nationale, and the Société des Indépendants.

Tanaka is now exhibiting at the Galerie Druet. The show will last another four weeks. The painter, small, wistful and *très rigolo,* watches the visitors coming and leaving. Occasionally he slips out a note-book and sketches one. If they buy a painting, he is pleased; if they don't buy a painting, he is pleased. It is all one to this artist whose work is being bought by individuals and academies all over the world. Prince and Princess Asaka of the Royal Family of Japan bought, at a previous exhibit, eight of his nudes. The Westernization of the Orient was symbolized by this purchase, because hitherto no nudes, white or yellow, had beautified the royal walls.

Nudes are the speciality of this artist. They preach the canons of female beauty. Though exuberant and natural, the depiction is so coldly rational that even the purity squads of Seattle finally forgave the artist for his vivid and uninhibited portraiture. At his present exhibit at the Galerie Druet, the fifty pictures evoke an emotional response that is quite natural, considering everything.

Wambly Bald
24 February 1930

All Montparnasse Assembles at Grave of Popular Artist

From garrets and sumptuous studios, in high hats and flowing ties, the ultra modern elite of Montparnasse turned out yesterday morning to attend the funeral of Jules Pascin, whose genius for 20 years inspired their art and whose generosity paid for their drinks.

Pascin, a naturalized American, committed suicide Monday. As an artist he was perhaps the most wanton and most zestfully voluptuous of any modern painter. His canvases were Gargantuan yet subtle orgies of rich color. In his Arabian Nights apartment in Montmartre he reigned like a fabulous caliph over the Bohemians of Paris. He killed himself because at 45 he had tasted all the joys of life and wanted to go out in a blaze of glory.

Like some old Roman esthete he opened the veins in his arms and caught the spurting blood in a scented bowl. He then hanged himself, and three days ago the police broke in to find the bloated and decaying corpse.

The funeral was worthy of his life and death. The long cortege which wound through the dusty streets to the grimy proletarian cemetery of Saint-Ouen included every nationality, and every walk of life. Side by side with sniveling little models were long haired expatriates escaped from Greenwich Village, and bored, wealthy Americans who play at patronizing the arts.

Widow Collapses

The most famous artists in Paris were present—the Japanese Fujita, Chagall, Kisling, Braque and Marcousis. There was also Aicha, an exotic mulatress model whom Pascin discovered one night while walking the Boulevards, and whom he made famous. There were simple services according to the Jewish orthodox rites. The painter's American wife, Herminie David, collapsed beside the grave and had to be carried off.

Pascin was born a Bulgarian Jew. According to the legend popular in Montparnasse, he was the natural son of the Emperor Franz Joseph. He went to America while a youth and there married. Pascin's precocious genius achieved success almost from the start. He alone of all great modernists lived to realize a fortune from his paintings.

Twenty years ago he moved to Paris and started a life of fantastic Oriental opulence. His parties in the Montmartre studio were famous throughout Europe. He spent thousands on his parties and gave thousands to charity. It is said he never passed a beggar without giving him at least a 100 franc bill. He dressed in the height of dandyism but always wore a 1900 model bicycle cap even to formal ceremonies.

8 June 1930

Harrison, Famous Painter, Wants To Die by Starlight

Pleading in his delirium that he be permitted to pass out with the stars, Alexander Harrison, the oldest American painter in the art colony of Montparnasse, is about to breathe his last. The shutters of his studio in the Rue de Vol de Grace have been thrown wide open that the wish of the dying man be granted. He is 77 years of age.

For years Mr. Harrison was addressed as the "Grand Old Man of Montparnasse." Tan and graceful and always very friendly, the white-moustached figure was one of the idols of the younger artists who always called upon him for instruction and guidance. Until three years ago, he was a regular frequenter of the Café du Dôme, where he held forth with his friends until age began to sap his health. He became absent-minded and in time was a victim of recurrent aphasia.

The fame of the American painter is internationally established. Born in Philadelphia, he came to Paris 50 years ago. In 1885, he received honorary mention at the Paris Salon. Then he began exhibiting in Brussels, Ghent, Munich, Berlin, London and other European art capitals.

Most of his work has been carefully preserved in his atelier. The spacious balconies are littered with the work of 50 years. Often chided for this by his painter friends in Montparnasse, Mr. Harrison would never tire of telling them of his disagreement with Whistler. One of the favorite *bon mots* of Whistler was: "To destroy is to remain." Mr. Harrison believed that an artist should never destroy his earlier work and today hundreds of paintings in his possession attest to the artistic evolution of the American painter.

20 September 1930

American Artist Wins Praise for His Work in Wire

Works of art executed in wire, wood, tin cans, sheet zinc, whitewash, house paint and other materials, which Leo Stein, internationally recognized art critic, yesterday characterized as being far more interesting and successful than the recent productions of two of the most famous French moderns in the world, are being shown by Alexander Calder, young New York artist, in the Galerie Percler, 38 Rue la Boetie.

Blasé amateurs, artists and critics, wearily wandering up and down the Rue de la Boetie in search of something new and refreshing, dropped into the Percier gallery by ones and twos yesterday afternoon while *The Tribune* reporter was there. After one glance around, they took off their hats, fanned themselves, looked at one another in pleased surprise, and appeared refreshed.

Works Are Witty

Many of the works shown by Calder are extremely witty. His abstract compositions in wire, sheet metal, wood and other materials are, according to Leo Stein, more complete and satisfying in their realization than the recent abstractions of Pablo Picasso. Mr. Stein, it is well known, was one of the "discoverers" of Picasso, and is reputed to have made a fortune by buying his works when the latter was still unknown.

In addition to the abstractions and drawings in India ink, there are wire characterizations of such well known figures as Kiki, Ozenfant, Miro, Mary Einstein, and Ferdinand Léger.

Calder's work obviously amuses and refreshes those who see it, but he is not being taken as a joke in France, as one may learn by reading the introduction to the catalogue of his show, which is by F. Léger who writes, in part:

"Before his recent works, which are transparent, objective and exact, I think of Satie, Mondrian, Marcel Duchamp, Brancusi, Arp, those incontestable masters of an inexpressive and silent beauty. Calder belongs to this line.

"He's a 100 per cent American.

"Satie and Duchamp are 100 per cent French.

"What a small world it is! "

Don Brown

2 May 1931

Art Becomes Aerial, Marinetti Tells Those Who Like Arty Theories: Height Counts Most

"As a result of the airplane, a new race of human beings is evolving; and with this new race, it goes without saying, we have a new art, an art that is no longer terrestrial but aerial, produced by beings who no longer live upon the earth but in the air, in the vast and pathless expanses of the unknown. Reality no longer exists; it has been pulled up by the roots. We are living in unfamiliar dimensions, at the extreme limits of the human consciousness. As a result, all human art is detached, hanging, swaying, ascending and descending spiral-like in the air, waiting to be hung up like a coat on a peg on the hatrack of the unknown."

The speaker was His Excellency, Filippo Tommaso Marinetti, venerable and thundering Father of Futurism, that once made Paris' Left Bank ring with manifestos and such, back in the days when he was emitting his own Italian version of a Barbaric Yawp. The audience in the rooms of the Dante Alighieri Society of Paris, at 12 Rue Sedillot, in addition to the Italian intelligentsia of the city, displayed a sprinkling of American debutantes and dowagers, a number of French countesses and at least one lady who looks as if she might be a Duchess.

For Signor Marinetti, like M. Tristan Tzara and others, has long since become distinctly *chic* and *mondain* and all that sort of thing; and when one goes back to Bryn Mawr, one really must be able to take him up in a serious way over the calculus and the cocktails.

Duce's Right-Hand Man

As for the Jovian Filippo Tommaso, now a member of the Royal Academy of Italy and by way of being Il Duce's right-hand man for the arts, he looks like the well fed pastor of a fashionable metropolitan church. The only thing that would tend to keep him from looking the part is his southern vitality and his smouldering effervescence.

Samuel Putnam

29 May 1931

Left Bank Artists Express Views of Rivera Row

A round robin of boos and cynical comment was the way American artists living on the Left Bank reacted to news of the art scandal at Radio City, wherein Nelson Rockefeller fired the mural painter Diego Rivera for refusing to do as he was told—take out the figure of Lenin from his panel.

Some of the Montparnasse painters thought publicity was at the bottom of the affair; others expressed the opinion that "money should never dictate to art"; still others felt Rockefeller was guilty of bad tactics in pre-emptorily ordering the artist to yield to his wishes.

"It just goes to show how little a few thousand dollars mean when big money decides to shut up Communism," said William Einstein, a member of the Abstraction Creation group. "Rockefeller, by his act, informed the world that he is really worried about what might happen unless disturbing ideas are suppressed. It was bad tactics on his part because he showed his hand."

Charles (Shorty) Lasar, who is considered the dean of all painters living on the Left Bank, remarked: "The eternal scrap between art and politics will never be settled—just like the disarmament conference. I think Rockefeller is a bad politician. He should have fought Rivera in the courts, and of course he would have won. Then, after he had won the case in the courts he could have played the big-hearted Charlie act, and paid the artist off with a great big bonus."

Other American artists said Rockefeller "should have hired an American to do the job in the first place."

18 May 1933

Music

American Jazz Called Symbol of Bolshevism

Jazz, booze and bolshevism: all three are one and the same. Some people prefer Jazz, which is the successor to alcohol in America. Europe as a whole prefers booze. Russia has bolshevism.

This is the view of Herr Doktor Siemens, one of Germany's leading art and music critics, who takes the subject very seriously in an article just published in a leading review here.

"America is said to have given up liquor," says the critic, stressing the "said" slyly. "It is no longer necessary to have alcohol: America drinks jazz. Jazz music creates drunkenness without the help of alcohol, a nice drowzy jag and not so expensive."

The critic then discovers that jazz has suddenly arrived in Berlin. Two jazz outfits, one from Paris, the other from Coblenz, are at present giving performances. The white haired gentlemen who make trips to Bayreuth for the Wagner festivals and who can tell the three Strausses apart the moment they hear the first note, have condescended to listen to the jazzers. Some were horror-stricken. Others, says Dr. Siemens, are writing learned theses to prove that jazz is "the symbol of the new terrible bolshevik age."

Dr. Siemens, however, has a word of defense. "Jazz," he says, "breaks up all pretense of dignity. The proud Prussian officer, the university professor, will never dance jazz. I wish our cabinet members, privy councillors and politicians would be forced by law to dance a jazz publicly once a week. Wouldn't they become human: nice and funny human beings?

"If the Kaiser had been forced to dance jazz the world catastrophe would never have happened. But that was impossible. It was easier to be a German Kaiser than to dance an American jazz."

George Seldes
15 March 1921

Notes of the Music World

Monday evening, an explosion of uncontrolled modernity transpired at the Salle Pleyel. Its crepitations were compositions for the violin, the violin and voice by Mr. Ezra Pound, and sonatas for piano, piano and violin, and a string quartet, by Mr. George Antheil. The performers were Miss Olga Rudge (violinist), Mr. Yves Tinayre (tenor), Mlle. Madeleine Portier (altist), M. Robert Meyer (violinist), M. Maurice Lechevalier (cellist), Mr. Antheil (hammerer of the clavier), and Mr. Ezra Pound (at the pages).

This concert, according to certain announcements in some of the local press, promised to be "iconoclastic," "revolutionary," and very rough on "tradition." Who made the promise we do not know, but we regret to say that it was not kept. Mr. Pound's compositions for violin—"Musique du XVe siecle," "Musique de Java recorde," "Fiddle Music, First Suite," and "Strophes de Viollon" can hardly be called radical. Seeking inspiration in the musics of long ago is not a new practise, although the practise has often given birth to new things. The violin pieces of Mr. Pound, which were by far the most interesting and pleasing numbers on the program, are, if one understands the architecture of "horizontal" music (splendid specimens of which are even found in the works of one J.S. Bach), a high-tide of melody. If Mr. Pound has a place among modern composers, it must be among the tuneful ones. He does not abjure melody. And, to add insult to injury, neither does he abjure emotion, which one hearing of the "Strophes de Viollon" quite suffices to prove.

The hubbub for which Mr. Antheil was responsible was quite unsolicitous of the welfare of the auditory nerve. Uninformed persons might easily be deceived into calling his compositions "ultra-ultra modern," but anyone who is at all informed on the development and tendencies of music would not make such a mistake. Mr. Antheil, in his "Sonata for piano," and "Second Sonata for violin and piano," obstinately refuses to recognize the piano as a musical instrument. He depotentiates every beautiful thing of which it is capable. His effort is to be anti-scriptural, but he is only impotently dissident.

His quartet for stringed instruments, which had its first performance Monday evening, is not confusingly subtle. For the most part it is enormously dissonant. We more than once thought the fiddlers were playing out of tune, but they really weren't. They were simply trying out some very common chords, bits of melody snatched from here and there, and making known to a numerous audience, Mr. Antheil's scorn for original melody, for euphony, emotion and straight thinking. Every so often the players encountered an ingenious detail and a few measures that were traitorously euphonious, but they were not of long enough duration to interfere with the serving of Mr. Antheil's Gargantuan feast of cacophonies.

This inspection of Mr. Antheil's "music," re-convinces us that he is a young "Pagan suckled in some creed outworn." If he would endeavor to say something new (or even something old in a not too old way, as Mr. Pound has) instead of endeavoring to say something revolutionary, his product would come closer to intriguing the intelligence than at present it does.

Irving Schwerké
9 July 1924

Why A Poet Quit The Muses

Ezra Pound's music reminds me of Rousseau going out at a late age and painting the leaves of the trees all a little larger so that one does not have to paint so many leaves.

Ezra Pound starts out upon the art of music a little frantically; a little hectically; a tree is to him a tree with a certain technical capacity as a tree; the same with a telegraph pole. And he is always concerned with some musical lion or tiger with which he invariably gives a marvellous meaning to a whole landscape; his colors are glaring and glassy; the octave takes on the piercing quality that we have expected eventually from Stravinsky's music and have not received while that worthy has been for sometime engaged in easier fields.

Pound's whole music has a mediaeval intelligence, a brilliant intelligence although it is not intellectual. Nothing could be quite so plainly music and so free from intellectualism. But it is mediaeval by preference; by thought. I am convinced that no other music today is so completely free from the developments of music during the last three or four hundred years, yet the music is as tight and as built up upon inner and strict laws of its own, as if it were built upon hundreds of years of musical tradition.

I have insisted that Pound is mediaeval by preference and by thought. I have seldom read such a clear and simple statement of the theory of harmony as recently appeared in his article recently published in the *Transatlantic Review*. With one stroke it brushes away a world of imbecilities carefully cultivated and cherished by impotents since the times of Bach. And there it makes for once the clear and bright statement of what "harmony" really is and means, and its sole practical significance. "Of course! " One always finds a man of talent very much "of course." The thing has always existed. And so did Rousseau's trees, carriages, and basket-ball players. And with this clarity about rhythm, which was born in him, and harmony, which he could see as "of course" as the nose on his face, as clearly as Rousseau could see that trees were round . . . it is with this that Ezra Pound makes a kind of music that is quite as different from other precious things of this time as anything I know of . . . as different as the members of Satie and Co. are alike to one another . . . as different as Rousseau was from the theoreticians of an age just past . . . and their piles of sunlight, resembling one another from a slight distance like so many new peas.

I find Pound's analogy in Rousseau. He seems the only man of the age who has started out writing music *round* so that there is air behind it . . . as he can clearly hear . . . and as Rousseau could clearly see. Pound's music, coming as it has, from a technically untrained musical talent that has been festering to express itself in real music all of his life, is a phenomena existing outside of our sphere of music for some time yet to come. To those musicians who have half an eye, it will be quite clear that the technique side of "Le Testament" is hectic, gawky, and from a viewpoint of modern musical technic, really annoying; nevertheless it will be apparent that it is a work of colossal talent; a genial work; a work gaunt and bare, but with a new richness, and an approach that is as new as new planets. The chief interest to young musicians is: Ezra Pound, musically, is a poet who wanted all of his life to become a musician, and has become one in such a curious manner that his music seems to have no connection with the last three or four hundred years at all! Every moment one is reminded of Rousseau painting his trees and telegraph poles round . . . just because the others were too stupid, in their mathematical filteration of light, to see things as they were . . . at any rate the way Rousseau saw them which was after all the most important. Musically Pound has with Rousseau, in the present mixed and impotent period of the world's musical history, an identicality which will in the course of time have some little influence upon the world of creative music . . . in fact, I feel safe in saying, a great deal. Every really new work which brings an entire new technical world into being is sure of influencing the work of the future, for it seems that from the technical manner of approach artists can most easily steal from one another, for technicality is the uppermost, the most superficial manifestation of an artist, and if he be a great artist beneath and outwardly rich in technical inventions . . . he will be robbed grandly and hilariously for years to come. Pound is a gold-mine of new technical means, and stands out sharply against the whole sum and substance of the present moderns in musical composition, who are at best a bunch of false-noters on the old masters who were true musical geniuses and inventors. Even Stravinsky has taken his place among them . . . his new pianoforte concerto sounds like a stupid new German work influenced by a second-rate or third-rate German "ultra-modern" who is jinking up the good old hearty counterpoint of Bach with a couple of "just stinkingly ultra" (as the Café du Dôme phrase has it) discords now and then. They are all of no account.

George Antheil
14 September 1924

"Ballet Méchanique" To Wipe Out Big Orchestras, and Audiences Too

Paris will hear the strident screech and crash of giant machines evocative of modern industrial America very shortly when George Antheil, American musical rebel, and Ferdinand Léger, well-known French painter of machines, present the "Ballet Méchanique."

For the first time in the world, dynamic music, which is "unlike any other music ever written," will be played on four player pianos simultaneously, with electricity as the motive power and a further volume of sound supplied by four electric bells, and two electric motors driving a steel propeller and a wooden rattle respectively. Two tins will act as gongs to complete the orchestral equipment.

The first half of the music was written early last year by Mr. Antheil and was completed recently, taking about two months to write in all. He conceived the idea for this new form of music at the same time that Picasso, the famous French modern painter, evolved his new cubism, leaving the new classicist period absolutely.

Mr. Antheil explained to *The Tribune* yesterday that he was firmly convinced that one could not go on digging up old forms of music and, after the titivating about a little bit, turn it into a new melody. "We must all concentrate on something absolutely new," he declared.

His "Ballet Méchanique" is written to music that resembles machinery's strident noises. It has no nuances and keeps at the same pitch throughout the twenty minutes. It is just as if you were to listen to the notes of circular saws biting their way through steel mixed with the crash of a steel die plant.

"It begins at a high tension and stops suddenly at high tension, although thousands of notes go to form the body of the sound. The music changes every second just like the position of water in a whirlpool changes all the time, yet the mass of water remains the same, just as does the mass of music," the young composer explained.

The whole ballet will last twenty-five minutes and will be conducted by Chester MacKee, another American. During the playing a film of machinery will be shown, which will also prove startling. The film was arranged by Mr. Léger, who also did some designs for the Swedish ballet.

The picture is composed of disconnected photos of different pieces of giant machinery photographed in action. They were taken on a moving chute, so that the audience will get a sort of swirling feeling that Mr. Antheil believes may be almost too much for it when accompanied by the music.

It is Mr. Antheil's firm conviction that shortly all music for orchestral recitals will have to be produced mechanically, as you can get the most perfect reproduction of the original score in this manner.

"A conductor does not want temperamental players in an orchestra," said Mr. Antheil. "All he wants is a player to carry out the orders of the music perfectly or, in other words, he wants a mechanical player.

"It costs several thousand dollars to give a single recital with a symphony orchestra. With that money you could build a whole mechanical plant and still have money in hand and, what is more, have the composition perfectly rendered.

"The composer puts all his spirit into the original score and goes over it again and again perfecting it, so that when he has finished he wishes it played just as he left it."

Roger Fuller
21 January 1925

Stravinsky Predicts Musical Future for America; Jazz Thrilled Him

Bringing with him the vision of America as the land of the future for music, M. Igor Stravinsky, famous Russian composer and iconoclast of rhythm, arrived in Paris from the *Aquitania* last night, after being lionized in New York, Chicago and other cities of the North American continent during a triumphant stay of more than three months.

"I expect your country to bring us the new things in music," he told *The Tribune* at the Gare St. Lazare. "Your skyscrapers impressed me as leading to new visions in art. What work! What energy there is in your immense country! "

M. Stravinsky categorically denied as a "foolish canard" the story widely printed after his arrival in New York a few months ago that a violent storm during the voyage had inspired him to write a new symphony in which the roar of the storm-swept seas was to be the rhythmic motif.

"How could I be expected to do anything as silly as that?" he said. "My work grows in me, but not in this fashion."

American jazz gave him a real thrill, he admitted, although he said he had heard much of it before going to America.

"It brings something of the elementary—the way it is presented in the United States. The music of the future will have to take it into account, no matter what the tendency of the composer.

"The work of the American composers is full of interest. I was especially impressed with a new ballet by John Alden Carpenter from whom many things may be expected.

"I cannot say enough for the hospitality shown me in America. Everywhere I was received with the greatest kindness and understanding. The American people are really music-conscious. There is a great love for music there, and it was astonishing to me to notice how much they reacted to modern music. My houses were always sold out to the last place."

Eugene Jolas
21 March 1925

Advancing the Interests of American Artists in Europe

The number of American "artists" actively engaged at the present time in an effort to convince Europe of their right to a place in the sun, is by no means inconsequential, and it increases more rapidly than one would dare imagine. One after the other they come and go, the American artists—a recital here, a recital there, an operatic engagement or two, or perhaps an orchestral, and then most of them disappear and are heard from no more. The careers of only a few run successfully from one season into the following. Not many of the Americans who "make themselves heard" on this side of the Atlantic are ready to assume the responsibilities a public life entails. Most of them (the truth is unpleasant but cannot be made known too quickly) give mediocre, unenlightened performances, and the unforgiving waves of the jealous musical sea are not slow to wash the names of these ill-advised persons from its sand.

In Europe, as in America, the prerequisite to success is what is known in a certain expressive parlance as "the goods," only that Europe is less suddenly convinced. Those American artists who possess the goods referred to usually arrive at establishing themselves in the esteem and affection of audiences all over Europe and of course do so by dint of hard, ceaseless work and incessant improvement of their talents. The past record of American musicians in Europe discloses too many conclusive examples in substantiation of this assertion to allow of any question. Americans have provided European opera houses with some of their finest singers and singing, and the same is true of a number of our instrumentalists and teachers. But the positions these artists occupied (and still hold) in the Old World, were not won by the advertising, the bluff, the proclaiming-from-the-housetops business which, within recent years have come to characterise the artistic antics of so great a proportion of the Americans abroad. They mounted by virtue of the quality of art they delivered. Years ago the "work" produced the publicity, nowadays the publicity is supposed to produce the work. What can it avail an artist, the influence of friends, a packed hall, etc., if his artistic stature is less than it should be, if he does not measure up to the standards of his chosen Muse, not to mention transcending them? What an impetus would be given to their art if they realized that by their music, not by their *réclame* are they finally known!

There is great fault in the attitude of most Americans who seek foreign musical careers and there is reason to despair of ever seeing it corrected. So many claim recognition, believe they have a sort of divine right to it. Why? Because they are Americans! Fiddlesticks! The music is the thing and nationality is outside the question. Let the vital-spark musician come along, and be he Russian, African, Turk, American or what not, his "interests" are likely to advance smoothly enough and his place be made. Naturally, there are many obstacles to overcome, but one of the proofs that an artist merits a foothold at the top, is that he overcomes them.

Today the chief hindrance to the American artist in Europe is the presence on the concert platforms and operatic stages here of an extremely large number of Americans who are unprepared, either by Nature or Man, to play the roles they have the pretention to. Sparingly trained before leaving the United States, a few months of study in Europe and they develop the recital complex and needs must give a program. A few weeks of coaching on an opera score and not even the prices they must pay for the privilege can prevent them from making what in nine cases out of ten is their first and last debut in opera. They forget, if indeed they had it to forget, that it takes years to make a career but only one bad public appearance to upset a career. The cocksureness of the misguided group under consideration is as wonderful as it is pathetic. Not one of them would ever be guilty of stopping to think that Europe has, in some things at least, the wisdom that goes with her age, for if they thought at all, they would be doing other things than carrying on their unjustifiable flirtations with Music.

Not so long ago (and it is still true to a certain extent) some of the best artists to be heard in European lyrical theatres were Americans, but now there is a tendency to close the doors upon Americans. This for a variety of reasons, all of which, except the most unpleasant one, are known to and rehearsed by Americans interested in such things. Everybody is aware that the European artist has a different struggle to make a living and that he does not welcome the thought of having his post filled by a foreigner; but few Americans ever attach any importance to the many deplorable operatic fiascos that have been perpetrated by Americans in Europe, and yet that is the sore spot most in need of doctoring. So many failures have been the harvest in recent years, that American artists have been given a very black "black eye." Directors are becoming afraid to engage them or to allow them the use of their theaters. One American *chute* abroad is infinitely more harmful to us than a dozen at home. Every misstep made by American "artists" in Europe is dangerous to the fairness of our name and impairs the progress of those who deserve to shine, those who really can render service to our artistic reputation and standing.

The interests of American artists in Europe can be completely advanced only when every American artist or would-be artist who performs here is *so* genuinely American that his *amour-propre* makes it impossible for him to offer Europe anything but the best. American aspirants to musical honors should become truer to the idealism of their country. Then they will never incur the risk of besmirching her musical record.

It is no doubt splendid for the American to "try-out" in Europe, but in so doing, the American would be a better American if he first made sure that he had something good enough to try out. Mediocrity is mediocrity, bluff is bluff, no technic is no technic, bad diction is bad diction, lack of musicianship is lack of musicianship, low ideals are low ideals. They can never be hidden by an Uncle Sam passport, any more than that precious document can prevent the positives of the aforenamed negatives from winning recognition in Europe or anywhere else. Europe, like the character in the book, "is willing," but Americans have but little to expect unless every last one of our "artists" right now begins to form the habit of bringing nothing but the finest musicianship, the clearest thought, the highest ideals they can to Europe. The place for them to begin the work of elevation is at home.

The Americans who have been successful in Europe are comparable to the musicians of any nation that might be named, and they are the ones who give America the name she deserves. We need such artists and need them by hundreds. The mediocre many make it difficult beyond computation for the deserving few, and the great sorrow, so far as American interests in Europe are concerned, is that, as yet no way has been found to keep our "second-raters" out of the European public eye.

Irving Schwerké
17 May 1925

Influence of Jazz in American Music
Greatly Over-rated, Says Koussevitzky

Young America is today before the blossom-time of its musical history, and a native school of composers is emerging with astounding rapidity.

But jazz as a vital factor in the evolution of American music is tremendously overrated, and is merely an external element which will only add to the American musical consciousness, without being a primary thing.

This is the radical impression brought back to Paris by M. Serge Koussevitzky, famous Russian modernist conductor, who has just returned from America after eight months of triumphant wielding of the baton in the principal cities of the United States.

"There is a tremendous musical movement in the United States," M. Koussevitzky told a *Tribune* reporter yesterday. "America is hungry for music and this desire for music is developed in a way never to be met with in Europe.

"Jazz has not the importance we usually connect with American music. It is not the last word that great country will have to show in new rhythms."

Speaking of American composers, M. Koussevitzky expressed himself as astounded at the creative force now being exhibited in the United States.

Deems Taylor, Aaron Copland, Alexander L. Steinert and the late Charles T. Griffes are among the composers, who, in his opinion, are best expressing the American idea with accents never before heard.

"I cannot say that I have been particularly impressed with the work of the men who seek to express merely the external elements of the American scene," he continued. "Noise? We have noise in Europe, too. Noise is not a prerogative of America. . . .

"I find, on the whole, that Deems Taylor has the American spirit more emphatically developed than any other composer there. His 'Through The Looking-Glass' is a master-piece. My personal opinion is that he has all the elements that—we might say—distinguish the American character from the European: great flexibility and a certain youthfulness.

"I am particularly attached to Aaron Copland's work. Although in a purely technical way he has not yet reached perfection, I might say that he has enormous talent, a deep culture is felt in his music . . . and his emotions, for those who can follow, are profoundly stirring.

"He has used jazz rhythms in a curious way—in a movement deeply tragic, which gives a remarkable impression."

Eugene Jolas
31 May 1925

Arthur Honegger

Monsieur Arthur Honegger is only thirty years of age, but already he has made considerable stir in the world of music. He is hailed by those who wish to be in the vanguard of all the arts as one of those who are freeing music from ancient trammels and making it the instrument for a new expressiveness, something which will sum up the jazz-automobile-radio-and-quick-lunch age.

Recently M. Honegger had the first performance of his greatest achievement so far, his opera "Judith," at the opera in Monte Carlo. It was a great triumph; the success of this work, when it goes abroad, seems to be assured, with the opera-going public at any rate, whatever the critics may say about it. In speaking about his ideas of musical composition, just after he had finished conducting his own opera, M. Honegger showed that he has some well thought out ideas about modern music.

According to M. Honegger, the chief obvious defect with operas hitherto has been their terrifying length. Evidently a just enough remark; every one knows that dreadful uneasiness, pervasive and communicated, which creeps over an audience during the last interminable hour of a Wagnerian performance. So M. Honegger has gone behind modern opera, back to the opera bouffe of the early Italians. Eliminating the packing which he finds so unnecessary, and reducing his work to what is just about essential to tell the story, M. Honegger has made a short work of "Judith," although it has three acts. The idea of doing this composition came, in a way, from M. Raoul Gunsbourg, director of the opera of Monte Carlo, who requested that M. Honegger do something for the opera of that city.

The libretto of "Judith" was by M. Morax. M. Morax also wrote a poem with which M. Honegger composed another great work "Le Roi David." This, together with his symphonic poem called "Pacific 231," were his principal achievements before "Judith." "Pacific 231" should satisfy the most revolutionary enemies of traditional music. It uses every possible musical device to express the spirit of the age of big machines, and in particular to express the trials and aspirations of a huge locomotive. It is curious that when the most eminent (and possibly "advanced") musical critic of England is howling for "pure" music—that is, music which borrows nothing from any other art and which shall symbolize nothing—composers like M. Honegger should be bent on doing just the contrary, on trying to express in music not only the spirit of the age, but even to give the feeling of its complicated machinery.

With "Pacific 231" what it is and with "Judith" breaking as many as possible of the established operatic conventions, M. Honegger's reputation as an original young composer is now established. His tendencies and his opinions about contemporary music have, however, been known for some time. He first became famous as a member of that school of theory called "the six," young men who were convinced that the Debussy tradition in modern French music had gone quite far enough, rebelled against it, and started to do something new. It must give people older than thirty, who are not musicians themselves and have not the leisure to follow the latest fashions in the arts, a strange sense of the passing of time to hear that Debussy is already quite old-fashioned. Possibly fifty years from now there will be a revival of Debussy, but, for the present, he is suffering the fate of all artists whose peculiar style has just been in vogue. And it seems such a short time ago since it was quite "cultured" to know and admire Debussy.

M. Honegger, strange to say, is not going to the United States. He has been offered huge sums to come to America to conduct in some of his own compositions, but seems inclined to refuse these offers, for the present at least. Instead, he will probably go to Russia, where, he thinks, he may find new material in the conditions which are the result of the gigantic upheaval in that country and the travail through which it now is passing.

2 March 1926

Notes of the Music World

It was a looseness of language to call the S. M. I.'s seance of Wednesday evening "Concert of American music." In the interest of exactitude, it should have been called "Concert of Music by American Composers," or something to that effect. It was, for the most part, a presumptuous parading of immaturities. One listened in vain for a single measure whose ethnic quality might have won it a claim to the title American, but there were measures to spare that were only more or less fortuitous dilutings of the European musical tendencies that rejoice in the name Modern.

Another such performance cannot be contemplated without misgivings. It was chaos of incredibilities. With all their superabundance of gesture, these American composers disclosed nothing Wednesday evening that can be taken for genuine experimentation in design, decoration, sonority, or the subtle things of spirit that distinguish the musician-composer from the composer who is not a musician. The young men in question undoubtedly have talent but it remains for them to prove it. They need to discover if they have anything to say, and if they have, if it is worth saying. They need to learn to think, not new thoughts, necessarily—no one expects the impossible, even from American composers—but how to think steadily, along one line and to carry a musical thought to a logical conclusion, logic and conclusion being two things they have conspicuously not yet associated with musical ideas. The public exhibition of their pointless cacophonies can have done no good to the cause of American music, and I for one regret that the concert took place.

The program was performed, graciously and artistically, by Mme. Ada MacLeish (soprano), M. Samuel Dushkin (violinist), M. Aaron Copland (pianist), The Krettly String Quartet, and a small orchestra conducted by Mr. Chester MacKee.

"As it fell upon a day," for soprano, flute and clarinet, of Aaron Copland, is monotonous in color and rhythmically uninteresting. The same composer's "Nocturne" and "Serenade" for violin and piano, were effective in their way, but created no particular mood or atmosphere worth remembering. For aught I know, this may be the highest praise, so assiduous are the musical youth of the day in their practices of negation.

"Sonate d'Eglise," of Virgil Thomson, is of the earthiest modernism. A fine example of crass emulation and the stiffness that results therefrom. Each of its three parts—*Choral, Tango, Fugue*—puerile in its noisiness.

George Antheil's "String Quartet" is traitorously tonal, and Mr. Antheil has almost turned poetic in his choice of themes. One may not have liked what Mr. Antheil says in this quartet, but he certainly knows how to say what he wants. There was apparent in this music a gratifying technical mastery of means, some harmonic passages full of flushed and melting color, but was lacking the polyphonic richness and inventiveness essential to all chamber music.

The hall, which held a large audience at the beginning of the concert, held a small one at the end.

Irving Schwerké
10 May 1926

George Antheil's Ballet Stirs Huge Audience to Plaudits and Catcalls

The carefully upholstered Theatre des Champs Elysées vibrated to strange and beautiful sounds yesterday afternoon, some of which were and others were not on the program arranged by Mr. George Antheil, composer. When the climax was reached, the much-discussed *Ballet Méchanique,* the audience was divided spiritually into two belligerent and opposing camps which, however, perhaps fortunately for the health of many music lovers, were so scattered geographically as to be in no position to do battle.

The composer was at the mechanical piano, which controlled also a number of fans, propellors, xylophones, and other articles for producing sound. The loud parts went best, because they sounded more like what the audience expected, but when the dynamics were reduced to mezzo-forte and the principal interest should have been diverted to the rhythm, the "contras" began to act up. They whistled, clapped their hands, and some of them who thought that enough damage was being done to the aural sense, put up their umbrellas and turned up their coat collars.

Pound Remonstrates

"Silence, imbeciles! " shouted Ezra Pound, with the French inflection, although the audience was anything but French.

"Get out if you don't like it," yelled another "pro," and his suggestion met with some favor.

But, after all had been said and done, the combatants filed out peacefully, after Antheil had been greeted with an applause so uproarious as to leave no doubt in his mind that his tonal seed had not all fallen upon stoney ground, and there was an atmosphere about the theatre most wholesome for the art of music. Everyone knew they had been somewhere. Whether one liked it or not, one was not able to guess what was coming next.

Mr. Antheil showed more humor in the arrangement of the program than did any of the amateur entertainers on the other side of the footlights. He began with the Freischutz overture, and followed it by a Handel *Concerto Grosso*. Then came the Antheil Symphony in F, which even those most hostile to the idea of expending musical possibilities did not fail to enjoy. Because of the impossibility of getting together the proper instruments, the *Ballet Méchanique* was not well presented, but enough was done to give an idea of its contents and spirit.

20 June 1926

Paris Audience Thrilled by Antics of Paul Whiteman's Jazz Orchestra

Paul Whiteman and his orchestra took their first Paris audience by storm, when they played at the Theatre des Champs-Elysées last evening.

The program presented by Mr. Whiteman was entirely unconventional. It consisted of pieces composed or arranged for jazz orchestra, not to forget jazz pieces for two pianos, two wind instruments blown by one man, for bicycle-pump, etc.

With the Whiteman organisation on duty, the health of jazz music is bound to improve. It is to be hoped that all French and other misguided jazz-players will go to hear Mr. Whiteman, and learn that jazz is not a riot of noise but something much more insinuating and subtle, and, it is to be feared, for them inimitable.

The most interesting number he presented was Gershwin's "Rhapsody in Blue." This piece is a serious attempt to use the resources of jazz to artistic advantage. It is largely, although not entirely, successful in this. It has a pleasant Oriental flavor, contains an interesting play of themes and ideas, and in spite of the monotony of its limited coloration (which is the great weakness of all jazz) is far from being tiresome. It made a big hit with the auditors and was received with great show of applause.

Irving Schwerké
3 July 1926

Literary And Artistic Paris Cheers Rendition of Antheil's Symphony

The concert at the Salle Gaveau last evening, better to acquaint the musical public with the works of George Antheil, the American composer, was an event of extraordinary brilliance. Musicians, writers, critics and artists from all quarters of the world exchanged greetings in the lobbies and directed their hearty applause to Mr. Antheil, who was forced repeatedly to rise and bow at the conclusion of his Symphony in F.

James Joyce sat in a *loge* at the right of the stage, in a characteristic pose of absorption and detachment, as if his mind contained the music, and had taken it to a sphere seven times removed in order to enjoy it. Serge Daghlieff, director of the Russian ballet, was nearby, Honegger and Darius Milhaud, prominent members of the group of French musicians known as "The Six," also were in attendance.

M. Leon-Paul Fargue, Maxim Jacob, M. Jacques Benoist-Méchin, Olga Rudge, Adrienne Monnier, Sylvia Beach, Pedro Figari and Girard Bauer, and M. Pruneres, director of the Revue Musicale, were present, not to mention Myron Nutting, who is working on a portrait of Joyce, Ivan Opfer, recently returned from Copenhagen, M. Tihyani, Hungary's foremost painter, Eugene Jolas, American poet, Pierre Loving, Bravig Imbs, and numerous others. Mrs. Christian Gross had a group of distinguished guests in one of the loges, and throughout the crowded hall were many persons prominent in the society of two continents. In order to beautify for the eye that which was designed for the ear, Poiret reserved front seats for his mannequins.

The orchestra was directed by Vladimir Golschmann, who achieved ideal results, either with Debussy, Antheil or Stravinsky. The Sinfonietta for five instruments was performed by MM. Chantome, Dherin, Dumoulin, Moyse and Vignal. It is one of Antheil's early compositions and is interesting both for its own sake and because it contains the germs of ideas he develops in the Symphony.

The Symphony was enthusiastically received. Its outstanding characteristics, contrasted with other modern music, is the integrity of its design. It proceeds in a direct line, with no spectacular devices to distract attention from the whole in favor of one of its parts. The restraint, in dynamics, in instrumentation, and in tempo, is truly remarkable. Antheil does not shake a theme to death, as a terrier shakes a rat. He often indicates a musical idea, and leaves the hearer to carry it out. But as the symphony proceeds, the themes attain more and more momentum and significance.

His debt to the masters of the early eighteen hundreds is evident, and he retains their old solidity and vigor without being a slave to their restricted orchestra or arbitrary harmony.

Elliot H. Paul
17 October 1926

U.S. Prodigy Re-triumphs With Paris Orchestra; Hundreds Are Turned Away

For the second time in a week, Yehudi Menuhin, ten-year old American violin wonder, swept musical Paris off their quavers, when he appeared with the Lamoureux Orchestra. In spite of the fact that the hall had been sold out early in the week, about two hours before the doors opened, a long line of eager humanity was waiting, hoping for the possible return of tickets. But none were turned in, and these hundreds of patient admirers of violin playing when it is young, were invited to contemplate the "S.O." sign and to take their disappointment elsewhere.

Inside the hall the atmosphere was one of extreme tensity. It is safe to say that, never in its history, has the air of the Salle Gaveau felt the current of so much human electricity. It was refreshing, to say the least, to see a Paris audience keyed up to such an expectant state of excitement, for in this town of musical plenty, thrills seem to be the commodity concert customers have the least contact with. Respectful attention was given to the Mozart *Symphony in G minor*, to the faded *Tableaux flamands* of Chapuis, and to the *Tombeau de Couperin*, by Ravel, all conducted in praiseworthy fashion by Paul Paray, but Mozart and Company were not what the audience had come to hear. They had come to hear young Menuhin and it was he who fired their imagination and gave it the outing of a lifetime.

When the little boy appeared, the hall shook with applause. The only calm person in the place was the juvenile soloist. He handed his violin to the concert-master for tuning, gave the conductor the "ready" sign, and proceeded to give a delivery of the Tschaikowsky concerto, which, for technical finish, musical feeling, breadth of style and quality of tone, defied understanding. In an artist who has gone through years of apprenticeship and "arrived," such playing *is* understandable, but when the performer's years are ten, there is nothing to do but marvel. Well on in the first movement of the concerto, Yehudi snapped a string. To judge by the concerted gasp of the spectators, their hearts broke with it. But here again, the calmest person in the house was the soloist. After receiving back his fiddle from the concert-master's repairing hands, he continued the movement from the point of the accident and set a new example for composure and *sang froid*. The ovation he won needs no describing. . . .

Yehudi Menuhin should give a recital for professional performers only. It would do most of them good to learn how musical music sounds when it is free of twenty or thirty years of artists' egoism (usually passed off as personality), when it is nowhere touched by pretense or affectation. Those who heard the boy have reason to rejoice, for it is after all an uncommon privilege to hear the things Providence reveals to babes and keeps from the grown and wise.

Irving Schwerké
13 February 1927

Roy Harris

Harris is a westerner. In our national music he complements Copland, being the spirit of the fields, the deserts, and all the great out of doors, while

Copland, like certain other equally significant young composers, expresses the Twentieth Century industrial age concentrated in New York City.

The holder of a coveted Guggenheim Fellowship, Mr. Harris will match his compositions against those of even better known young Europeans when the Roth Quartette, with M. Louis Cahuzac and Mlle. Nadia Boulanger, performs his Sextette for clarinette, the strings, and piano at the Salle Gaveau. He will have stiff competition, for the other first auditions on the program have been composed by Joaquin Nin, Florent Schmitt, Louis Aubert, Ch. Koechlin, Jacques Durand, and Renée Hansen. Will he prove to French critics as he did to Olin Downes that his music is "beyond the excitements and banalities of the day? " It is here that he himself wishes to engage battle, for he is proud that so far neither cleverness nor extreme technical facility have been remarked in his compositions, desiring above all to express in the modern manner ideas and musical moods that grow, not out of a passing phase of life, but from such fundamental elements as trees, rain, the sand, the sea, and all that blooms without the city.

Such a determined stand can only have come from the expression of some deep native influence. Harris has developed something of a complex against the city, yet from this complex comes the creative energy which builds itself into his symphonies and his original Andante.

And through it all he insists upon ignoring the crash of traffic, the trip of riveting hammers, and the rumble of the underground. In nature he finds the permanent element which he wishes to express, carrying some familiar note to a posterity which will perhaps have outgrown the modern industrial age and come to regard both it and its art as curiosities merely. The rhythm of a tree is as complex as that of any machine. It is an equally adequate subject for modern musical technique. For the musician, who deals in forms, rhythms, colors, and moods unlike those of the novelist, Harris finds that the rural life is psychologically essential. Energy and health lie in the country, and from it comes a bracing, tonic force. This concept, highly personal in a machine age, Harris explains by his need to bring into harmony his racial heritage, the modern environment, and that musical technique which all advanced composers employ. He seeks a coordination which will have continuity, not crystallization, with the past. To him city life is reiteration, country life is variety. A creative talent inspired by such unusual convictions must nourish itself upon close analysis and make discoveries foreign to the urban mind.

William Leon Smyser
5 May 1927

Gershwin Picks *Americans in Paris* for Subject of Next Jazz Symphony

George Gershwin, now in Paris, is writing a new symphony, the subject of which is *Americans in Paris*. The subject is to be handled lightly, in the spirit in which many Americans come here, to play, carefree and happy.

He has with him his sister, Frances, and his brother, Ira. The latter writes his lyrics. Mr. Gershwin believes in modern music, but not in the way in which it is written.

"The emotions are neglected and the appeal is only made to the intellect. This is unnatural because our emotions are the means with which we understand and feel music."

After *Americans in Paris*, Mr. Gershwin will start on some new ideas for Broadway shows, taking as a basis the various phases of French life that he intends to study. Also, in the near future we may expect to hear the second *Rhapsody in Blue*, but as yet Mr. Gershwin will not give any clue to the subject.

3 April 1928

They Might Have Been Stars, But Lacked Courage, Hallie Stiles Says; Star Tells Why Opera Failures Crowd Montparnasse

What price do American boys and girls—particularly girls—who come to Paris with dreams of becoming opera or concert stars pay for success? How many of them ever see their dreams realized? How many of them, broken in spirit and health, with singed wings and shattered illusions relinquish their dreams and go home or become sodden wrecks sinking from degradation to degradation in Montparnasse dives?

The answer is not cheerful. Most of the Young American girls and boys who come to Paris to seek a musical career are foredoomed to failure. For the few, however, with the courage and strength necessary to endure the privations that an aspiring singer must undergo there is a glorious reward. So declared Miss Hallie Stiles, brilliant young American singer who has achieved a remarkable success at the Opéra Comique here, in an exclusive interview with *The Tribune* yesterday.

Miss Stiles described how, after months of toilsome study she at last received the coveted invitation to sing at the Opéra Comique.

"When it came time for me to sing," she related, "I didn't have a cent. For three days my cook had been buying me food out of her own money. The morning after my appearance I woke up to find that I had achieved a far greater success than I had ever imagined and there was easily $500 worth of flowers in my apartment. Even so I had to borrow two francs from the cook to buy coffee for breakfast.

"That is the sort of thing a young singer must expect to undergo. Alas, most of them are not prepared, I have seen hundreds of American boys and girls come over here fully expecting to be great opera singers within six months.

"A great many of our boys and girls who come over here have not had enough vocal training in America. They aren't ready for Paris. They get some rich man to furnish them backing, thinking that within six months at the most they will be on the road to fame.

"Some of the most pitiful human wrecks in Montparnasse and Montmartre are girls who once had a brilliant future ahead of them but lacked the patience or endurance to perfect their art. They wanted to become stars overnight. God only knows how many such cases there are."

25 November 1928

Antheil Given Ovation after Premier
Of Opera *Transatlantic* in Frankfort

The world creation last evening in Frankfort-am-Main of *Transatlantic*, the opera by the American composer, George Antheil, attracted an audience that packed the theatre and among whom were seen musicians, writers, journalists and other artists from every corner of Europe.

The audience gave the newborn opera, the American title of which is *The People's Choice*, a rousing reception of enthusiastic and unreserved approval. After the first act there were four curtain calls for the entire troupe and three after the second act. After the third act the composer and the conductor were called to the stage and given an ovation.

It was one of the most brilliant successes in modern operatic history. Later in the evening a banquet in honor of Antheil was given in the Frankforterhof Hotel, at which time the young composer received the congratulations of his interpreters and scores of his admirers.

Plot Melodramatic

On the supposition that people like opera plots that have action in them, Mr. Antheil cast *Transatlantic* in a melodramatic mold. There is ample play of "and the villain still pursued her." The story is distinctly American. It centers around a presidential election, the amours of the president-elect as well as those of the political boss providing the heart interest of the piece.

The way Mr. Antheil told the story in music, together with the magnificent way in which it has been staged by the Frankfort Opera, makes *Transatlantic* one of the most exciting spectacles on the operatic stage today. Certainly it is one of the most convincing theatrical essays that the young school of any nation has to boast of. It reveals one of the outstanding talents of the time and is an opera of which America should be proud.

American Ditties Used

Orchestrated in a manner which a short time back was considered ultramodern, but which today sounds quite classical, the score of *Transatlantic* discloses how theatrical and emotional present day rhythm and idioms can be when worked with by a composer whose technique and insight are big enough to get out of them what Antheil has. That is, amazing variety of rhythmic inventions, harmonic puissance and melodic flow.

Motives from some well-known American popular ditties are employed as thematic material and with felicitous results. It is dynamic throbbing music and the tunes are the kind that everybody wants to whistle.

Irving Schwerké
26 May 1930

American Negro's Tone Poem *Africa*
Scores Success in Concert Here

The Saturday afternoon concert of the Pasdeloup Orchestra added another item to the history of American music in Europe by giving the first performance in France of the tone poem *Africa,* by the American Negro composer William Grant Still.

The work made a deep impression and was enthusiastically received by the large audience, and Richard Lert, who conducted, gave a reading of the difficult and penetrating composition that was perfect in detail and made felt the essence of Still's music, so sincere, so curiously and beautifully orchestrated, so unaffectedly, even primitively lyrical. If I had a regret, it was that Still was not present in person to approve his interpreters and to receive the plaudits of the crowd.

The work of Still is another evidence of the high summits to which the American Negro musician is soaring, and it must not be supposed that the American Negro composer is without ancestry, that he has no tradition when he has the example of men like Edmund Dede, Joseph White and Coleridge-Taylor to cheer him on.

William Grant Still was born in Mississippi in 1895. His life has been one of constant struggle, and also of progressive attainment. Part of his musical education he obtained under the guidance of Ernest Bloch and two or three other teachers, the rest he has by instinct. Among his compositions are *Puritan Epic, Darker Africa* (tone poems), *Afro-American Symphony, Sahdji* (ballet), *La Guiablesse* (Negro lyrical drama); *From the Land of Dreams, Levee Land, From the Black Belt* and *Log Cabin Ballads* (for chamber orchestra).

Africa is a tone-poem in three parts, the first and third of which were heard at the Pasdeloup concert. It is an American Negro's conception of the land of his ancestors, is based largely on folk-lore and was influenced by the composer's contact with American civilization. In mind's eye, the composer beholds not the Africa of reality but an Africa mirrored in fancy, and radiantly ideal. The first movement is called *Land of Peace.* In the opening measures the music establishes an atmosphere of pastoral repose and quiet. In contrast with it is spiritual peace, indicating the influence of America for the idiom is that of the spiritual. After its announcement by the horns, this theme is sung by the various choirs of the orchestra, passes through various formal color and key changes, works up to a concluding and expressive climax.

In *Land of Romance,* the music is tinged with ineffable sorrow, Africa is pictured as a land of fanciful and mysterious romance. The third part is *Land of Superstition.* Contact with American civilization has not yet enabled the composer to overcome his inherently superstitious nature. Superstition! This is the inheritance that binds him to the past, the heritage by which it is possible for him to form accurate notions of Africa, far-distant, far-removed, yet ever near and present.

Irving Schwerké
5 February 1933

Theater

Cocteau Ballet

Verily, at the Théatre des Champs-Elysées, one is not bored.

After the "noise-makers" concert of Friday night we were ready for an extravaganza of any proportions, but Jean Cocteau's ballet, "Les Mariés de la Tour Eiffel," is a delicious piece of buffoonery, in which the tentatives of "Le Boeuf sur le Toit" which M. Cocteau presented last season are brought to a successful and highly diverting development.

The audience came to be amused and expected as much from the house as from the stage. Therefore they shouted and cat-called and whistled and booed, and between these noises and the applause of the enthusiastic portion present, the appropriate music that accompanied the piece was almost indistinguishable.

After the ballet a man in the gallery arose in his place and yelled an impassioned harangue down at the delighted audience, calling them many things that the censor deletes, because of the approval manifested, and insisting on his own conspicuous sanity, as evidenced by his violent impatience with spectacle and spectators.

Jean Cocteau by Picasso

"Are you a Dada or an anti-Dada?" shouted one excited man to the orator. But pandemonium drowned question and reply and the answer to this is lost to us forever.

The curtain rises on a platform of the Tour Eiffel, done in a modern manner, naive in design, but insipid in color and particularly infelicitous in contrast to the costumes. At each side of the stage is a huge megaphone, from which alternate voices kept us informed of what was passing on the stage, and what was about to pass; a proceeding that was welcome, for the incoherence was complete, if amusing.

A wedding party arrives, in costumes of extreme drollery, and the ballet is built around the adventures that develop during the wedding feast. A photographer takes their picture, after many attempts, for each time that he opens the apparatus, an unexpected apparition makes its appearance, instead of the little bird that he promises. An ostrich, a lion—such an amusing lion! all front quarters and wide eyes—a bathing girl from Trouville, a mischievous little boy and many other personages.

A host of wireless dispatches arrives and dances about to a clever ritournelle by Germaine Taillefer. Each performer wears a mask and the impassivity of their heads, while they caper about in pantomime and dance, is irresistibly comic. The piece finishes, as it should, with entire inconsequence. The wedding party goes off in a train made by dragging a screen across the stage, painted to represent a railroad coach, and the photographer examines his camera while the proprietor restores order to the restaurant.

To those who see nothing but nonsense in all modern productions we recommend an evening at the Champs-Elysées this week. The ballet is diverting in the highest degree, and the audience even more so.

22 June 1921

Nudity and the Imagination

Those persons whose standards of morality, in the theater, are based on the number of square inches of skin concealed from the public gaze, are likely to receive the shock of their lives at the Casino de Paris. On the other hand, those whose psychological insight extends far enough to encompass the truth that nudity, or comparative nudity, in its actuality, annihilates the imagination, will be bored by the displays that are supposed—by some theater directors—to be most alluring.

The most destructive group of women that ever appeared on the American stage wore skirts to the floor and long trains. They left wreck, ruin and murder in their wake, they were the Floradora Sextette. I doubt very much if the ladies who appear at the Casino de Paris in costumes scarcely larger than a special delivery postage stamp will ever cause the slightest ripple in the most precarious of domestic establishments.

Voilà! Two or three of these Casino houris are perfectly nude to the waist, others go even farther. The charms of some are visible through perfectly diaphanous draperies. All have bare legs—*cela va sans dire.*

But this is not a moralistic treatise, far from it, the purpose being merely to set forth certain brief suggestions relative to a psychological condition. And speaking of psychology, it seems pardonable also to wonder what these charm-displaying girls think about when not before the footlights. Have they, or the ones responsible for their appearance, artistic purposes? Art may be well served by nudity, to be sure, when it is perfect in outline; but how rarely is it perfect in the actuality of the stage!

Confessing ourselves to be sophisticated and but mildly curious over the preceding issue, let us pass to other points in the present show at the Casino de Paris, with its extremely popular song of the hour, *"Il faut Savoir tout Prendre avec le Sourire,"* which gives the spectacle its name. After passing through a desert of mediocrity of outworn music, dances, posings, millinery and fragmentary gowns, we come to a bright flowery and fragrant oasis, in the person of M. Maurice Chevalier.

When you try to catalogue M. Chevalier, that is another matter. You think of a half dozen of the best American and English comedians and try to compare him with any one of them. It can't be done; and then you can only decide that he embraces some of the best elements of all of them. He is screamingly funny when perfectly silent; he can put over dialogue with tremendous zest; with but little vocal attainment, he is yet able to make a song, especially the "Smile" thing, into an original triumph. And finally he can dance and do acrobatic stunts with the best. Unusual and talented person, this M. Chevalier.

Sharing honors almost equally in the dancing line is J. W. Jackson, who looks like an American. There are also several other dancers and comedians quite worth while in the show. Finally comes Poiret as exhibited in the lavish and original costuming of the concourse of "Grandes Amoureuses." All that can be said of Poiret is that even if he designs a gown of a distinct period, it has marked distinction, and you know instantly that no one in the world could have done it except Poiret.

The Casino show is inordinately long and, as indicated, has many ordinary spots. It has run a long time, but it has high spots enough, probably, to keep it going for many weeks yet. And that M. Chevalier is the highest spot of them all.

Wilbur Judd
27 June 1921

Bernhardt Dies in Arms of Son; Sacrament 'Mid Movie "Props"

Quietly and unreluctantly, Mme. Sarah Bernhardt died in the arms of her son Maurice last night at 8:15 o'clock. Her family and a few friends prayed beside her bed.

Her devoted granddaughter Lysiane, Mme. Louis Verneuil, was certain that she saw a faint smile of joy break through the thickening shadows over the tragédienne's face.

Mme. Verneuil with Mme. Bernhardt's great grandson, little Maurice Gross, M. Arquilliere of the Comédie-Française, and Mme. Peyronnet of the Théatre Sarah Bernhardt, were in the room when the end came. The elder granddaughter, Mme. Gross, had gone to her own home shortly before.

The last sacraments were administered to Mme. Bernhardt at 3:10 o'clock yesterday afternoon while the servants moved the motion picture cameras, electric cables and lighting apparatus from the house into a van.

The double symbol represented her acceptance of defeat at the last, for although she had not spoken since ten o'clock in the morning, Mme. Bernhardt shook her head negatively every time the family suggested clearing the house of the studio apparatus.

When it became apparent that the great artiste was sinking into silence, the granddaughter, Lysiane, Mme. Louis Verneuil, hurried in her limousine to a priest. Father Risser of the Church of Saint-Francis de Sales returned with her, encountering the departing symbols of "Divine Sarah's" earthly career.

Responds To Sacrament

Leaving the house, Father Risser said that though she was motionless and speechless, Mme. Bernhardt showed unmistakable recognition in her eyes, responding to questions during the sacrament with a slight pressure of her hand.

At the same time that the call was sent for the priest, calls were sent to the Roslands and other life-long friends of the dying tragédienne.

Mme. Rosland, known to France as "Rosemonde," arrived hurriedly, accompanied by her son, Maurice. Descending from a taxi-cab, the dramatist's widow, weeping convulsively and unable to walk alone, was half-carried into the house by her son.

They were admitted to the sick room, where Mme. Bernhardt recognized them and attempted to smile.

Immediately afterwards Mme. Bernhardt went into a coma from which she did not recover.

Professor Labbé, an Academician and one of the world's greatest kidney specialists, arrived at six o'clock to hold a consultation. As he left, he said gravely, "We can only wait for the end now."

Lysiane, her granddaughter, with M. Louis Verneuil, and Dr. Marot, were at the bedside during the last moments.

Dies In Son's Arms

Mme. Bernhardt did not regain consciousness and died in the arms of her son.

Her grandson, Gross, went immediately to a florist and came back with an enormous bunch of lilacs in mauve and white and placed it on her bed. Mme. Perronnet of the Théâtre Sarah Bernhardt and M. Arquilliere of the Comédie-Française came to the house shortly after her death.

From the Elysée Palace to the tenements of Montmartre and La Villette Paris mourned last night.

Around the three story house on the Boulevard Pereire a motley assemblage waited for hours, unwilling to believe that so much which seemed permanent of the glory of France had passed forever.

Again and again old men and youths, rich and poor alike went to Mme. Bernhardt's door, demanding, "Is it true, monsieur? Can it be true? "

Fullest funeral arrangements were made by Mme. Bernhardt herself in recent years. Belle Isle was chosen as her last resting place, where the jagged rocks rise high into the air, overlooking the sea like a monument raised by nature to the greatest of her kind.

The famous rosewood coffin purchased thirty years ago, lined with its delicate mauve satin chosen by the artist herself, is to be used for the funeral.

In that rosewood box Mme. Bernhardt sometimes slept, years ago, telling her friends that "Death must hold no terrors for me." From this incident, and from the legend which grew up that she never travelled without her coffin, the expression "le cercueil de Sarah Bernhardt" entered the French language as a phrase to describe the macabre and the weird.

Vincent Sheean
27 March 1923

The Odéon Rejuvenated

For a good hundred years any reference to the Odéon as being far, far away, or devastatingly dull, or perpetually empty, was as much a sure-fire joke in France, as any allusion in America to the dirt of Pittsburg or the long-haired men and short-haired women of Greenwich Village.

American visitors too in years not long past found inspiration for a sort of incredulous glee in the ancient bag of tricks so dear to both actors and audience, in the antiquated and dilapidated settings reminiscent of the old ten-twenty-thirty in America. It was not many years ago that I saw "Les Misérables" at the Odéon in a set of flapping flats and with a consumptive death song that would have done honor to a never to be forgotten American melodrama of my youth in which I clearly remember that the young wife was diabolically got off the stage by being told to go upstairs where she would find "powder and everything to make a bride bright, happy, and comfortable."

But times have changed; and during this last year a director of the New York Theatre Guild remarked to me that Americans had no conception of the achievements of Gémier at the Odéon. It is to Gémier, first of all, naturally, that we must look for an explanation of the tremendous progress which the second national theatre of France has shown in recent years. Gémier, who believes in the democracy of the theatre, who seeks to reconstitute those national and universal qualities which belonged to the public entertainment of the ancient arena and the mediaeval square, and has by that token liberated himself from the formula of strict naturalism in the theatre, has, with his combination of a community ideal and a renewed method of mise-en-scène, accomplished great changes in a short time. It was not without long preparation that Gémier came into the execution of his theories in the official position of director of the second state theatre. After long experience with Antoine, acting and directing in regular theatres, in music halls, in small fashionable theatres, in advanced theatres, at the Cirque d'Hiver, he had perfected a careful technique in acting, tried out his theories in almost every conceivable genre, and kept in close contact with the public.

Even today we find at the Odéon a welcome variety of the modern and the classic in the French repertoire; and to the English speaking public it offers a range from Shakespeare to O'Neill. Among the works of more recent French dramatists given at the Odéon is Lenormand's "Le Simoun," a drama laid in the oppressive heat and enervating stillness of the African desert. The atmosphere is created at the start and largely maintained throughout by the dancing, singing, and acting of the negro player Habib Benglia, in the role of a minstrel. Gémier as a father haunted by the problem of incest, builds his portrayal soundly from scenes of precise realism at the beginning to the lyric exaltation of tragedy at the end. The play is a combination of interesting psychological insight with very obvious melodrama: Gémier and Benglia lift it above its normal plane of significance.

Typical of the Odéon treatment of a classic is the dramatization of Voltaire's "Candide" by Marches and Vautel produced in a Guignol setting devised by Fuerst. Visually the result is most pleasing. Inside the proscenium frame is set up a miniature stage with its own elaborate, painted columns, portals, and draperies; and a curtain upon which are painted the dancing forms of Candide, his beloved Cunegonde, the philosophic Doctor Pangloss, and the ancient unknown female who shares their adventures. The scenes are a jolly set of inventions like colored toys: romantic intimacy, gaudy grandeur, and the post-card picturesque are parodied with pleasant humor. Against this fantastic background and with the more or less music-hall character of the acting, the satire is thrown into strong relief; and how thoroughly up to the minute it is.

Shakespeare is well represented in the Odéon list of plays. "The Merchant of Venice," which is the backbone of the Shakespearean repertoire, has come to be a supreme example of non-literal adaptation. Retranslation from a translation; jazzed up, as we might say; it is as far from the original as the requirements of immediate popular appeal might, in certain opinions, lead an Elizabethan text. Gémier, though his comparatively simple setting of steps leading to a back platform, easily masked for small interiors and quickly adapted to open square or judicial chamber, would make scene shifting very easy, nevertheless does not give us the Shakespearean swift alternation of scenes which amounts almost to simultaneity. He arranges the play, suppresses whole scenes, and puts in others. In some cases too he rewrites characters; and he introduces an enormous amount of special stage business. The Prince of Morocco becomes a figure of burlesque, his every action duplicated with miniature bombast by a tiny page of his own color. The solitary Tubal becomes a whole group of Jews, fellow-conspirateurs of Shylock. Gémier's own interpretation of Shylock is closer to the aspect of the Jew as seen through mediaeval eyes. It is a figure of tremendous vitality, but confined to the realm of thwarted villainy; there is perhaps a touch of pathos in his complete humiliation, but there is no suggestion of the dignity of racial martyrdom which Anglo-Saxons have of late read into the role. The spectacular element in the production is the interpolation of two violent mob scenes. The carnival becomes a wild nocturnal celebration, with colored lights, costumed and masqued crowds swirling up and down the stage steps and in and out of the house: a kaleidoscopic effect of color, movement, revelry. Shylock reeling home from the night's feasting, is attacked by the mob, shoved and dragged into a circle, taunted by rhythmic gibes, until he collapses at the end of the scene. In the trial scene the mob gathers about him, threatening him in chorus, a refrain which rises higher and higher till he drops to his knees and signs away his estates. Many of Gemier's innovations here partake rather too much of the nature of added attractions, arising from no interpretive necessity. Yet better any of these things than the curse of dull pedantry.

O'Neill's "Emperor Jones" was a presentation of particular interest, of course, to Americans. The whole atmosphere of the production was entirely different from that of the New York performers. Fuerst's settings, Benglia's acting in the title role, the movement and essential quality of the presentation were totally dissimilar to the corresponding elements in the American version. Gilpin's swagger and realistic bravado in the earlier scenes were in no way paralleled here. The setting for the first act—plaster-white walls broken by two low arches, a scarlet throne in the center—was an expression of the Emperor's attitude toward his surroundings rather than a realistic background, and Benglia's acting was here an interesting French stylization of the Emperor's temporary grandeur. As the scenes in the forest progressed, scenes laid in a black and white wilderness of forms largely reflective of the fears of the protagonist, Benglia's portrayal became more and more intense. Plastically his performance surpassed Gilpin's. In the moment when he climbs slowly to the slave block, and again when he is driven to the spasmodic dance of the primitive, he attains a rare and complete realization of emotional expression through the use of the body. In general, though the exigencies of translation and presentation before a foreign audience with preconceptions of its own, and the failure in the use of external means to preserve the tension of the monodrama somewhat weakened O'Neill's drama, it had a production at the Odéon which attained a significance rare in such transfer from the stage of one country to that of another. Americans await with justifiable interest the production of other American drama at the rejuvenated Odéon.

Florence Gilliam
4 May 1924

The Most Parisian of Paris Theatres

Why do American visitors in Paris pursue, with an enthusiasm which must eventually be disillusioned, the French revues of the type to be found usually at the Folies Bergères and the Casino de Paris? The French frankly preserve these institutions as an allurement for the foreigner; yet, in the case of Americans, could be no quicker or surer method of convincing the visiting population that the Parisian stage is inferior to their own. For it is just in this kind of production that the American theatre particularly excels. The Ziegfeld Follies, The Greenwich Village Follies, The Shubert Passing Shows, the revues and extravaganzas and other entertainments of this kind which a single season produces in New York, far outrank the Parisian brand.

They are more up to date; they have prettier girls; they are often funnier; they are usually better set, better costumed, better lighted; and they move always with a mechanical perfection and a magic ease unknown in the French revue of the same type. The summer visitor after going the round of these performances in Paris either becomes inarticulately bored, or seizes the first opportunity to say that the celebrated Parisian stage has been overrated.

It is not that I would solemnly advise more serious fare for the casual visitor; though a whole season in Paris would reveal much that is worth while in the legitimate drama. But for light summer entertainment there is so much better stuff to be found in the small, so called "chic," theatres in Paris, of which the Daunou is a typical example. It is true, of course, that certain visitors whose comprehension of French does not work at lightning speed, naturally pass up these smaller and more Parisian entertainments for spectacles in which the comprehension of the eye is the chief requirement. But such a choice is not really necessary. Quite aside from the amusement to be derived from the quick repartee and the witty local allusions of these more intimate comedies, there is plenty to charm the eye and ear of the most casual spectator. The settings and costumes are likely to be distinguished examples of current French taste. There are luxurious interiors on a small scale; pleasant fantasies restrained and simplified for scenes out of doors. And these theatres make a specialty not only of spectacular costuming but of perfection in fashionable dress, even when turned to purposes of comic effect. Often too there is music of that pleasant melodic quality so much more characteristic of the French composer than the repetitions, adaptations, and imitations of American jazz tunes with which the big revues manufacture many of their scores. The love scenes of the small comedies have just as much or more romantic charm than those of the big spectacles. And, as for following the action, theatres like the Daunou give, of course, the customary outline of the plot (in one, two, or three languages), and the comic gift of the most finished Paris comedians is conveyed by attitudes, gestures, intonations delightfully comprehensible even to those who do not grasp the subtleties of the dialogue.

Florence Gilliam
25 May 1924

Black Birds May Be Hit of Summer Season in Paris

Black Birds, the all-Negro show which has started at the Moulin Rouge, bids fair to become the big hit of the Paris summer season.

Although brought here by Mr. Lew Leslie primarily to appeal to the tourist trade and the resident British and American colony, this typically American show has caught the fancy of the French. And this is no little compliment to the talent of the players, for they must "put over" their songs and dialogues in a language not understood by a goodly portion of the audience.

Josephine Baker, colored entertainer who was the toast of Paris two years ago, did it, but hers was but one act in a revue predominantly French. The Black Birds must maintain the interest for an entire evening—and they are doing it superbly.

They are assisted by a red hot jazz band, the world famous jazz of the Plantation Club in New York. There are more than 100 artists in the Black

Bird company, including the popular stars, Adelaide Hall, Ada Ward, and Tim Moore, all well known on Broadway.

Another show which should prove interesting to Americans is *Maya,* in English, at the Studio des Champs-Elysées. This play, it will be remembered, was prohibited in New York after having scored a success in almost every European capital. The play is a psychological study of the life of a public woman and her clients. This piece, which is by Simon Gantillon, is a masterpiece in its way. The English translation is by Sibyl Harris.

The last performances of *La Castiglione,* with Mme. Ganna Walska in the title role, are announced for this week at the Comedie Champs-Elysées. Mme. Ganna Walska has scored a great triumph in her Paris debut. This is one show that should not be missed.

The English Players are out to establish a new record with *Journey's End* at the Theatre Albert Ier. This is a powerful war drama dealing with the reactions of a group of English officers in the trenches on the Somme while waiting for the big German offensive of March, 1918 to break. The three star roles are excellently acted.

10 June 1929

Pirandello on the Movies

This is a terrible crisis. Whenever the stock market slips down a few more points we wail and conclude that the old economic system has gone to pieces and nothing remains but financial anarchy.

Similar conclusions are applied to the theatre. Every time we sit in a half filled house before a mediocre play unenthusiastically performed for an indifferent audience—not a rare occurrence in these unhappy days—we feel forced to the opinion that the art of the theatre is dead and the talking movies have buried it. Putting plays on the stage, we sadly reflect, will soon be as placid an occupation as imitating medieval stained glass.

It is therefore comforting to meet a person who is not a professional optimist, who stands among the highest in the intellectual and artistic worlds, who has given much of his life to the theatre and who says without hesitation that the art of the stage is eternal—depressed by temporary world-wide economic troubles and harassed by bad conditions in particular countries, but certain of a great future, despite apparent competition by a new kind of spectacle which should not really conflict with it.

This person is Luigi Pirandello, the Italian dramatist.

Pirandello is a swell fellow. Samuel Putnam, editor of *The New Review* and translator of some of Pirandello's works, took me to see him last week at Pirandello's place in the Avenue Victor-Emmanuel III. Pirandello is 64 years old. He has a little pointed grey beard at the bottom of a tanned, creased, round face, and his eyes are unaffected, friendly, simple and honest. There is no hooey in him whatsoever.

He first became known in America years ago by the production of his *Six Characters in Search of an Author,* which was successful less because our countrymen understood it than because it was different from the plays to which they were accustomed; and since then all our intellectual circles have considered him a topnotcher. In spite of this, he really is a great man.

"The play is an eternal form," said Pirandello. "People will always want to see and hear the living actor. A shadow, a bad reproduction, will never satisfy them."

Pirandello has hopes for the American theatre, although it is hard to pin him down and find out definitely what those hopes are. Virtually, the only American playwright he knows is Eugene O'Neill, but he is going to the United States presently to see the work of other men. He esteems highly the later works of O'Neill, and is sorry that Europe knows chiefly such earlier plays as *The Emperor Jones, Anna Christie* and *The Hairy Ape.* He spoke in praise of *Strange Interlude,* but admitted that it was not a success in Germany because Freudian phenomena and inner sexual conflicts are old stuff in that country. Europe considers O'Neill elementary, Pirandello said, with an air of agreeing with Europe; yet he still believes O'Neill to be a man of promise.

The stage in Paris also presents hopeful possibilities to Pirandello, in spite of what he considers a bad season this year. Steve Passeur is the new author who impresses him most—a young man still full of defects, he said, but with force and something to say.

In Italy the theatre is in dreadful shape, in Pirandello's opinion. It is controlled by trusts who do nothing but buy up cheap foreign productions for importation. "But I believe that Signor Mussolini will be able to do something to improve this situation, just as he has bettered conditions in other fields," he said.

All this, while hopeful, is not forcefully so. Pirandello, up to this point in the conversation, spoke without great enthusiasm.

Then he was asked about the talking pictures and their effect upon the stage.

"They cannot hurt the theatre," he said. "Formerly the theatre did harm to itself by imitating the movies; now the movies are making the mistake of imitating the theatre.

"Naturally, in small towns, where great actors cannot go, the talking pictures serve a purpose in bringing their shadows to people who otherwise would never see them. But in the big cities they will never do as a substitute.

"The movie people make a fatal error when they try to imitate literature. You cannot put a novel of Dostoievsky or Tolstoi on the screen. It is too complicated. It requires too much thought. It only puzzles the public; it does not please them. The movies must leave literature for the novel and for the stage, and develop their own art, particularly suited to them.

"The talking motion picture machine is a worker of miracles, in itself, it does wonders and astounds the people. The problem is to find inventions of the spirit worthy of this machine."

R. L. Stern
31 May 1931

Little Magazines and Little Presses

Pierre Loving and *The Transatlantic Review*

We dropped in on Pierre Loving the other day and discovered him busy hammering away at his typewriter. We immediately found our interest whipped as we glimpsed some excerpts from the essay which appealed to us as extremely timely and discerning. Without further ado we appropriated the manuscript for our readers and here it is:

". . . it is nothing less than astonishing that a review, printed in English, as broad and unfettered and experimental as was *The Transatlantic,* should have held out as long and as lustily as it did. It had certain flaws—it would be truer to say, no doubt, that it had certain noble stigmata; probably it had both in equal parts. But it did not perish because of its flaws. No, the stigmata, which brought undeniable canonization in their wake, were beyond doubt the cause of its physical death. And yet there were grievous flaws. What the review chiefly lacked, according to one careful reader, was a—how shall one phrase it? —well, a stronger abutment of the editor's conscience in its pages. To be more exact, in the details of its pages. Mr. Ford's own literary personality, from which we have learned to expect much, was too little visible in the body of the magazine; it was niggardly relegated to the modest type of the *Chroniques* in the back. Surveying the definite achievement of *The Transatlantic,* we may safely record, I think, that its fiction was on the whole far superior to its articles or its verse, even though some excellent verse was published. I remember distinctly the verse of Mr. Adams, a poet I never . . . heard of before. But the fiction was often matchless. In the work of Ernest Hemingway and in that of Nathan Asch, Mr. Ford introduced two interesting young writers to the . . . public. Beyond these discoveries . . . the pervasive tone of the review—or rather what should have been the pervasive tone—was compacted into the editor's causerie. Save for the *Chroniques* of the editor, despite its loose stride, its air of feverish experiment, the general make-up of the magazine gave one a sensation of incurable drift. The feeling somehow clung, even after one had narrowly scrutinized the individual contributions and found some of them good, especially the short fiction which was hard to tally anywhere else. But the sense of adventure and play in letters was worthily fed in *The Transatlantic*. Discriminating readers will always be thankful for that."

Eugene Jolas
18 January 1925

La Maison des amis des livres
Chez Adrienne Monnier

Words, Words, Words!

Surrealisme has captured as its chief citadel *Commerce*, the magazine of the *avant-garde* published under the guide of Mlle. Adrienne Monnier at the *Maison des amis des livres*. M. Louis Aragon . . . gives a strange explanation of surrealisme in the last number of *Commerce*, under the title of *"Une vague de Rêve."* Among other things, he says: "I lived in the shadow of a great white building decorated with flags and echoing with cries. I was not allowed to leave this chateau, nor its society, and those who stepped up the staircase produced an atrocious cloud of dust on the doormat. . . . But slowly I unraveled other most definite beliefs. . . . They can be reduced to very little. 'The tendency of every being must be to persevere in its being' is one of their favorite formulas . . . the ignoble expression 'enchanted with finalisme' suffices for them to condemn

Adrienne Monnier

everything. Then they inaugurate paragraphs of their intellectual lives by this phrase which they like: 'Let us take the veil from words.' They never suspect that such methods drag them to the realizations of hypotheses, and hypotheses *a posteriori*. Their spirits are hybrid monsters, etc." In reading the article one comes dangerously near the feeling that, after all, the philosophic background of the new consciousness is not new. . . . For we have heard those accents before. . . .

Eugene Jolas
8 February 1925

The Middle West and Mr. Ford Madox Ford, etc.

There is a sharply personal article in the *Literary Review* of the New York *Evening Post* in which Mr. Ford Madox Ford . . . silhouettes the literary physiognomy of his friend, Ernest Hemingway, and other writers. Mr. Ford expatiates interestingly on the qualities of the American literary youth of today, and benignly points out the objective egotism of the Middle Western writers. What he says about Ernest Hemingway bears quotation: "The best writer in America at this moment (though for the moment he happens to be in Paris), the most conscientious, the most master of his craft, the most consummate, is my young friend Ernest Hemingway. . . .

Hemingway, with immense labor and excruciating thought and knowledge, turns out a short paragraph. . . . That would damn Mr. Hemingway if it were not for his youthful bloodlust which is an admirable derivative. . . . Mr. Hemingway writes like an Angel; like an Archangel; but his talk—his manner—is that of a bayonet instructor. He never gets very far from the spirit of Berlud!"

Introducing Miss Gertrude Stein's New York

Intense interest is being shown in literary circles at the forthcoming book *The Making of Americans* by Gertrude Stein to be published by the Contact Editions . . . Mr. Robert McAlmon, the director of the Contact Editions, told us recently that he expected Miss Stein's volume to be the beginning of a new literary epoch. "Because of the timorousness of commercial publishers," Miss Stein's work has only appeared in brief extracts in the *Transatlantic Review*. It will be issued in four to six volumes, appearing over a period of a year or more. Among the books published by this firm are volumes by Bryher, Mary Butts, Ford Madox Ford, Ernest Hemingway, Mina Loy, Ezra Pound and William Carlos Williams.

American Writers in Paris May Organize

Ever since the *Transatlantic Review* became extinct, the Anglo-Saxon literary forces now "exiled" here have been without cohesion. We just learn that a group of young Americans is preparing to launch a new magazine which is to be the expression of the modern American consciousness, and, which, we are told, will take a militant attitude toward the so-called Middle Western school of writers. This new group, loosely connected, is bound together apparently by the ambition to express creatively the abstraction of their age.

Eugene Jolas
8 March 1925

From a Litterateur's Notebook

This Quarter is out at last, and it seems to me that simple statement of its contents is the highest praise which may be extended to its editors, Ernest Walsh and Ethel Moorhead. This time, it was printed in Milan. Its advent is a literary event of the highest importance and familiarity with its pages will be necessary to those who wish to keep pace with modern artistic achievement.

The prose contributions are by James Joyce, Ernest Hemingway, William Carlos Williams, Djuna Barnes, Robert McAlmon, Kay Boyle, Morley Callaghan and Ethel Moorhead. Ezra Pound heads the list of poets, followed by Emanuel Carnevali, Raymond Knister, Ernest Walsh, Kenneth Fearing, Eugene Jolas, Robert Roe, and Carl Sandburg.

One of the principal services rendered . . . is the publication of copious extracts from the scores of George Antheil, which will enable musicians to break through the utter drivel which newspapers have published about his work and to examine it for themselves.

Nothing contained in the volume is so trivial that it can be summarized. . . . I cannot resist, however, saying a glad word because Dr. Williams is on the list. He has always seemed to me one of the few men in America who is completely sane, who sees things with a clarity which may be used almost as a standard of right-thinking. My test for queer people would be a measure of their degree of disagreement with Williams. His article sums up America, without hope or abuse, sentimentality, cleverness, or regret. After reading it, Sinclair Lewis and H. L. Mencken will gather up what few goods they each hastily and simply hide, flee from the face of mankind, dissolve like snails in rock salt. Either that, or they will fail to see anything in it.

There are two American poets I regret were not included. . . . They are Gertrude Stein and E. E. Cummings, but the former has recently published a tremendous novel (which she wrote years ago, I believe) and the latter is staggering from the effect of having won the Dial prize.

Elliot H. Paul
31 January 1926

Ernest Walsh, Poet and Editor, Dies in Monte Carlo at Age of Thirty-One

Literary Paris was dismayed yesterday, when news was received that Ernest Walsh, poet and editor of *This Quarter,* was dead. . . . The poet died in Monte Carlo after a lingering illness. The news of his death came as a distinct shock to his numerous friends in Paris, who, although aware of his delicate health, were unprepared for the sudden end. It was generally stated that American literature loses in him one of the most brilliant poets of the younger generation, as well as an *animateur,* who has left his stamp on the literary history of his age.

Up to a few days before his death, he was still at work, dictating letters to unknown poets in every part of the world, writing poetry with a hand that was already weak, discussing details for the third number of *This Quarter.* . . . The third number of *This Quarter,* by many regarded as the most brilliant and advanced magazine in the Anglo-Saxon world, will be issued in the near future, and will in many ways be a monument to the genius of the young poet. This number will contain a plethora of his last writings, and will be his farewell to the world.

Walsh placed himself in the front-rank of the modern literary movement, when he, together with Miss Ethel Moorhead, launched *This Quarter* in the early part of 1925. The magazine by the sheer force of its dynamic quality—in contradistinction to the emasculated quality of most of the modern magazines—created a sensation on both sides of the Atlantic. It was violently attacked by the reactionaries and academicians. Several months later this number was followed by a second one, representing also some of the more radical of the younger poets and writers, including Ezra Pound, James Joyce, Ernest Hemingway, Robert McAlmon.

American literature loses in Ernest Walsh an intellectual whip. He opened up many channels for expression and facilitated the emergence of writers who were suppressed by a commercial criticism.

Eugene Jolas
26 October 1926

Pound's *Exile* Is Published

After an inexplicable term of silence, Ezra Pound, aggressive American poet, critic, prosateur and defender of the original in art, has launched from his retreat at Rapallo his long-promised magazine *Exile*. Mr. Pound warns the unwary that his publication contains nothing except what is personally interesting to himself and that it is not likely to interest anybody who has no fault to find with the current condition of letters in England. Those who accept these conditions may purchase *Exile* three times a year until the editor "gets bored with it."

The first number contains several selections the quality of which may be taken for granted by the prospective purchaser who is acquainted with Mr. Pound's judgment. The editor himself, Ernest Hemingway, John Rodker and Guy Hickok are among those represented. The magazine is for sale at the Titus bookshop, just back of the Dôme, for 10 cents a copy.

11 March 1927

Magazines in General and One in Particular

Since the discontinuation of *This Quarter,* there has been no outlet— dubiously excepting *Dial* and *Vanity Fair*—for the writer whose expression is shaped into an untried form. There has been no editor willing— or, perhaps, able—to allow a contributor to choose his own material and treatment, none to take a chance on an unrecognized talent. If he would see his work in print, the writer was forced to conform to the petrified criterion of a magazine's public or as in the case of the *Mercury,* mimic the editor.

With practically every American editor trapped in a blind-alley plugged by commercial interests, the advent of *transition* in Paris is of exceptional interest both to writers and to readers, for the program of this new literary magazine is joyfully devoid of gags and shackles. Circulation being a secondary matter, the artistic opinions of a business office are not required: being published in France, there is no risk of busybodies suppressing an issue because of an offending phrase. In short, there is no irrelevant machinery between the editor's desk and the linotype machine.

Elliot Paul and Eugene Jolas, who are responsible for *transition,* assume without rehearsal the role of creative editors. Both are alert to the manifestation of new influences and methods; both through their own writing have shouldered the problems that block the way to self-expression; the prejudices of each are visible only at the point where originality ends and bad writing begins. If the writer is articulate, they respect his full right to say what he wants about subjects of his own choosing.

The creative editorship of MM. Paul and Jolas does not evidence itself by personal dominance of the magazine. It is more subtly displayed in the tolerance and firm judgment with which they have selected the contents. If for a moment their discrimination may seem to be on vacation, it may be as a purposeful test of the reader's wariness, for a self-respecting editor is justified in hoping for the mental cooperation of his audience.

This tolerance and good judgment are, I believe, a far more reliable indication of *transition*'s worth than the excellent stories and poems that fill the first issue. After all, many manuscripts have accumulated and no laborious research would be needed to find sufficient material for an issue or two. But the maintenance of a high standard and a consistent avoidance of the dull imperatively demand a sound and sensitive editorship.

The April number of *transition* has about it nothing of the belligerent radicalism of *Secession* nor the passive correctness of T. S. Eliot's *Criterion Quarterly*. In range it extends from the advanced writing which represents the latest stage of James Joyce's evolution to the conservative but richly woven prose of Ludwig Lewisohn. Each narrative and poetic contribution represents a personal tendency caught at a high degree of perfection. This insistence on uniform quality rather than uniform style is the most reassuring sign that *transition* is well immunized from arteriosclerosis.

Robert Sage
20 March 1927

A Transitional Phenomenon

Let us look at *transition*. Here is the most ambitious effort of the young, and, in the usual sense, unsuccessful writers among the exiles.

The first number is out and may be taken as an earnest of what is to come. For purposes of examination, the poetry may be put aside. It is all pretty innocuous. Mr. Jolas is to be felicitated on his already well-known talents as a translator, and all the verse might by a candid judge be said to

Eugene Jolas

possess the quality known as poetic. So much the worse if it mean little to the average reader; this is probably what the verse of the near future will be like.

The old emotions, or modes of expressing them have gone stale. Landscape poetized and made to flow with the flux of the soul, the theme of so many lyric poets of the century past, now seems unreal. The young men of our day are surveying, rather than external nature, the dark mysteries of the psyche. Hence grotesque juxtapositions of mood, the nausea of conflicting emotions, even the empty play of clashing words and ideas.

It is the prose that may be examined and the esthetic theory behind it defined. In this number of *transition,* we may roughly divide the prose into the intelligible and the unintelligible.

Of the former stand out the opening pages of Mr. Lewisohn's latest contemplated novel, in which he shows that he is a real story teller. It is interesting to note that he has begun with the old-fashioned preface, for even when he is telling a story, Mr. Lewisohn is fundamentally a moralizer. . . .

But obviously the main dishes on the bill are those of Mr. Joyce and Miss Stein. They are supposed to be the leaders of this group, blazing trails down which the less hardy may run. In passing, I should make no pretense to pass judgment on the totality of Mr. Joyce's work. That would involve complete knowledge of it, to say the least. What I am concerned with is this particular chunk of intelligibility as an illustration of an esthetic theory.

Mr. Joyce has deliberately chosen to break the ordinary social contract between author and reader. This fundamental concept of the old esthetic code being neglected, Mr. Joyce can have no complaint if intelligence (the intelligence that brings order out of chaos) condemns his writing as nonsense. If the past course of literary history can be relied on, this writing may be exceedingly interesting as an ephemeral phenomenon; but it will remain as an eddy in the current.

But it may be interesting to examine this work, and, so far as that be possible, to describe it. The idea of communication is flouted; the essential, and the only essential is that the writer shall express himself. The unwary reader who may try to make of it what ordinary intelligence calls sense is losing his time.

. . . the art of Mr. Joyce is not primitive. It is a highly sophisticated backwash of romantic irony, the germs of which may be seen at least as far back as Tieck, and the very concept of which may have come into the world of western thought when Kant obfuscated the whole theory of knowledge.

The time and even space elements have been lost sight of by Mr. Joyce. His obvious aim is to reproduce the flux of consciousness through the human mind. It takes little introspection to see how interesting this is and how impossible. Here is figured, to some extent, that which makes of every man who is ever so little self-conscious, a criminal and a philanthropist, a sadist and a masochist, and a thousand other personalities at one and the same time. But the attempt to photograph the psychologic stream, besides being dull, is futile; that stream runs too swift. Even Mr. Joyce in some way practices selection.

Mr. Joyce's technical devices correspond to what he is trying to accomplish. Examine them; out of an occasional conglomeration of words, or out of the whole, it may bring some comprehension. Take, for example, the willful mispronunciations which they evoke. These float to the consciousness of every man alive every day, and are shown in the conscious deformations of children, once they have passed the stage of baby talk. Frayed nerves, or exuberant vitality (at least in the case of the children) is behind all this. With it goes another trick of Mr. Joyce's, one common to adults with an encumbered vocabulary, and too much mental luggage, and which, incidentally, is used by the laboratory psychologists in certain sorts of mental tests. It is the telescoping of words and images, what, when it was done with words alone, was in the old rhetoric called *crasis.* Mr. Joyce gives one a real jolt when he jams together 'enemy' and 'inniskilling' to make 'inimyskilling,' or 'memorial' and 'marmor' to make 'mormorial.' Those nourished on the humanities remember the first instance they encountered this when they found 'kagathos' for 'kai agathos.'

All of which does not alter the truth about the whole. Mr. Joyce may be a deliberate mystifier, and having a good laugh, but I doubt it. He might as well be one. His writing is a negation of the constructive effort which has always been necessary to narrative art. Nor in detail is he enrichening the language. Neither English nor any other living tongue can absorb neologisms at the rate with which Mr. Joyce turns them loose.

Alex Small
10 April 1927

Notes of Montparnasse

Mr. Wyndham Lewis's *The Enemy* is a very serious publication, and it pays considerable attention to America and American writers, and particularly to the writing group of expatriates now in Paris. . . . Mr. Lewis is in dead earnest, and he writes none too consecutively. What he has to say is stimulating and pertinent, but it has more the effect of a series of electric flashes rather than a steady flow of light turned on the subject at hand. He begins with a bold challenge to the bookshops of the Left Bank, which he accuses of being agents of Joyce and of the "Super-realist and Dôme sodalities," which with overstressed truculence he is attacking. Then he gets on to his work, and devotes much space to considering *transition* as the mouthpiece of the American expatriates. Here Mr. Lewis makes the error of regarding *transition* as merely a vehicle for the latest writing of Mr. Joyce (whom he thinks does not belong with that group but is a phenomenon *sui generis*), and Miss Stein, with whom he has little patience. He seems to have not noticed, or to have disregarded as unimportant, the highly interesting experimental work being done by some of the less known poets and story-writers who contribute to *transition*.

Lewis points out the intelligent youth of our day are not concerned with being revolutionary. Rather they have been infected with the terrors of their fathers, and rather than rushing into experiment, are more concerned with defending the bits of property and the bourgeois morality which still are left of their heritage.

This brief indication may tempt you to read an article which is worthwhile, and which contains much more than I have mentioned. And I hope it might arouse Mr. Elliot Paul, who is named specifically, to a rejoinder, in which he would be bound to state Mr. Lewis's ideas more clearly than the latter does himself.

Alex Small
12 October 1927

Footnotes: *Exile*

While the publication dates of the fourth *This Quarter* and the final number of *The Little Review* are still floating indefinitely somewhere in the near future, Mr. Ezra Pound's *The Exile* has unexpectedly made its third appearance in Paris via the American mails to fill up the interim. Those responsible for the reading matter in this issue are W. B. Yeats, John Rodker, R. C. Dunning, Payson Loomis, Morley Callaghan, Clifford Gessler, Howard Weeks and Herman Spector—also Louis Zukofsky, E. P. and Ezra Pound, who still writes occasionally under his own name.

It is Mr. Pound's habit to leave his stamp quite clearly on his undertakings, and the third *Exile,* like the first, is very decidedly Poundian, in spite of the heterogeneity of the contents. The editor editorializes, poeticizes, comments, warns and criticizes so insistently that his personality—and he has a personality whether you like it or not (I don't)—quite dominates Senator Yeats' correct verses, Mr. Dunning's cautious rhymes, Mr. Callaghan's skillful realism and Mr. Rodker's terminating pages of *Adolphe*. In fact, Mr. Pound reserves the *pièce de résistance* of the number for himself, for Louis Zukofsky, the creator of *Poem Beginning "The,"* shorn of his fake nose and whiskers, can be nobody in the world but Mr. Ezra Pound . . . attempting to spoof his favorite friend, The Public. And the gesture is almost perfect . . . this *Poem Beginning "The,"* smothered in a maze of documentation that makes T. S. Eliot and Marianne Moore look like amateur footnoters, is a cold-and-calculated piece that leaves few footholds for adverse criticism.

There are several interesting things in *The Exile,* but it's difficult to shake Editor Pound, who follows you right on through like a guide in a museum.

Robert Sage
13 May 1928

A New Mythology

When a young and lively magazine called *The New Yorker* made its appearance some years ago, it was eagerly and immediately acclaimed and became straightway an immediate success. The reason for this popularity was primarily that it filled a certain need for the smartening-up of humor. It was a need which was just beginning to be felt and one that established magazines in a similar vein were still unaware of. It spoke of the people who for the moment held the public's interest, and dealt with them with exactly the quantity of wit or appreciation that Carl Van Vechten or sophisticated contemporary opinion accorded them. In this way *The New Yorker* has followed a brilliant career, and because of its uncanny ear for things in "good taste" that are taking place, and its remarkable knack of commenting cleverly upon them, it has earned its well-deserved reputation of being a valuable record of the point of view it records in America.

The point of view in question, however, makes achievement a limited thing. It leaves no field for revolt, for mystery, or for the existence of, for instance, what Eugene Jolas began calling in the very first issue of his magazine *transition* a new mythology. By this mythology is meant the creative work of people who do not necessarily serve as dinner-table topics but who have in some way wanted to contribute to the durable quality of the age into which they have come. It is not an easy thing to announce the actual presence of something generally unperceived, and to persist with vigor and enthusiasm in seeking out evidence of its existence in the face of indifference, and in many instances, of hostility. To make this search over a period of two years the basis for the appearance of a monthly review is obviously an enormous task.

That Eugene Jolas has succeeded is no longer a matter of doubt. The tradition of insecurity which "art" magazines have established by their tendency to spring up like mushrooms and die out as quickly again has been, with the general opposition of the press, another drawback to the success of *transition*. But now with the appearance of No. 15, the third quarterly issue since its change from a monthly appearance, any doubts as to its permanency and as to its value should be put to rest. This number, under the sole editorship of Eugene Jolas, does at least one definite and important thing. Apart from what it offers as pure reading matter, its collection of articles on photography by Jean-Georges Auriol, L. Moholy-Nagy, and Robert Desnos, and the series of reproductions of the work of Eugene Atget, Man Ray and Moholy-Nagy, give it a documentary value of unusual interest.

It is doubtful whether the dual perception which has from the very first run through the pages of *transition* could have existed in the attitude of one born and reared in an old country. But because of the confusion and variety of Eugene Jolas' experiences he is sensitized to two civilizations. This has made it possible for him to respond to what we have come to consider the purely American product, that is the unimaginative and homely school of writing, as well as to the fantasy and the "beyond realism" of the modern European writer. The presentation of opposed schools in writing in the pages of one periodical has in itself established the fact that "modern" is by no means a descriptive term, and that the inspiration of each new writer stems from the old mythology of his own land.

There is no reason why such an admission could create a sense of confusion. Rather is it a fresh thing to read a magazine which is making no attempt to create artists all of a piece. The experimental vocabulary of James Joyce has no relation to the intense and direct prose of Robert McAlmon, or either of these to the solemn loyalty Peter Neagoe gives romance. Nor need the biting cynicism of Matthew Josephson touch the quality of Harry Crosby's hymns, or the realism of Atget's photographs impinge upon a universe seen only through the eye of Man Ray's camera. Any one of these contributions is more than a comment upon what New Yorkers will say over the tea-cups this week, and if they be less than fables for a new mythology, let us enjoy them as some of the best reading our time has offered, and leave the rest to another age to decide.

Kay Boyle
10 March 1929

Swan Song of *The Little Review*

The final number of *The Little Review* has appeared, the most interesting literary document of years. Margaret Anderson and Jane Heap are voluntarily discontinuing it, Margaret Anderson because "even the artist doesn't know what he is talking about. And I can no longer go on publishing a magazine in which no one really knows what he is talking about. . . ."

F. B.
1 September 1929

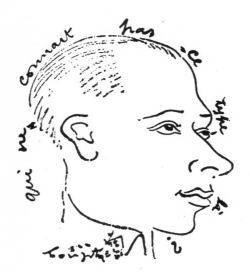

Henri Broca

Boy Grows Up to Edit
"The Chief Organ of Montparnasse Society"

If Montparnasse has an "official" life, Henri Broca is the animator of it. Broca is the publisher, editor, reporter, copyreader, and artist for *Paris-Montparnasse,* the magazine which styles itself as the chief organ of Montparnasse society; the monthly which has Man Ray as staff photographer, Fujita, Kiki, Kisling, André Salmon and Broca as perpetual subjects for articles. About this handsome, athletically built man clusters a large group of artists and writers who look to him for their diversions. If there is "nothing doing," Broca creates something.

Montparno
10 December 1929

Nancy, the Last of the Famous Cunarders, Steers Her Hand Press into the Stormy Literary Seas of the Montparnasse Surrealists

In the Rue Guénégaud, near the Seine—both the river and the street—Jacques and Henry are this week setting up a hand-printing press. This is an important item of news for all those who write in the ultra modern vein, or the near ultra, for the press belongs to Nancy Cunard and from it will come, beginning soon, a long list of books chosen from this group of writers. Until this week, the press has been functioning in Chapelle-Réanville under the name of the Hours Press. The name will remain and so will the master printer—Nancy Cunard.

Last June the town of Chapelle-Réanville heard that one of its residents, an English girl, had purchased a printing press and was hard at work. This was the beginning of the Hours Press. Miss Cunard had decided that certain writings by moderns looked better in books than in manuscripts. So she bought a printing press and went to work. All the type she sets herself, her two partners, Jacques and Henry, having other duties on their shoulders. She has ideas about printing, in regard to type, size and form which no one seems to know where she learned. No doubt, they just came to her, as she herself did to the print shop.

Since the June day when the font of type was put into place in the French village, Miss Cunard has published four volumes: *One Day* by Norman Douglas, *Perronik the Fool* by George Moore, *The Eaten Heart* by Richard Aldington, and a French translation of the Lewis Carroll story, *The Hunting of the Snark,* which was done by Louis Aragon. All of these have been marketed.

But Chapelle-Réanville is, after all, a long way from the center of affairs. Telephones function rather sporadically, and the mailmen have habits all their own. So the Hours Press is now being established in the midst of things. From its new location, it will issue sometime in the future a long list of poems or writings. Among the first to be composed will be the *Collected Cantos* of Ezra Pound. Following these will be *Four Unpublished Letters to Catherine* by Laura Riding; a series of very modern poetry in de luxe style by Walter Lowenfels, Bob Brown, Roy Campbell, Richard Aldington; a war story not decided upon; the first poems of Brian Howard, something by Harold Acton, Robert Graves, David Garnett and Iris Tree. Covers for these volumes will be done by Hilaire Hiler, Elliott Seabrooke and Eugene MacCown. All publications are limited editions, most of them in 16-point type of from 12 to 20 pages.

Several poems by Miss Cunard have appeared from other presses. She contributed a poem to an anthology called *Wheels,* and has had another poem printed in a separate edition. This poem, *Parallax,* is well known on the Left Bank. Two more are to be issued soon in London. The title of this book will be *Poems (Two).* It is being printed by the Aquila Press with cover designs by Seabrooke.

In coming to Paris, Miss Cunard is really returning home. The Left Bank was her home for ten years until she got the bee for printing and decided to do it at her home in the country. Actually, she has never been alienated or expatriated, for she made frequent visits to the center of literarydom.

Montparno
26 January 1930

Passing of *transition*

An American writer in Paris has just performed an act almost without precedent in the annals of modern literature. He has deliberately killed, in the zenith of its success, a magazine which he created, owned and edited for three years. The murderer's name is Eugene Jolas, and his victim is *transition,* the last issue of which is just off the press.

Eugene Jolas has decided to discontinue the publication because he feels it has served the purpose which its name indicates and because he wishes to devote his time exclusively to personal literary work. He is *par excellence* a writer of the future, of the new international world which contemporary statesman and intellectuals are striving to create, for he writes with equal talent in three languages: English, French, German. His determination to concentrate his energy on producing works of his own is therefore altogether natural and full of promise.

The amazing thing is that Jolas has killed *transition* when he might have sold it profitably. He has refused alluring offers made by several noted American publishers. . . . He declined them because he feared that in their hands it would inevitably become a commercial undertaking. . . . But it seems best . . . to let its creator and destroyer speak for himself. Here is Jolas's editorial swan song, as he chanted it the other day for *The Tribune,* to whose staff, like so many of his collaborators, he once belonged:

"*Transition* was not an anthology, like most modern magazines, but a review with a dialectic, a review that was out for an ideological revolution. Against the sordid objectivism of the Middle Western school of literature, *transition* placed the subversive action of the imagination. It tried to encourage a new sense of the fabulous in modern terms. By withdrawing *transition* from the scene of literary action I feel that we have reached the immediate objectives of our attack. We have disintegrated the philistine notion of a pragmatic world and have tried to give an impulse to a liberated form of expression. We experimented with explorations into the pre-logical or instinctive world through the dream and the fairy tale, we took cognizance of the evolution of the senses produced by modern machines and attempted to adjust Form to these kinetic recognitions, we tore asunder the academic philology and made composition again a thing of individual evocations.

"There is nothing on the horizon just now to encourage any continuation of literary action. The hoax of the New York "New Humanists" is not made to rouse our fighting blood. The mercantile spirit of literary reportage now rampant among the American "New Objectivists" is not exciting. The half-a-dozen writers in America whose minds could interest us are too absorbed in the economic struggle and compromises of various kinds to make their collaboration at all effective.

"I gave up *transition* with a heavy heart. It was a magnificent adventure. It has brought me many good friends and a plethora of still better enemies. Contact with the *genus literatus* has not always been a pleasant one. The megalomania of the individual writer, the jealousies and envious side-glances, make frequently the job of the editor a particularly difficult one. But I feel sure I have tried in these three years of intellectual warfare to be just and sometimes even generous."

It was at the end of 1926 that Eugene Jolas first conceived the idea of gathering together the radical forces in international literature. At that time the *Dial* was publishing its polite prose, opening a gap for the philosophy of Irving Babbitt. In France, *This Quarter* . . . the only revolutionary journal of the arts, had not appeared for a long time. Ezra Pound's *Exiles* was still unborn. T. S. Eliot envisaged in his *Criterion* a new academism. *The Little Review* appeared at long intervals.

In the winter of 1926, after returning from America to Paris, Jolas invited Elliot Paul, who like himself was then working on *The Tribune,* to join him in launching *transition. . . .* An unusual feature about *transition* is the fact that it was conceived and executed by newspapermen. It was a real newspapermen's venture. . . . In the course of events, Jolas invited Robert Sage to join Paul and him as associate editor. Other *Tribune* contributors were Leigh Hoffman, M. C. Blackman, Edgar Calmer, Emily Holmes Coleman, and Waverley Root. As Jolas himself is fond of remembering, there is not a little truth in the statement that *transition* was in many respects "an offshoot of *The Tribune.* "

B. J. Kospoth
25 May 1930

First Venture of Anonymous

Some time ago the foundation in Paris of a new publishing house devoted exclusively to the publication of anonymous works by authors idealistic and daring enough to sacrifice the publicity of their names was announced in these pages. The mysterious firm in question—for even its founders wish to preserve their anonymity—has just issued its first anonymous volume. It is a play entitled *U.S.A. With Music,* and it is a very nice looking book. While everything else about their undertaking is anonymous, the publishers have been compelled to make the concession of giving their house a name, and thus *U.S.A. With Music* bears the imprint of Carrefour Editions, 18 Villa Seurat, Paris.

Paris is the Mecca of American literary venturers. We do not know the names of the gentlemen, or ladies, concerned in the Carrefour Editions, but it is evident that they are Americans. One of the founders, it is hinted, is a patron of the arts who has "distributed several millions worth of books in America." At the time of its inception, Carrefour issued a proclamation called *Anonymous*, which should be read before reading its first volume, as it explains the aims and hopes to which it owes its existence. The following program was set forth in this interesting document:

"*Anonymous*, just issued in Paris inaugurates an international movement for anonymity in the arts to combat what an English author calls 'that infernal personality mongering.' *Anonymous* puts the stress on the artist's work, not on his name. It does away with the 'superman in the spotlight.' The work stands or falls by itself. The audience has no name. It is anonymous. The artist, by renouncing his name, establishes a common bond with the audience. At a time when the world needs a unifying and universal faith, *Anonymous* supplies a common basis for belief, a belief in creation."

It would be manifestly unfair to attempt to judge from the first volume whether this ideal of *Anonymous* has been realized. *U.S.A. With Music* is interesting enough to arouse curiosity as to the identity of its author.

21 September 1930

Limited Editions for Connoisseurs of the Fine Art of Book Making

To my prejudiced mind there is no minor art which has the fascination of typography. Fine printing, the designing of beautiful books . . . has about it a certain dignity. . . . An exceptional book has a double appeal: that of its content, and that of the manner in which it is presented.

The new publishing house which goes under the name of Harrison of Paris has avoided the pitfall of so many publishers of fine editions by realizing this double character of the book. . . . The new firm, under the unusually capable supervision of Monroe Wheeler, has realized the ultimate aim of the craftsman of books: to dress first-class work in a garment worthy of it. The presentation is subordinate to the content only in the sense that the book to be printed is chosen first for its intrinsic worth and is then designed in the manner which will best bring out the full flavor of that content. That the house has not fallen into the too common error of the typographer who violates the fundamental rule of his art by making his decorative details obscure the main lines of his subject is indicated by the very clear editorial plan which it puts forward. Its texts, it explains, fall into four groups: great popular works, of which the Bret Harte work is an example; major poems, among which the present edition of *Venus and Adonis* takes its place; "human documents," meaning such volumes as

Thomas Mann's *A Sketch of My Life,* one of the volumes now under consideration; and original works hitherto unpublished, of which Glenway Wescott's *The Babe's Bed* is the only title so far announced.

Of the three books *Venus and Adonis* is, to my mind, the most beautiful volume—quite fittingly. The richness of the binding . . . makes it a handsome book. . . . But it would be difficult to praise too highly the restrained good taste of the text pages, set in the handsome Cochin face in a bold size—14 point—with parallel rules in blue at the top of each page. It requires an artist to run his sheets through the press a second time in order to use a single touch of color; once the second color is ordered, few printers can repress the temptation to splash it all over the page.

I have rarely seen such uniform good taste, intelligence and artistic sensibility displayed by any publishers of limited editions as are manifested in these first offerings of Harrison of Paris. So long as this standard is maintained, there need be no hesitation in accepting this imprint as a guarantee of an important book perfectly printed.

Waverley Lewis Root
16 February 1931

The New Review

They are talking about "White Magic." In the cafés, they are talking about "the new middle ages." They are talking about "the new objectivism" and the secrets of "Zang-tumb-tumb." There is another war. The writers are fighting it out in the second issue of *The New Review,* published in Montparnasse. Samuel Putnam, Ezra Pound, Hilaire Hiler, George Antheil, Louis Zukovsky, Herman Mueller, T. F. Tracy and Lincoln Gillespie are in the army.

Samuel Putnam, in an exhaustive and caustic exposé, wherein he scores the births and deaths of the "isms" since the war, traces the ancestry of the "Revolution of the Word." One might go back away behind the Renaissance. One might go to Aristotle, Quintilian or anywhere. The American champions of the word are too late, says Putnam. "As for the American-in-France self-advertised advance guard movement, it merely fastened parasitically upon the French. Their ideology is not to be taken seriously, but their seriousness is. The past decade was one of whiners, professional miaowlers."

The champions in *The New Review* seem to agree on a discipline and clarity in letters. This makes for intelligibility and reconstruction. Emphasis is on the "object," on the sacramental significance of "reality."

Wambly Bald
14 April 1931

Book News and Reviews

Three Stories and Ten Poems Reviewed

Three stories and ten poems is very pleasantly said. So far so good, further than that, and as far as that, I may say of Ernest Hemingway that as he sticks to poetry and intelligence it is both poetry and intelligent. Roosevelt is genuinely felt as young as Hemingway and as old as Roosevelt. I should say that Hemingway should stick to poetry and intelligence and eschew the hotter emotions and the more turgid vision. Intelligence and a great deal of it is a good thing to use when you have it, it's all for the best.

Gertrude Stein
27 November 1923

On American Writing

To the English reader there must of necessity appear a note of ugliness in all late-American work. Nevertheless, beginning with the *Spoon River* of Mr. Masters which, but for the war, must have taken all England by storm, there has . . . appeared a new sense in American literary work. *Spoon River*, the *Poor White* of Mr. Sherwood Anderson, *Main Street* and *Babbitt*, differing immensely as they do in literary value, are all of them united in one characteristic. They possess the historic sense.

One used in one's haste, and before the war, to say that Americans knew nothing—and they probably didn't and it did not help them. They pursued, as far as writing was concerned, knowledge along European, and mostly purely English lines. . . . And when my young friend Mr. Robert McAlmon tells me that I shall never be able to write because I know too much he is probably in the right of it, being real America getting back on Concord. Salvation by millennial eurhythmics will never overrun Europe because Europe is old enough to know that there is no short cut to salvation—but as long as you are young enough not to know that dead sea fruit and its taste you have still youth enough to do something ugly and alive. And ugliness and aliveness came into the American writing world with an immense rush during the war, at some period when we ourselves had our eyes fixed on other things.

They were, those qualities, already due and overdue. The first American writer, Stephen Crane, had exactly the qualities of Mr. McAlmon himself.

As far back as the late nineties of last century he was persuading himself that he knew nothing but was ready to storm any literary position. Then came Mr. Pound! And heaven knows what Mr. Pound knows or does not know, since—his verse apart—he is always so intent on bashing on the head some caitiff hound or other that the interjections he meanwhile lets drop are singularly inscrutable.

Under the shadow of Mr. Pound's imprecations, however, there was growing up a whole, violently experimenting group that found expression between the parti-coloured covers of the *Little Review*. And when the mists that surround contemporary history have rolled together it will appear that the queer *Little Review* made the beginnings of real American literature a possibility. It was the trying over ground for all sorts of badnesses, outrages, tastelessnesses and experimentalisms that a literature must get out of its system before it can begin to live; and merely by its sporadic and thwarted attempts to put Mr. Joyce before the American writer the *Little Review* did immense things for America. Mr. Joyce is not nationally American but then he isn't, heaven knows, from any possible point of view, English—and he is the greatest literary influence of the day. He has for good or ill introduced at last into literature the note of complexity that is the note of the life we live. You may not like *Ulysses* but you cannot get away from it any more than, if you are destined to be a commuter resident in Manhattan Beach, you can get away from that, dislike your surroundings how you may.

And the note of post-war American writing is its complexity—the complexity of its handlings and its perception of the complexity of all modern problems. Black, it seems to say, may still be black and white; but if, on one *Main Street* or another, your air is forever obscured by a dust of automobiles, bootlegging parties, white enamel bath-room fixings and all the rest of the ingredients of Civilisation, what can your inner, your private life be but all-of-a-speckle!

Ford Madox Ford
17 February 1924

A Few Friends

The publishing list of the Three Mountains Press consists of six works selected by my friend Mr. Pound as marking the high-water mark of English literary psychology and execution of the present-day—these works all having been published in Paris and being all by writers who have been profoundly influenced by the curious, indefinable, unmistakeable spirit of workmanliness that breathes in the Paris air. Mr. Pound has selected three English and three American writers for publication under his aegis. I will leave out of account the three English writers: any English Critic—I mean Reviewer—would tell you that he had never heard of one of them. I will also leave out the *Indiscretion* of Mr. Pound himself. Dealing as they do with family history in an American society of two decades or so ago they may, for all I know, occasion personal discomfort to the actual present reader—and, if he dislikes that at first, he may, and with some reason, go on disliking it. The *Great American Novel* of Dr. William Carlos Williams—unless the reader happen to be a Great American Novelist—and the *In Our Time* of Mr. Ernest Hemingway do not, I imagine, start with any such handicaps. Each of these works is distinguished by a singular, an almost unsurpassed, care of handling, Dr. Williams in a mood of fantasia presenting you with a sort of madly whirling film in which Greater America flies over, round and through your head whilst Mr. Hemingway gives you minute but hugely suggestive pictures of a great number of things he has seen whether in the days when the late war was a war of movement, or in the gardens and presence of the King of Greece, or again in the *corridas* of Southern Europe. Mr. Hemingway stays in Paris and his work is in the hardest and tightest tradition of the French, inspired with a nervous assiduity that is the American contribution to the literary forms of today. Dr. Carlos Williams is a practising physician in the United States who dashes now and again through Paris on his way somewhere. So, if the American reader will pardon the gaucheness of a phrase that I cannot think how otherwise to put, his work is more European. For whereas French work on the whole retains the aspect of hard chiselling that distinguished even their most impressionist writers, Europe around Paris has developed Impressionism almost to its logical ends, so that to read Dr. Williams is to be overwhelmed by the bewildering remembrances that, with their blurred edges, are all that remain to us of life today. To read Mr. Hemingway is to be presented with a series of—often enough very cruel—experiences of your own that will in turn be dissolved into your own filmy remembrances. Dr. Williams, in short, presents you with a pre-digested pabulum of life, Mr. Hemingway with the raw material. These are the two main literary trends of today and each of these writers in these several ways is singularly skillful. I daresay both of them might distress a quite lay reader, for that is a branch of diagnosis in which I am singularly inexpert.

Ford Madox Ford
24 February 1924

Tristan Tzara

We have a great many reasons for being grateful to M. Tzara. He began by being the inventor of Dada and the Dadaist Movement—a movement which, conducted with much and salutary extravagance, did a great deal towards bringing international minds back from the contemplation of after-war circumstances to the consideration of the Arts. Nothing else could have done that particular trick and nothing else was at the moment so necessary or so valuable. It was as if, worried as were our minds by the endless details, the endless alternatives of tidying up the trench and wire-soiled map of the world, the odd manifestoes of Dada really burst themselves upon our attentions. You had at some moment or another to look away from Affairs and then, inevitably, your eye fell on one or other sheet decorated with unbelievable capitals; woodcuts of life-size eyes; cylinders; wheels. . . .

It is of course obvious that a Movement that was so much a matter of clamorous voices and of so relatively little actual production must more or less quickly come to an end. . . . Its participators must in the end get to work and in order to work they must go away from the noise of the shoutings. So, after several glorious rows and a Congress or two, Dada ceased; but it is a tribute to the vitality of the races that produced it that it ever existed at all—and it is a symptom that precisely in the countries where its extravagant periodicals more or less humourously flourished you find an art-life more or less vigorous. So international Paris fairly hums; New York—or it may be Chicago or the West-Middle-West—lets off an occasional rocket; and from the South Latin nations there comes the sound of cheering—or of imprecations; whereas to go to London is like going into an efficiently hermetic telephone-box. You are in a twilight, you hear nothing. For London was the one city in the world that could be got to take no notice at all of Dada. I believe only Mr. F. S. Flint the poet paid attention to its existence, since he wrote a monograph on French poets mostly Dadaist. And the *Athenaeum* soundly flagellated Mr. Flint and then died of the effort.

So, for Dada alone we owe a good deal of gratitude to M. Tzara, and, personally, I owe him a good deal more, for by either his writings or his conversations—either by agreeing or very forcibly differing I do manage to set my critical eye as to Parisian artistic activities. He droops, as it were, about the boulevards and in and out of studios, and where you see him there, you may be certain, there will be something or other going on!

Ford Madox Ford
11 May 1924

The Uncertain Feast

We have had some opportunities of meeting the younger men and women who are seeking the quiescent atmosphere of an Old World civilization in order to realize their creative dreams. Most of them are intensely American in a very real sense. Their immense, astounding country has left its impress on their souls. They are here in answer to a Romantic call and they sharpen their memories against the background of a crepuscular magic. They write their novels and poems and plays from this distance and give us a silhouette of modern America. Miss Solita Solano, whose *The Uncertain*

Feast has just been brought out, is one of these highly gifted American writers who live in France.

The Uncertain Feast seems to us to be a vital contribution to the complex problem which America presents today. Although written by a woman, it has not the usual feminine garrulity that makes women writers produce enormous volumes without feeling or insight. Her story is told in sharply chiselled sentences and stark evocations of moods. She has "measure" and analysis. She stands over the corpses of emotions and dissects them without shuddering. To be sure, in the portraiture of women and their enigmatic banalities she is less successful than in the pathological introspection of men's minds and souls. Her women always seem slightly unreal, but when she begins to paint men, she gives us unforgettable impressions of keen understanding.

Miss Solano is the poet of emotional crises. Over her book hovers the phenomenon of *Ulysses*. But she has forged her own style . . . kinetic . . . tremendously evocative of New York . . . the rush of the subway is in every ideation of her heroes and heroines.

Eugene Jolas
28 December 1924

A Neglected Masterpiece

The award of the Dial Prize to Edward Estlin Cummings brings to mind one of those misfortunes which cause publishers to grow prematurely grey and authors to turn in upon themselves until they become bad company for their friends.

In 1922, Boni and Liveright, published Cummings' *The Enormous Room*. Considered commercially, it was an absolute failure, and its lack of critical success was even more astonishing. Word was passed around that it was a "war book" and that was the end of it. The comic relief corps of New York columnists, headed by Heywood Broun and guarded in the rear by F.P.A., found that it touched a bit too directly upon the human sensibilities and that there was nothing in the "plot" which fitted the phrases to which they had grown accustomed. The man who set himself up as champion of the American language and who lets his followers believe that his ear is always attuned to catch the vigorous rhythms of the common speech, none other than Mr. Mencken, admitted having tried to read the book but did not notice that what he had always publicly hoped would be done had been accomplished, namely, the real literary employment of the piquant cadences of everyday American speech.

Cummings has the peculiarly tenacious sort of mind which does not allow itself to be overpowered by the ridiculousness and illogic of a situation until he has captured it in words. His story concerns his spiritual development while confined as a suspect by the French government during the war. There is nothing indignant about the book, but it is pervaded with a triumphant note, recalling the remark of Dostoyevsky that "man can survive where the hog would perish, will laugh when the gods go mad."

Elliot H. Paul
21 February 1926

Ernest Hemingway

Hemingway's New Novel

The brilliant English and American colony in Paris thinks that Ernest Hemingway is one of its white hopes. He has published two books, one a collection of short stories and the other a satirical whimsy caricaturing the modern school of novel writing. He now appears with a full length novel, *The Sun Also Rises,* almost coincident with the news that he is quitting Paris and coming back to Oak Park, Ill., to live.

The Sun Also Rises is the kind of book that makes this reviewer at least almost plain angry, not for the obvious reason that it is about utterly degraded people, but for the reason that it shows an immense skill, a very honest and impassioned conviction about how writing should be done, a remarkably restrained style, and is done in an amusing and clever modern technique, a sketching in with conversation and few modelings of description and none of rumination. Why then be angry at it? Because the theme itself is so gestury. Just as it was a perfectly fair criticism to say that *Main Street* was a picture out of proportion to gain an end, so it is also fair to say that *The Sun Also Rises* is entirely out of focus. The difference between them is that although *Main Street* did gain an end of parts, *The Sun Also Rises* leaves you feeling that an artist has just done something to be smart.

The heroine of *The Sun Also Rises* is another lady of *The Green Hat*, except that she is a little more outspoken and a little heavier drinker. All of the characters are prize old soaks, and it is for the drunken conversation that a great many of the passionate admirers will tout the book. It is funny, you have to admit that. One of the times that the vine does the talking is a dissertation on the modern writer and it is keen and witty. But most of the time the picture is so trivial. It isn't that you mind its being drunken or of a sort of hypercivilized crudity, but you do mind horribly having a man who has obviously the talent that Hemingway has doing just that sort of thing. Except for the fiesta, which is vivid and gross and impressive and worth doing, the book is concerned with such utter trivialities that your sensitiveness objects violently to it. The wasting of a genuine gift on something that is exactly what you would expect a mediocre young man from Oak Park, Ill., and not one with real talent, to write about Paris is what makes you unhappy. Every young man from every Oak Park in the United States probably gets just such an angle on the group of rotters that are to be found in any city any place, and he always writes about them. But rarely with such results. Hemingway can be a distinguished writer if he wishes to be. He is even in this book, but it is a distinction hidden under a bushel of sensationalism and triviality.

Fanny Butcher
19 December 1926

From a Litterateur's Notebook

There is already a faint line of demarcation in American literature between the writers with aesthetic sense and those who conceive writing in terms of patience. The former are few and unpopular, are not quite sure of themselves and often grow less so for want of encouragement and understanding. The latter become more convinced each year that they shall inherit the earth. Their books sell in large numbers, they are praised by men like themselves employed by periodicals and called critics, their output is steady, their place in the community respectable. Most of them write a "daring" book supposed to have been derived from memories of childhood, ending with a transient love affair with some Greenwich village girl whom they fail to disguise for the sake of the gate receipts.

When the second book comes along, it is ordinarily built around the theme that dealings with prostitutes are not always completely satisfactory and that the variety afforded by non-promiscuous maidens is refreshing. By that time some business-like clerk in a book store or stenographer in a publishing house decides that the young man will be a good provider and the next book is an apology for married life and an attempt to justify the author for failing to speak to the Villagers who used to give him gin and loan him money.

There is another school who sneer at autobiographical writing and pretend that the source of their inspiration comes from the life which is completely external. They write short stories about a middle-Western plumber having his photograph taken on the lawn, etc., standing just behind the photographer and performing the same function not nearly as well. Also they see American progress on a large scale, and trace families through three or four generations.

It is not their subject matter, meagre as it is, which excludes them from the possibility of ever producing significant work, but the manner in which they conceive their compositions. Much is said about their manner of writing, but what matters their manner if the thing is a mistake from the beginning.

The elementary principles of art are too simple for them. They write, not to express themselves, but to express what their readers express orally day after day. Instead of stimulating thought, they are careful to limit the scope of the story's influence. Books are "college books," "books of rebellion," "sex books," or what not. The buyer and the seller must know in advance what they are like, and the extent to which the author conforms to their expectations measures the success of the book.

The devices used by Sinclair Lewis, for example, are not difficult to discover. He restates each point nine times, so that the dullest mind could not fail to grasp it and retain it. There is a conversation about pressing pants, for instance, then the author's comment about the banality of pants, then the pants are brought in and the author comments about the manner in which the pants are brought in and establishes the fact that they are invariably brought in the same manner and that the manners of the bringer-in do not change from time to time. The same technique was used in the old-fashioned burlesque shows, except that the pants usually fell off the Dutch comedian.

Of course, a reasonably impressionable person is dead tired before Lewis gets his hero clothed. A suggestion would have been enough. But in the same way in which imitators of good writers are not as good as the original, imitators of bad writers are not as bad as their masters. This brings us to Louis Bromfield. He has endurance and many friends, but I have yet to discover the germs of art in his writing. He does not see things as an artist, and he does not copy the methods of those who see things as artists. Because his stories have a chronological and geographical sweep, they are commonly supposed to "be on a large scale." The flimsiest sort of reasoning would show that the opposite is the case. In order to get so many generations and countries into a book, the scale must be very small. If scale counts, an ordinary road map would outweigh El Greco's "St. Peter and St. Paul."

Bromfield writes in cliches, uses words and phrases shamelessly which have been squeezed dry of all meaning, has all the faults of Dreiser with none of the latter's virtues. But the way he writes is not important. If he had artistic vision or was susceptible to aesthetic impressions, there would be hope that he might learn to express himself without resort to the literary second-hand stores and auction sales. His main concern is not to study his subject, but to ascertain that no one shall be in doubt as to what he means. In *The Green Bay Tree* he was struck with the fact that a non-conforming lady did not end in the police court and felt no remorse for having lived sensibly. There is scarcely a page on which this is not reiterated or reinforced. *Early Autumn* shows no improvement. No future books are likely to show an improvement, since the error lies at the beginning of the first one.

Elliot H. Paul
2 January 1927

Gertrude Stein

Gertrude Stein has been writing for twenty-five years. Volumes have been printed about her, in American and English magazines, but the same editors who have welcomed essays and anecdotes concerning her have refused consistently to publish examples of her work. Up to the time Sherwood Anderson, in his preface to *Geography and Plays,* reassured the imaginative public, the wildest notions as to her personality and activities were current. "As there is in America an impression of Miss Stein's personality, not at all true and rather foolishly romantic, you will perhaps understand something of my own surprise and delight when I was taken to her to find instead of this languid impossibility a woman of striking vigor, a subtle and powerful mind, a discrimination in the arts such as I have found in no other American born man or woman, and a charmingly brilliant conversationalist."

Anderson's words punctured one ridiculous legend, but they were soon repeated and distorted until they constituted another. Facts regarding Miss Stein's life began to leak out. It developed that she had been born in Pennsylvania, had been graduated with high honors at Johns Hopkins where she displayed unusual brilliance in scientific fields, and, more recently, had driven a Ford during the entire years of the World War, first on the French and then on the American fronts.

That a writer, and especially a writer editors found it difficult to understand, should be equipped with a healthy set of nerves and a strong body was considered most astonishing. Miss Stein's normalcy then became her principal eccentricity. But the critics, who had been floundering for years, daring neither to dismiss her writing as a joke nor to hail it as a new kind of art, seized upon Anderson's theme and have exploited Miss Stein's charming personality, world without end. The literary product was never mentioned. Even Miss Stein's lesser countrymen, upon learning how magnificently she had "done her bit," forgave her everything in the way of poetry and overlooked the fact that she found it more comfortable to live outside Those States.

Recently, however, Miss Stein has come in for a little genuine appreciation. Because young writers have not had it dinned into their heads that her work was great stuff, they have assimilated a certain amount of it naturally and easily, so that today many of them show her influence. Gradually the icefloe of tradition has cracked, so that clear water now shows between those who write to tell the world something and those who write to create something within the covers of their own books.

Miss Stein's goal became the employment of words as an abstract medium. Having stripped stories of narrative and description, and purged characterization of incident, she proceeded to another refinement of her product and moulded her typical situations and universal qualities into pure patterns.

Before discussing *As A Wife Has A Cow A Love Story,* which seems to me to approach the ideals of Miss Stein's art most closely, a word should be said regarding *Composition as Explanation,* in which she makes important contributions to the literature of aesthetics which is shockingly meager.

Critics have written libraries full of stuff about specific books or authors or groups or periods or what not, but comparatively little has been said about the fundamentals of the art of writing, still less has been expressed concerning the art of reading. The latter cannot be neglected much longer. Happily the things called classic have reached a volume which precludes the possibility of their inclusion in a single brain. Consequently, cultured non-creative men need no longer talk and act alike.

Miss Stein has definite ideas as to the usefulness of the classics. They are important because they are beautiful, and for no other reason. As a guide to modern composition, they are utterly without value and the mere holding of the notion that classics might be studied with a view to perfecting technique would preclude a person from ever making a work of art, except by accident. Works of art spring from minds which appear immature sometimes because of an abnormal specialization of articulative functions. But having been created, they transcend whatever puerile ideas their creator may hold concerning them. So a discussion of artists is nearly always unsatisfactory. Dwelling upon particular works of art has a definite limit, and there is left only as a subject for study the things which beautiful creations of all periods have in common.

Hasty people are often misled by a title. Mr. Edmund Wilson, the anonymous clerk on *The Dial* who deigned to notice the book at all, and all other American reviewers decided, erroneously, that *Composition as Explanation* was merely an attempt on Miss Stein's part to explain her own work. Nothing could be farther from the point. She uses her own work and development incidentally, as illustrations, but the book is an exposition of certain fundamentals of aesthetics which needed badly to be stated. What she says would apply to Nathaniel Hawthorne or Li Po. . . . It was left for Miss Laura Riding, American poet residing in England, to discover this, and to appreciate it.

It is characteristic of Miss Stein that of the twenty-odd years she has spent in writing, only a few months have been consumed in writing about writing. "No one formulates until what is to be formulated has been made," she says. "Composition is not there, it is going to be there and we are here."

The falsity of the time element in writing has occupied the attention of the best modern writers for some years, and a wide range of experiments have been performed with a view to freeing writing from the curse of chronology. In painting, no such problem exists. No one cares which part of a canvas was painted first. In music, the problem is equally acute and George Antheil, particularly, has attempted to compose in such a way that, although the music must pass the ear, as it were, in a series of points forming a line by means of memory, the effect shall be architectural and a dimension analogous to space shall be involved.

A musical composition, if properly enjoyed, is enjoyed as a whole, reconstructed *in toto* from memory after having been heard. Its beauty lies in the fact that it does not have to be rearranged but merely remembered. Miss Stein realized that a prose composition should also possess this quality and that the time in the composition, not the time consumed by the things suggesting the composition, determines its form.

Writing about a thing which has happened, which is complete and without active time, may be compared to painting. Writing in a continuous present, as Miss Stein does, of things happening and beginning again and again, is more like music, in so far as its formal problems are concerned. So her works have to be performed, and there are few trained or capable performers. I am not attempting to summarize the contents of *Composition as Explanation*. That is unnecessary because Miss Stein has stated what she had to state. I can only indicate the book as one which is good to be studied and in which may be found many statements of things which students and enjoyers will continue to feel.

Elliot H. Paul
19 June 1927

A Minority Report

Many significant American writers, after having passed through a long period of utter neglect, are obliged to go through a second and more trying ordeal during which they are praised extravagantly, but for the wrong reasons. Sherwood Anderson is an outstanding example of this. Because, like all honest folks, his philosophy at any given time is likely to reflect the kind of life circumstances are forcing upon him, he has attained a reputation for being naive. As matter of fact, Anderson is one of the most sophisticated men in Those States, and even his characters who approach nearest to being true children of nature are extraordinarily wise. My nomination for the most naive writer, not only for America but for the entire civilized world, is Ludwig Lewisohn, whose reputation rests upon the assumption that he has seen it all. Lewisohn's credulity gives his work a quality which is certainly valuable, and he has demonstrated time and time again that sincerity, however far removed it may be from actual facts, will sustain an artistic structure.

But Ernest Hemingway has suffered more from the careless terminology of reviewers than either of the above-mentioned writers. Of course, before his work was known or widely commented upon, he wrote "naturally," assuming that everyone else did. When things began to be printed about him, Hemingway was assured from every side that he was vigorous and unaffected. He tried to laugh it off, but gradually found himself growing self-conscious about the "he-man" stuff. When a man is told from every side that he is natural, it makes it very difficult for him to remain so. Hemingway has done it. He has preserved a proper contempt for those who would like to raise themselves a little higher by clinging to the tail of his comet. But there are signs of a struggle. The "vigorous" parts of his work are at times dangerously near over-emphasis, resulting from his just determination not to be forced out of his natural course.

The quality for which I value Hemingway's work is his extraordinary delicacy, and his patience in putting it into words. I mean delicacy of treatment, not the tenderness he feels for his characters nor the good-will they often bear toward one another. It is not the fact that he has a splendid ear for the rhythms of American speech which places Hemingway in the front rank of American writers, although this is gratifying. It is his sensitiveness to the currents of human understanding and the hopelessness of human misunderstanding which makes the clouds break so often in his skies, revealing great blue distance beyond.

Elliot H. Paul
18 March 1928

Countee Cullen Declares Poetry a Matter of Personal Taste, Not One of Definition

Countee Cullen, the American poet, has been in the Latin Quarter for the past two years working on two long poems, something the author of *The Black Christ* has never tried before. This gifted young Negro has some interesting ideas about his art.

"Poetry," he says, "is entirely a personal matter and no one has ever been able to define it. Shelley's defense of it misses the mark. I don't think it ever will be bottled up and wrapped into a neat package. If verse does not strike the roots of you, for you it is not poetry. But it may be for someone else. I have this brought home to me in my reviews. One critic praises one poem and another calls the same piece insipid and banal. Entirely a personal matter, it is.

"Poetry should not be criticized excepting in a broad way. There should be as many ideas about a poem as there are individuals. Everyone should judge for himself whether for him a poem is good or bad and not permit a critic to decide for him. Criticism is a secondary art, anyway, an art of the frustrated.

"I don't like free verse. I never wrote but one poem in that manner, and that was my first one. Verse comes out of me rhymed and metered. Free verse does not fit me and I think but few really good poems have been written without form." Cullen appeared to be amused as he thought of that first poem in free verse. He assumed the air of a tired old man of 90 thinking back across the years to a misty past.

Cullen came abroad two years ago on a Guggenheim fellowship. He dedicated himself during this time to producing two narrative poems in a romantic vein. He expects to return to the United States in the fall for a tour on which he will read his poems. This is not a new thing to him, for he has read his works before audiences many times before.

Montparno
5 March 1930

Is Sex Necessary in America?

The whole United States, I learn by way of various weekly magazines and newspapers, is laughing over a book called *Is Sex Necessary?* by James Thurber and E. B. White. . . . I recommend it to Americans living abroad for reasons herewith. The book is of interest to us over here not merely because its subject is the whole American scene, viewed from the angle of sex. That, of course, if the book is well done, is enough to make a lot of us buy it. But there is also the fact that after living in Europe a while the tendency of most of us is more and more to look at America panoramically; to discuss America as if we were foreigners; and to compare Americans with Europeans, probably with an eye to finding out what is wrong with us, if anything.

Is Sex Necessary? offers more than a chance to sentimentalize about the dear homeland, with its hot and cold running water, its self-confidence, its money and its naivete. The book is more, too, than a howling parody on the psychology works of Adler, Freud, Jung etcetera in best-selling English translations. It is finally and completely successful, in my opinion, because it shows up the people who right now are laughing loudest at this commentary on—the people they know.

Edgar Calmer
27 April 1930

Lewis and Dreiser: Who Deserved the Nobel Prize?

The Nobel committee having, apparently, decided that for reasons politic or otherwise America must receive the literary award, succeeded in narrowing the field down to two contestants—Theodore Dreiser and Sinclair Lewis. They chose the lesser man. Their justification . . . lies in the peculiar terms of the deed of gift. The Nobel award . . . is not offered purely for literary merit. It recompenses literary work for its utilitarian aspects, a highly appropriate aim for a prize established by the inventor of so useful an article as dynamite. The author rewarded is assumed to have performed some "service" (whatever that may mean) through the influence of his works. The excuse for giving the prize to Lewis rather than to Dreiser is, then, his position as a critic and satirist of certain aspects of American life. Mr. Lewis, then, by delineating the dullness of Main Street, the unintelligence of Babbittry and the hypocrisy of evangelists, has performed a service.

The Ostrich Society

It does not invalidate the argument that it is founded on a mistaken premise. Society does not want to be told about its failings and man does not want to correct his faults. Babbittry flourishes more strongly than ever, and the Babbitts go about laughing at their replicas with Mr. Lewis' book to sustain them. The error is Mr. Nobel's, not Mr. Lewis'. There is no reason why the latter should be penalized because the former was obsessed by the strange delusion that man can be made better merely by pointing out his faults to him.

It might be suggested that merely to provide humanity with a work of art is to do it a service. In a sense, this is true. The artist does himself a greater service, however, and from a restricted viewpoint (one, say, that confines itself in time to the space of a generation or so) may actually do considerable harm to the society about him simply by providing it with a work of which the implications are socially or morally upsetting. If the donor of a literary prize wishes to reward aesthetic achievement, he will be wiser to eschew such extraneous ideas as the good which a work might do. He will, indeed, be wiser not to offer any prize at all, since the theory that a prize jury can be gotten together which will infallibly select the greatest writer, painter, composer, sculptor of its time is another of those idealistic illusions which hard fact has contradicted. We find, then, that as between Dreiser and Lewis the Nobel Prize committee acted correctly in awarding the prize to Lewis under the peculiar conditions established for that award. What may seem strange to certain of my readers is the contention . . . that the award would have been justified as well on purely aesthetic grounds—the contention, that is, that Lewis is a greater writer than Dreiser.

Dreiser-Polyphemus

The origin of this opinion is not difficult to find. It lies, no doubt, in the comparative stature of the two writers. Dreiser is a big man; he blunders heavily and clumsily through massive, formless works, which, no doubt could be rewritten by a cleverer man so that they would read much more smoothly and easily. But the force which permeates them would be lost. This is something to be felt, not to be demonstrated. It is the energy of a mind showing itself through its creation; it is something apart from technical skill, apart from superhuman avoidance of defeat. A great artist, indeed, is almost always a man who has great failures as well as great successes to his credit. He is not a perfected human, he is an exaggerated human. His faults are magnified along with his merits. They are often, indeed, manifestations of the same force. . . . It is a question of scale. Dreiser is a titan, and Lewis is not.

Difficult as it must be to compare two writers on different degrees of the ladder, we may arrive at an estimate by comparing their success in their chosen manners. Dreiser's weapon is the bludgeon; it is an instrument that does not call for *finesse*. He strikes heavy blows with it, inelegant but crushing; he uses his weapon perfectly according to its technique. Lewis is wielding the scalpel. It is an instrument that calls for deftness, dexterity, a sensitivity of touch. Mr. Lewis' merits are great; but it does not reduce them to point out that his touch is not sure, that his writing does not have the fineness that his particular instrument demands. Lewis is sometimes awkward, less so than in Dreiser; but awkwardness does not matter with the bludgeon, and it does with the scalpel.

Those who put Dreiser below Lewis are evidently confusing craftsmanship with art. Lewis reads more smoothly than Dreiser, but . . . the test of great writing is not the ease with which it glides into the mind—and out again. It would be more accurate to gauge its greatness by the turmoil which it causes in forcing its way into the mind; and for that purpose rough edges are certainly no handicap.

Waverley Lewis Root
17 November 1930

A Review and Which Smells Like a Novel

Lucy Church Amiably: A novel of Romantic beauty and nature and which Looks Like an Engraving, by Gertrude Stein. Published by The Plain Edition an Edition of first Editions of all the work not yet printed of Gertrude Stein, Paris.

You can read sometimes *Three Lives.* Sometimes you can you can read sometimes *Conversation as Explanation.* You can read even you can read sometimes you can you can read if you have time sometimes you can read *The Making of Americans.*

You cannot read *Lucy Church Amiably.* Not even sometimes.

As an authoress writes a book a punk story.

Can you read much of this. She said can you read much of this. Can you read much. Of this on page nineteen. Nineteen and two is twenty-two. Twentyone twentytwo twentythree. Read much:

> To leave on the thirtieth and to arrive on the second and to be on the way on the fourth and to be settled by the fourteenth and to be having word of their decision on the sixteenth and to be forgiven on the seventeenth not twice but once. This makes it as noiseless as ever.

But not noiseless enough.

Some parts of *Lucy Church Amiably* are more difficult than others. . . . There is an explanation. When a wife has a cow a love story there should be an explanation. With *Lucy Church Amiably* there is an explanation explanation is is called Advertisement. It is less difficult than other parts of *Lucy Church Amiably*.

Advertisement

> Lucy Church Amiably. There is a church and it is in Lucy and it has a steeple and the steeple is a pagoda and there is no reason for it and it looks like something else. Beside this there is amiably and this comes from the paragraph.

> Select your song she said and it was done and then she said and it was done with a nod and then she bent her head in the direction of the falling water. Amiably.

> This altogether makes a return to romantic nature that is it makes a landscape look like an engraving in which there are some people, after all if they are to be seen there they feel as pretty as they look and this makes it have a river a gorge and inundation and a remarkable meadowed mass which is whatever they use not to feed but to bed cows. Lucy Church Amiably is a novel of romantic beauty and nature and of Lucy Church and John Mary and Simon Therese.

This is less difficult than other parts. This is more simple. But then it is all simple. She said by repeating you can change the meaning you can actually change the meaning.

Repeat.

But then it it it is all simple. It is all simple. It is all simple. It is all. Simple.

Waverley Lewis Root
9 February 1931

Since the Death of D. H. Lawrence

D. H. Lawrence is sharing the ironic fate of most great artists whose genius has strayed beyond the outposts of contemporary imagination. During his lifetime, critical appreciation was withheld or charily meted out in small and infrequent doses. But, with the death, the attitude of aloofness magically evaporated, and now, but fifteen months later, Lawrence is ranked with the gods.

The treatment Lawrence received in his native isle was particularly hypocritical. He was too disturbing, too rebellious, too sharp-tongued for the polite, literary gentleman of London . . . an alarming fellow best put in his place by silence. But Lawrence dead was no longer a trouble-maker; he was a great Englishman who could at last be made a safe subject for rhapsody. And how dear old London rushed to the feast! A frantic search was instituted for all the unpublished scraps of his manuscript that might be lying about. The entire hierarchy of English letters began writing learned analyses of his work. In all the resulting clamor, Lawrence was abruptly metamorphosed from an outlaw into a saint, from an erratic artist into a genius.

There was much that was cheap and nauseating about this hasty posthumous appreciation. Ten years ago Lawrence already had to his credit such books as *Sons and Lovers, The Rainbow, Women in Love, Aaron's Rod,* and *The Lost Girl.* Either he was a genius then or he was not a genius when he died. The mere fact of his death had no effect on his merit. The truth is, I fear, that the London gentlemen are again committing an excess. Lawrence is today being overrated to about the same extent that he was previously underrated. There can be no doubt that he was a very great artist, probably the greatest English novelist of his generation. But he was an imperfect genius. He had rare qualities and grave shortcomings.

Robert Sage
5 July 1931

Kay Boyle Writes Novel of Quality Too Rarely Found

Since the accidental inception of this page, an effort has been made to maintain a high critical standard, and not to slip too often into the error of praising the mediocre out of sheer fatigue of condemnation. The book reviewer . . . is apt to succumb to the temptation to let his standards relax and praise simply competent work because day after day he finds nothing better to write about. But if he makes the mistake of exalting the mediocre, he finds himself without words when something of the first water really comes his way.

It must be admitted that the attempt to maintain a high standard has very often failed of success on this page as on others. The unconscious dulling of standards by a succession of neatly manufactured but essentially empty books has not been the only cause. The embarrassing element of personal friendship with authors sometimes enters, or even, shameful confession, a consideration of the reaction of a review on an advertiser. Advertising men have never been noted for their clear and piercing logic.

Hence this long preamble to a review of Miss Boyle's latest book, *Year Before Last,* which is as near perfect as any novel which has been discussed on this page since William Faulkner's *Sanctuary.* . . . Miss Boyle's writing is as tense and as vivid as that of any of the select company of modern authors who are really doing something with language. . . . But it is not a question of style or of her use of her tools that makes her book important; it is rather perhaps that, despite her technical skill, her language remains always a tool, a means of expression, and not the end in itself. Her words glow and bite and eat their way into the soul because there is feeling and fire and emotion behind them.

The plot of the story is beside the point. It is a love story, and in an age when every young girl knows all about copulation it is good to come once in a while upon a woman who still knows something about love. The reader is made to feel the strength and the all-possessing force of that love, and with the woman of Miss Boyle's story suffers from the bitter specter of incurable disease that pursues relentlessly and inescapably the young man whose life is so deeply felt and so vigorous that death stalked him as a quarry worthy of the hunt. This is a book to get drunk on. There are not many such.

Waverley Lewis Root
4 July 1932

Italians Want No Advice from Hemingway on American Writers

The ridiculous sensitivity of Fascist Italy to criticism, or, more exactly, her ability to discover criticism where none is implied, has just led to another explosion in the case of Hemingway. Samuel Putnam, editor of *The New Review,* who, as a translator from Italian, is interested in contemporary Italian writing, sponsored an international jury whose purpose was to choose the three best American and the three best Italian books of the year, not to award them prizes, but simply to present to each country the works picked from the other's literature, with the intention of bringing about a mutual acquaintanceship with the best works of the two nations. . . . For the American jury, Mr. Putnam selected William Faulkner (whose acceptance has not yet been received), J. G. Grey, Harry Hansen, Eugene Jolas, R. Ellsworth Larson, H. L. Mencken, Gorham B. Munson, and, as you have already divined, Ernest Hemingway.

With the announcement of the choice of Hemingway, the storm broke. The *Giornale di Genova* devoted a column to selections from Hemingway's writings to demonstrate that he was inimical to Italy, citing such passages as one in which a Fascist traffic officer pockets 25 lire extracted from a motorist. . . . Remarking somewhat nonsensically that "the literary importance of Hemingway is entirely aside from the point," certainly an odd way of looking at the matter, since his only function is to give a literary opinion, the *Giornale di Genova* assumes mistakenly that Hemingway is to pass on Italian works, and ends by calling on his Italian companions on the jury to protest. Evidently pressure was brought to bear on them, and the Italians began flooding Putnam with letters asking him to get them out of the fix in which they found themselves, the patriotic motive of wishing to introduce Italian writers to America being, apparently, no counterweight to the heinous sin of having even so distant a connection with an American writer who had denied that perfection is an attribute of all things Italian. "There appeared to be nothing to do," Mr. Putnam writes, "but withdraw Hemingway's name. This I have just done on his behalf, for the reason that I was sure that that was what he would want done."

Thus an effort for mutual understanding between two nations is vitiated at its inception by the chauvinism and intolerance of a mentality which offers poor recompense to those who try to understand and sympathize with it. Italy intolerantly rises in wrath against Hemingway, missing his basic understanding of and friendliness for Italian character, because of a few isolated and unimportant passages in a long book, which could hardly do any harm to the Fascist State (unless it is indeed vulnerable) while Hemingway, who has suffered direct attack from Italy and might very well be expected to refuse to join any group with amicable intentions towards that country, is ready to forget about that and serve with the American part of Mr. Putnam's jury. . . . Hemingway had already made his choice, which may be interesting to Americans, if not to Italians. He picked *1919* by John Dos Passos; *Conquistador* by Archibald MacLeish, and *The American Jitters* by Edmund Wilson. "Am no judge of masterpieces," he wrote to Putnam, in offering this list. "Above are three best books I have read during the year—all have faults—all are *damned good*."

Waverley Lewis Root
21 November 1932

Expatriates Show Their Mettle in Neagoe Anthology

Americans Abroad is a book that cannot be reviewed. It contains short stories, poems, and some contributions unclassifiable as either, by 52 American writers, some of them more or less definite expatriates, some only eligible for membership in this volume because of protracted periods of residence abroad. A general review cannot possibly be adequate, and space forbids writing 52 reviews.

One or two generalizations may be hazarded however: first, that the selection is a good one, and gives one to wonder if the scorn poured out upon expatriates should not be suddenly dried up at this demonstration of how many of the important names in the latest group of American writers are more definitely associated with Europe than with America.

The selection is not all of unpublished work, as I had supposed it would be. My first reaction to that discovery was disappointment; the second the reflection that perhaps that accounts largely for the high quality of the contributions. Writers asked to participate in such an anthology as this are apt, if an unpublished piece is demanded, to hand over something which they have not been able to dispose of elsewhere, often for excellent reasons.

The merely freakish and the out-and-out idiotic, which for some reason apparently cannot be entirely eliminated from English publications on this side of the water, are kept to a minimum in this volume, and the pleasant poems which on analysis possess no meaning worth troubling about are also very few. In short, there is good value for one's money in the nearly 500 closely printed pages of this book.

Waverley Lewis Root
19 December 1932

McAlmon's *Indefinite Huntress*

Dear Mr. Root: I have just read your review of Robert McAlmon's book of short stories, *Indefinite Huntress,* which seems to me most unfair. So much is blamed upon Ernest Hemingway that I think his name should be used more sparingly and, at any rate, only when one is quite sure. If there be really any debt owed, it is owed by Hemingway to McAlmon, who wrote these tales long before Hemingway had written any at all.

Last week I wrote a review of *Indefinite Huntress* for an American publication, and I wrote in this review: "How much McAlmon owes to older men (such as Dreiser) is more than negated by the extraordinary debt of influence so many of his contemporaries owe to him; at least a half dozen names come to mind. Because I recognize in McAlmon the sound and almost heedless builder of a certain strong wing in American letters, I can see Hemingway only as the gentleman who came in afterward and laid down the linoleum because it was so decorative and so easy to keep clean." Or words to that effect.

There is also the question of Faulkner's style. I don't agree with you for a moment when you say that Faulkner writes barely and cleanly. At the present time I am in a state of enthusiasm about Faulkner's *Light in August*—I don't know when I've been so stirred and astounded by a book. But at whatever page you may open it, you find sentences so charged, so involved, so rich, so weighted, that it seems a far, far cry to Hemingway or anything like him. . . .

Kay Boyle
17 December 1932

Season's Most Brilliant Book Is Gertrude Stein's Biography

I wonder how Gertrude Stein feels about having written a best seller. My guess, on the evidence of this book, is that she is pleased. She does not appear to have taken refuge in the theory, dear to unappreciated writers, that if a book has a wide circulation, the reason for its popularity must be vulgarity. It is not true that best sellers are necessarily bad books. It is equally not true that best sellers are necessarily good books. It is not goodness or badness, but the sort of goodness or badness that decides whether a book is going to appeal to a wide public or not. There are, besides, extraneous features, such, for instance, as timeliness. In this case one such factor enters, I think. That is curiosity. Gertrude Stein has for so many years been a legendary figure, and one unapproachable by the general public because of the direction in which her work turned, that now that she has written something which the public can understand, the public is paying its dollars to find out what all the mystery was about.

Not much mystery will be found in this book. Its clarity is crystalline. The style remains recognizably that of the author of *As a Wife Has a Cow a Love Story* or *An Instant Answer,* but it is that style plus the desire to convey meaning. Miss Stein has all but eliminated punctuation, but her sentences are so perfectly phrased that no punctuation is necessary. They can only be read in one way.

The style recalls also *Three Lives,* but with added richness. Despite the remarkable qualities of that early book, it quickly became monotonous in effect. *The Autobiography of Alice B. Toklas* never becomes monotonous. If the difference is the result of the passage through what most critics have chosen to call unintelligibility, that period may be considered to have been justified. That part of Miss Stein's work never appealed to me, but perhaps she was doing what she remarks painters sometimes do when they turn to still life because they find the human body unpaintable; and yet, she finds, everything that they have to say can be said in dealing with the human body. In the same way, she has been for years dealing with words to a large extent independently of their meanings; but now she demonstrates that her own technique is a thousand-fold more effective when she employs meaning.

Descent to Avernus

It appears to me that after *Three Lives* and *The Making of Americans,* Gertrude Stein dived into a tunnel, emerging briefly with *Composition as Explanation,* and then disappearing again until she popped up with the present book. The result is such that I hope from now on she stays out of the tunnel, or, to use the comparison from her own book, that she keeps away from still life.

One quality that this book possesses which will no doubt surprise those who have classed her with the deadly solemn persons who are usually to be found in the business of concocting word patterns is wit. Having heard Virgil Thomson working on his music for her *Capital Capitals,* I was prepared for this revelation, probably an easier task for a musician than for a reader; for after all what Miss Stein seems to have been trying to do with words for many years is to wring them dry of literary meaning and use them as notes in a sort of spoken music. My own opinion is that notes serve much better for this purpose, but Miss Stein's banishment of connotations from her words is one of the chief factors in producing the clarity of the present book. There is no ambiguity about her words, no ragged fringes of meaning adhering to them. Her vocabulary is simple and precise. It is directed to the intellect, not to the emotions. Connotative words are useful to arouse emotion—which often means speciousness—while still preserving the semblance of reporting fact. Miss Stein holds to the fact. It is curious that, being so constituted that she has chosen to remove from her words all appeal to the emotions and leave in them only what speaks to the intellect, that she has then tried to arrange these emotionless words in patterns calculated to avoid arousing the intellect and to speak directly to the emotions. It is significant also that in seeking to reach the emotions she has failed, in seeking to reach the intellect succeeded.

It is because the emotions are somehow deftly avoided in Miss Stein's writing that this book impresses one with its wit rather than with its humor. . . . Many of Miss Stein's witticisms are applied to well-known writers or artists whom everybody knows. Sometimes they are second-hand, as when she quotes her servant Hélène on Matisse. . . . Picasso gets the credit for a good many of the pithy remarks with which the book is filled. It is he who is quoted as saying that "when you make a thing, it is so complicated making it that it is bound to be ugly, but those that do it after you they don't have to worry about making it and they can make it pretty, and so everybody can like it when the others make it." It is he also who said to Gertrude Stein, "He is very nice, your brother, but like all americans, he shows you japanese prints. *Moi j'aime pas ça.*" And finally Picasso said of Braque and James Joyce that they are *"les incomprehensibles que tout le monde peut comprendre."*

More Victims

But if Gertrude Stein is ready to quote the witticisms of others, it is not because she is not quite capable of producing them herself. She says of Wyndham Lewis that he was "tall and thin, looked rather like a young Frenchman on the rise, perhaps because his feet were very French, or at least his shoes. He used to come and sit and measure the pictures. I can not say that he actually measured with a measuring-rod, but he gave all the effect of being in the act of taking very careful measurement of the canvas, the lines within the canvas and everything that might be of use." . . . Tristan Tzara appears later: "I have always found it very difficult to understand the stories of his violence and his wickedness, at least I found it difficult then because Tzara when he came to the house sat beside me at the tea-table and talked to me like a pleasant and not very exciting cousin." On Ezra Pound she is rather hard. "Gertrude Stein liked him but did not find him amusing. She said he was a village explainer, excellent if you were a villager, but if you were not, not."

On Hemingway

Hemingway gets considerable attention, perhaps because his proper placing seems to trouble Miss Stein somewhat. . . . Hemingway and Miss Stein did not agree on E. E. Cummings and Sherwood Anderson. Hemingway "accused Cummings of having copied everything, not from anybody but from somebody. Gertrude Stein who had been much impressed by *The Enormous Room* said that Cummings did not copy, he was the natural heir of the New England tradition with its aridity and its sterility, but also with its individuality. . . . Gertrude Stein contended that Sherwood Anderson had a genius for using the sentence to convey a direct emotion, this was in the great american tradition, and that really except Sherwood there was no one in America who could write a clear and passionate sentence. Hemingway did not believe this, he did not like Sherwood's taste. Taste has nothing to do with sentences, contended Gertrude Stein. She also added that Fitzgerald was the only one of the younger writers who wrote naturally in sentences."

Of Robert McAlmon, Gertrude Stein says: "McAlmon had one quality that appealed to Gertrude Stein, abundance, he could go on writing, but she complained that it was dull." Of Glenway Wescott: "He has a certain syrup but it does not pour." Of Elliot Paul: He "was a new englander but he was a saracen, a saracen such as you sometimes see in the villages of France where the strain from some Crusading ancestor's dependents still survives. Elliot Paul was such a one. He had an element not of mystery but of evanescence, actually little by little he appeared and then as slowly he disappeared."

The brilliance and cleverness of this book will be evident from these citations. Its greatest cleverness is not in quotable passages, but in its whole scheme—in its presentation as the autobiography, not of Gertrude Stein herself, but of her lifelong companion, Alice B. Toklas. It is not only that this allows Gertrude Stein to say things about herself that it would be difficult for her to say in the first person, for she has done a much finer piece of work than simply to write of herself arbitrarily as if she were someone else. She has actually entered completely into the character of Alice B. Toklas writing of Gertrude Stein, so that when her friend's admiration for her is put down on paper it seems to bear the unmistakable stamp of verisimilitude, a sincerity which makes it evident that this is Alice

B. Toklas' opinion of Gertrude Stein, not Gertrude Stein's opinion of Alice B. Toklas' opinion of Gertrude Stein.

So regarded, the work is a *tour de force*—a description generally used to indicate not a strength but a weakness. One wonders if this beautifully executed indirect approach is not a sign of a certain weakness. It permits the writing of an autobiography without self-revelation. After reading this book, one knows the life history of Gertrude Stein, one still does not know Gertrude Stein. She is seen as an outsider, a very intimate outsider, but still as an outsider sees her. I do not think she wants to reveal herself.

Waverley Lewis Root
9 October 1933

Ex-Tribuner Is Author of Novel

It is always a pleasure to those of *The Tribune* staff who remain here in the dark house to learn of the accomplishments of those who have returned to the outside world. Wolfe Kaufman served several terms on this newspaper; the pleasure of receiving a book from him for review is doubled by the fact that this is a pretty good book.

Tender Cheeks is a novel about Broadway bums, the kind who hang around in front of the Automat and then move across the street awhile to stand in front of the Palace, and those whose lives are a vague amalgam of indecision, rest periods in the subway at night after they have panhandled a nickel, attempts to chisel a cup of coffee from each other, and moderate suffering from cold and hunger.

Kaufman is in a position to observe them, for he is on the New York staff of *Variety*, the theatrical weekly, than which nothing is more Broadway. This book is not, however, a job of reporting; it is a true creation.

R. L. Stern
1 October 1934

VI The Second "Paris Tribune" and Other End-pieces

The slow decline and then the decease of the Paris *Tribune* "was one of the saddest things that could have happened." So wrote Paris *Herald* reporter Al Laney. It marked the termination of "an epoch in the lives of Americans in Paris," Laney concluded, "and it was impossible any longer to ignore the fact." Writing of the period when the *Tribune* and *Herald* were competitors in Paris, he admitted that the *Tribune*'s reporting of the life on the Left Bank far excelled anything attempted by the *Herald*.

Laney's bittersweet conclusions find confirmation in the following reminiscences written especially for this book by six former Tribuners, whose recent excursions into the past appear to have been mostly pleasant. Lawrence Blochman, who once relinquished the management of the *Tribune*'s Riviera supplement to James Thurber, recalls when he found himself in the midst of a celebrated literary feud and creates an unforgettable cameo-portrait of exile Frank Harris, one of the principals. Louis Atlas evokes in the profiles he draws of Harold Stearns and B. J. Kosposh two qualities often identified with the twenties: fantasy and playfulness. Wambly Bald writes a final "farewell to Montparnasse" column in which nostalgia adds a haunting poignancy to both the time and the man; Ralph Jules Frantz, managing editor of the Paris *Tribune* from December 1929 to 31 November 1934, surveys the whole operation with dispassion but still with the accent of one who begins by writing: "Paris was a good place to be in the late twenties and early thirties." Irving Schwerké completes what he describes as the "hardest assignment" of his career by endowing both the era and himself with an infectious ebulliency; and the editor of the short-lived successor to the *Tribune*, Waverley Lewis Root, writing from Paris, recounts a scheme he designed to prove that, although the death of the "body" of the *Chicago Tribune* had occurred on 31 November 1934, it possessed an imperishable "soul" which he and other Tribuners labored to invest with new attire.

If it is true that a newspaper exists only by being read, then the final word belongs to a *Tribune* subscriber who, after reading the first number of Root's *Paris Tribune* dated 1 December 1934, sent him the following message:

> Please accept my fifty francs, my hearty congratulations and my sincere admiration of your enthusiasm and spontaneity in kindling the fire of the new *Paris Tribune* on the bier of the old *Chicago Tribune,* Paris Edition.
>
> Let nothing dampen your spirits (save it for your throats), and remember that Robert Louis Stevenson said, "It is a better thing

to travel hopefully than to arrive, and the true success is to labor."

Your present initiative is the surest proof anyone could want that the Americans still in Paris are alive and kicking.

Mary Knight
Paris, 1 December 1934

H.F.

The Sweet Madness of Montparnasse

Where are they now?

All dead, or nearly all. And the survivors with their dimmed memories, including myself, are only half-dead or maybe three-quarters which is an advantage over being all dead come to think of it.

With this happy note as a starter, let's try to go on.

First, the impressive names parading out of the euphoric past: Ernest Hemingway whose *The Sun Also Rises* was said to have explained Montparnasse expatriate life on the Left Bank of Paris back in the late twenties and early thirties of this hectic century . . . the self-confident Gertrude Stein who was classified as a fake by her art critic brother Leo; they refused to say even hello when they passed each other on some Paris street . . . F. Scott Fitzgerald who always looked miserable whenever he slouched all alone in a Montparnasse café; Hemingway said he had been "trying to lick" the problems of a novel festering in his brain for five years and was not succeeding . . . George Antheil, the cherubic-looking avant-garde composer whose far-out recitals sometimes started riots . . . Hilaire Hiler, artist, raconteur, pianist at Le Jockey night club, founder of the Neo-Naturist movement in painting, whose best talent was telling jokes in Dutch dialect . . . Link Gillespie, a brilliant cross-eyed screwball who made claim to invention of a new futurist vocabulary for the printed page, the words and paragraphs minced together, which he said topped James

Joyce in originality. Link often carried in his vest pocket hunks of Camembert cheese which he nibbled placidly while explaining his literary ideas . . . Samuel Putnam, an ex-newspaperman scholar and translator, always broke, who managed to borrow enough money to start his *New Review* quarterly with the encouragement and blessings of Ezra Pound and Ford Madox Ford. And there were others, so many of them.

We who lived in Paris in those years, some four decades ago, laughed out loud at such romantic tags as "Lost Generation." Lost my eye! We were just healthy young Americans who joyously made a switch to Paris without having to fight for it. Paris to us was the sunnier side of the street, that's all. It was the cultural center of the world. Also the freedom center and by that I mean freedom of the spirit if I may be permitted that original phrase. Paris had it all, with no nine-to-five nonsense for us. The always jumping sidewalk cafés, each an inspiring little whirlpool of culture and pleasure—that's where we really lived, not in our little apartments or hotel rooms in the Montparnasse quarter. And there was total indifference as to who you were or what you had accomplished.

We who worked on the Paris *Tribune* were all very rich, indeed, even though we rarely had a dime when payday came around. With the living cost very cheap we had very good eating, very good drinking (wine with all meals), very good comaraderie, also good wenching on occasion, and there were lots of occasions with so many impatient female tourists, usually school teachers, anxious for liberation in a foreign land. Maybe they were forerunners of today's women's liberation movement.

No, we weren't "Lost Generation" rebels at all; we weren't rebelling against anything. We just wanted to live well in that Alice's Wonderland environment. Certainly we weren't parasites; painters painted, writers wrote, others held down jobs such as ours as newspapermen on the *Tribune* which took just a few hours out of every wonderful day. I hasten to add that working under editor Jules Frantz could hardly be called a strain. All was smooth, easy, informal, clublike with Jules, and could be described as a pleasant part of the pleasant spectrum. Ever beckoning were the irresistible magnets of the outdoor cafés—particularly the Dôme, Coupole, Rotonde and Sélect—their carnival air floating over our discussions of art, literature, philosophy, and women. I guess that's why so few among us ever bothered to detach ourselves for some real creative work. We kept living for today, confident meanwhile that tomorrow or the day after would somehow convert us into great writers or great artists. Still there were tomorrow-looking exceptions, among them Henry Miller who preferred to labor in solitude and extreme poverty while gathering his notes and doing his so-many-pages-a-day writing until he finally came up with his *Tropic of Cancer* novel which made him world famous.

Apart from the Americans were avant-gardists Louis Aragon, Tristan Tzara, André Salmon, Brancusi, Zadkine, Fujita, and perhaps I should include Jean Cocteau who was only about ten percent avant-garde in his poetry and film making and ninety percent dilettante. And whom I once saw dashing nimbly from his table at the Rotonde. He crossed the sidewalk, hailed a taxi, waved goodby to his friends left behind, and was gone. And those left behind quietly continued their discussion of the future of Surrealism with its cinematic possibilities. There, and at other cafés, was where the cultural action was while the aproned garçons, darting among the tables with drink and food trays, helped enliven the scene. While you talked with friends, or just sat and looked, you saw and heard the sidewalk peddlers of art, rugs, and peanuts. There were the *flics,* as the cops were called, cycling around in pairs with their smart blue capes on their backs. There were the hustling *poules,* usually young girls from the provinces, who were everywhere. And the wide-eyed tourists, including celebrities from the States, trying to take it all in while they too milled around. Yes, that's where the action was, culturally and otherwise, so charged with vibrating interest that visiting celebrities were fast deflated like punctured tires. Here's a story. One day Sinclair Lewis, freshly exalted by winning the Nobel prize, dashed importantly over to the Dôme zinc bar with a cheery grin on his mottled face. While ordering a drink he let everyone know who he was. But that got him such indifference, such a freeze, that he didn't even finish his drink. Lewis looked confused, snorted once or twice, and hurried away. No one had educated him as to what living in Montparnasse was all about.

Joie de vivre! Maybe that sums up the meaning of our life in Paris. Maybe not. Then let's try the clarion sound of *C'est la vie!* which says a lot including the French concept of tolerance that extended even into romantic matters. For instance, a doddering graybeard fondling a young girl in public met with no sneers. That was his business and more power to him. The spirit of tolerance was all pervasive. When a man took a girl up to his hotel room the *concierge* (the manager, usually an old woman) not only never objected. She often congratulated him. *C'est la vie!* And a word about the brothels. They were just as much a part of Paris as the trees in front of the Dôme, the Luxembourg Gardens, the Louvre, Champs-Elysées, and the fish and flower markets on the streets. Not that any of us *Tribune* fellows had any need for them. But on occasion they were fun to visit for social reasons. We knocked off from work around two or three in the morning when most of the neighborhood cafés were closed. Well, nearby the *Tribune* was a lively open-all-night brothel where we could sit around and chat over a drink before going home. It was like entering any ordinary café unless you decided to take one of the available girls upstairs. It was fun watching the bold *poules* trying to entice the patrons even to the extent of leaping upon their laps. I say again to preserve our good name that we men of the *Tribune* never, or nearly never, gave in.

And I recall a Grand Opening in Montparnasse that created considerable stir. Word got around that the public was invited to a brand new whorehouse described as most ornate, most fashionable in every way with glittering chromium and ultramodern decor all over the place, and its name was the Sphinx. No art show *vernissage* in New York ever saw anything like it. The deluxe place was jammed. Sedate looking madams politely showed off the expensive furniture, wall-to-wall carpeting and big mirrors. And the champagne and food tidbits were free. The only tidbits not free were the beckoning *poules* themselves who solemnly declared that they had to charge double on opening night because it was such a big festive occasion. That's French thrift for you.

Now a turn of the kaleidoscope to catch more of the sweet madness that once was Montparnasse. Without getting dithyrambic. The interminable discussions about the stream of consciousness (et cetera) in contemporary literature, Joyce, Stein, Eliot, Pound, Proust. The *"Bon jours"* and *"Comment ça vas"* heard among those gathering at the street art shows. The violent flareups some nights when café garçons ganged up for heave-ho of a shouting drunk. Male and female tourists eager to come upon orgies anywhere and never finding out because there weren't any, none that I know of. The tourists, guidebooks in hand, determined to go to Les Halles for onion soup at 4 A.M., something mentioned in guidebooks. Vacationing coeds panting for sampling of quick love safely away from home. The dignified Russian waiters, usually with frayed collars, who claimed to have been Dukes, Arch-Dukes, at least generals. Jimmy, the ex-pugilist from Liverpool, who tended bar at the Falstaff where several times a night he would leap over the bar to put a noisy customer to sleep with one punch. After which, Jimmy always apologized, gently brushed the man off, and helped him into a taxi.

Who else? Well, there was the buxom earthy Kiki known to everyone as the Queen of Montparnasse. She was witty, lively, everyone's friend, and got Hemingway to write a preface to her slender volume of autobiography. And Colette with her dyed red hair who was usually surrounded by worshipful youths. Man Ray, the brooding painter who switched to photography and became renowned in that field. Paul Morand, the writer-diplomat whose early book, *Open All Night,* had been one of my favorites when I went to college. And James Stephens, the writer whose *Crock of Gold* was another favorite in my own early years. One day I cornered him, a dyspeptic-looking little man, at the Coupole where he sat mournfully over a vermouth-cassis. He complained that it was "so disgraceful" that so many young women "these days" lived "so loosely" and appeared to have "no morals at all." He should see them now!

Ezra Pound. That man had no sense of humor at all. Having arrived from his home in Rapallo, Italy, for a few days in Paris, he hailed a taxi at the Dôme to get him over to the American Library on the Right Bank. He asked me if I wanted a lift. I said sure; I was on my way to the Right Bank too. We sat in the taxi, chatting pleasantly for a few minutes, and then I casually said, "Mr. Pound, you and I definitely have something in common. Our names can be easily punned." That was all. I was just trying to make light conversation. Then I took a look at his outraged glaring face and thought he would explode. He stopped the taxi, opened the door, and said just one word, "Out!" So I got out. To this day I don't know what the hell he got sore about.

Ford Madox Ford, a big huffy-puffy Britisher, was another one. I casually mentioned in my *Tribune* column that he liked to throw parties at some *bal musette* where he enjoyed dancing with girls who were one-third his age and half his size. Which was true. Anyway, he never spoke to me again.

One afternoon there was a knock at my hotel room door. It was a *Tribune* colleague calling. With him was a skinny, shy bald-headed stranger whom he wanted me to meet. He said, "This guy just got here from Greenwich Village and you should know him. He's going to be a great writer some day." I looked at the emaciated fellow who gave an embarrassed grin, a cigarette drooping from his thin lips. "Is that so?" I asked him nonchalantly. "Well, he said it. I didn't," this man replied. I pressed the bashful Greenwich Villager to tell me more and finally got this out of him: "What I want to do is write stuff that has real guts, not just the phony sentimental stuff that's called realism today but something that gets right down to the bone, hard, honest realism, and I don't give a damn if it never gets published while I starve to death if need be. And I'm used to starving. It's got to be second nature to me. Ha-ha." I too laughed a brief ha-ha, and that is how I met Henry Miller.

The fellow who brought him over, Alfred Perlès, who is Carl in Miller's *Tropic of Cancer,* and Miller and myself became chummy some time after that, spent a lot of time together in the cafés. After a while the three of us practically lived together in a small hotel in the suburb Clichy on the Right Bank because we wanted to get away from Montparnasse for a while. And on Sundays we took long bicycle trips through the Bois de Boulogne. Little did I know then that Miller was pumping me for a character he was plotting in his *Tropic of Cancer.* Had I known I would have been more careful.

Because I kept telling this shy, ascetic-looking man fanciful stories about myself, usually sexual, just to get his reaction. He would look shocked and demand to hear more. "Do you know what happened to me last night when I ran into three Englishwomen at the Deux Magots? " I would begin, and his hungry ears were ready for the whole bit. The stories I related were nearly always fanciful, built up as I went along. And that's the way he colored me as Van Norden in his *Tropic of Cancer,* also using of course fancy of his own. I certainly was no depraved sex fiend as he made me out to be as a result of my apocryphal error with him. No saint either, come to think of it. Just another young American living in Paris, that's all.

Miller is still around.

But those others. Those many others, especially Hemingway who with a casual generous gesture directly affected my life. I got to know him at the little Dingo bar, around the corner from the Dôme, his favorite hangout when he stayed in Paris. Big, pleasant, cheery, talkative, he was about as literary looking as a half-back football player. He never talked about books or Isms. But get him started on sports, especially sports personalities, or fishing, and he would talk your ear off. Or about some near accident he had while skiing in Switzerland. Stuff such as that. And always that smile, that ironic smile on his healthy ruddy face.

One day, shortly after his return from Cuba where he had remained a long time, I spotted him coming out of the Luxembourg Gardens, and we talked. He fired questions at me. Where was everyone? The Dingo looked deserted. He had been back in Paris nearly a week and a lot of the old faces were gone. Where, back to the States? he wanted to know. I told him it looked that way, and rattled off names of those who had gone back. A slow exodus. Dwindling American colony. The expatriate dream had begun to fade. How about me? Did I feel like going back? No, I told him, I still liked it here and always would. Then he threw me this thunderbolt out of the clear blue sky: "If you change your mind I'll pay your fare." He told me where he was staying. "Drop over tomorrow and I'll lend you the money." He playfully feinted a punch at my solar plexus, laughed, and walked off while I stood there stunned. Questions buzzed like bees in my head. Go back to the States? Why not? What for? What have you got to lose? And so on. I was still in a kind of trance when I went to see him in his hotel room near the Café Flore next day. He wrote out a sizable check, handed it to me, and a week later, after saying goodbye to my *Tribune* friends I was on the boat. What if I hadn't run into him outside the Luxembourg Gardens? What if I had never left Paris? And as Gertrude Stein might have put it: what is what is what? What I now know is that we ex-expatriates, who are still around, will not forget our years on the Left Bank and the Right Bank of Paris. No one can ever take that away from us.

Wambly Bald
January 1971

Frank Harris, Bosie, and the "Tribune," Riviera Footnotes to a Great Literary Feud

That the *Chicago Tribune* nearly fifty years ago should have figured in the great literary feud growing out of the trial, conviction, exile, and death of Oscar Wilde may seem strange today, but I have read somewhere that truth is indeed strange. Let's begin at the beginning.

The *Chicago Tribune*'s European promotion staff did not indulge in the streetbrawling tactics of the circulation wars at home, but it was alert, in a more elegant way, to the challenge of competition. In the euphoric decade between the end of the First World War and the Great Depression, there were four major English-language dailies in Paris: the London *Daily Mail*, the European *Chicago Tribune;* the granddaddy of them all, the Paris *New York Herald*, and later the *Evening Paris Times*. However, when the beautiful people went south with the birds at the approach of winter, they had to wait twenty-four hours for the latest news of American and English stocks, bonds, and horse racing. The Paris editions rode the Blue Train. There was no air mail in 1923 when the *Tribune* stole a march on the opposition by creating a *Riviera Supplement* printed in Nice all winter to be wrapped around yesterday's Paris edition each morning. In addition to stock prices and sporting results, the four-page tabloid contained overnight world headline news and local items of music, art, tourist, social, and café-society activities from St. Tropez to Menton.

The supplement was produced at a French printshop on the Descente Crotti, an alley back of the Municipal Casino on the fringes of Old Nice which is (or was) a reasonable facsimile of Old Naples complete with flapping clotheslines. The printers knew no English and set type letter by letter. The makeup man, Monsieur Alavoine, occasionally got his luxuriant black beard caught in the quoins while locking up the front page. It was at the Imprimerie de la Descente Crotti that I first met Frank Harris.

Harris was publishing (privately) the second volume of *My Life and Loves* on the same presses that brought forth our daily prose. He was something of a minor hero to the "under thirties" of the 1920s, which meant most of the *Tribune* staffers in France. Few of us, I think, were aware of Harris's courageous stand as an editor against the Establishment and the Boer War, which had once earned him a prison term. But we were in favor of his fight against Puritanism in language, as exemplified by the first volume of *My Life and Loves,* and of course everyone had read his biography of Oscar Wilde. There was a flurry of excitement therefore when the man bringing corrected proofs back to the printer was recognized as Frank Harris.

Harris was in his seventieth year at this time, and old man to us, but he refused to admit it. He dyed his huge moustache black, wore white flannel trousers, made a point of running after street cars, and proudly showed off his young red-headed wife. It may have been a coincidence that he always showed up at American Express headquarters in the Rue du Congre to call for his mail while I was checking on new American arrivals. In his resonant bass voice he frequently held forth on the duty of American writers to get back to the English of Chaucer, as he was doing, by calling a spade a spade and a cunt a cunt. The startled school teachers on sabbatical who were writing home about the beauties of the Riviera invariably gathered up their papers and left the premises in embarrassment, whereupon Harris would allow me the privilege of buying him an Italian vermouth at the Savoy terrace on the corner.

Harris was always ready with literary advice for the young writer. "Never translate," he told me (before I had started on the first of the seventeen volumes to my credit). "It will spoil your English style. Never touch a woman while you're doing serious writing. She'll drain the energy that belongs to your work." He was dogmatic about everything.

In February 1925 Harris's dogmatism was shaken for perhaps the first time in his life. Reggie Turner, a close friend of Oscar Wilde's who had not spoken to Harris since the publication of the Wilde biography, came to Nice and surprisingly accepted Harris's invitation to be a guest at the Villa Edouard VII in the Cimiez quarter. Turner succeeded in convincing Harris that his melodramatic description of Wilde's death (in an explosive disintegration of his digestive tract) was untrue. Since Turner had been present at the death and Harris had got his information from Robert Ross, also present, he began to doubt other details that Ross had given him—the moving of Wilde's body to Père Lachaise cemetery, for instance, which Turner also called completely false. So when Lord Alfred Douglas, whom Wilde used to call "Bosie," came to Nice two months later, Harris sought to renew relations with him also. Bosie was another man who had refused to speak to Harris in nearly twenty years.

Lord Alfred Bruce Douglas was, like Harris, an accomplished literary brawler but usually for different reasons. He had not appeared in court (contrary to his wishes, he said) when his father the Marquess of Queensberry initiated the sex charges which sent Wilde to Reading Gaol. He was in Old Bailey on libel charges in 1914 for calling Robert Ross "a notorious sodomite." Ten years later he had publicly accused Winston Churchill, while First Lord of the Admiralty, of withholding the news of the Battle of Jutland to permit his Jewish friends to profit in the stock market. Churchill brought charges of criminal libel and Lord Alfred Douglas went to jail for six months. It was to expose his prison pallor to the sun of the Midi that Bosie was coming to Nice.

The Harris biography of Oscar Wilde had never been published in England because Bosie had threatened to bring suit for criminal libel if it were. He had objected to Harris's portrayal of the young Lord Alfred as an ingrate who had caused Wilde's disgrace and had then abandoned him on the Continent, penniless, in his mother's villa in Naples. Harris, who was not exactly in affluent circumstances himself in 1925 (he had actually inquired about the possibility of a job with the *Tribune*), saw a chance to have his life of Wilde published in England at last, if he could only placate Bosie. And after what Reggie Turner had told him, it was entirely possible that he had actually done Bosie dirt. The man who told Harris of Bosie's imminent arrival and the man who finally arranged a meeting was a reporter for the *Chicago Tribune*'s *Riviera Supplement*.

Archie Craig (referred to by both Harris and Douglas afterward as "a mutual friend") was a Scottish lad with excellent connections. He was related to the Brooke family which gave Borneo the White Rajahs of Sarawak, and his cousin, the Dayang Mudah of Sarawak, was the charming hostess of a villa on the Promenade des Anglais. He also enjoyed some sort of distant kinship with the Scottish Douglases. Archie realized the importance of his role as mediator and was afraid of failure because Bosie had repeatedly refused to meet Harris. He enlisted my help and I agreed, although I didn't see what influence I could bring to bear.

Frank Harris was also anxious that I should convey the message that he held Lord Alfred Douglas in high esteem, even though that esteem was somewhat qualified.

"As editor of the local English language daily," he told me as he sipped his *Turin sec* (courtesy of the *Tribune*) in the Ruhl bar, "you'll of course meet Bosie when he gets to Nice. You're going to meet the greatest living poet in the English language. I might even omit the adjective 'living,' because the sonnet he wrote on the death of Wilde is as fine as anything in our literature. But he's an awful shit-ass! "

Harris let me know that if he were convinced that he had indeed maligned Bosie, he would be glad to write a new preface to the Wilde biography.

It was in April 1925 just before the Supplement shut up shop for the season that Archie introduced me to Lord Alfred, also in the Ruhl bar. I found it difficult to associate the pasty face and bulbous nose of this slightly effeminate middle-aged man with the pictures I had seen of the extremely handsome young Bosie of the turn of the century. I told him I hoped he would agree to meet Harris.

"Frank Harris is an extremely clever man," said Bosie, shaking his head dubiously, "almost as brilliant as he considers himself. But he's dangerous. I don't trust him. I hope you haven't let him talk you into anything."

I told him that I was interested only in having the record set straight, and that I thought Harris was genuinely if belatedly anxious about the possibility of having been misled.

Bosie made a show of relenting only with the greatest reluctance, but when Archie triumphantly drove him and Harris to Saint Tropez for the weekend, he seemed too well prepared for his decision to have been spontaneous. As Harris told me on his return to Nice, Douglas had carefully preserved cancelled vouchers amounting to nearly a thousand pounds to prove that he had not left Wilde "penniless in Naples," as Harris had written, and that he had paid for Wilde's funeral in Paris.

"Oscar had lied to me, as he had to everyone else whenever money was concerned," Harris also said—and here I paraphrase Harris's characteristic idiom—that Bosie had also denied that there was anything sexual in his youthful intimacy with Wilde; that although they had exchanged kisses, there had been no physical contact beyond that.

Frank Harris kept his promise. In May 1925 he wrote the new preface, acknowledging without qualification his injustice to Bosie but implying that Robert Ross and his friends had deliberately deceived him.

"That I should have misjudged the foremost poet of this time is my keenest regret," he wrote; "that I could have believed that such noble gifts could go with corrupt meanness of character shows the malignant cleverness of his detractors."

Harris thought British publication of *Oscar Wilde: His Life and Confessions* was now assured. But Lord Alfred Douglas was not to be put off by mere apologia. He now demanded that the whole first version of the two-volume biography be revised and the passages unfriendly to him be deleted. Harris refused, objecting that to replate many pages would be an unwarranted expense that he could not bear.

That was the end of the matter as far as Harris was concerned. Bosie, however, was persistent. A few months later he wrote his own preface to Harris's new preface and had them privately printed together by the Fortune Press of London.

The *Chicago Tribune* disappeared from Europe in 1934, three years after Frank Harris died at the age of 75. Lord Alfred Douglas died in 1945. Archie Craig, the *Tribune* reporter who healed the Harris-Douglas feud at least for a month, is also dead. But the apologetic Harris preface still lives. One of the 225 copies of the limited edition can be found in the Rare Book Room of the New York Public Library.

Lawrence G. Blochman
September 1970

Harold Stearns; Sundays at the "Trib"

Harold Stearns wrote the racing column for the *Tribune*. Stearns wasn't just an ordinary racing man. He was an intellectual who liked horses because they were an easy and a pleasant pastime. It made him much too melancholy to think about himself or about other people, so he thought about horses instead. He went to the races, wrote his piece for the paper, and all night until the dawn he sat in the bar of the Café de la Renaissance in Montparnasse. He sat there drinking *coups* of champagne and explaining to a few friends who were interested just what had happened at Auteuil or at Longchamps that day.

He was a medium sized man, rather stocky, and he walked slyly, almost on his toes, like a cat. It may have been the champagne, the cognac and the *vieux cure* that make him seem buoyant. It always seemed to me that he was about to float off into space and I daresay I wouldn't have been at all surprised if he had. When he came into the office at the end of the afternoon to write his column on the races, he seldom spoke to anyone. He slipped into his chair without ceremony, avoided the usual preliminaries of fooling with the typewriter or fussing with paper, and quickly tapped out his copy. Then he went downstairs for an apéritif and headed for Montparnasse and the Café de la Renaissance. Quite often he dispensed with dinner entirely. I'll always remember him as he sat there in the office at the typewriter, or at the Renaissance bar. He was a figure in complete repose.

In the office one afternoon, one of the boys looked over at Harold Stearns and said: "The Hippique Buddah."

And from that day, Harold Stearns was known as the "Hippique Buddah."

Well, I liked Stearns because he was quiet and as dignified as a man could be in his circumstances. He let people alone in that small, crowded office, and this was a quality much to be appreciated. It amused me, too, to see the way he handled money, like a child, when money came his way. For instance, a couple of times during the year he would find some old friend to stake him to a bet. Some of these old friends were wealthy and the bets they placed were substantial. On such occasions, Stearns was liable to make a big killing at the track.

When luck was with him, when the horses did come in, he would appear at the office wearing new clothes and new shoes and his three-day growth of beard was gone. He smiled now and was more sociable. These outward signs of prosperity lasted for about a week. Within a week the new clothes were shaped to their owner's personality and the usual three-day beard growth was again in evidence.

Stearns only talked about the races when he sat at the Renaissance. And then he spoke only in monosyllables, and in a low voice, with a minimum of effort. He shifted his weight from one side of the bar stool to the other, to relieve his cramped muscles. He sat there, the "Hippique Buddah," looking neither to the right nor to the left, but into the mirror behind the bar. In that mirror, he saw the world—his world—revolve. He saw the people who came into the café and those who went out. He saw the sun set and he saw it rise. He saw the drunks quarreling and he saw the lovers kissing, all in that mirror.

Once an intoxicated fellow threw a chair and broke the mirror and my friend Stearns disappeared from the Café de la Renaissance for two days until the mirror was fixed. It was as though the world had come to an end for two days.

After he had been sitting at the Renaissance bar for about eight years, Stearns' behavior underwent a slight change. He began to talk occasionally of a filly he said he now owned. Someone had bequeathed it to him, or he had won it on a bet, or he had bought it on one of his rare winning days. As a matter of fact, I really don't know how he came into possession of that colt, because I never was able to get the real story out of him, and I didn't really want to.

But I liked to hear him talk about it because, even though I never saw the animal, I was almost certain that she existed. I liked to believe in that filly. No one else had seen her either but Stearns had so consistently informed us as to her steady growth that we all believed in her. Sometimes I would drop into the Renaissance early in the morning, on my way home from the paper, and I would find Stearns at his usual place, at the bar. I would stand there looking right at him while I talked but he would look at me in the mirror. It got so I began to think the people in that mirror were more real than the people outside of it.

"I went out to see the filly today," Stearns said.

"When are you going to bring her out? " I said.

"Dunno yet."

Silence, then:

"Costs me a pile of dough."

"What does it cost to keep a horse? " I said.

"I got a bill for 7,000 francs today," Stearns said.

"All for that filly? " I said.

"Food and stable care. Also trainer's bill," he said.

I looked over to the shelf where the *soucoupes* were piled high. They represented Stearns' unpaid drinks. Champagne *coupes* at five francs a *coupe*.

"A hell of a lot of money to keep up a horse," I said.

"Worth it."

"How many months does that bill cover? "

"Three months."

"Your filly eats damn well," I said.

"Eats like a sonovagun."

"When are you going to race her? "

"Takes time yet. Gotta wait."

Sometimes he did speak exultantly of the day she would make her debut at the track. I began to think about that filly quite a lot. Every time I saw Stearns he talked about her. He talked about her growth, about her food and her health and the way she ran and how she had become very friendly with a stable dog. Of course we never thought of her as growing up. We couldn't imagine her growing up. For us she would always be a filly, even if she got to be fifteen years old.

Well, he went right on talking about her like that for five years. And then one day he just stopped talking about her.

Don't ask me why. I really don't know why Stearns stopped talking about her. I heard from one person that the filly had broken a leg and had to be shot. I heard from someone else that she had been sold. I heard from another source that she had been poisoned. I heard many other stories, but they were all hearsay. Nobody really knew for sure. I never asked Stearns himself for the real story because it wasn't the kind of thing you could talk about. Someone even remarked that the colt had committed suicide. That's how people talk. And they don't care what they say. All I know is that I felt pretty bad when my friend Harold Stearns stopped talking about that filly. I felt as though someone I liked very much had gone and died.

There were a lot of reasons why I couldn't discuss that filly with Stearns. In the first place it was too delicate a subject. I hadn't seen the animal so I didn't know just what she was like. Of course I had pretended all along that I knew what she was like, so now I just had to go on pretending that I knew what had become of her.

You see, this wasn't a horse I had seen, that I could refer to by name. In a way, it was all my fault. I had never insisted on going to see that filly. I had never asked him to show me a picture of her. And now she was only a mythical thing. And you can't ask a man what has become of a mythical filly, because you'd feel like a damn fool, wouldn't you?

And then Stearns might have thought I was checking up on him, that I didn't believe in his horse. He was a sensitive person and I didn't want him to think that I doubted his word. So I just tried to forget all about that filly although every once in a while when I think of Stearns, I can't help but think of that colt, too. Maybe she's alive after all. If so, I hope she's being well treated wherever she is.

Sundays at the *Trib*

Our Sundays in the *Tribune* office were cheerful. The place belonged to us. We on the day staff could come and go as we pleased. There were three of us in the office—Kospoth, the city editor, and two reporters. We had a leisurely lunch at a good restaurant, then we sat on the terrace of the Café des Trois Portes and had coffee. Later in the afternoon we went upstairs to write a few pieces from the French papers. The city editor sent down to the stereotype room the mats of the Gumps and other comics and features that regularly appeared in the paper. And the work for the day was done, as far as the day staff was concerned. The night staff came in later to put the paper out.

I guess what helped make our Sundays more interesting was that Kospoth was no ordinary fellow. He was a man of about 50. He had worked as a newspaperman in almost every capital in Europe, had reported the campaign of Wrangel's army, and had had a few other important assignments in his day. Sometime during his travels in the Near East he had married an oriental woman who had been a lady in waiting to a princess.

In spite of a certain elegance in manner and speech, despite his culture which was somewhat *ancien régime,* he was very much at home on the paper. We called him "The Sultan," or "The Mahatma" amongst ourselves. The height of his achievements, besides knowing many languages, was the wearing of a monocle.

That, we thought, was something.

The bit of glass gave him a certain austerity, and it awed even those of his critics who occasionally tried to infer that Kospoth wasn't doing his share of the work. And yet he did fit into the picture of the *Tribune* much more than I at first suspected.

In the first months that I knew him, the American aviators by their trans-Atlantic flights had aroused a great interest in aviation. This craze for flying was felt even in our office. We began to experiment with aeronautics. We carried on these experiments with gliders made of copy paper or cardboard and weighed down with paper clips. The windows of the editorial room gave on a large schoolyard and we took to sending these paper airplanes out of the window, across the yard, challenging one another to see whose plane would go the farthest.

Kospoth observed this child's play indifferently for a while but soon was making paper gliders of his own. On Sundays he would stand there on a chair, paper airplane in hand and call upon us to admire his skill in launching the thing. He tried it in the room a few times and found that it went into a nose dive because the tail wasn't weighed down sufficiently. Accordingly, he affixed a few paper clips to the tail and declared it was ready to take off.

The bit of paper went soaring across the yard, turned slowly and fell into a tree. We watched it not without a certain interest.

Kospoth then fetched his gloves and his cane and fedora and went down to the Café of the Three Doors for his middle-of-the-afternoon apéritif.

Louis B. Atlas
January 1971

Now He Is a Music Critic!

I was happy to be invited to contribute a chapter to this book on my great love: the Paris *Tribune,* the world's dizziest newspaper. "Tell about your work as music and dramatic critic of the *CT,*" the letter said, thus giving me the hardest assignment I have ever had. "Where to begin," that was the question. Sacha Guitry came up with the answer. I once had asked him if he was in favor of kissing a woman's hand, to which he replied, "I certainly am! You have to begin somewhere! "

And somewhere in the present case, was that I went to Paris for a vacation of three weeks and stayed there well-nigh onto twenty-five years. The "vacation" was terminated during World War II when the Nazis confiscated my household and monies. I escaped to Portugal, from thence on a refugee ship to America. The years 1921-1934 were the time of my life, principal credit going to the Paris *Tribune,* "Europe's American Newspaper."

My first article for the *Tribune,* published 6 May 1921, was on the Berlioz *Requiem,* at Notre-Dame Cathedral, in commemoration of the hundredth anniversary of the death of Napoleon I; the last was a review of a new Henry Bernstein play at the Gymnase, entitled *Espoir.* Little could I have imagined what were to be the consequences of that initial coverage.

During the many years I was with the *Tribune,* I had only one desire, namely, to do the best job I could under the circumstances, and to amuse myself as much as possible while doing it. The performers who came under my scrutiny were fortunate in that I have always tried to handle "the rod of criticism with the tenderness and reluctance of a parent"—I think this is from Gibbon. "Be that as it such," as a beloved matron used to say, my *Tribune* tenancy accomplished two things for me: it won me many friends in many corners of the globe, and it provoked the ire of a numerous, implacable crowd. I was a young boy when my great friend and teacher Moriz Rosenthal instructed me: "You must arrive at the point where neither blame nor praise can harm you." I don't think I lost much time in "arriving." Later on, Bill Roger's, "Cheer up! there ain't anybody that everybody likes! " also came in handy. With experience, I learned how to avoid the sting of bees—is this Gibbon again? —and became accustomed to the buzzing of hornets as well as the laudations of friends and admirers.

People made quite a pastime of "writing in" for or against me. I was immune to both types of attention. The paper printed many of these missives, especially the vituperative, damn-you-Schwerké kind. Some were so vicious the paper did not dare to print them, and there was one that was written on a piece of toilet paper nine inches long—quite a feat in itself, I thought. I took meticulous pains to send a thank-you word of reply to every correspondent who gave his name and address.

But everybody did not express his contumely by penning a Letter-to-the-Editor. There was a small group of French journalists and musicians who, on occasion, gave vent to their disdain by dubbing me *Le Presque Parisien Monsieur Schwerké*. Being Gallic, it was necessarily very subtle! They had no way of knowing that I was not one bit interested in showing how *Parisian* I was, but in showing how *American*. Yes, writing and being on the *Tribune* staff was an enriching experience in multitudinous ways, always excepting of course the lucrative. You have no idea how heart-warming it was to be told that, when a prominent American society dame was asked, "What does Schwerké write for? " she had replied, "Practically for nothing."

I loved, still love the French, and they were more than generous in their acceptance of me. My *grand souci* was to understand, appreciate, learn from them, ever mindful that I was a guest in their wonderful country, that they didn't owe me a blessed thing, and that there wasn't a blessed thing that I could do for them. We got along swimmingly. They sensed my attitude, knew it was sincere, and doors that otherwise would have remained closed, were opened to me. All the established denizens of the French professional worlds took me under their wings and, in many instances, really fathered me. On 1 May 1930 France awarded me the *Officier d'Académie* decoration; 1 April 1937, the *Officier d'Instruction Publique* decoration; 30 July 1951, the *Legion d'Honneur*—all three for "services rendered to music in general and to French music in particular."

Between the two wars, Paris was the music capital of the world. A sweeping statement? Easily substantiated by quoting from statistics which I published annually in the *Tribune* and elsewhere. During the 1925-26 season, for instance, New York had a total of 1,156 musical performances, while Paris had 3,394. During the 1926-27 onslaughts, New York had 1,218, while Paris came limping in with a mere 2,978.

When I took over the music department of the *Tribune*, it was, to all intents and purposes, non-existent. Within a few years it had become the most widely read music reporting sheet in Europe, for the *Tribune* went everywhere; and when it closed, Schwerké was said to be the Dean of its writers—a distinction of which (can you blame me?) I am inordinately proud. In serving the *Tribune* I took one, and one only, stand, that was, to let people know that I was *only the representative* of a great newspaper, THE PAPER must come first. Some naughty-minded creatures, need it be affirmed, thought that this was only my way of attitudinising for effect, that "great" was one big joke, *c'est en crever de rire*. Oh, well. . . .

For super-abundance, no city in Europe or America could compete with Paris. My *Tribune* term of office witnessed 86 full-size ballets, 255 operas and operettas, and hundreds of new plays. *En plus,* there were innumerable salons, societies, and groups which, every five minutes, were putting on concerts of new music; orchestras that brought out new scores at every session; composers who were individually presenting *soirées* or *matinées* of works not yet dry on the manuscript; Ida Rubinstein, who annually staged her many-million-franc productions at the Opéra (most opulent things you ever saw!); pianists, violinists, cellists, singers, ensembles, exponents of the saw, of this or that or the other—all hoping to impress Paris and find success within her gates.

Paris had a public for everything, even modern music manifestations in the dank, back rooms of bistros, where you were sure to find *le tout Paris* in elegant evidence. Nothing daunted, I did my part by inviting large coteries of retainers to my studio to partake in the *leres* of works by Alexander Steinert, Quincy Porter, Alexander Tansman, Georges Migot, and others, presented by the most capable interpreters. As usual I received my share of abuse: for some I liked "this modern stuff" too much, for others I did not like it at all. However you may want to take it, I think I can safely say that I have forgotten more "modern"—and other music, too! —than others have ever dreamed of. Discontent with old ways is endemic to the human mind, and no one can say that I ever had a *parti pris* against listening.

Time, on which you can always count, will winnow this epoch without prejudice—an epoch as hectic as it was exciting and stimulating, an epoch productive of a glut of worthless music and of much music that was, and still is, purveyor to the human heart, its language so simple in its complexities that the most untutored listener can receive something from it. Excepting the loners, the Paris modern-music scene consisted of *cliques,* clans, *chapelles,* and groups of experimental, innovative, *avant-garde,* and ultra-apostles of the arts of tone, sound, and noise. Belonging to, or not belonging to this or that set, disrupted many a social gathering and friendship (you know how the French like to argue!), spoiled the hilarity of many a party, upset the decorum of many a concert. "Do come," silly hostesses who entertained with modern music, would urge prospective guests, "the music will be awful, but we'll have *so much fun.*" Aloof to anything that smacked of cultism, I rode unscathed through *Sturm und Drang* and back again.

I was on friendly terms with innumerable composers from many countries, one of whom was George Antheil, *l'enfant terrible* of those now far-distant days. No one, I surmise, ever had more extensive coverage in the *Tribune* than Antheil, or deserved it more than he. I was responsible only for the articles in which I reviewed his music, sometimes pro, many times con. We were friends, and in the bigness of his nature, he knew that he could not tell me what to write any more than I could tell him what notes to put down. For reasons which we never could fathom, the Latin Quarter clique—they assumed the attitude that they owned him heart, body, and soul—worked and worked on George, trying to create enmity between us, and they came within a hairbreadth of succeeding; but here let George carry on by means of quotations from letters he wrote me at various times:

This letter is just to repeat what I said: namely, that I have from the beginning considered, even as you have, that we were the best of friends, and I sincerely hope that we may remain so. I have always known that you held my well-being at stake: consequently I have read everything you have ever written about me as a friend. . . . Thanks for your gentle rebukes. . . .

I have spent too much of my young life with the madmen, the literati, the painters, the theoreticians of my age. 1926 was an exceptional year, and fairly comfortable. But all the rest held disappointment, intrigue among the silly little Café du Dôme crowd, and all the hideousness of which the present day American Latin Quarter is capable. . . . The letter coming in this morning's mail brought me real joy also, for it made me realise that you have been a friend of mine from the beginning, and saw through things years ago, which I only began to learn recently. . . . Dearest Irving, if you could only have gone through my sufferings two years ago when I realised that the gang who had been exploiting me left me flat at the first loud cry of "Wolf." . . .

I should like once and for all to go definitely on record *against* this legend which records it that you have been down and against me. I know of it, but I confess that I am not quite sure why and where it originates. During the past five years you have been a very devoted friend, and anybody who says the contrary is either a liar, a fool, or plain coo-cuck. . . . You have been one of the first *real* critics (in contradistinction to the would-be's, of which the Latin Quarter is full) who first appreciated my talent publicly. Certainly you were the first in the English language. . . . You have been practically the only real critic who writes for the papers of my own native land, who has ever given me a single kind word, and I shall not forget it. . . .

Dearest Irving, I read your criticism on the front page of the *Tribune* [26 May 1930 first world performance of Antheil's opera *Transatlantic,* at Frankfort]. Irving, I can say only one thing: for years I have regarded every word and criticism of yours purely constructive[ly], and, as you know, from year to year have tried, *in my own way,* to profit by your always deep and instinctively right advice. Consequently your criticism of the other day will always mean much more to me than you can ever suspect. . . . My most heartfelt thanks to you, who have proved, all these years, the truest and firmest of friends.

Sunday evenings when I was not away from Paris, my studio was open house for any artists who, perhaps at loose ends, had no better place in which to sit around and just do nothing. No one was ever "invited"—word was passed from one to another, and it always was a great satisfaction to me how many turned up. One said, "I think we ought to call these evenings *Schwerké's Société des Nations Musicales.*" The appellation would have been apropos, for many were the times when fifteen, twenty, and more nations were represented. What gibbering and gabbeling! What fun it was to hear such a *mélange* and medley of tongues! For nourishment, a samovar was kept on a steady boil—no one ever counted their cups of tea—and there were piles of Russian ryebread tartines. A free and easy *désinvolture* prevailed, an unceremoniousness *sans borne aucune.* Did someone feel like playing piano, he went to the Bechstein and played; did someone feel like singing, it was not difficult to dig up an accompanist. What did it matter whether the group listened or not? The gab-fest didn't mind the music and the music didn't mind the background conversations; though there were moments when a mysterious hush would come over the room, subdued by the magic spell that a Sarkissoff at the piano was casting over us all. "What an oasis," Kandinsky would exclaim, "Here, *daragoy* Irving, we are relieved from all strain and effort, here we can relax and feel 'unconventional.'" To which Madame Kandinsky would acquiesce, with her characteristic, *"Et voilá, et voilá!"*

As much as I enjoyed these informal "assemblies," and not to slight them in the least, nothing—so far as I was concerned—surpassed the *soirées* that artist friends gave in my studio, the heart-warming feature of the compliment being that they *offered* to give an "evening" for my friends and me. I never had to ask them, or even suggest or hint that they might make such a contribution to the pleasures of a handful of their admirers. The guest-list was seldom more than twenty, and after the music, there were cakes, sandwiches, and champagne. Aino Acté, John Brownlee, Nicolai Orloff, Victor Labunski, Arthur Shattuck, Nina Kochetz, the Belgian Piano-String Quartet, Albert Spalding, André Benoist, Andolfi String Quartet, Paul de Lestang, Richard Hageman, the Hewitt String Quartet and Quincy Porter, Eleanor Spencer, Harriet MacConnell, Arthur Laubenstein, the Loiseau String Quartet, Jan Hambourg and Adolphe Hallis, René Leroy, Joaquin Nin, Conchita Supervia, *e tutti quanti.* What unmitigated joy it was to hear them in an intimate setting, in surroundings in which they were certainly at their best! The transcendent séance in all this long list of unforgettable outpourings, came when my old friend and teacher, Moriz Rosenthal, wrote me from Athens, "If you will have my *Gaveau grand* brought to your studio, I'll be happy to play for you and your friends, date to be chosen." I had to read the letter three of four times before allowing myself to believe it. My friend of (almost) a life-time, *the* teacher and pianist for whom I had more admiration and gratitude than all the others put together, would play *chez moi.* The mere anticipation of it made me so happy I was like to explode!

At last the eventful evening came, the guests had taken their places, I went around to make sure that they all were comfortable. They were, and I could finally bring in The Master. Upon entering the room, he stopped short and whispered in my ear, "Isn't that handsome woman over there the famous actress, Mary Anderson? I used to know her, oh, so long, long ago." I guaranteed that he was right in his surmisal, that it *was* she and no other; upon which Rosenthal went over to her, made a deep bow, kissed her hand, and said, "Why, Mary Anderson, are you still alive? " Without losing so much as a split second, she retorted, "Yes, I am, Mr. Rosenthal, and you? "

If he ever outdid himself, Rosenthal accomplished it that evening—at least in *my* books. There was a charm, a tenderness, a warmth, an enveloping communicativeness that an artist can never attain on a concert platform. Not only did Rosenthal play work after work from his prodigious repertoire, but a score of other numbers that he never used in public, holding our ears, minds, and emotions in a state of happy and equal enchantment.

Early in the evening, prior to his sitting down to the piano, I "presented" Moriz to the gathering, ending with an expression of my boundless gratitude for his friendship and understanding, for the many things I had learned from him, "and how proud I am. . . ." "Yes, yes, *yes,*" Rosenthal cut in, "my young friend cannot be any prouder of me than I am of him. You see," he said, taking great care to enunciate slowly and very distinctly, "you see, *mes chers amis,* I taught Irving so well to play the piano that now he is a MUSIC CRITIC! "

Irving Schwerké
February 1971

The Second "Paris Tribune"

It was towards the end of October 1934 that Jack Hummel, publisher of the Paris edition of the *Chicago Tribune,* called me into his office. He held out to me the flimsy blue sheet which in those days identified a cable. "Read this," he said.

I started to read. It began: HUMMEL HIGHLY CONFIDENTIAL SHOW THIS TO NO ONE STOP. I stopped, of course, and handed the cable honorably back. Or rather, come to think of it, I did not stop. I continued: PAPER SOLD TO HERALD STOP CEASE PUBLICATION WITH NOVEMBER 30 ISSUE STOP MAKE EQUITABLE ARRANGE-MENTS WITH STAFF. It was signed MCCORMICK.

It is not usual to announce beforehand that a newspaper is about to disappear. As a rule, the staff learns about it when they are engaged in preparing the last number. It is psychologically disastrous to inform newspapermen that they are working in a vacuum. A newspaper is an ephemeral production at best. It is produced with blood, sweat and tears, in the heat of action, appearing at the moment of its making to be the most important creation of the human mind; twenty-four hours later it has become inferior wrapping paper.

In the face of this obvious fact, newspapermen continue, with enthusiasm and devotion, to perform their daily tasks, because the newspaper, despite the perishability of any single issue, is after all a continuing creation. The Paris *Chicago Tribune* of November 1 might be wastepaper on November 2, but the Paris *Chicago Tribune,* no date, would continue forever. Or so we have assumed. Now suddenly, it became known that there would be a Paris *Chicago Tribune* of 30 November, but no Paris *Chicago Tribune* of 1 December nor any other thereafter, forever and forever, amen; for Colonel McCormick had signed an engagement not to revive his paper at any time in the future. Suddenly the task of putting out a daily paper for the next month had become pointless. Nobody was interested any more—least of all the staff.

The brunt of whipping the staff on to bring out a daily paper all the same fell upon me. The managing editor, Ralph Frantz, was on vacation in the States when the blow fell. That left me, as news editor, in charge (managing editor was the highest post we had), until he was able to get back, a week or two later. (There was no transatlantic plane service in those days.) Getting out the paper under the prevailing circumstances really required a Simon Legree, a role for which I was badly cast. The prevailing feeling seemed to be that since there would be no paper 1 December, what did it matter if there were no paper, say, 5 November or 21 November? To me it seemed to matter greatly. I had a suspicion that nothing would please the business department better than to have us miss an issue. If the editorial department failed to produce a single day's issue, the business department would have a legitimate reason for withholding severance pay.

MAKE EQUITABLE ARRANGEMENTS WITH THE STAFF, the Colonel had instructed. The business department, an organization of incredible pettiness, seemed to have interpreted this as meaning that the less they paid out, the more grateful the Colonel would be, and the more the business management might therefore expect from him. This, I am convinced, was not the case. The Colonel had many faults, and enormous ones, but niggardliness was not among them. He had a sense of grandeur. During the two years that I worked for the foreign service of the home paper, I recall, my instructions were that wherever I went, I was to travel by the best available accommodations and put up at the best hotels. A representative of the *Chicago Tribune,* the Colonel maintained, could not accept anything less than the best.

This was not quite the spirit of the business office of the Paris Edition, which had always paid beggarly salaries, pointing out that we had the advantage of working under French law, which guaranteed us all sorts of security, including abundant severance pay. (I was entitled myself, if my memory is correct, to something like three years' salary, because of length of service, the fact that I worked nights, and the importance of the position I held.) But now the time had come to pay off on those promises, and the business office had suddenly discovered that the same benefits were not provided by law to newspapermen working in the United States (at vastly superior salaries) and they therefore saw no reason why they should be afforded to us. STAFF MAKING UNREASONABLE DE-MANDS, the business office cabled to Chicago, when we suggested that the obligations of the law should be fulfilled.

As a matter of fact, not much was done either in the field of demanding or of offering. Up to the last day, none of us knew whether we would be paid a penny; it seemed more likely that we would all be thrown out into the street uncompensated. We heard a rumor (I do not know to this day whether it was true or not) that the *Chicago Tribune* was quietly transferring all its funds to the London office, so that we might sue and win in Paris, but there would be no assets to attach. This atmosphere of impending disaster did not encourage diligence in putting out the paper. I fought a nightly battle (along with Frantz, when he got back) to get a paper out. On two occasions one other man and myself wrote and produced the whole paper alone, with everyone else roaring drunk and uninterested in cooperating. We spent a good deal of our time during this month chasing the drunks downstairs to the bar again to get them out from underfoot; after two or three evictions, they would stop bothering the few workers. We were on the fifth floor, and there was no elevator.

The habit of setting bonfires in the wastepaper which accumulated nightly on the floor mounted during this month to the point of arson. Twice I saved our morgue from becoming fuel for the flames. A morgue, I should explain, for those unused to newspaper language, means the files. Our morgue was our pride. Its brown paper envelopes, stuffed with clippings, brochures, references and the like covered two walls of the city room, floor to ceiling, and was minutely cross-referenced in the card catalogue which accompanied it. I considered that the contempt I felt for the Paris *Herald* was fully justified when, after taking over the paper, they threw the morgue away. As a matter of fact, I believe I am correct in saying that to this day the morgue of the *International Herald Tribune,* successor to both the old papers, contains only clippings from its own issues, as though they were the repository of all the wisdom of the world.

I am told that on the last night, the ritual bonfire reached such proportions that it looked for a moment as though the whole building might be burned down. I say I was told, for I do not know. I was not in on the death. November 30 happened to fall on my normal night off, and I took it. I was sore. I was sore at the staff which had obliged me to fight it every night for a month to get the paper out, despite the interest everyone had in preserving his right to compensation. This extenuating effort had been furnished against the background of other demanding activities. Two or three days after Hummel had showed me the Colonel's cable, the United Press phoned to offer me a job, and I started at once, putting the *Chicago Tribune* to bed at about 2 A.M., and then moving over to the U. P. office to work until 8 A.M. I was also the Paris correspondent of the Copenhagen *Politiken,* at that time the largest paper in Scandinavia. As though this were not enough, I had also taken on another very special job. What it was appeared on 1 December 1934.

On that day, the *New York Herald* appeared, announcing that it was now the sole American newspaper in Paris and that the Paris *Tribune* was no more. And also on that day the subscribers to the supposedly extinct *Chicago Tribune* received in the mail the *Paris Tribune,* whose articles were signed with the same bylines they knew from the *Chicago Tribune,* along with certain features of the dead paper—and, what was worse, much of its advertising.

I was of course not present at the conversations which followed between the business managers of the *Tribune* and those of the Paris *Herald,* but they must have been fun—or would have been for me. Apparently the interlocutors were not amused. "We have bought and paid for your paper, and it's still coming out," the *Herald* people roared. "Stop it! " "How can we stop it? " the *Tribune* people answered. "We've fired all those people. We can't control what they do."

To me, the most amazing feature about the replacement of the *Chicago Tribune* by the *Paris Tribune* was that the secret of its preparation had never leaked out. It fell like a bomb on the heads of the businessmen who thought they had sold, or bought, the *Chicago Tribune.* And yet, during the month when I had been working to put the new paper together, dozens of people had to be let in on the secret—the people who were to write it; the people who were to print it (the same company which was printing the *Chicago Tribune*); advertising solicitors; the Bell Feature Syndicate, which gave us permission to continue to run, without pay, the crossword puzzle and Culbertson's bridge column; a hundred or so advertisers; and, most important of all, the people in the mail room, who were putting in overtime running labels for us through the *Chicago Tribune*'s addressing machine. This was undoubtedly actionable, but the *Chicago Tribune* was not in a position to go into court.

The Paris *Herald* must be credited with having made things easy for us, though that was hardly its intention. No sooner had the deal to buy the *Chicago Tribune* been consummated, than the *Herald,* with indecent haste, notified its advertisers that since it now had a monopoly on reaching American readers, it was increasing its advertising rates. We only had to go to them and say: "Take one ad a week with us (the *Paris Tribune* was a weekly, in tabloid format, a poor thing but enough to break the monopoly) and you will save the extra money the *Herald* is asking you to pay seven times a week—for they can't raise their rates as long as we exist." The amount of the hike the *Herald* had announced was sufficient so that advertisers were ahead of the game if they advertized with us. They saw the logic of this situation, and accordingly we ran the publicity of all the steady advertisers—shipping lines, travel agencies, stores, movie theatres, and so on.

The *New York Herald* subscribed to the news service of the United Press, for which I was now working. It suggested to the United Press that it might find itself able to get along without United Press news unless some way was found to make me stop publishing the *Paris Tribune* (for though the new *Tribune* printed no listing of its editors, there was little mystery about who had started it, especially as I had signed the front page editorial announcing the new publication). I wish I had a copy of that article now. Will Barber had it framed and gave it to me, but it was left behind when I got out of Paris in a hurry in June 1940, a few jumps ahead of the Nazis. Its general theme, I believe, was that a newspaper is not a piece of property to be sold like a chunk of real estate, but the intangible creation of the minds of the men who write it. The amount the Paris *New York Herald* paid for United Press service was not impressive, and all my boss said was that if my name were not publicly connected with the *Paris Tribune* that would relieve the pressure on him. So I stopped signing what I wrote; but the paper went on.

It did not go on for very long—two months, but that was enough. By the end of that time, the *Chicago Tribune* foreign news service had taken on four of the fired men, the *New York Herald* had found places for four more, and the others had taken care of themselves. Severance pay had also been handed out—not as much as we were entitled to under French law, but not too bad a settlement. For this last, I think the pressure of the *Paris Tribune* deserves no credit. I understand that payment had been decided upon before the paper shut down; why the business department thought it advisable to keep this a secret from the staff is almost impossible to understand—except, perhaps, on the theory, amply supported by its relations with the editorial staff throughout the years, that it could only with difficulty resign itself to the prospect of parting from any money.

Somewhat to my surprise, the recipients of severance pay checks included me. It is true that the manager who handed it to me remarked with satisfaction that it would have been much larger if I had been a good boy. Besides this, all it cost me for having been a newspaper publisher for two months was $100, the deficit on the first issue. The others paid for themselves. For this modest sum, the *Paris Tribune* achieved its object. Without regrets, I allowed it to die.

Waverley Lewis Root
January, 1971

Recollections

Paris was a good place to be in the late twenties and early thirties—the period between World War I and II. And the *Chicago Tribune*'s European Edition was a happy place to work, despite the low pay and often inadequate news sources.

Compared with the cultural aridity of much of the United States at that time, Paris offered a rich variety of music, art, literature, intellectual discussion, and cosmopolitan mores. There were those who fled to Paris because of another form of American aridity, known as Prohibition. In place of watered whisky, bathtub gin, and needle beer, expatriates in Paris found an extensive choice of alcoholic beverages available, from genuine scotch to wine, champagne, and beer, not to mention the wide range of French apéritifs, cordiales, brandies, eaux de vie, etc.

At the time I reached Paris at the beginning of December 1925, three American dailes were published there—the morning *New York Herald* and the *Chicago Tribune* and the afternoon *Paris Times*. There was also the *Continental Daily Mail,* an offspring of the *Daily Mail* of London. The Continental edition usually had one or two Americans on its staff.

For many of those working in the editorial departments of the Paris English-language papers, especially the American ones, the job was merely a bread-and-butter proposition, providing a steady income while they pursued what they considered more worthy activities—writing, painting, composing, studying. But there were always a few pros on the staff who kept the papers functioning, no matter how much time their colleagues devoted to the muses.

And even for those American newsmen not bent on pursuing an artistic career, Paris had much to offer culturally. For example, the *repetitions generales* (final rehearsals) of the great Paris orchestras were usually held on Saturday mornings, with the admission charge only a fraction of what was charged for the formal concerts on Saturday and Sunday afternoons. It was not uncommon for two or three newsmen to spend the early morning hours drinking and then attend an orchestra rehearsal. On one such morning in 1926 I returned to my hotel on the Rue de Lille about 11 A.M. to find that in my absence a thief had ransacked my room and taken everything portable, including my typewriter.

For those who liked art, the fare was also abundant. In addition to the vast Louvre with its priceless old masters and sculpture, and the smaller Luxembourg Museum, whose offerings were slightly more modern, there were a number of other museums, such as the one devoted exclusively to works of the sculptor Rodin. There were also countless art shops where paintings of all types were on view, from old masters to the far-out experimenters of the twenties—dadaists, cubists, and many other avant-gardistes.

As for literature, there were several small publications printed in English to which any aspiring writer could submit his efforts, with a fair chance of seeing them in print. Included among these were *This Quarter*, published by Edward Titus, then the husband of Helena Rubenstein, the beautician; the *New Review*, operated by Samuel Putnam; the *Boulevardier* of Erskine Gwynne; *Story Magazine*, published by Whit Burnett and Martha Foley.

As for *transition* (lower case *t*, please), probably the best known and most successful, it was conceived and born in the offices of the *Chicatrib*, as the European Edition of the *Chicago Tribune* was known because of its cable designation. Co-founders of *transition* were Eugene Jolas, trilingual poet and writer, and Elliot Paul, novelist, raconteur, musician, and bon vivant. Both were on the *Chicatrib* when *transition* was conceived, but Jolas left the paper to devote full time to the budding periodical. Soon joining them as associate editor was Robert Sage, another *Chicatrib* colleague who, years later, was to win acclaim for his book about Stendhal, a project he was already considering back in *transition* days.

The *Chicatrib* rented space in the building of *Le Petit Journal*, a Paris morning daily. The building, fronting on the rue Lafayette, covered half a square block. A side entrance for delivery trucks was on the rue Cadet, and the rear of the building was on the rue Lamartine, from which there was access to the *Chicatrib* offices. The *Chicatrib* occupied the entire third floor of the rear half of the building. Coming in from the rue Lamartine side, anyone seeking the editorial department would have to traverse a long corridor, at one side of which were the various business departments—advertising, circulation, and, most important, the paymaster. Finally came the editorial department, and beyond it, the office of the Paris correspondent for the parent paper in Chicago and his staff.

Those working for the parent paper were the elite—they were paid in dollars and enjoyed expense accounts that were fairly liberal for that era. Those working for the *Chicatrib* were paid in francs—every two weeks. Pay was quite low, amounting to about $15.00 a week for ordinary news personnel, and not much more for higher echelons. But the money went a lot farther than it would have gone in New York, or elsewhere in America. At least it could have.

However, custom decreed that on every bi-weekly payday, most of the staff would gather in a nearby bistrot for several rounds of drinks, and then, breaking up into smaller groups, head for favorite restaurants where francs were spent lavishly on food and drink, with emphasis on the latter. The result was that, for most of the staff, the remaining thirteen days until the next payday were rather lean. Fortunately, a favorite bistrot on the rue Lamartine, officially named Le Rendezvous du Petit Journal but known to all as Gillotte's, the name of the owner and his wife, extended credit. The first thing most of us did when we received our pay was to head for Gillotte's and pay our debts—we knew that was necessary to assure our having food and drink for the next two weeks after our payday binge. To the credit of most of those who worked for the *Chicatrib,* the Gillottes lost very little over the years from unpaid debts.

The editorial department of the *Chicatrib* consisted of one large room. There were two windows in the outer wall, overlooking the playyard of a girls' elementary school on the rue Buffault. Opposite this wall was the entrance from the corridor. Just outside the entrance and forming part of the wall on that side were two phone booths with headsets for taking long-distance calls. More than one staffer, having imbibed well but not too wisely, was found asleep in one of those booths.

A wall on one side of the room separated us from the business departments; the other side wall separated us from the rooms of the parent paper's Paris staff.

The main piece of furniture in the editorial room was a huge circular table, with a semicircular indentation on one side where the news editor sat. Around the rim of the table sat the workers who were used interchangeably as rewrite men and copy editors. In one corner was the managing editor's desk, in another corner the sports editor's desk, while the financial news desk occupied a third corner.

The society editor worked at a desk outside the newsroom on the other side of the corridor, adjoining a separate section partitioned off for use of P. & A. Photos, then owned by the *Chicago Tribune-New York Daily News.* There were a couple of other typewriters and desks in the society editor's section at which reporters worked if they still had copy to grind out after the night side came on duty about 8 P.M. During the day, the reporters worked at the same typewriters on the rim used later by the night side. The city editor in daytime occupied the same slot occupied by the news editor at night.

The paper in the late twenties, and even up to the time of its merger with the *New York Herald* near the end of 1934, seldom had more than three reporters. One man usually covered the American Embassy and consular offices, the American Chamber of Commerce in Paris, the weekly luncheons of the American Club, and various other American groups such as the American Legion and the Veterans of Foreign Wars. The latter two organizations usually were involved in bitter rivalry, and the paper was often unjustly accused of showing favoritism to one or the other, depending on which had gotten the most space in any particular week. Another reporter covered ship news, meeting the boat trains from Cherbourg and Le Havre, interviewing notable arrivals at the Gare St. Lazare or finding out where they were staying so they could be interviewed later. A third reporter was usually available for general assignment. With the large number of Americans living in Paris or traveling in France, there was often news involving romances, divorces, accidents, even an occasional murder. When the general assignment reporter was not tied up on spot news, he was usually assigned to working up features.

As for national and international news, our sources were quite limited.

The parent paper maintained a correspondent in New York, and just one small part of his job was to send us a very skeletonized summary of the major American news stories of the day. This file usually arrived about 10 P.M. via Commercial Cable, the overseas service of Postal Telegraph— that is, it arrived around 10 P.M. if there were no breakdowns in the cable or land lines between New York and Paris. Once the skeleton summary of a few news stories arrived, the entire staff got busy, expanding maybe a two-sentence item into half a column or more. This was a real feat since at that time the Paris paper didn't even have a morgue, as a clipping file was known. (I started one when I became managing editor in December 1929, and it had reached respectable proportions by the time the paper was merged.)

The parent paper's correspondents in Europe and Asia filed their stories through the London bureau, which forwarded them to Chicago. To take care of the Paris edition, there was a leased wire, available for about one hour, from London to Paris, and most of the stories sent to Chicago were also put on this wire for the Paris edition. The stories, written in cablese, came on narrow strips of blue tape pasted onto sheets of orange paper, each sheet about six inches wide and five inches deep. All these stories also had to be handled by the rewrite copyreading staff, but they were usually out of the way before the cable from New York arrived. The wire from London came into the Bourse, the Paris stock exchange, where the government telegraph service had a receiving center. The copy was brought to us by a one-eyed cyclist named André who, when he dallied en route with the copy, always had some wonderful excuse for being late.

The New York cable and the wire from London were our two major news sources, but the French newspapers also provided us with some of our news. Extracting this, of course, required considerable skill on the part of our rewrite staff, who had to have a working knowledge of French. Sometimes a staffer didn't know French quite as well as he thought he did, and the result could be either amusing or embarrassing.

When Marshal Foch died, the French papers were full of news about the state funeral which brought royalty and top statesmen from many countries which had been allies of France during World War I. One rewrite man took all this mass of material and wrote a very competent story about the funeral. In fact, my predecessor as managing editor, Bernhard Ragner, congratulated the man on his work. "But," added Ragner, "every time you came upon the word *deuil* in the French clippings, you translated it as *threshold*, and still your story read well." *Deuil,* of course, means *mourning,* while *seuil* is the French word for *threshold.*

Whereas in America the proofreaders belong to the printer's union, over there because of the language difference, proofreaders on English-language papers were adjuncts of the editorial department. In my ten years on the *Chicatrib* we had an interesting collection of characters in the proofroom. One was an aspiring opera singer, an Australian protege of Dame Nellie Melba. He always had an opera score open before him which he studied every minute he could steal from his proofreading chores.

Elliot Paul was hired originally as a proofreader but his talents were so obvious that he soon was brought upstairs to the editorial department. When I joined the paper near the end of 1925, the head proofreader was a man we called "Beaver" Chambers—he had a first name but no one ever used it, and now I don't even recall what it was. Chambers' favorite tipple was rum, and Papa Gillotte had a cask of very old rum which he reserved for Chambers and others of the *Chicatrib* staff. Because Chambers consumed so much of this rum, we nicknamed it "rum cham-bair," the French pronunciation of Chambers' name. Somehow Bob Sage did not realize that this was a nickname, and on one of his frequent walks around Paris, he dropped into numerous bistros, in each one asking for "rum cham-bair," only to be told that they had never heard of it.

Chambers finally lost his job as head proofreader, for what reason I no longer recall. The proofroom was headed for a while by a man named Lawrence, a former Navy chief petty officer who retired on a pension at a comparatively young age. The final boss proofreader, and the one I remember best, was Robert Fox, a dour Scot who didn't even know how to read or write when he entered the British army in World War I. But he was persistent and he came out of the service with an excellent knowledge of the English language, which he was constantly striving to improve during the post-war years. His knowledge of words and correct grammar was excellent, but once in a while American idiom would baffle him. However, he wasn't stubborn about it, and when he had questioned some usage and was told it was correct, he accepted the statement and added the fact to his knowledge of "American" as distinct from "English."

Of all the proofreaders, the one who gained the most fame later was Henry Miller. He gives a version of how he was severed from that job in *Tropic of Cancer*. However, the facts are somewhat different. He had a chance to go on a trip to Belgium with some friend paying all the expenses and he took off, without asking for leave of absence or a word of explanation. His friends Alfred Perlès and Wambly Bald, both proofreaders at the time, never told me that Miller intended to return, so after about ten days I hired a new man to fill the vacancy. Miller returned a few days later and didn't seem too upset when he learned that the job was no longer open.

Wambly Bald obviously should have been on the editorial staff, but he repeatedly turned down my invitations to move upstairs. He worked very hard on his weekly column and I, for one, don't buy Perlès' story that Miller sometimes wrote Bald's column for him.

The editorial department had its interesting collection of characters, too, some of whom went on to other more important careers. Among the many, to name but a few, were: William L. Shirer; Sterling Noel, now editor of the Hearst newspaper in Baltimore; Ephraim Gomberg, executive vice-president of the Philadelphia Crime Commission; Ned Calmer, CBS broadcaster and novelist; Bert Andrews, who headed the N. Y. *Herald Tribune* Washington bureau, and broke the story of the Whittaker Chambers "pumpkin papers" in the Alger Hiss case; Wilfred Barber, who won a Pulitzer prize posthumously for his coverage of the Ethiopian-Italian war for the parent *Chicago Tribune;* Wolfe Kaufman, novelist and Broadway press agent; Reynolds Packard, novelist and foreign correspondent; O. W. Riegal, head of the journalism school at Washington and Lee University; Waverley Lewis Root, gastronomic expert and writer; George Seldes, writer and polemicist; Vincent Sheean, foreign correspondent and writer; Martin Sommers, once foreign editor of the *Saturday Evening Post;* Edmond Taylor, foreign correspondent and writer; James Thurber, artist and writer; Gregor Ziemer, writer and broadcaster.

As I said at the beginning, life in Paris was good in those years. The hours were short and the work was not hard. The day side usually worked from about 9 A.M. to 5 P.M., though sometimes a reporter had a night assignment, for which he got compensatory time off. The night side hours were from 8 P.M. until 2 A.M., though except for one man on dog watch, usually chosen by lot, most of the staff was free by 1 A.M. In case of a major news break between 1 and 3 A.M., there was no difficulty in rounding up a staff since some of the boys could always be found in one of the neighborhood bistros, which stayed open all night.

While the night side hours were shorter than those of the day side, the night staff worked under considerably more pressure, since they had to transcribe cables, rewrite stories from the French press, expand brief cable items from America into longer stories, and edit copy and write headlines. Usually the same person did not edit and write a head for a story he had previously written. Letting another person edit the copy and write the head usually provided a double check.

And that reminds me of an incident that happened before I became managing editor. Ragner, my predecessor, was in a hospital for surgery, and I was temporarily in charge. That meant I sat in the slot until about 11 P.M., after which I went down to the composing room to supervise the makeup. When I went downstairs, one of the senior rewrite men replaced me in the slot. It just happened that this man earlier in the evening had transcribed an Athens dispatch, received via London, about a lad in the Greek capital who was in love with a movie star, who spurned his attentions. In despair, the lad shot himself but fortunately the wound was not serious. In rewriting the story, our man added the totally unnecessary phrase, "so tonight he is safe in the arms of his mother instead of in the arms of Jesus."

Apparently the rewrite man had figured that another staffer would edit the story and blue pencil the phrase. But as it happened, the item got to the bottom of the pile, and when I phoned from downstairs for some shorts, the same man who had written the item wrote a head for it and sent it down, without rereading it. It also happened that there was a small hole at the bottom of Page One into which that story just fitted. When the paper came off the press, we checked headlines and the leads of major stories, but no one thought to read every line of a short at the bottom of the page.

Ragner was a regular church-goer, and when he received a complaint from a church-oriented reader, just after his return from the hospital, his anger was considerable. The offending rewrite man, already on probation because of other lapses, was fired. He later got a job on the *Paris Times,* but he didn't last long there because in translating from the French the word "petit-fils" he made it "little son" instead of the correct "grandson."

The *Chicatrib* had a fairly liberal attitude toward drinking. Staffers could come to work with a few drinks under the belt so long as they proved competent to do their work. Anyone with too much to drink who kept others from working was sent home. One thing that *was* frowned on was a continuing binge, but there were very few cases of that during my ten years on the paper. The other staffers felt uncomfortable when there was a real alcoholic temporarily on the staff. We all drank pretty freely after work, and with an alcoholic there was always the fear that if you asked him to have one drink with you, you might start him off on a binge that would last for days. As soon as a man became identified as an alcoholic he was severed from the staff.

There were a number of big stories during my Paris years. One I particularly recall was the Lindbergh trans-Atlantic flight in May 1927. Ragner sent Bill Shirer and me to cover the expected arrival at Le Bourget. When we sought guidance on what angles of the story each of us should cover, Ragner replied: "There'll only be one story and whichever of you gets back first will write it." I'm sorry to report that Shirer beat me back, so it was his story that was used. My offer to write a secondary story to go with the main story was rejected by Ragner. I think the *Chicatrib*'s failure to give more extensive coverage to that epochal story was a major blunder, but I wasn't even news editor then.

We usually brought out a special edition when there was a major heavyweight title fight. We would get a round-by-round account by cable and have alternate headlines set, covering all possible results. Then, when we got a flash giving us the fight's outcome, only a few lines of type had to be set. The correct eight-column banner line was dropped in, the page locked up, and the presses would start rolling within twenty minutes. Sometimes, after getting out such a special sports edition, some of my colleagues and I would peddle the papers in night spots frequented by Americans. The sale was quite brisk, and offers to buy us drinks were so numerous we had to reject some invitations.

I remember well the elections of 1928 and 1932. Hoover, as expected, won over Al Smith in 1928, though many on the staff hoped to see Smith win because he was a foe of Prohibition. The election of 1932 was more exciting. America was in the grip of the Great Depression, which even we in Paris felt. There was no longer a great influx of American tourists, and the paper's advertising declined. When the United States went off the gold standard, the exchange rate of the dollar suddenly fell from 25 francs to 15. However, since we were paid in francs, this change had little effect on our living costs in Paris. But for anyone who had to send money to America for insurance payments or other obligations, it suddenly took almost twice as many francs to buy the amount needed in dollars.

With Mussolini strengthening his grip on Italy, and Hitler beginning his Nazi regime in Germany, along with the drying up of the American tourist influx, the economic outlook for the poor old *Chicatrib* grew steadily gloomier. Circulation was gaining in 1934, but advertising was not keeping pace. Salary cuts were made, starting at the top, but this was not sufficient. It took more and more dollars from the parent paper to make up the deficit in francs.

One of the biggest sources of revenue for the paper in its more prosperous years was resort advertising. But Mussolini with his strict currency controls virtually shut off the *Chicatrib*'s revenue from Italian resort advertising, and the situation with regard to advertising from Germany was even worse. Furthermore, the Nazi regime had little use for the *Chicatrib* which, in its news columns, reported Nazi excesses.

The more foresighted among us realized there was no longer room for two American newspapers in Europe—the *Paris Times* had already succumbed near the end of 1929, right after the stock market crash. But, with our circulation gaining, some of us hoped that Colonel Robert R. McCormick, owner of the *Chicatrib*, might decide to buy out the rival Paris *New York Herald*. There are reports that he had such a solution in mind, but when he went to New York and saw the Reids, owners of the *New York Herald Tribune* and its Paris paper, he found the Reids were not interested in selling their Paris outlet, so he asked whether they were interested in buying his Paris outlet, and they were.

I was visiting my home in Ohio when I received a cable from Jack Hummel, general manager of the *Chicatrib*, telling me the paper had been sold to the Reids. Oddly enough, I had been in Chicago just a few days earlier, and had visited the Tribune Tower to see the Colonel and other executives of the parent paper. I didn't get to see the Colonel, being told that he was in New York on business. The cable informed us what that business was.

Before returning to Paris, I contacted the *Tribune* in Chicago about a job there, and was told they had a place for me. But I had to return to Paris to wind up my affairs and see the Paris paper through the last few weeks of its independent existence. I was flattered when the late Larry Hills, then general manager of the Paris *Herald*, offered me a position second only to his managing editor, the late Eric Hawkins. But I declined with thanks because I felt it was time for me to return to America.

The final night of the *Chicatrib*'s independent existence was a wild one. Somehow we managed to put out the paper despite an excess of drinking and the influx of *Chicatrib* alumni, there for the "death watch." Once the paper was off the press, the party almost got out of hand. Some of the younger, wilder members of the staff thought it would be fun to burn out the editorial room, and Waverley Root and I were kept busy putting out small fires which had been playfully set.

Finally, about 5 A.M., I managed to get everybody out and locked up the place. And so the Paris *Chicatrib* passed into history, although for a year the name *Chicago Tribune and New York Daily News European*

Edition appeared in smaller type under the name *New York Herald* at the top of the front page of the merged paper. Then, a year later, the surviving paper's name was changed to the *New York Herald Tribune European Edition.*

Although I had a good job awaiting me in Chicago, I decided to work in New York, so I joined the staff of the *New York Herald Tribune,* where I remained for thirty-one years, except for three years abroad during World War II. I resigned in April 1966, the day before the start of the strike that caused that great paper's demise.

Ralph Jules Frantz
October 1970

A Paris "Tribune" Who's Who

ATLAS, LOUIS, a rewriteman, a reporter, and a remarkably talented caricaturist, with an unfortunate penchant for anonymity, was also a regular *Tribune* columnist ("Anything Can Happen") from 1931 to 1934. Shifting to the *Herald* after the *Tribune* closed, he stayed on in Paris for a year before returning to the United States and a position with O.P.A. For many years a Washingtonian, he is now Chief of the Press Section, European Branch, I.P.S.-U.S.I.A.

BALD, WAMBLY, a graduate of the University of Chicago, tried being a sailor, a farmhand, a beachcomber and, for a time, a hermit in the Mohave Desert before migrating to Paris in 1929 and joining the *Tribune* as a proofreader. Resisting the urgings of Managing Editor Frantz to join the editorial staff, Bald settled for the proofroom and the amalgam of good living and imaginative reporting that went into his weekly "La Vie de Bohème" column. His record of Left Bank dramas ended in 1934 when he came back to America and became a reporter for the *New York Journal-American,* and, later, a feature writer for the *New York Post.*

BLOCHMAN, LAWRENCE served the *Tribune* in Paris and as editor of the Riviera Supplement (Nice in winter) from 1923 to 1925. With more than forty publications to his credit, his novels *Bombay Mail* and *See You at the Morgue,* the Dr. Coffee stories, and a biography of Dr. Squibb proclaim his versatility and endurance. A student of French literature and language, he has translated, among others, Simenon, Misserand, and Daniel-Rops.

BODENHEIM, MAXWELL, a Chicagoan whose arrival in Greenwich Village in the twenties many considered an event, but whose sudden appearance on the Left Bank was haughtily ignored—despite his flamboyant attire that included a red beret—wrote several articles for the *Tribune* on the subject of Montparnasse. Bodenheim's sojourn in Paris was understandably brief.

BOYLE, KAY, an occasional contributor to the *Tribune*'s pages, assisted Eugene Jolas on *transition* and was a close acquaintance of Alex Small and Harold Stearns. The latter appears in Miss Boyle's novel *Monday Night.* As secretary to Bettina Bedwell, Paris fashion correspondent for the *Chicago Tribune* and *New York Daily News,* Miss Boyle ghostwrote many of her boss' columns, enlivening their content by inventing a prince who roamed Paris shopping for beautiful things for his wife.

317

BROWN, DON, one of several Tribuners who first saw Europe with the A.E.F., doubled as *Tribune* reporter and artist, interviewing and sketching visiting celebrities at the Crillon or in Left Bank cafés. In 1931 Brown had a one-man exhibit at the Galerie Jeune Peinture, which prompted one critic to write that it revealed a painter of "extraordinary vitality, originality and vision, [one] destined to achieve a position in the front rank of contemporary artists."

CALMER, EDGAR (NED), a Chicagoan whose first newspaper job was reporting for the Paris *Tribune*, fraternized briefly with the *transition* group in the late twenties before joining the *Herald* and eventually the Foreign News Service. A CBS correspondent during World War II and an occasional novelist, he has written nostalgically about newsmen in Paris in *All the Summer Days.*

ETTLINGER, HAROLD, admittedly ambivalent toward the diverse attractions of Paris, remained a *Tribune* rewriteman long enough to explore the life of the city in several columns and features. Finally exasperated by the usual monetary squeezes, he left the paper in the early thirties and joined the AP as European correspondent. His auto-biographical book, *Fair, Fantastic Paris*, describes his *Tribune* days (it "was like no other paper on earth") affectionately and amusingly.

FORD, FORD MADOX, whose "Literary Causeries" appeared in the *Tribune*'s Sunday Magazine Section in 1924, spent most of the same year editing *Transatlantic Review* with one-time reporter Ernest Hemingway in a tiny office lent by William Bird, a practicing journalist and printer and publisher of Three Mountains books, to whom Ford dedicated his novel *No More Parades.*

FRASER, GEOFFREY, that rarity, an Englishman on the *Tribune* staff, worked as a rewriteman for two years in the early twenties before starting an international news feature service in Paris. Later he became a correspondent in Berlin and Geneva for several British newspapers, and after World War II he reopened his feature service. Fraser published fellow Tribuner Imbs' first book of poems.

FRANTZ, RALPH JULES, whose long career with the *Tribune* as rewriteman, copy editor, news editor, and managing editor he has recalled in these pages, has just retired from active newpaper work. His last position, which followed over three decades on the *New York Herald Tribune* staff as telegraph and suburban editor, was with *The Record* (N.J.). Membership in the Newspaper Guild of New York, the Overseas Press Club of America, and the present secretary of the O.P.C.'s Correspondents Fund, of which he was a founding trustee, are among the important posts held by this veteran journalist.

GILLIAM, FLORENCE, one of the *Tribune*'s theatre critics, arrived in Paris in 1921, and before the end of the decade had become Paris correspondent for *Theatre Magazine, Theatre Arts,* and Erskine Gwynne's short-lived magazine, *The Boulevardier.* With her husband, Arthur Moss, she published *Gargoyle,* the first English-language review of arts and letters on the Continent. Her services to France and to American organizations in France (described in her book *France*) span the last forty years, and include leading positions in the American Women's Group in Paris, American Catholic Women's Organization of Paris, and American Aid to France, in recognition of which she has been awarded the Médaille de la Reconnaissance Française and membership in the Legion of Honor.

HOFFMAN, LEIGH, secretary to the *Tribune*'s Foreign News editor, performed a good deal of the "drudge work" on the night desk for several years in the twenties, and contributed to *transition.*

IMBS, BRAVIG fibbed his way into a job at the *Tribune* with claims that he had worked for the *Tribune* in Chicago and could speak fluent French. Temporarily eluding detection by befriending a few sympathetic colleagues willing to cover up his shortcomings, he was finally unmasked, fired, and then reemployed in the *Tribune*'s advertising department and proofroom. A poet (*Eden: Exit This Way*), he was for a time a favorite of Gertrude Stein's, who, along with other Montparnassians, is described in Imbs' *Confessions of Another Young Man.* Following a distinguished career as an OWI radio correspondent and broadcaster during World War II, he lost his life in an auto accident in France.

JOLAS, EUGENE, whose journalistic apprenticeship included jobs with the *Waterbury Republican,* the *New York Daily News,* and the editorship of an army newspaper in 1917-18, wrote a lively literary column ("Rambles through Literary Paris") in the mid-twenties in addition to being a rewriteman. Completely trilingual (though an American citizen, he was a native of Lorraine), Jolas founded *transition,* a magazine devoted to investigations into language innovation, which included among its contributors, besides several *Tribune* staffers, James Joyce, Gertrude Stein, Kay Boyle, Hart Crane and Archibald MacLeish.

KOSPOTH, B. J., a quiet, self-effacing man, the kind, as a friend wrote, one "could know a great deal about without really knowing anything about him at all," joined the staff in the early twenties and remained with the paper until 1934, serving as diplomatic correspondent, city editor, and art critic specializing in Left Bank painters. After a tour with the *Herald,* Kospoth moved on to the *Tribune*'s London bureau.

MILLER, HENRY, the *Tribune*'s most famous proofreader, lived so ascetically during his newspaper days that few besides Wambly Bald and Alfred Perlès knew of his prodigious literary output, then still unpublished. Not cut out to be a journalist and not really interested in holding the *Tribune* position, he one day—following months of punctual arrivals and departures—failed to appear. Ten days later, editor Frantz, assuming Miller had returned to America, hired a replacement, only to have Miller turn up almost immediately, ready for work. Nothing could be found, however. Miller's *Tropic of Cancer* contains his version of the episode along with some amusing descriptions of *Tribune* colleagues.

PAUL, ELLIOT, alternately a proofreader, assistant night editor, and occasional book and music critic, memorialized Left Bank life and himself in *The Last Time I Saw Paris* and *Springtime in Paris*. A better than average accordionist and pianist, a compulsive but losing poker player, a fabricator of outlandish hoaxes, a gourmet with imperial tastes, and an inspired improvisator of "social gatherings" at the *caveau* in rue de la Huchette, Paul epitomized "la Vie de Bohème." His antics, told and retold with embroidery throughout the Quarter, and his commanding physical appearance—rotund, bearded (some found a resemblance to Henry VIII), often sporting a black hat and swinging a cane—overshadowed his literary accomplishments as novelist (five published novels by 1930, with more than a score to come), associate editor of *transition*, and self-proclaimed interpreter of Gertrude Stein's writings.

PERLÈS, ALFRED, was a "downstairs guy" (the epithet was used to distinguish the editorial staff, "upstairs guys," from the printers, linotypists, and proofreaders—of whom Perlès was one—who rubbed elbows a floor below). His accomplishments as part-time columnist and prime mover of the paper's Port Edition are unmentioned in Henry Miller's freewheeling account of their newspaper days (*Tropic of Cancer*). Perlès's own evocation of the time, *My Friend Henry Miller*, concludes that it was the "most fertile period of our life in Paris."

PUTNAM, SAMUEL, a Chicagoan, though never a *Tribune* staffer, wrote features for the paper from time to time and was a familiar figure among the Left Bank literati and newsmen, once even entrusting an edition of his magazine, *New Review*, to Henry Miller and Alfred Perlès. An able translator (Cervantes) and a specialist in Brazilian literature, Putnam also wrote *Paris Was Our Mistress*, an engrossing and informative account of life in Paris between wars.

ROOT, WAVERLEY, although a young and inexperienced newsman in the Paris of 1927, succeeded William L. Shirer as *Tribune* news editor. The appointment was explained partly by a letter of introduction Root carried to the Paris-based correspondent of the New York *World* that served to promote the bearer, at least in the eyes of the hiring *Tribune* editor, to a "trained, big-time New York newspaperman." Root's weekly book reviews fermented a few memorable squabbles, with the critic taking on several irate correspondents at once, but more often they garnered compliments from satisfied readers, including occasionally Ezra Pound. After the *Tribune* closing, Root spent three years with the United Press, shorter periods with *Time,* the Mutual Broadcasting System, the *Daily Mirror,* and a ten year stretch as Paris correspondent for the *Washington Post.* An experienced translator, ghost writer, and occasional historian (*The Secret History of the War*), he has recently written of that most sacrosanct of newsmen's memories of Paris, French cooking.

SAGE, ROBERT, was described by a colleague as a "man of infinitely discreet jest, wondrously sober in his folly." Scholarly and literary (he was an associate editor of *transition*), he remained a *Tribune* rewriteman until 1934 when he moved to the editorial staff of the *Herald,* where he stayed until the occupation. One of the few Americans to reside in France during the war (he lived quietly in the country with his French wife), he rejoined the *Herald* in the mid-forties as travel editor, providing, in the opinion of Managing Editor Hawkins, "solid, colorful news of events of interest to tourists." In 1954 Sage published a new translation and edition of Stendhal's *Private Diaries.*

SCHWERKÉ, IRVING, the Tribune's veteran music critic from 1921 to 1934 and a musician himself, also served as Paris correspondent for Italian, British, and American music journals. He organized the first all-American concert (Paris, 1929) and music festival (Germany, 1931), in addition to lecturing, concertising, and writing numerous books. Deserving of the honorary title, "Ambassador of American Music in Europe," he has since 1942 maintained a studio for teaching of piano, voice and violin in his native town of Appleton, Wisconsin.

SELDES, GEORGE, while head of the *Tribune*'s Central European Bureau in Berlin, had occasional pieces published in the Paris *Tribune.* He started his career with the *Tribune*'s Army Edition, first as a $25-a-week reporter, then as managing editor (pay: $28.00 per week), a position he left after one week to become John Steele's assistant on the paper's London Foreign News staff. In 1920 he moved to Berlin. Seldes' numerous books include *Tell the Truth and Run, You Can't Print That,* and the recently reissued *Freedom of the Press.*

SHEEAN, VINCENT, hired by the *Tribune*'s Foreign Press chief in 1922 as a "general handy-man" whose duties included reporting for the *Tribune,* got his first byline, as well as his "identity," for an account of the death of Sarah Bernhardt. Informed that his initials J. V. were unsuitable as a newspaper signature, he was ordered to use Vincent, his second name, thus acquiring, as he later wrote, a "name like a mask" behind which he has worried ever since. Graduating from handy-man status to the Foreign News Service in 1931, he began his colorful career as foreign correspondent by covering the Peace Conference at Lausanne.

SHINKMAN, PAUL, a reporter and columnist ("Latin Quarter Notes") on the *Tribune* in the mid-twenties, joined the paper's Foreign News Service in London in 1927.

SHIRER, WILLIAM L., perhaps the *Tribune*'s most illustrious alumnus, worked as a reporter on the newspaper while writing occasional features and even "Who's Who" columns before joining the *Tribune* Foreign News Service. His experiences as journalist, radio commentator, and international correspondent in Europe in the thirties and forties are vividly recalled in *Berlin Diary*, and his *The Rise and Fall of the Third Reich* and the recent *The Collapse of the Third Republic* are important contributions to contemporary history.

SMALL, ALEX, a *cum laude* graduate of Harvard who had tried advanced study and teaching in France, surprised and impressed everyone, notably Colonel McCormick, by turning out first-class reporting almost as soon as he had joined the *Tribune*. His reward for this was a biweekly column ("Of Fleeting Things") that permitted long absences from Paris as well as an unlimited range of topics. Alex Small's talk, described by Edmond Taylor as "an indefinable blend of Samuel Johnson, Brooks Adams, Rabelais, and Xenophon, with traces of Thomas Hardy and perhaps Ambrose Bierce," often took aim on the claims of the "machine age" (he had a Menckenesque distaste for the fetish of progress) and the boasts of American exiles, principally the "*transition* crowd" whose members he regarded as "symbiosis in an advanced stage." Small finally deserted Paris completely (he was city editor for awhile in the 1930s), joined the *Tribune*'s Foreign News Service, reporting the opening events of World War II, and finished his career on the staff of the parent *Tribune* in Chicago.

STEARNS, HAROLD, the former *New Republic* reporter, author of *America and the Young Intellectual*, and editor of *Civilization in the United States*, descended on Paris in 1921 and at once attuned his New England temperament (purposefulness, accomplishment and moral integrity) to long evenings of cerebral silence and pleasurable apathy in Left Bank cafés, and to the post of *Tribune* tout, where as "Peter Pickem" he advised the local horsey set to "play to place." His career of dreamy indolence, briefly interrupted when he quit the *Tribune* in 1929 for a similar post in the Paris office of the *Daily Mail* and the more prestigious sobriquet of "Lutetius," came to an end in 1932 with his return to America and the publication of several articles recanting nearly all he had said in defense of exile. However, in his autobiography, *The Street I Know*, published in 1935, Stearns showed a more positive side of expatriation. A gentle, whimsical, fey character, Stearns appears in Kay Boyle's novel, *Monday Night* and briefly in Hemingway's *The Sun Also Rises*.

STERN, ROBERT L., held several positions with the *Tribune* in the thirties—city editor, rewriteman, and copy editor—as well as serving as Paris correspondent for *Variety*. In 1935 he joined the *Herald*. At present he works as a copy editor on the staff of the New York *Daily News*.

TAYLOR, EDMOND L., with a tour on the St. Louis *Globe Democrat* behind him, turned up in Paris in 1928 seeking, as he wrote later, "more journalistic opportunity." Hired on as a *Tribune* reporter and feature writer, he bided his time in Montparnasse, observing his picturesque colleagues and the Quarter's habitués, while waiting for an opportunity to join the Foreign News Service. It came in 1930. As the *Tribune*'s chief correspondent in Paris, Taylor reported the major events leading up to World War II, reflections on which comprise the substance of his recent book *Awakening from History*.

WARREN, LANSING, joined the *Tribune* in the early twenties. A tall, quiet, efficient, humorous man, he used his "Dear Pard" column to spoof naive American visitors experiencing the surprises of Paris for the first time. Before joining the Paris bureau of the New York *Times,* Warren had become city editor of the *Tribune* and for a time assistant to the managing editor. Following World War II, he resumed his career as journalist in France.

Index